MW00786217

THE MEESE REVOLUTION

THE MEESE REVOLUTION

THE MAKING OF A CONSTITUTIONAL MOMENT

STEVEN GOW CALABRESI

Clayton J. & Henry R. Barber Professor of Law
Northwestern Pritzker School of Law

and

GARY LAWSON

Levin, Mabie, & Levin Professor
University of Florida Levin College of Law

Foreword by
MARK R. LEVIN

Encounter
BOOKS

NEW YORK · LONDON

2024

First American edition published in 2024 by Encounter Books,
an activity of Encounter for Culture and Education, Inc.,
a nonprofit, tax-exempt corporation.
Encounter Books website address: www.encounterbooks.com

Manufactured in Canada and printed on
acid-free paper. The paper used in this publication meets
the minimum requirements of ANSI/NISO Z39.48-1992
(R 1997) (*Permanence of Paper*).

FIRST AMERICAN EDITION

LIBRARY OF CONGRESS CATALOGING-IN-PUBLICATION DATA

Library of Congress CIP data is available online under the following ISBN
978-1-64177-429-1 and LCCN 2024033727.

DEDICATION

STEVEN GOW CALABRESI
Dedicates his work and co-authorship of this book to
T. KENNETH CRIBB JR.
Without whom many of the events described in this book would not have happened and to
JUSTIN BRAGA
Without whom this book could never have been written.

GARY LAWSON
Dedicates his work and co-authorship of this book to
PATTY, NATHANIEL, AND NOAH
Without whom none of the events described in this book would have mattered quite as much.

EPIGRAPH

*"[O]ur peculiar security is in the possession of a written Constitution.
Let us not make it a blank paper by construction."*

— THOMAS JEFFERSON

Letter from Thomas Jefferson to Wilson Cary Nicholas,
September 7, 1803

*"On every question of construction [we should] carry ourselves back
to the time when the constitution was adopted, recollect the spirit
manifested in the debates, and instead of trying [to find] what meaning may be squeezed out of the text, or invented against it, conform
to the probable one in which it passed."*

— THOMAS JEFFERSON

Letter from Thomas Jefferson to William Johnson,
June 12, 1823

*"I entirely concur in the propriety of resorting to the sense in which the
Constitution was accepted and ratified by the nation. In that sense
alone it is the legitimate Constitution. And if that be not the guide
in expounding it, there can be no security for a consistent and stable,
more than for a faithful exercise of its powers. If the meaning of the
text be sought in the changeable meaning of the words composing it,
it is evident that the shape and attributes of the Government must
partake of the changes to which the words and phrases of all living
languages are constantly subject."*

— JAMES MADISON

Letter from James Madison to Henry Lee,
June 25, 1824

TABLE OF CONTENTS

FOREWORD

PROFESSORS STEVEN CALABRESI and Gary Lawson have authored an exquisite book that eloquently describes one of the most important constitutional battles of our time—that is, whether those responsible for upholding and interpreting the Constitution will do so faithfully or will usurp it through various contrivances to enshrine within the law itself the progressive ideology. For decades, the progressive ideologues went unchallenged and their impact on American jurisprudence was both omnipresent and monopolistic. But with the election of President Ronald Reagan, and his appointment of Edwin Meese III as the 75th attorney general, that was about to change.

Ed Meese spent his life in all aspects of the law and emerged as the statesman with the intelligence, courage, and fortitude to launch and lead a movement to reestablish constitutional republicanism and challenge what became the activist acculturation and socialization of the legal profession. It was a daunting undertaking. The American Bar Association and other legal organizations, law schools and law review articles, legal scholars and journals, legal analysts and commentators, and, of course, justices and judges, were marinated in the ideology and self-righteousness of judicial activism and supremacy. And they were not about to easily surrender their primacy and domination over constitutional interpretation and adjudication, especially not to traditionalists or "originalists" who might set back or at least slow their Progressive Project.

During my tenure in the Office of Presidential Personnel at the Reagan White House, my portfolio included vetting potential judicial nominees. I worked closely with Ed's staff, including Kenneth Cribb and John Richardson, who served as top aides to the then counsellor to President Reagan. Years earlier, Ed had been Governor Reagan's top legal adviser in California, and President Reagan relied on his judgment and advice for decades. When Ed moved to the Department of Justice, I was invited to join his team. Eventually, I served as Ed's special assistant and, ultimately, chief of staff. Thus, I write as someone who had a close working and personal relationship with Ed and observed his superb stewardship of the Department of Justice.

Although the department is a vast enterprise, with tens of thousands of employees involved in nearly all aspects of our society, and the magnitude of the responsibilities of an attorney general can intimidate if not overwhelm most mere mortals, Ed embraced his responsibilities with vigor, prudence, and his usual optimism. But he had no illusions about the difficulty of not only managing such an immense bureaucracy but refocusing it from an unwieldy, ever-growing, increasingly ideologically driven operation with growing police powers back to its traditional mission of upholding the rule of law, defending civil liberties, and protecting the nation from enemies foreign and domestic.

Ed rejected the idea that the purpose of the department, the law, and the Constitution was to serve those individuals and groups seeking to fundamentally transform America into some kind of utopian society, along the lines prescribed by Rousseau, Hagel, or even Marx, unencumbered by the Constitution's firewalls, which exist as an impediment to the would-be masterminds' designs, their hoped-for centralized yet ubiquitous Leviathan, and the mobs or factions they would birth through demagoguery, propaganda, indoctrination, welfarism, and, if necessary, threats and intimidation. He witnessed that Progressives were intent on weakening if not undoing the Constitution's construct, taking special aim at such foundational principles as separation of powers and representative government. Ed was acutely aware that this heresy was marketed in self-righteous declarations about democracy, justice, equality (or is it equity?), modernity, reasonableness, and progress, and the simultaneous repudiation of the Constitution and those who drafted, adopted, and ratified it. Indeed, the Framers and their masterpiece were portrayed as throwbacks to a bygone era, and the eternal principles that undergird the American experiment, concisely set forth in the Declaration of Independence, were quaint but antiquated, useless ideas and parchment for present-day challenges in an advanced, industrialized society. Therefore, the Constitution must be viewed as a necessarily "living and breathing" document as it impedes societal advancement and human development.

Of course, Ed knew this was nonsense. Dressing up centralized tyranny as progress and empowering elitists to lord over society is antithetical to enlightened self-government and a dynamic civil society. But how do you impose this utopia on a public that would never knowingly sanction it? The answer, at least for the Progressives, was through the judiciary. After all, the judiciary is designed specifically and uniquely to be insulated from the public. Supreme Court justices and lower federal court judges are not subject to elections, serve for life, and operate in a cloistered, opaque environment, answerable to no one. That is intentional. The job of judging is, in fact, supposed to be more paint by numbers than abstract art. That is not to say that issues before courts are uncomplicated or cases are always cut and dry. And there are times when adjudication by justices and judges is compelled. However, this underscores that a small handful of lawyers in robes ought not jump their constitutional lane into the lane of the elected branches. As Ed would explain time and again, unlike Congress, where the House is divided into electoral districts and the Senate is comprised of two senators from each state, such representation was of no concern among the Constitutional Convention's delegates when designing the Supreme Court. The appointment and mission of the justices would not require a political formulation given the nature of their authority. Discerning what the Constitution compels, through its text and the intention of those who authored it, is utterly unrelated to the geographic, societal, and cultural diversity of the country. Justices and judges are expected to exercise their review role cautiously and wisely, not as some kind of oligarchs, members of a super legislature or politburo, free to dispense orders and rewrite the Constitution at will.

Ed Meese is not only a constitutional scholar and accomplished leader, but a stellar historian. He explained the birth of the Progressive movement in the late 1800s and its ideological loathing of constitutional republicanism, limited government, and dispersed powers, which were firewalls against their efforts to reengineer man's nature and remake society. And he knew that for Progressives, the courts were the key to slowly but surely changing the relationship between government and the individual, to the detriment of the individual. Indeed, the early Progressive intellectuals, among them Woodrow Wilson, who as president of Princeton University in 1908 wrote *Constitutional Government in the United States*, made clear their intentions. He wrote that "the courts are the instruments of the nation's growth, and that the way in which they serve that use will have much to do with the integrity of every national process. If they determine what powers are to be exercised under the Constitution, they by the same token determine also the adequacy of the Constitution in respect of the needs and interests of the nation; our conscience in matters of law and our opportunity in matters of politics are in their hands." Wilson added that "if they had interpreted the Constitution in its strict letter, as some proposed, and not in its spirit, like the charter of a business corporation and not like the character of a living government, the vehicle of a nation's life, it would have proved a strait-jacket, a means not of liberty and development, but of mere restriction and embarrassment."

It was William F. Buckley Jr. who famously said, "I am obliged to confess I should sooner live in a society governed by the first two thousand names in the Boston telephone directory than in a society governed by the two thousand faculty members of Harvard University." Indeed. Of course, justices and judges are of flesh and blood. Their black robes and wood empaneled courtrooms, and the respectful references to a justice or judge as "Your Honor," do not make the man or woman wiser, smarter, or better. They do not change their fallibility. There have been only 116 Supreme Court justices in our nation's history. Their character, ethics, intelligence, morality, and mental fitness have spanned the human spectrum. Some have been racists and antisemites. Some have refused to retire despite the onset of dementia. Some have been lazy and unfit, relying on their clerks to write their opinions. Others have been exceptional, insightful, and intuitive. But few are Solomonic and none are godlike. And the Supreme Court's history reflects it all. There have been decisions worthy of high praise. But there have also been judicial disasters. And when the High Court gets it wrong, and becomes more political and activist than judicial and prudential—as it did in *Dred Scott v. Sandford* (slavery), *Plessy v. Ferguson* (segregation), and *Korematsu v. United States* (internment)—the effect can shake the nation's foundations and the damage can be everlasting. And in each of these notorious examples, a small handful of justices jumped through extra-constitutional hoops to reach their preferred outcomes.

During his decades in the law, Ed Meese witnessed how the federal government grew massively in reach and authority, and that governing power had shifted dramatically away from the people and their representatives to a vast and pervasive administrative state. Thus, so much of the nation's governance was controlled by unelected bureaucrats and judges, or the permanent government. He knew that the progressivism was devouring constitutional republicanism, due in large part to the acquiescence or active support of the judiciary. Ed saw, as I wrote in *Men in Black*, that activist federal judges had abandoned their constitutionally designed roles to take over "school systems, prisons, private-sector hiring and firing practices, and farm quotas; they have ordered local governments to raise property taxes and states to grant benefits to illegal immigrants; they have expelled God, prayer and the Ten Commandments from the public square; they've endorsed severe limits on political speech; and they've protected virtual child pornography, racial discrimination in law school admissions, flag burning, the seizure of private property without just compensations," and more. "Courts now second-guess the commander in chief in time of war and confer due process rights on [terrorist] enemy combatants. They intervene in the electoral process." Hence, it is difficult to find any area of life where the judiciary does not meddle and sit in final judgment.

The Wilsonian view, which has poisoned most of our legal institutions, was now the dominant view coursing through all aspects of our legal system. And Ed realized it led in one direction: the abandonment of traditional constitutional jurisprudence for the institutionalization of the progressive ideology as the standard through which law is practiced and judicial reasoning and decisions are made. It was a seismic and successful revolution that profoundly and perilously altered our constitutional construct and, consequently, our republic. And it was in this environment that Ed Meese determined he had a much bigger task as attorney general of the United States than the already huge job of running the Department of Justice. Through top department appointments, new legislative and policy initiatives, refocusing the department, crucial (now historic) public speeches and debates, and the nomination of highly qualified individuals to the federal courts who had previously demonstrated their loyalty to traditionalism and originalism, Ed launched a legal and constitutional counterrevolution, pushing back against progressivism and judicial activism, that remains as vigorous as ever. Without Ed's leadership, the battle would be over, having never been seriously engaged. Originalism, Ed Meese heroically argued, is the only legitimate means by which the Constitution is to be interpreted. And this remarkable book provides the historical, definitional, and philosophical context for Ed's case—our case—and the movement he launched and led to save our republic.

It was the honor of a lifetime to serve with Ed Meese, my mentor, teacher, and dear friend. Now, for the rest of the story.

— MARK R. LEVIN
Former chief of staff to Attorney General Edwin Meese III

INTRODUCTION

THE MEESE REVOLUTION

O N JULY 9, 1985, thousands of lawyers from all over the United
States gathered in Washington, D.C., for the annual meeting of
the American Bar Association (ABA)—the nation's largest and most
powerful association of lawyers. As the attendees looked at the schedule
of events, they saw that they were to be welcomed by the new fifty-four-
year-old attorney general of the United States, Edwin Meese III, who
had been confirmed by the Senate just four months earlier.

Ed Meese was known in 1985 for his devotion to President Ronald
Reagan, his boundless energy, and his rock-ribbed conservatism. Some
ABA attendees were no doubt curious to see whether this former state
prosecutor, San Diego School of Law professor, and best friend of a
movie star turned politician was really up to the job of serving as attorney general of the United States. Everyone probably expected a
welcoming speech full of pablum about the importance of the lawyers'
guild, pay increases for judges, and respect for the rule of law (with no
definition of what that might mean). Little did they know that they were
about to hear one of the most important legal speeches in 235 years of
American history—a speech that has reverberated throughout American constitutional law for the last four decades and that has radically
changed the course of our republic in ways that few today appreciate.

Attorney General Ed Meese had come to the ABA's annual meeting
to announce that the United States Department of Justice under his
leadership would adhere to what he called the original intentions of
the Framers of the United States Constitution when interpreting that
document. It would no longer follow the example set by Supreme
Court justices such as William J. Brennan Jr. and Thurgood Marshall,
who treated the document as a "living constitution" whose meaning
changed with times and trends.

Mr. Meese's speech excoriated the Supreme Court for its appalling
performance during the just concluded 1984–1985 term. That surely
raised some eyebrows. There have been other times when Supreme

Court cases were criticized by executive branch officials (or soon-to-be executive branch officials) in major policy addresses. Chief Justice Marshall's broad construction of federal power to create a bank in *McCulloch v. Maryland*[1] was challenged by Andrew Jackson in an 1832 veto message; the pro-slavery opinion in *Dred Scott v. Sandford*[2] was criticized by Abraham Lincoln in the Lincoln-Douglas debates; the anti-economic regulation opinion in *Lochner v. New York*[3] was vigorously attacked by Theodore Roosevelt; and the anti–New Deal opinions of the Hughes Court from 1933 to 1937[4] were publicly rebuked by Franklin Roosevelt. But these were relatively rare events. Today it seems commonplace to hear executive officials lambaste the Supreme Court—as did, for example, President Obama in his 2010 State of the Union Address, with some of the justices sitting in the audience. But for most of our history this was not a normal occurrence. Attorneys general, in particular, were typically reticent about making broad public statements concerning constitutional law. Mr. Meese's speech was different.

After some general remarks that may have lulled some ABA attendees into thinking that they were hearing the usual fluff, Ed Meese laid into the Supreme Court's decisions on federalism, the constitutional division of power between the state and national governments, blasting the Supreme Court's pro-national power decision in a 1985 case called *Garcia v. San Antonio Metropolitan Transit Authority*.[5] This case held that federal labor laws, such as minimum wage laws, applied to state government employees as well as to private sector employees, overturning (by a 5–4 vote) a contrary decision issued nine years earlier (also by a 5–4 vote) finding that Congress had no constitutional power to tell state governments how to run themselves.[6] Meese explained that "[o]ur view is that federalism is one of the most basic principles of our Constitution. By allowing the states sovereignty sufficient to govern we better secure our ultimate goal of political liberty through decentralized government."

Meese found a few federalism cases from the just-finished Supreme Court term to praise, but he made it abundantly clear that he thought that the Supreme Court needed to make radical changes in its approach to federalism, which is among the most important subjects on which the court rules. Overall, it is fair to say that former professor Ed Meese gave the 1985 Supreme Court a grade of F on federalism.

Meese gave the Supreme Court what amounts to a solid B for cutting back a bit on the exclusionary rules of *Mapp v. Ohio*[7] and *Miranda v. Arizona*,[8] which prevent prosecutors from using in court evidence obtained through illegal searches or from confessions made by suspects who had not yet been told of their right to remain silent. (Meese would later argue that these anti-prosecutor cases should be overruled altogether.) But he then blasted the Supreme Court for its rulings on the Constitution's First Amendment "religion clauses," which forbid the government from either establishing religion or prohibiting its free exercise. Meese said the Supreme Court was too hostile to religious liberty. He noted that "to have argued, as is popular today, that the [First] amendment demands strict neutrality between religion and irreligion would have struck the founding generation as bizarre." Ed Meese effectively gave the Supreme Court a grade of F on its religious liberty case law as well.

All of these critiques were just a warm-up—or, more precisely, specific applications—of the main point of Meese's speech, which was that the Supreme Court was getting wrong answers because it was asking the wrong questions. The court was careening about as a kind of self-made super legislature, sometimes leaning liberal and sometimes leaning conservative, instead of studiously and dispassionately ascertaining the actual meaning of the Constitution. Attorney General Meese was not asking for new policies. He was asking for a new method of judicial decision-making.

In urging the Supreme Court to change its approach to deciding cases, while announcing that the executive through the Department of Justice was changing its own way of looking at the law, the new attorney general called the Supreme Court's 1985 case law "incoherent" and "adrift." Worse yet, said Meese, "In considering these areas of adjudication—Federalism, Criminal Law, and Religion—it seems fair to conclude that far too many of the Court's opinions were, on the whole, more policy choices than articulations of constitutional principle. The voting blocs, the arguments, all reveal a greater allegiance to what the court thinks constitutes sound public policy than a deference to what the Constitution—its text and intention—may demand."

What was needed to get the Supreme Court back on track, Meese maintained, was nothing less than a new "Jurisprudence of Original

Intention": a jurisprudence based on the original meaning of the text of the Constitution and not on the policy views of the judges interpreting it. As Meese explained, "The permanence of the Constitution has been weakened. A constitution that is viewed as only what the judges say it is, is no longer a constitution in the true sense."

Meese then added, in two of the most important sentences ever spoken by an attorney general, "It has been and will continue to be the policy of this administration to press for a Jurisprudence of Original Intention. In the cases we file and those we join as amicus, we will endeavor to resurrect the original meaning of constitutional provisions and statutes as the only reliable guide for judgment."

In other words, Attorney General Meese's July 9, 1985, ABA speech was not just a speech about abstract legal ideas. It was a public announcement of a sea change in the litigating and brief-writing policies of the Department of Justice (DOJ), as well as in the method by which the executive branch would interpret the Constitution and laws when the DOJ's Office of Legal Counsel (OLC) gave legal advice to the president or other executive actors. And henceforth all Reagan administration judicial nominees would ideally be originalists.

Attorney General Ed Meese would go on to give more than thirty speeches laying out the original meaning of various parts of the Constitution, and the DOJ would produce thirty monographs on the original meaning of parts of the Constitution and hold three academic conferences on that subject. The Meese Justice Department would be a giant law school that would teach the courts and the bar "originalism"—the doctrine of constitutional interpretation that is held to some degree by six justices of the Supreme Court in 2024: Chief Justice John Roberts, Justice Clarence Thomas, Justice Sam Alito, Justice Neil Gorsuch, Justice Brett Kavanaugh, and Justice Amy Coney Barrett.

It may be hard today to appreciate the truly revolutionary nature of Attorney General Meese's speech. At the time Ed Meese gave this speech on July 9, 1985, there was no member of the Supreme Court who was remotely an "originalist." Supreme Court constitutional decisions frequently did not even quote or acknowledge, much less follow, the text of the Constitution. Perhaps a tiny handful of first-term, Reagan-appointed lower federal court judges, such as Robert Bork and Antonin

Scalia, would describe themselves as "originalists," but you could probably count them on both hands. Not a single tenure-track member of
any law school faculty anywhere in the United States was publishing
serious work developing an originalist theory in 1985. Originalist law
professor Robert H. Bork of the Yale Law School had by then resigned
from the Yale Law School faculty in disgust. The most significant originalist in 1985 was Raoul Berger, who in 1977 wrote a book called *Government by Judiciary* that foreshadowed some of Meese's criticisms of
the court a decade later. Mr. Berger was briefly a law professor from
1962 to 1965, but when he did his famous work on constitutional law in
the late 1960s and 1970s, he did not hold a tenure-track appointment at
a law school.[9] And while future Supreme Court justices Antonin Scalia,
Clarence Thomas, and Sam Alito were active in the law during that time,
none had by 1985 written any significant works on originalism.

Ed Meese put originalism on the map in high-stakes national politics.
His speeches were often covered on the front pages of newspapers, in
a pre-internet world in which getting on the front page was crucial. Ed
Meese's speeches sparked a national conversation, which drew public
responses from liberal Supreme Court justices William J. Brennan and
John Paul Stevens, as well as from prominent liberal legal academics—
or at least those committed enough to the academic enterprise to take
him seriously and respond.

Today, the Supreme Court has at least six justices who treat the
Constitution's original meaning as important to at least some of their
decisions—and a few who treat it as the single most important consideration in their decisions. Even Justices Elena Kagan, Sonia Sotomayor,
and Ketanji Brown Jackson, whom no one would call originalists, take
originalism more seriously than anyone on the Supreme Court—and
almost anyone in the legal academy or the bar—would have taken it in
1985. The lower federal courts, and the state courts as well, are filled with
self-described originalists. The legal academy remains largely hostile,
often openly so, to originalists, but roughly one hundred law professors,
including tenured faculty members at institutions such as Yale, Harvard, Chicago, Stanford, and Columbia, self-identify as originalist. Any
lawyer today who does not know how to make a persuasive originalist
argument has no business arguing constitutional law cases, and any law

school that does not train its students to make persuasive originalist arguments, alongside other kinds of constitutional arguments, is committing a form of educational malpractice.

As this book will explain, none of this would have happened without Ed Meese. Every development over the last four decades that has led to the modern successes of originalism can be traced to Ed Meese. Never before or since in American history has any one attorney general so thoroughly transformed the legal culture. By contrast, four decades after Franklin D. Roosevelt's most powerful attorney general, Homer S. Cummings (1933–1939), had left office, nobody in the Jimmy Carter administration probably even remembered his name, much less what principles of law he had stood for.

U.S. constitutional law has been transformed since Ed Meese gave his ABA speech, and the man who is the most responsible for that transformation does not get the public credit and recognition that he deserves. When people think of originalism in constitutional law today, they usually associate the idea with former justice Antonin Scalia or with such brilliant contemporary Supreme Court justices as Clarence Thomas and Neil Gorsuch. But Attorney General Meese argued for originalism before Justices Scalia, Thomas, or Gorsuch did. In fact, it was Ed Meese who deliberately gave Justice Antonin Scalia the bully pulpit of the Supreme Court from which to expound on originalism, a topic Scalia had not publicly addressed prior to becoming a Supreme Court justice.

Most importantly, as we describe in detail in chapters 6 and 8, Ed Meese created the opportunities for two generations of originalist scholars, judges, and government officials to develop their own originalist ideas. Ed Meese promoted originalism before any of the hundred or so law professors who are now developing and debating it had done so, and he seeded the ground that made subsequent work on originalism possible. Ed Meese put the full political weight of the transformative Ronald Reagan presidency behind the idea that the original public meaning of all written legal texts is the only legitimate meaning of those texts.

Ed Meese's influence did not end with his resignation as attorney general in 1988. Over the past three and a half decades, Meese used his perch at the Heritage Foundation and on the board of directors of the Federalist Society to help promote debate and discussion of originalism and the rule of law in general. He has both inspired and facilitated younger generations of scholars, as well as younger generations of activists in and out of government, such as Lee Liberman Otis, Leonard Leo, and David McIntosh, who worked post-Reagan to put originalists on the Supreme Court, inferior federal courts, and even state courts. The fruits of those tireless and selfless efforts are evident. The 2021–2022 Supreme Court term saw *Dobbs v. Jackson Women's Health Association*[10] (which overruled *Roe v. Wade*[11]); *New York State Rifle & Pistol Association, Inc. v. Bruen*[12] (which reaffirmed the Second Amendment right to carry a gun outside your home subject to reasonable regulation, which had first been recognized in 2008 in an opinion written by President Reagan's finest Supreme Court appointee, Antonin Scalia[13]); *West Virginia v. Environmental Protection Agency*[14] (which places policymaking authority primarily with Congress rather than with executive agencies); and *Kennedy v. Bremerton School District*[15] (holding that a high school coach can pray by himself on a public school playing field). The October 2022 term yielded *Students for Fair Admission, Inc. v. President and Fellows of Harvard College*,[16] which limits the ability of colleges and universities to discriminate on the basis of race in admissions. These results were unthinkable in 1985. However one evaluates these decisions (depending on one's point of view), they are enormously consequential, and they are the direct result of the Meesian constitutional revolution.

It remains to be seen how long-lasting and profound this revolution will be. Will it outlast the 2024 presidential election and threats of court-packing or will it endure for twenty or forty years or more? Whatever the future brings, the modern Supreme Court case law demonstrates that a constitutional revolution has happened. This book aims to show *how* it happened—and that all roads lead to Ed Meese.

At this point, Ed Meese would immediately say that all of his accomplishments were really the work of his boss President Ronald Reagan, his predecessor William French Smith, and the capable people who populated his Department of Justice divisions and staff. Ed Meese is such a modest and devout person that when the meek inherit the earth, he will own all of the land west of the Mississippi River. Notwithstanding his protestations, however, Ed Meese's transformational tenure as the most influential attorney general in American history *is his own accomplishment.* While he, of course, had invaluable help from President Reagan, more than a bit of help from his predecessor, and a good measure of help from his Justice Department loyalists and judicial nominees, Ed Meese was the indispensable man in promoting, publicizing, and legitimating both originalism and the Reagan Revolution. No other attorney general has *ever*, in 235 years of American history, played such a leading intellectual role in transforming the theory of American constitutional law as did Ed Meese, while at the same time serving as the chief aide and counsellor to President Ronald Reagan. That is why we have called this book *The Meese Revolution.*

Attorney General Meese's uniqueness is shown by the fact that his outstanding predecessor as attorney general, William French Smith, published a book on his tenure as President Reagan's first attorney general entitled *Law and Justice in the Reagan Administration: The Memoirs of an Attorney General* (1991), which never once mentions the word "originalism." Think about that. The word "originalism" never appears, not even once, in William French Smith's autobiography of his important more-than-four-year tenure as Ronald Reagan's first attorney general. Attorney General Smith's judicial philosophy, as revealed in his book, was to favor what he called "judicial restraint"—the idea that courts should not strike down too many laws or executive branch actions, even the ones that were unconstitutional. As we explain in chapter 5, there is a profound difference between a jurisprudence of *originalism* and a jurisprudence of *judicial restraint*, even if much of the bench, the bar, and the academy still does not grasp the point.

When Smith was attorney general from 1981 to 1985, the leading originalist thinkers, law professor and then judge Robert H. Bork and gadfly Raoul Berger, also often emphasized "judicial restraint" or "original intent" rather than the original public meaning of legal texts in criticizing wrong court opinions. Bork and Berger were initially reacting against the excesses of the High Warren Court (1962–1969) rather than formulating a deep interpretative theory of the law. Bork and Berger saw their advocacy of judicial restraint and original intent as primarily a restraint on judges—a forced crouch by the courts—rather than as a method for accurately determining the meaning of a legal text. One might say that Bork and Berger were in the 1970s and early 1980s judicial *conservatives* but not necessarily judicial *constitutionalists*.[17]

Ed Meese had read and was influenced by Bork and Berger's scholarship, which accounts for his July 9, 1985, reference to a "Jurisprudence of Original Intention." As we will see later in this book, Meese shifted to the idea of adhering to the original *public meaning* of constitutional and other legal texts at about the same time that Judge Antonin Scalia argued for this approach in a speech on "Original Meaning" delivered on Saturday, June 14, 1986, at the Attorney General's Conference on Economic Liberties. Two days later, following the advice of Ed Meese, President Ronald Reagan nominated Scalia to be an associate justice of the Supreme Court, replacing William H. Rehnquist, whom Reagan nominated to succeed the retiring Warren Burger as the new chief justice of the Supreme Court. This made possible William Rehnquist's federalism revolution in the Supreme Court's case law and Antonin Scalia's defense of textualism, formalism, and originalism in constitutional law and statutory interpretation.

None of Ed Meese's distinguished predecessors as attorney general over the course of more than two centuries successfully altered constitutional theory or theories of judging during their tenures in office. Some of them, like Robert Jackson, went on to highly distinguished careers as Supreme Court justices, while Roger B. Taney went on to a disastrous career as a Supreme Court chief justice who helped cause a civil war. But there is no "Robert Jackson approach" to constitutional interpretation, just as there never was a "Roger Taney approach" to constitutional interpretation. Some attorneys general like John Mitchell succeeded in helping to change one line of Supreme Court case law, such as criminal procedure, but John Mitchell never put forward a comprehensive theory of the role of a judge or of legal interpretation. (He just wanted guilty crooks sent to prison and kept there.) Homer S. Cummings was attorney general from 1933 to 1939, and he helped cause the Supreme Court's revolutionary doctrinal changes in 1937. Robert F. Kennedy was attorney general from 1961 to 1964, and he led a revolution in civil rights law. But neither Cummings nor Kennedy nor any of the Supreme Court justices they helped appoint put forward a whole theory of the role of a judge or of legal interpretation in the way that Ed Meese did.

The relatively modest role of attorneys general in legal development throughout American history is not surprising. First, it must be remembered that from 1789 until 1870, the attorney general was only a part-time government officer, paid much less than a federal cabinet member's salary, with a handful of staff, no control over federal prosecutors, and no Department of Justice to assist him in carrying out his duties. One would not expect much from such an unimportant officer, and the early attorneys general were bit players in the theater of American constitutional law and Supreme Court justice selection.

Second, even after the creation of the Department of Justice on July 1, 1870, the office was more administrative and political than intellectual. Many distinguished people have held the position, but they have not been the engines of fundamental changes in legal theory. The closest competitors to Ed Meese in this respect are President Franklin D. Roosevelt's (FDR's) four very able attorneys general: Homer S. Cummings, Frank Murphy, Robert Jackson, and Francis Biddle. Collectively, they changed the legal culture through the New Deal, but the real verdict of history is that they tore down a pre-1937 legal culture without offering a coherent replacement. In contrast, Ed Meese both tore down the 1985 legal culture and offered originalism as a replacement.

Three of FDR's attorneys general wrote books on the Supreme Court crisis,[18] but none of them articulated a formal and novel theory of constitutional interpretation or of judging. Even FDR's Supreme Court appointees, who put in place most of the framework for modern constitutional law, had no common judicial philosophy, and they fought bitterly with one another about everything once the pre-1937 jurisprudence had been overruled. Activist New Deal justices like Hugo Black, William O. Douglas, and Wiley Rutledge almost never agreed with judicial restraint New Deal justices like Felix Frankfurter, Stanley Reed, and James F. Burns. Three other New Deal justices, Harlan Fiske Stone, Frank Murphy, and Robert Jackson, had no identifiable methods of deciding cases. Compare this with the more consistent methodology (even when they often disagree on results) of post-Meese justices like Antonin Scalia, Clarence Thomas, John Roberts, Samuel Alito, Neil Gorsuch, Brett Kavanaugh, and Amy Coney Barrett.

So why did Ed Meese become the country's only attorney general to successfully lay out a new and coherent philosophy of judging that has been taken up and used by six out of nine current Supreme Court justices, half the lower federal courts, countless state court judges, and one hundred or so law professors? Three major reasons come to mind.

First, Ed Meese is a first-rate intellectual. He was a former adjunct law professor at Berkeley School of Law, and he was, for four years, a full-time law professor at the University of San Diego School of Law. He loved to read, and he was the happiest when he was in an academic setting where debates were going on all around him, powered by a super-bright faculty who cherished ideas. Ed Meese loved public policymaking, and he loved legal debate. The Meese Justice Department was thus something like a conservative-libertarian law school or think tank of the best and brightest right-of-center legal minds in the country. Former Intercollegiate Studies Institute president Ken Cribb was the intellectual leader and dean of this law school, with the formal title of counsellor to the attorney general. Ken's fabulous interpersonal skills made him the social glue that held together the high-powered alpha males and females on the civil side of the Meese Justice Department.

Second, Ed Meese's young team, mostly aged twenty-six to forty-two, was put to work on judicial selection, which is discussed at length in chapter 9; speech-writing, which is discussed in chapter 7; the writing of legal monographs or law review articles on the original meaning of legal subjects and the organizing of academic conferences, which is discussed in chapter 8; conservative and libertarian criminal law topics, which is discussed in chapter 11; the writing of strictly originalist Office of Legal Counsel (OLC) opinions guiding the executive branch in the positions it took on all legal issues from 1985 onward, which is discussed in chapter 11; and, finally, fighting off attacks on originalism in the briefs filed by the Solicitor General's (SG's) Office, which is discussed in chapter 10. Attorney General Meese brilliantly used his conservative-libertarian law school of a Justice Department to produce originalist judges, speeches, academic conferences, policy monographs, criminal law policies, OLC opinions, and briefs before the Supreme Court. The energy and productivity of the Meese Revolution was truly a force to behold.

Third, Ed Meese was successful because he was, in essence, Ronald Reagan's right-hand man and counsellor. He could speak and act with the authority of the president 100 percent behind him. Consider, for example, the following never-before-published story.

Fast-forward to the third week of February 1987—one year and six months after Attorney General Meese's ABA speech. The National Security Council staff, which was supposed to be, but in fact was not, under the control of White House chief of staff Donald Regan, had been publicly caught selling U.S. arms to the Iranian government. Certain members of the national security staff, acting on their own, undertook this initiative. The purpose of the arms sales was to secure the release of American hostages in Lebanon while diverting the profits to aid an anti-communist insurgent group in Nicaragua called the Contras. This was contrary to the spirit, if not the letter, of a federal law called the Boland Amendment, which had outlawed aid to the Contras by the Reagan cabinet departments and agencies but not specifically by the White House national security staff.[19] Congressional Democrats, who had majorities in both houses of Congress, were furious. The firing of the National Security Council staffers at fault did little to mollify them. Talk of impeachment was in the air, and the embattled Donald Regan quietly let President Reagan know that he wanted to retire as soon as a replacement was available. President Reagan, then seventy-six years old, faced the greatest and gravest crisis of his presidency.

Attorney General Ed Meese was out in Arizona, speaking to a meeting of U.S. attorneys, the top federal law-enforcement officials across the country. Meese's phone rang. It was President Ronald Reagan. The president told Meese that Donald Regan had secretly decided to resign. The president asked Ed Meese to help him in working to find a successor. Ed Meese said that he would be happy to do so but that he was currently in Arizona meeting with the U.S. attorneys. President Reagan replied, "I will immediately dispatch a National Guard jet to pick you up and to bring you back to Washington, D.C."

Meese boarded the National Guard jet and spoke again with Reagan on a secure phone line. Their first instinct was to hire former Nevada senator Paul Laxalt, an old friend of Reagan's, for the job, but unfortunately Laxalt was not interested. Laxalt then suggested that Reagan consider liberal Republican, and former Senate majority leader, Howard Baker, who had been a presidential candidate in 1980. Reagan thus had Howard Baker in mind when he talked to Meese. Meese pointed out that Baker was revered on Capitol Hill and that the appointment of a liberal Republican White House chief of staff would end all talk of impeachment. Reagan and Meese were intrigued by the idea, but they both agreed that there were two big questions that needed to be answered. First, would Senator Baker be willing to leave retirement to serve as White House chief of staff for the last two years of a lame-duck presidency? And, second, would Senator Baker be comfortable following and implementing policies that he had disagreed with as a presidential candidate in 1980 and later as Senate majority leader?

Meese met and talked with Howard Baker as soon as he could after landing in Washington, D.C. Senator Baker told Meese that he would like to serve as President Reagan's third White House chief of staff and that he was comfortable following Reaganite positions even if he had previously opposed them. Meese called the president and told him that Howard Baker was willing to serve, and Ronald Reagan hired him on the spot and was hugely relieved.

Steve Calabresi was in the attorney general's office with Ken Cribb, Ed Meese's rock-ribbed conservative counsellor and chief of staff, when Meese returned from the White House to the Justice Department. With a satisfied smile on his face over a job well done, Meese told Steve Calabresi and Ken Cribb that he had just helped Ronald Reagan hire Howard Baker to serve as Ronald Reagan's third White House chief of staff. Cribb was quietly furious at the ascendancy of a liberal Republican, but Calabresi suspected that Meese's decision had averted impeachment and made possible a Republican victory in the 1988 presidential election, as turned out to be the case.

Ken Cribb then urged Ed Meese to go right back to the White House and to capitalize on his goodwill with Howard Baker to get Cribb appointed assistant to the president for domestic policy with a 2nd-floor West Wing office, so that he could keep an eye on what Howard Baker was doing. Meese agreed that that would be a good idea, and when Meese returned to the White House, he found Howard Baker unpacking boxes in the chief of staff's office. Baker readily agreed to the appointment of Ken Cribb, and Cribb and Baker developed a very harmonious and successful working alliance. Conservatives in the Reagan administration were reassured by the knowledge that Cribb had an office in the West Wing.

The first point of this story is that when President Ronald Reagan needed help with a very serious problem that could have led to his impeachment, he turned to his loyal chief aide and counsellor, Ed Meese, for a solution. This showed that Ronald Reagan trusted Ed Meese. Meese's modesty and his desire to credit Ronald Reagan for everything good that Meese did gave Reagan total confidence in Ed Meese's bona fides. Once, when some fake news scandal was raised about Ed Meese, Ronald Reagan wisely dismissed it out of hand saying, "If Ed Meese is not a good person, then there are no good people in the world." Ed Meese had the complete trust and confidence of President Reagan, and quite rightly so.

The second point of this story is that no attorney general in history, with the possible exception of Robert F. Kennedy, President John F. Kennedy's brother, has had as much policymaking clout outside the Justice Department as did Ed Meese. Ed Meese was on the National Security Council (NSC) for all eight years of the Reagan administration, including when he was attorney general, and he helped formulate a hardline foreign policy and a huge buildup of the U.S. military forces. Meese's hardline allies on the NSC, like Secretary of Defense Caspar Weinberger and CIA director William Casey, ensured that the more moderate Secretary of State George P. Shultz and White House chief of staff, and later Treasury secretary, James A. Baker III did not prevent the implementation of President Reagan's foreign and defense policies. Meese liked and respected both George Shultz and Jim Baker, who were both vital parts of the Reagan administration. But Reagan and Meese came into office on January 20, 1981, committed to the view that Soviet communism should be rolled back and not merely contained. They wanted to win the Cold War, not to engage in détente. And, they did win the Cold War without a shot being fired!

In President Reagan's second term, Ed Meese chaired the Domestic Policy Council in addition to serving as attorney general and was the controlling member of the National Security Council along with Bill Casey and Caspar Weinberger. Meese helped to shape all the domestic policy options that were presented to President Reagan for his consideration during Reagan's second term.

President Ronald Reagan was a transformational president like President Franklin D. Roosevelt, but the liberal media and academy studiously avoid mentioning his name even today. Ed Meese was associated with *every* great thing that President Reagan did. Along with people like Bill Casey, Caspar Weinberger, and (yes) George Shultz, Meese played a key role in the peaceful winning of the Cold War; along with President Reagan and Martin Anderson, he argued for the tax-rate cuts, which set off the greatest economic boom in American history; he helped facilitate President Reagan's launch of the Strategic Defense Initiative to protect against incoming nuclear missiles; and he advised President Reagan to appoint William Rehnquist to be chief justice and Antonin Scalia and Anthony Kennedy to be associate justices. Ed Meese was Ronald Reagan's right-hand man and counsellor de facto for all eight years of the Reagan administration. Ronald Reagan made all of the important policy decisions himself, but Ed Meese helped shape and implement them whenever he could.

* * *

THIS BOOK is primarily an intellectual (and to some extent an oral) history of Ed Meese's role in the triumph of originalism in legal interpretation, which necessarily discusses to some extent Meese's role as President Reagan's right-hand man and counsellor de facto. It is a story that is not widely known but to which Steve Calabresi was privy because he worked as a special assistant to Ed Meese from June 1985 to March 1987 and then for four months as an aide in the 2nd-floor West Wing office of Ken Cribb when he first became assistant to President Reagan for domestic policy. Both of us have also been privileged to work for decades with Ed Meese on the board of directors of the Federalist Society.[20] Steve Calabresi saw firsthand how Ed Meese and Ronald Reagan institutionalized their charisma and power into the Department of Justice, the Federalist Society, and the wider legal culture. He saw how Meese's legacy as attorney general and continued energy afterward shaped, and continue to shape, the discussion and implementation of originalism. It is long past time that Ed Meese's story be told. He is much too modest to tell it himself, so the job has fallen on his loyal and devoted follower (and that follower's friend and frequent co-author).

Most of this book will focus on Meese's role in changing the legal culture. It would require a whole separate book to explain Meese's larger role in the Reagan Revolution. But because the Reagan presidency is now outside the lifetimes of many people today, and because many people have incentives to lay claim to the enormous accomplishments of the Reagan presidency, there are six more episodes, most of which are hitherto unknown to the public, wherein Ronald Reagan followed Ed Meese's advice on a critical matter and Meese changed the course of American history. These episodes, some of which we discuss in more detail in subsequent chapters, help set the context for the rest of this book.

First, Ed Meese was hired to be the chief of staff to Governor Ronald Reagan's highly successful 1980 presidential campaign. Meese was entrusted with this key role by Reagan from the beginning, as a result of the extremely close bond he had formed with Governor Reagan as his legal affairs advisor and chief of staff in California over a seven-year period from 1967 to 1974 when both men worked closely together in a small office every day. A presidential campaign's chief of staff is crucial to the campaign's success. Meese's first historic accomplishment, which led to the Reagan Revolution, is that he helped get Ronald Reagan elected in the first place.

Second, in one of the most underappreciated moves in recent American political history, Ed Meese and Michael Deaver introduced William J. Casey to Ronald Reagan, who was so impressed by Casey that Reagan hired him to be campaign chairman after firing John Sears from that job during the New Hampshire primary of 1980 for mismanaging the campaign and for having caused Reagan to lose the Iowa caucuses. Bill Casey was a spectacular campaign chairman, and he went on to play a major foreign policy role in the Reagan administration as director of the CIA, where he and Meese were key players in the winning of the Cold War.

Third, shortly before the 1980 Republican Convention in Detroit that nominated Ronald Reagan for the presidency, Richard Wirthlin, the campaign's pollster, commissioned a poll to determine which potential running mate would most help Reagan in the general election campaign against President Jimmy Carter and Vice President Walter Mondale. Among those considered were George H. W. Bush, Gerald Ford, Howard Baker, Robert Dole, John Connally, William Simon, and

Paul Laxalt. Gerald Ford entertained the idea of running as Reagan's vice-presidential candidate if he could be in essence co-president, with Henry Kissinger reinstalled as secretary of state. Those terms were unacceptable to Reagan, but Ford had publicized their negotiations, so Reagan had to act fast to forestall talk of Ford. Reagan made an unprecedented appearance on Wednesday night of the convention, ahead of his speech accepting the presidential nomination, just to clarify who his running mate would in fact be.

A meeting was held in Reagan's hotel suite in great haste to fend off speculation about former president Ford being Reagan's running mate. Those in attendance included Ronald Reagan, Richard Wirthlin, Richard Allen, William J. Casey, and Ed Meese. Wirthlin's polling revealed that Bush or Ford would help Reagan the most as a running mate against the Carter-Mondale ticket. Ed Meese considered Bush to be more reliably conservative than Ford, Baker, Dole, or Connally, and Meese thought that picking Bush would win over the moderate Gerald Ford wing of the party. Meese also thought that Bush's character and manner made him the right man for the job. Meese recommended to Reagan that he should pick Bush to be his running mate for these reasons, and Reagan was persuaded by Ed Meese to pick Bush. The Reagan-Bush ticket swamped Carter-Mondale, and it caused Republicans to win a majority in the Senate for the first time since 1954. Reagan also swept in enough Republican congressmen that, with the help of conservative southern Democrats, he had a working majority in the House of Representatives.

Bush turned out to be an outstanding vice president and won a presidential term of his own from 1989 to 1993 with Reagan's critical help. The Bush-Reagan legacy then led to the election of a third Republican president, George W. Bush, who served from 2001 to 2009. Ed Meese set this whole train of events in motion by persuading Ronald Reagan to pick George H. W. Bush as his running mate. Meese and Bush Senior became good friends and allies.

Fourth, after Reagan won his first term in November 1980, he asked Ed Meese to run his transition team. Presidential history scholars have praised the Meese-run transition as one of the best in American history. With the help of Pendleton James, Meese ran a tight and effective transition for less money than Jimmy Carter had spent on his presidential transition four years earlier—not accounting for the astronomical Carter-era inflation. Meese played a role second only to that of President-Elect Reagan in hiring Ronald Reagan's first cabinet and his entire White House staff.

Fifth and sixth, in addition to filling the administration with talented and brilliant Reaganites from the academic and corporate world, Meese also baked into the agenda for Reagan's first year his epochal tax cuts, which slashed income tax rates across the board, and an enormous and badly needed increase in military defense spending. Martin Anderson developed the idea for the tax-rate cuts during the 1980 presidential campaign. Reagan's promises to cut taxes and radically boost defense spending could easily have been lost in the halls of Washington during the transition. Instead, thanks to Ed Meese, we saw during the Reagan years passage of the Economic Recovery Tax Act of 1981, which lowered maximum marginal tax rates from 71 percent to 50 percent—and, eventually, in 1986, with Jim Baker's invaluable help, to 28 percent. This launched a global economic boom that has lasted for four decades, and which may well outlast the United States' recent bout of economic folly. We also saw hugely increased U.S. spending on national defense, launching an arms race that bankrupted the Soviet Union, which had invaded the Islamic country of Afghanistan. Indeed, it has been reported that Reagan persuaded the Islamic governments of Saudi Arabia and the other Gulf States to flood the world oil market to decrease the Soviet Union's main supply of revenue, which was oil and gas reserves.[21] As a result of the arms race and low oil prices, the Soviet Union went bankrupt, and Mikhail Gorbachev had to sue for peace and tear down the Berlin Wall. This is how Reagan won the Cold War.

No one other than Meese's closest aides knew the power Ed Meese had, because Meese always gave the credit for all his many and huge accomplishments to President Reagan or others. He never leaked to the press so as to build himself up at the expense of the president or anyone else. Ed Meese quite rightly believed that leaking information given to you in confidence to the press is profoundly immoral and a betrayal of trust. Thus, almost no one in the 1980s had any idea how much power Meese wielded behind the scenes. The exception was his staff, headed up by Meese's right-hand man Ken Cribb, and fleshed out with others including Steve Calabresi, Steve Matthews, John Richardson, Mark Levin, Becky Norton Dunlop, John Harrison, David McIntosh, and Ann Rondeau. This means that the public history of the 1980s is in one fundamental way incomplete.

Even after Ed Meese resigned as attorney general to become an important player at the Heritage Foundation, the Federalist Society, and the Hoover Institution, he secretly intervened on three very high-level public policy matters, about which we say more in the conclusion, where his recommendations made history.

First, President George W. Bush learned from Ed Meese and Leonard Leo that conservatives would not support the nomination of President Bush's White House counsel, Alberto Gonzales, to the Supreme Court. Meese and Leo gave the George W. Bush administration four names of people they thought would be good Supreme Court appointments: John G. Roberts, Samuel Alito, J. Michael Luttig, and law professor Michael McConnell. Bush followed Meese's and Leo's advice in nominating John Roberts to be chief justice, but after Alberto Gonzales had become attorney general, Bush departed from it to nominate White House counsel Harriet Miers, a personal friend of Bush from Texas, to a second slot on the Supreme Court. Conservatives publicly rebelled in a fury, and Bush was forced to withdraw the Miers nomination. A chagrined president then nominated Samuel Alito as his second Supreme Court pick, and Alito was confirmed.

Ed Meese thus not only helped recommend to President Reagan that he appoint Chief Justice Rehnquist, Justice Scalia, and Justice Kennedy to the Supreme Court when he was attorney general. He, in effect, also helped George W. Bush to appoint both Chief Justice Roberts, an alumnus of President Reagan's White House Counsel's Office, and Justice Alito, an alumnus of the Meese Justice Department. These justices, together with President Donald Trump's three splendid appointees, Neil Gorsuch, Brett Kavanaugh, and Amy Coney Barrett, put in place a six-justice originalist majority on the Supreme Court. Indeed, it was Justice Samuel Alito who wrote the 2022 opinion overruling *Roe v. Wade*.

Second, when it became clear to President George W. Bush that we were mired in a quagmire of a civil war in Iraq, Meese served as a member of a small advisory commission, chaired by Reagan White House chief of staff and former Treasury secretary Jim Baker, known as "The Iraq Study Group," which met from January 2007 to July of 2008. Ed Meese worked closely with former conservative Democratic governor and senator from Virginia Chuck Robb to argue that the United States should not withdraw all troops from Iraq, as the Democratic Congress was arguing, but that we should instead send more troops into Iraq, as the general in command of the troops had recommended, and extend the term of service of all those currently in Iraq in a "surge" to vanquish the terrorists. Ed Meese, Chuck Robb, and Jim Baker persuaded President George W. Bush that the "surge" was the right way to go, Bush implemented it, and it worked.

Meese's third great post–Reagan administration service to the nation came in the fall of 2007 when President George W. Bush's second attorney general, Alberto Gonzales, became ensnared in a scandal over the partisan firing and hiring of chief federal election law prosecutors, which caused both congressional Democrats and Republicans to demand that he resign or be impeached and removed. This put George W. Bush in a very difficult situation, because any successor nominee as attorney general would have to be of impeccable ethical integrity, be confirmable by a Democratic majority in the Senate, and not upset George W. Bush's Republican base or challenge his administration's conservative policies and executive orders. The vice chair of the Senate Democratic Caucus at the time, Senator Chuck Schumer, recommended that George W. Bush nominate a brilliant conservative federal district judge in New York City, Michael Mukasey.

The George W. Bush administration was intrigued by this idea, but officials were nervous that Democrat Chuck Schumer was proposing it, and they did not want someone disloyal or unqualified to serve as the administration's attorney general. The second Bush administration asked Ed Meese secretly to interview Judge Mukasey and report back with a recommendation. Ed Meese secretly interviewed Judge Mukasey, and Meese became convinced that he was of impeccable integrity, brilliant, and jurisprudentially and politically conservative. Bush hired Judge Mukasey, and he went on to do an excellent job as attorney general. After he left office, Judge Mukasey joined the Federalist Society's board of directors, on which he served with great distinction until May 2023.

* * *

WE HAVE WRITTEN this book in part to fill in for the lack of an autobiography, which Ed Meese is too modest to write. His 1992 book, *With Reagan: The Inside Story*, gave Ronald Reagan all the credit for everything that Meese did. This was a characteristically kind and loyal thing for Ed Meese to do for his best friend, but it muddies the historical record, and, more seriously, it muddies the truth.

There is an excellent 116-page biography of Ed Meese by Lee Edwards, *To Preserve and Protect: The Life of Edwin Meese III*, published in 2005 by the Heritage Foundation, which we urge you to read. We have learned from reading it, and we have relied on it in our book. It is an excellent traditional biography. Our book differs from Lee Edwards's in four respects.

First, this book is not really a biography. It is an intellectual history that includes some biographical elements, because the history that we tell has one specific person at its center. This is first and foremost a story of ideas and their genesis, development, and influence. The biographical aspects are incidental.

Second, we emphasize Meese's success as attorney general in radically changing the way in which people today, four decades later, talk and write about U.S. constitutional law. Ed Meese launched an intellectual revolution, but he was too modest to take credit for it. As a result, others like Justice Antonin Scalia, who began speaking and writing about originalism only in 1986, well after Ed Meese's pathbreaking speeches on originalism were given, got most of the credit for having invented the originalist approach to legal interpretation. That is not wholly a bad thing: Justice Scalia was an intellectual giant and one of the most influential people ever to sit on the Supreme Court. But the truth is that Ed Meese was there first, and he was *more* of an originalist than Justice Scalia, plus he was responsible for Scalia's appointment to the Supreme Court. He was just very modest about what he had done.

Third, our book differs from biographies in a way that lawyers and law students will appreciate but which may puzzle other readers. Our book describes at some length speeches by Ed Meese and President

Reagan, Office of Legal Policy monographs, and Office of Legal Counsel opinions. We have described and occasionally quoted at length from the speeches to let Ed Meese and Ronald Reagan speak in their own words to the more than half of the U.S. population that is too young to have heard them or to remember them. We have described the Office of Legal Policy monographs to show the extent to which Ed Meese's Justice Department functioned as a conservative and libertarian law school. We have described the Office of Legal Counsel opinions because they are examples of originalism, Ed Meese's jurisprudential philosophy, originalism put into action in the DOJ in 1985–1988, before Justices Antonin Scalia and Clarence Thomas started issuing originalist opinions on the U.S. Supreme Court.

Fourth, we establish that Ed Meese was in every way Ronald Reagan's alter ego and right-hand man. In doing this, we are acting as dispassionate reporters and not as Meese acolytes. We both served in the Reagan administration, and we know from our own personal experience that it was President Reagan who ran the show and made all the important decisions, assisted critically by Ed Meese. But Ed Meese helped President Reagan make the decisions that the president wanted to make, and then he saw to it that those decisions were executed.

On October 8, 2019, Ed Meese was awarded the Presidential Medal of Freedom by President Donald J. Trump. This medal is the highest civilian award of the United States, and it is awarded to recognize "an especially meritorious contribution to the security or national interests of the United States, world peace, cultural or other significant public or private endeavors." It was established in 1963 by President Kennedy, superseding the Medal of Freedom that President Harry S. Truman established to honor civilian service during World War II.

Prior to receiving the Presidential Medal of Freedom in 2019, and the Bradley Prize in 2012, Mr. Meese had received no public acknowledgment for his enormous role as an intellectual leader in the process of profoundly changing American constitutional law. Nor would he ever seek it. Ed Meese cared almost not at all for money, he did not seek fame, and he wanted passionately to serve his country and client. Ed Meese never cashed in on his time in government by litigating cases before the judges he helped to appoint, by lobbying, or even by writing a best-selling "tell-all" book. Meese was hardworking, happy by nature, and devoted to his wife, whom he had met in high school. During his tenure as the nation's 75th attorney general, Ed Meese was the subject of scorching criticism from the press and the legal academy, which either made fun of his pathbreaking speeches or hounded him for alleged ethical improprieties, *none* of which turned out to be true. But those who do not understand Ed Meese's role in shaping American law do not understand American law.

When we started writing this book, we asked Ed Meese what President Reagan's and his own vision had been for the administering of the DOJ during the three and a half years between February 25, 1985, and August 12, 1988, when Ed Meese served as attorney general. Attorney General Meese responded by saying that both President Reagan and he saw the key elements of his job as appointing originalist judges, who would follow the law and not make it, and as administering equal justice under law. The two ideas are related, since the first obliges judges to follow the law and not their policy preferences and the second obliges judges to rule for the party who has the law on his or her side and not for someone the judges personally like. Taken together, this is what it means to have a government of laws and not of men—that is, the rule of law.

A wise man once wrote that ideas have consequences. Ed Meese's ideas had consequences. A constitutional lawyer who had gone into a coma on February 25, 1985, and regained consciousness on February 25, 2024, would certainly be aware that something monumental had occurred. Such a modern-day Rip Van Winkle would have gone to sleep in a world where constitutional law consisted of multifactor balancing tests, where the Supreme Court declined to enforce constitutional limits on federal power or even the separation of powers, where *The Federalist* was never cited, and where the original understanding of the public meaning of the words of the Constitution was irrelevant and ignored. He would have awakened to a world with far fewer multifactor balancing tests; significantly more vigorous policing of constitutional limits on federal power and the separation of powers; routine citation of *The Federalist*, along with 18th-century dictionaries; and five and one-half justices out of nine on the U.S. Supreme Court who are self-professed originalists: Associate Justices Clarence Thomas, Samuel Alito, Neil

Gorsuch, Brett Kavanaugh, and Amy Coney Barrett, with Chief Justice John Roberts apparently not quite ready to join the party but able, in at least some important cases, to form a six-person majority on the Supreme Court. It would be vividly apparent to our newly awakened lawyer that something quite radical and revolutionary had happened in American constitutional law.

Ed Meese happened. The rest of this book explains how and why.

PART I

RONALD REAGAN'S RIGHT-HAND MAN AND COUNSELLOR

CHAPTER ONE

EDWIN MEESE III: A LIFE OF SERVICE, FAITH, AND FAMILY

ED MEESE'S FAMILY history is in one sense unremarkable in that it follows a familiar pattern of so many families who immigrated to America in the mid-19th century. In another sense it is quite remarkable, because it shaped such a remarkable man.

Edwin Meese III was born on December 2, 1931, in Oakland, California, to Edwin Meese Jr. and Leone Meese. Hermann Meese, Ed Meese's paternal great-grandfather, had arrived in St. Louis from Germany in the 1840s. Exactly where in Germany Ed Meese never learned, and growing up during World War II he was not particularly inspired to find out. A carpenter by trade, Hermann Meese moved to San Francisco in 1850—by covered wagon, as family rumor had it. Once settled, Hermann wrote the father of his true love in Germany to ask permission to marry her. Permission was granted. Ed Meese's great-grandmother Katherine sailed around Cape Horn (the Panama Canal had not yet been built) to finally reunite with her betrothed in San Francisco.

The Meeses were among those devout German Lutherans who escaped forced membership in a united Prussian league of churches by immigrating to America. Hermann founded the Lutheran church in Oakland and served as its president. The *Los Angeles Times* described the new attorney general's origins in a May 4, 1986, feature, with some exaggeration, in this way: "Their Lutheran sect, known as the Missouri Synod, is considered one of the religion's most conservative branches. It is known for its Biblical literalism, its strict hierarchy and its typically uninvolved attitude toward government. An insular people in many ways—they developed the second-largest parochial school system in the country—Lutherans have close family and clan ties and a strong aversion to flamboyance."[1]

Edwin Meese Sr., Ed Meese III's grandfather and Hermann Meese's son, died when Ed was just a year old, but he followed in his father

Hermann's civic footsteps, serving as city councilman and treasurer for the City of Oakland and as president of the Oakland Lutheran Church. Michael Meese, Ed Meese's son, remembers his grandfather telling him that Edwin Meese Sr. walked through San Francisco after the 1906 earthquake and that it was the only time he ever saw his father cry.

Young Ed III idealized his public-spirited father, Edwin Meese Jr., who served as president of the Kiwanis Club, commander of the American Legion, chairman of the Alameda County Red Cross, and a leader of the Boy Scouts. According to the *Los Angeles Times*, Meese Jr.'s dedication to service "easily overrode traditional Lutheran antipathies for government. The Meeses, more than many of their neighbors, became a family as patriotic as they were pious."[2] Patriotism and politics seemed to arise naturally from the freedom in the United States. In Prussia, it had been downright dangerous to adopt political or religious views that strayed from the party line.

Ed Meese's grandmother on his father's side, Cornelia Meese, lived to be 101. Of Dutch rather than German background, she read to Ed Meese as a little boy. This affected him profoundly, as he became a lifelong reader—reading has always been Ed Meese's main hobby. He remembers reading history, biographies, adventure tales, and stories about firefighters as a child. At one point, Meese and his three younger brothers all came down with measles. Cornelia sat in the hallway between two bedrooms in which they convalesced two to a room, reading to all four boys.

Ed Meese's grandparents on his mother's side, Frank and Gretchen Feldman, were also of German and Lutheran background. They lived close by, and Meese recalls that they would regularly stop by for lunch on Sunday at their house on the way home from church. Ed was also close to his mother's brother, Uncle Henry, and his sister, and Ed's godmother, Aunt Margaret.

Like his father and grandfather before him, Ed's father, Edwin Meese Jr., served as president of the Lutheran Zion Church in Oakland, and for twenty-four years he served in government as treasurer and tax collector of Alameda County. These jobs were nonpolitical, nonpartisan roles that didn't violate the Lutheran imperative to stay out of politics. Meese's mother, Leone, he told us, "was a homemaker who was very active in the parent-teachers association. I had three younger brothers, so there were four boys born within five years, and she had plenty to do at home, but she too was active in the local community." Meese recalls his parents with nothing but affection: "I could not have had a better role model than my father. My parents were very kind, very generous people."

Ed was close to his three younger brothers—Myron, Clifford, and George—who were all within five years in age. "I was the oldest of four," he told us. "One brother, Myron, was handicapped by spina bifida, so he walked on crutches and with braces his entire life. My folks took such good care of him that he had a normal life. He out-lived by three times the lifespan the [doctors] predicted for him at birth, to fifty-seven years old."

George Meese, the youngest of the four Meese brothers, laughs that Ed was a tough act to follow. "Ed was always very bright and did well at school. We were raised during World War II, so we used to play soldiers in the backyard, with foxholes in the backyard, which upset our parents a little bit, but we enjoyed playing war. Things were very, very safe then. Everybody knew the neighbors. Of course, that made it hard to do anything bad, because everybody knew you. Ed thought we should have a newspaper in our neighborhood, which we called *The Weekly Herald*. I was copy boy. Ed, of course, was the editor. Cliff, a reporter. I forget what Myron was. But every week, our newspaper went out to a few neighbors, with a little news article on what we all were doing during that week. Ed was always a leader. In Cub Scouts and Boy Scouts, of course, we all followed along after him."

Ed Meese attended Oakland High School, a public school, where he was one of three valedictorians of the class of 1949. There he met Ursula Herrick, a Methodist from an Episcopalian family. Both were members of the debating and public speaking club, the Forensics Society. Ed's father had also been a debater in his day. One of Meese's teachers recommended that he take a summer school class with the Junior Statesmen of America. A Yale College alumnus judging the program's championships urged Ed Meese to apply to Yale College, and so, on a lark, he did.

Ed Meese was admitted to all three colleges to which he applied—Stanford, Berkeley, and Yale. Since Yale had given him a partial scholarship, he went in spite of the fact that it was three thousand miles away from home. He enrolled in Davenport College, which was then one of the ten original residential colleges.

Meese says his political views were largely formulated at Yale. He roomed with one of his high school debate partners. As freshmen, they both joined the Yale Political Union and tried out all four Yale Political Union parties: a Labor Party on the far left, a Liberal Party, a Bull Moose Liberal Republican Party, and the Conservative Party. Both young men chose the Conservative Party. "And, so from that point on I did a considerable amount of reading," Meese says. "At the time, *Human Events* was practically the only conservative publication. Then later on, shortly after I graduated, *National Review* started up, so I read that, and different authors, Russell Kirk always having been one of my favorites."

Other works particularly influential to him were Friedrich Hayek's *The Road to Serfdom* (1944)—and later *The Constitution of Liberty* (1960), and the three-volume series on *Law, Legislation, and Liberty* (1973–1979)—and the work of Ludwig von Mises. Hayek and von Mises are both theorists of seminal importance to the conservative (and libertarian) movement.

At Yale, he was elected the chairman of the Conservative Party of the Yale Political Union and, in his junior year, president of the Yale Political Union, which was unusual since the job usually went to seniors. He was also chosen as chairman of the Yale Debating Team. He credits history professor Rollin G. Osterweis, the Yale debating coach, as a key influence. (Eventually, Osterweis taught Meese to mark in red lines in the text of a speech where to pause to take a breath and what words to say loudly for emphasis. It was a classic debater's trick that served Meese well given his lifelong love of debate).

The issue of that day was whether the Republican Party in 1952 ought to nominate Senator Robert Taft, an isolationist traditional conservative, or General Dwight D. Eisenhower, the general who had helped win World War II and supported an actively anti-communist foreign policy. Meese describes himself as a natural Taft conservative who thought Eisenhower was the best candidate and isolationism the wrong policy in a world threatened by communist dictators in the U.S.S.R. and China. "For a person like me, there wasn't much difference between Eisenhower and Taft. Today, they would probably both be on the same side pretty much on most issues," he remarks. Meese's high school sweetheart (and future wife) Ursula Herrick's father had attended West Point with Eisenhower, and they knew and liked each other. President Eisenhower ultimately appointed Ed Meese's father-in-law as postmaster of Oakland.

During his first year at Yale in 1949, Meese joined ROTC in the Field Artillery Branch of the U.S. Army and the Lutheran Student Association ("a very active group of Lutheran students," he said) and managed the track team. Meese graduated in 1953 with a BA in political science and great gratitude to Yale for familiarizing him with the East and with people and lifestyles quite different from those of his hometown in California. Returning West, he enrolled at the Boalt Hall School of Law at Berkeley starting in 1954, but he was called up for active duty by the Army Reserve after his first year at law school. He served for two years with a field artillery battery whose weapons included a 240-millimeter howitzer, a bulldozer, and other equipment. This triggered a lifelong interest in logistics and operations.[3] He completed active duty in 1956, then re-enrolled in law school at Berkeley, where he won the moot court prize in his second year and later a California moot court state championship.

He and his high school sweetheart Ursula Herrick, the smart, pretty graduate of a one-year program in business at Harvard-Radcliffe, married in 1959, a year after he graduated from law school. They had kept in touch since high school and saw each other summers in Oakland, working together in the same recreation department for a couple of summers. They were married in an Episcopal church in September 1959, when Ed and Ursula were twenty-eight years old—considered unusually old for marriage for the time. They began honeymooning at Lake Tahoe, Nevada, but when it started to snow, they hightailed it to Los Angeles, with Ed suggesting a visit to the new L.A. Police Headquarters building. Laughingly, Ursula agreed, and so in Los Angeles they took a tour. The next day they followed up with Disneyland, specifically Sleeping Beauty's castle and the wonders of the deep in Captain Nemo's submarine. Ursula Meese admits to this day that Ed "can't drive by a police or fire department without slowing down."[4]

After graduating from law school in 1958, Ed joined the Alameda County District Attorney's Office as a law clerk, later serving as a colleague of D. Lowell Jensen, who later served with him as his deputy attorney general. Both used to practice riding around in the police cars, taking in the scenes of cases they were trying. Ed Meese continued the practice when he worked for Governor Reagan, and he maintains an abiding love for the police and the good work they do.

Meese's experience as a trial attorney trained him to synthesize and summarize complex ideas and usably reconstruct the action items to be drawn from any meeting. Almost everyone we interviewed about Ed Meese would independently mention this as one of his greatest skills, drawn on at almost every cabinet meeting during Ronald Reagan's presidency. He would distill the decisions taken and what action items had been approved. The power to do this is akin to the power to set an agenda for a meeting. Meese's ability to succinctly and precisely summarize the contents of panel discussions at symposia is legendary. So many of his former aides in the cabinet and the Justice Department commented on this unique talent that we asked how he had learned how to do it. He attributed it to trial lawyering, which requires one to organize information for a jury "in a way that leads toward a decision by showing the arguments on both sides, or sometimes, several sides." Ed Meese's academic and appellate lawyer subordinates at the Justice Department had never tried cases to juries, and so Ed Meese's talent at summarizing the evidence for a jury was foreign to them. It was in this way that Ed Meese saw he could be most helpful to the president. "And, being evenhanded meant that I could then work with all the members of the cabinet, my colleagues who are on the cabinet, in order to come to as good a solution as possible" and make the best possible recommendations to the president.

Ed Meese worked for three years prosecuting felonies and capital crimes. In 1961 it happened to be his turn as deputy district attorney to present information for the general sessions of the state legislature as representative of the Law and Legislative Committee. This led to Ed's making friends and acquaintances in the California legislature.

Then came a series of incidents caused by anti–Vietnam War protesters, Black Panthers and other militant groups, and events arising out of the anything-goes hippie culture of the day. During the 1964–1965 academic year, the so-called Free Speech Movement broke out at the University of California at Berkeley. It was the first major civil disobedience movement on college campuses in the U.S. of the 1960s, and many more were to follow. A takeover of the university administration building had resulted in the arrest of 773 people, with Meese being the leading figure in pursuing prosecutions.

Ronald Reagan was elected governor of California in 1966 on a law and order platform, particularly with respect to left-wing radical campus groups. By the time Reagan won the 1966 California gubernatorial election, Ed Meese was a major figure in prosecuting those who had staged a takeover of the Administration Building on the Berkeley campus. After Reagan won the governor's race in 1966, a state senator recommended Meese for a Reagan staff job. "We later found a telegram that he had sent to the governor. So that's how I was invited to come up and meet with the governor," Meese said.

> I had no idea of looking for a new job. I liked my work and my
> job, and I wasn't looking for a new one, but I was interested to
> meet this new governor whom I had never met before. We met
> in his office and talked for about a half hour. I was so impressed
> by him, his friendly personality, but also his amazing knowledge
> of matters of criminal law, the death penalty, extradition—which
> was a big issue from the governor's standpoint—and more. These
> were things I knew well only because by then, I'd been working for
> eight years in the district attorney's office. When he surprised me
> by offering me the job, I surprised myself by accepting. All I could
> think of while traveling the seventy-five miles back to Oakland
> from Sacramento was how I was going to explain having a new job
> to my wife. But she has always been great, very supportive, so even
> though we'd just had our third child, a daughter, we moved to Sac-
> ramento—and I was very fortunate to have had that opportunity.

Meese joined Governor Ronald Reagan's staff as legal affairs secretary in 1967 under Reagan's chief of staff William Clark Jr., formerly Reagan's executive assistant, with Michael Deaver as his deputy. Meese was so well regarded that in 1969–1974 he took over Clark's role after Clark was appointed to a California state judgeship. He worked to keep Michael Deaver as his deputy after Clark left, with success, and they became life-long friends and later close colleagues in the White House. Meese was a leader in the crackdown on the May 15, 1969, firebombing of Wheeler

Hall, in which a dozen buildings were vandalized and firebombed by Berkeley radicals.[5]

The chaos of the counterculture and antics of the anti–Vietnam War radical left in the 1960s and 1970s—its advocacy of recreational drug use, "free love," "blame America first," and its antipathy to religious and family values, free markets, and private property—appalled Meese, as they did other conservatives. Countering it drew Meese and Reagan together.

"Many people contributed to Governor Reagan's effectiveness and success during his eight years in Sacramento, but one person became so essential that the press teasingly referred to him as the 'assistant governor,'" said Lee Edwards of Meese's role as Governor Reagan's chief of staff.[6] Reagan biographer and journalist Lou Cannon memorably called him "Reagan's geographer" and confirmed Meese's compatibility with Reagan which enabled him to speak for Reagan to others with authority.[7]

We asked Ed Meese if Governor Reagan had considered challenging former vice president Richard M. Nixon for the Republican nomination in 1968, as many at the time had urged him to do. Meese replied, "[V]ery much so." But he and Bill Clark, then still chief of staff, were "very much opposed." They felt that Reagan had a lot left to do in California, and that he wasn't really ready yet for the presidency—"but if it had come along, he would have accepted it," Meese said. "In his own mind he really wasn't seeking the job," but did hold out hopes of bringing the Rockefeller and Nixon wings of the party together someday.

What about Governor Reagan's 1976 decision to challenge President Gerald R. Ford's reelection bid? To that Meese replied that he thought Reagan liked Ford as a person. Reagan worried that Ford had continued the big government policies he had inherited from his predecessors—Richard M. Nixon, Lyndon B. Johnson, and Franklin D. Roosevelt. "You see, the major change in the government of the United States came in different phases," Meese explained. "The first phase was Franklin Roosevelt in the 1930s, where giant steps were taken toward big government. In many respects the New Deal was a departure from basic constitutional values, which was evident in the creation of the big alphabet agencies that combined legislative, executive, and judicial power all in the same agency—and in the tremendous growth of the federal government and usurpation of functions which up until that time had historically been handled by the states or localities, or by individuals or individual private sector firms." Governor Reagan saw Lyndon Johnson's Great Society as a second phase in governmental change, following FDR's New Deal. He considered the Nixon and Ford administrations to constitute a third phase in institutionalizing Johnson's Great Society rather than trying to roll it back, as they should have done.

Reagan also was deeply concerned about the acceptance by some of communism as an alternative form of government with which we needed to coexist rather than unrelentingly oppose. Prolonged détente with the Soviets was, Reagan felt, wrong, both in theory and in practice. As he saw it, the Soviets were cheating, so it wasn't really détente, but just allowing them to continue their aggression.

Meese served as a policy advisor for Reagan's 1976 presidential campaign against President Gerald Ford, full-time for the last three months or so. In this period, he was in the inner circle of the campaign leadership. He was present and supportive when Governor Reagan announced liberal Republican senator Richard Schweiker of Pennsylvania as Reagan's running mate if he got the 1976 GOP nomination to run for president. Picking Senator Schweiker as his running mate was a Hail Mary pass, but Reagan fell just a few delegates short (1187–1070) of receiving the Republican nomination that year.

From 1974 to President Reagan's 1980 presidential campaign, Meese worked in the private sector and taught at a criminal law center that he formed at the University of San Diego with the help of the Scaife Foundation. He also served as vice chairman of California's Organized Crime Control Commission. In this period, he became good friends with a libertarian colleague, Bernie Siegan, a defender of constitutionalizing economic freedom[8] as in a famous case called *Lochner v. New York*, and a constitutional consultant to the Bulgarian government after the fall of Soviet communism. Meese got him nominated by President Reagan to the U.S. Court of Appeals for the Ninth Circuit, but unfortunately Siegan was not confirmed by the Senate.

Ed Meese loved teaching and being a law professor. He never really stopped teaching and learning. His son Mike said of him in 2021 that "what may not come through as prominently is that he really thinks of himself as a teacher. I think being a law school professor was very important to him because it is where he stays grounded and connected with folks. He's always learning and teaching, and especially reading. Unfortunately, by printing things out, he keeps Office Depot in business! The stacks of paper you remember from his desk in the Justice Department have followed him because he is really a teacher. People who meet him think they're going to be talking respectfully to a doddering old guy who's ninety-two. But he's as sharp and together as ever. And that's really from a lifetime of being a continuous student, and teacher."

Ronald Reagan, as we noted, fell short of the Republican presidential nomination in 1976 by a sliver. Four years later he tried again, with Ed Meese at his side. And they made history as the rest of this book sets forth.

On a personal level, Ed Meese's family was warmly welcomed by President Ronald and Nancy Reagan into their inner circles of closest and best of friends in the White House. On July 24, 1982, Ed and Ursula Meese suffered the devastating loss of their son Scott, who was a nineteen-year-old sophomore at Princeton, and who died in an automobile accident. Within ten minutes of Ed Meese's return to his White House office after this catastrophe, both Ronald and Nancy Reagan were in Ed's office embracing him with tears streaming down their cheeks. They urged Ed, Ursula, and the children to spend that weekend at Camp David to recuperate a bit. In 1983, Ed and Ursula Meese celebrated the wedding of their son Mike with Ed's father and mother in attendance. They celebrated the wedding of their daughter, Dana, in 1999.

On Thanksgiving Day 2023 the whole Meese clan gathered at their vacation lake house and celebrated together with their two children, Mike and Dana, and their spouses, and their five grandchildren and nine great-grandchildren with a tenth on the way. Ed Meese's life has truly been one of service, faith, and family.

CHAPTER TWO

THE REAGAN REVOLUTION

ED MEESE'S LASTING accomplishments happened primarily while he was serving President Ronald Reagan. Reagan's two-term presidency ended thirty-five years ago, before a substantial percentage of the country's current population was even born. An astonishing 50 percent of the U.S. population was born in 1982 or thereafter, and so for more than half of all Americans today President Reagan is someone they read about in (often shamelessly slanted) history books or Wikipedia entries but do not remember. Those who lived through the Reagan presidency in the 1980s did not always receive accurate information about it through the media, and there were facets of the presidency that were not known at the time even to staunch Reaganites who were able to pierce the media filters. But everything that Ed Meese did in the 1980s was in service to the vision and agenda that he shared with President Reagan. Accordingly, it is impossible to talk about Ed Meese without also talking about Ronald Reagan. It is no accident that Ed Meese titled his own book *With Reagan*.

Many Americans today cannot fully appreciate the awe in which millions of people held President Ronald Reagan during his two terms in office from 1981 to 1989. President Reagan was the leader of what his supporters called the "Reagan Revolution"—a massive change in the foreign and domestic policy of the U.S. government. It is impossible to convey in one brief chapter the scope and significance of the Reagan presidency,[1] but we will briefly describe the four key elements of "Reaganism" that Ed Meese tirelessly worked to develop and promote: a reconceptualization of the proper role of the national government; an economic policy premised on freedom, low taxes, and sensible regulation; a foreign policy focused on defeating rather than containing international communism; and a revival of constitutionalism in place of the inventive judicial policy-making that had characterized American constitutional law for decades. We will describe those elements largely through President Reagan's own words, which inspired people in a way that presidential words seldom do.

Before we talk about the Reagan Revolution, however, it is worth hearing a few words about Ronald Reagan the person. No one is better able to talk about Ronald Reagan than Ed Meese, as no one alive today knew President Reagan more closely and personally than did Counsellor to the President and Attorney General Ed Meese. Meese and Reagan were best friends and ideological soulmates. It is therefore fitting and appropriate to let Ed Meese describe who Ronald Reagan really was.

REAGAN

WITH RONALD REAGAN, Ed Meese told us, "what you see is what you got. ... He was through and through a genuine person in his beliefs, in his values, and in his actions." That authenticity, rare enough in politicians, surely contributed to President Reagan's enormous popularity. No doubt his generosity of spirit did as well; as Ed Meese explained, Reagan "was extremely generous, particularly courteous[, and] he respected everyone, even those people who were his opponents politically." Ed Meese is also generous to a fault, which perhaps explains why he added: "And, I think [as a result] no one could really hate Ronald Reagan. Even the press disliked his views and disliked his values to a large extent, but they had a hard time disliking Ronald Reagan." We can both attest that if one were on a campus in the 1980s (and perhaps even today), one would not have had to look far to detect hatred for Ronald Reagan.

President Reagan's generous and amiable spirit and good sense of humor infused his leadership style. As Mr. Meese described it,

> [W]hen he had to make a decision, he wanted to make a decision that the people who would have been on the other side would still appreciate the way in which he handled the situation. So ... he chose to spend a lot of time with his cabinet, because he wanted this interchange of ideas. ... [H]e used to say, "The more information I get, the better decisions I will make." ... And, when he made a decision, he would, rather than announcing it immediately at the cabinet meeting, he would say, "Let me think about that." ... And, then in the morning, the first thing he would do would be to call the people on the opposite side of ... his decision ... and let them know so they would not be blindsided. And then, he would thank them for their views. ...

Anyone who watched Ronald Reagan in action, even from a distance, saw someone of indefatigable good cheer and an extraordinary sense of humor. Three publicly known episodes stand out.

The first was tragic. On March 30, 1981, John Hinckley Jr. took six shots at President Reagan in an attempted assassination. One of the bullets hit the president on a ricochet. As he was being wheeled into surgery, President Reagan looked at his wife, Nancy, and said, "Honey, I forgot to duck."[2]

The second was both humorous and symbolic. On August 11, 1984, President Reagan was scheduled to give his weekly national radio address—a tradition that has been lost to modern technology. The speech itself began, "My fellow Americans: I'm pleased to tell you that today I signed legislation that will allow student religious groups to begin enjoying a right they've too long been denied—the freedom to meet in public high schools during nonschool hours." During the sound check before the speech went on the air, President Reagan ad-libbed a few changes in the opening line for the benefit of the sound technicians, deadpanning: "My fellow Americans, I'm pleased to tell you today that I've signed legislation that will outlaw Russia forever. We begin bombing in five minutes." As we will shortly see, Ronald Reagan did not accept the establishment consensus about détente with international communism.

The third was historic. In 1984, President Reagan ran against the fifty-six-year-old Walter Mondale. Reagan was seventy-three years old and was the oldest president, at that point, in American history (Joe Biden now holds that title). He would, moreover, be seventy-seven years old at the end of a second term. One of the journalists in the second of two presidential debates between Reagan and Mondale asked Reagan whether he was too old to be running for a second term as president, and Reagan gave the journalist a broad grin, smiled, and happily said: "I will not make age an issue of this campaign. I am not going to exploit, for political purposes, my opponent's youth and inexperience." Walter Mondale, the journalist, and the whole room roared with laughter. It is quite possible that, in that single moment, Ronald Reagan won his 1984 reelection as president by a landslide.

Ed Meese confirms that this sense of humor was a natural part of President Reagan's persona: "Ronald Reagan just enjoyed laughing.

He had a cheerful approach to life. Ronald Reagan's sense of humor was spontaneous."

Ed Meese experienced that sense of humor firsthand:

[William French] Smith, my predecessor as attorney general, and I…were both together at the time that I was taking over as attorney general, and Bill Smith was returning to California, having just retired. We were both on Air Force One with the president because he himself was going to California.... [Bill Smith and I were both asleep side-by-side in large reclining armchairs reserved for cabinet members traveling on Air Force One]. [T]he President saw us…, and he summoned the White House photographer to take a picture of both of us sleeping there. And, so about a week or so later…, I [received in the mail] this framed picture autographed and inscribed by the president, and it said:
"Dear Ed:
"See, I told everyone you could do Bill Smith's job and here is the proof!
Signed, Ron"

And I still have that [photograph] as a treasured memento of his sense of humor in my time with the president.

REAGANISM

ALL HUMOR ASIDE, the Reagan presidency inherited a catastrophic situation at home and abroad. During Jimmy Carter's presidency from 1977 to 1980, the economy was in shambles from Carter's disastrously anti–free-market regulatory policies,[3] generating a combination of high inflation, high interest rates, low economic growth, and high unemployment, dubbed "stagflation," that baffled even liberal economists. Interest rates in 1981, as President Reagan took office, were at 16 percent—almost three times the rates as of summer 2023—and unemployment was measured at around 7 percent—more than twice the 2023 level. Moreover, foreign affairs were going quite badly in 1980. The Soviet Union had invaded Afghanistan in 1979, and the government of Iran had seized and held as hostages, since November 1979, the U.S. ambassador to Iran and more than fifty other embassy personnel. President Carter's response to these crises was to give a speech on July 15, 1979, in which he blamed the American people for lacking confidence, chastised them for being concerned about material goods, and proposed mandatory energy rationing.[4] This disastrous address has come to be known as the "malaise speech"—an epithet that apparently came from Ted Kennedy and was picked up by Reagan.[5]

Carter's record on economic and foreign policy was terrible, so his campaign was mostly one of attacks on Reagan, suggesting that if Reagan were elected president, there would be a nuclear war. During the one 1980 presidential election debate on October 28, Carter launched into another such attack on television, claiming that Reagan opposed Medicare. Reagan responded by grinning, shaking his head, and saying, "There you go again," explaining that he opposed certain Medicare proposals because they were inferior to others that would better implement the program.[6] This lighthearted response to a desperate attack put Reagan ahead. Reagan ended his closing statement by asking Americans if they were better off in 1980 than they had been in 1976. He won the presidential election of 1980 in a 440-electoral-vote landslide.

The "Reagan Revolution," however, was not really about Reagan the person. It was about a set of ideas. Four sets of ideas were central to what has come to be called "Reaganism." We briefly describe—or, rather, let President Reagan describe—those ideas below at a high level of abstraction, leaving for elsewhere an account of specific policies that implemented those ideas.

Reorientation of the Role of the Federal Government

ONE KEY IDEA, and perhaps *the* key idea, was a reorientation of the role of the federal government. As President Reagan took office in 1981, there had been an increase in of the federal government's activity for a century, dating back to the Progressive Era, accelerating during the New Deal, accelerating again during the Great Society, and continuing unabated through the Nixon, Ford, and Carter years. In 1792, there were four major federal agencies: the Departments of War, State, and Treasury, and the Post Office. By 1980, there were thirteen executive departments and untold dozens of "alphabet soup" agencies, many of which exercise more power than some cabinet agencies and many of which were created in the two decades before Reagan took office. To be sure, presidents cannot unilaterally set budgets or create or abolish bureaucracies; only Congress can authorize those things. But presidents make proposals, define agendas, and help set the terms of discussion, through both talk and action. President Reagan was particularly adept at using speeches to lay out his vision of government. His audience was not just members of Congress, the bureaucracy, or the media but the broader public, and his vision emphasized basic principles more than the policies of the moment that flowed from those principles. Here is how President Reagan, through some of his most notable speeches, described his conception of the national government.

On January 21, 1981, the day after he was sworn in as president, Ronald Reagan gave his first inaugural address. It is a remarkable speech that bears reading in full, but five short passages stand out as encapsulations of President Reagan's guiding philosophy.

After describing the dire circumstances facing the country, President Reagan famously declared, "In this present crisis, government is not the solution to our problem; government is the problem." That may seem simple, but coming after a steady century of progressivism and its aftermath, it gave words to the sense of millions for whom government had become more an obstacle than a protector. In a direct rebuke to the elite consensus of the previous century, which entrusted ever-increasing power to self-proclaimed experts, President Reagan observed: "From time to time we've been tempted to believe that society has become too complex to be managed by self-rule, that government by an elite group is superior to government for, by, and of the people. Well, if no one among us is capable of governing himself, then who among us has the capacity to govern someone else?" This fundamental trust in free people rather than governmental control by those who think they know better is the essence of Reaganism. As Reagan explained, "If we look to the answer as to why for so many years we achieved so much, prospered as no other people on Earth, it was because here in this land we unleashed the energy and individual genius of man to a greater extent than has ever been done before. Freedom and the dignity of the individual have been more available and assured here than in any other place on Earth." Accordingly, said Reagan, "It is my intention to curb the size and influence of the Federal establishment and to demand recognition of the distinction between the powers granted to the Federal Government and those reserved to the States or to the people. All of us need to be reminded that the Federal Government did not create the States; the States created the Federal Government."[7] Even more basically, he observed, "[w]e are a nation that has a government—not the other way around."

In his February 6, 1985, State of the Union Address to Congress, President Reagan emphasized the revolutionary character of these thoughts on government by boldly announcing that "[f]our years ago we began to change, forever I hope, our assumptions about government and its place in our lives." His plan for the next four years was straightforward: "Let us resolve that we will stop spreading dependency and start spreading opportunity; that we will stop spreading bondage and start spreading freedom." Harkening again to the idea that government is not the solution, he added that "[e]very dollar the Federal Government does not take from us, every decision it does not make for us will make our economy stronger, our lives more abundant, our future more free." These views were grounded in universal principles applicable in all places to all peoples, not something tailored to the politics of the moment. "Our mission," said President Reagan, "is to nourish and defend freedom and democracy, and to communicate these ideals everywhere we can. America's economic success is freedom's success; it can be repeated a hundred times in a hundred different nations."

President Reagan carried out this universal mission even when speaking in forums unlikely to be receptive; on October 24, 1985, he told the United Nations General Assembly that "[w]e Americans do not accept that any government has the right to command and order the lives of its people."

President Reagan returned to these themes once again at the end of his presidency on January 11, 1989, when he delivered his Farewell Address to the Nation. This is also a speech worth reading in full, but among its many poignant passages was this: "Almost all the world's constitutions are documents in which governments tell the people what their privileges are. Our Constitution is a document in which 'We the People' tell the government what it is allowed to do. 'We the People' are free. This belief has been the underlying basis for everything I've tried to do these past 8 years."

Thus, President Reagan sought reconsideration not just of what government should be doing for (and to) people but also which level of government should be doing it. Both of these ideas, however basic they are to the country's founding, were truly revolutionary in Reagan's time, though Reagan perceptively said in his Farewell Address that while "[t]hey called it the Reagan revolution ... for me it always seemed more like the great rediscovery, a rediscovery of our values and our common sense."

Economic Policy of Free Markets and Free People

A SECOND ASPECT of the Reagan Revolution—stemming, as did all the others, from the first—was an economic policy premised on free markets and free people. President Reagan inherited a poor economy. The day President Carter was replaced by President Reagan, the inflation rate in the United States was 13.5 percent, interest rates were 15.6 percent, the unemployment rate was 7.2 percent, and the United States' gross domestic product (GDP) was $3.211 trillion dollars. By comparison, in January of 2020 (before the coronavirus and the various governments' panicked responses to it temporarily intruded on our world), the inflation rate in the United States was 2.3 percent per year, interest rates in the United States were at 1.75 percent, the U.S. unemployment rate was at 3.6 percent, and U.S. GDP was $22.111 trillion dollars. In other words, under President Reagan and his five successors, the U.S. gross domestic product increased by $18.901 trillion dollars in only thirty-nine years, and the 1970s combination of high inflation, high interest rates, and high unemployment has been forgotten even by many who lived through it. Sadly, in 2024, high inflation and stagflation are returning to the United States as a direct result of President Biden's fervent efforts to undo the Reagan Revolution.

President Reagan's inaugural address diagnosed the economic problems, which began with "a tax system which penalizes successful achievement and keeps us from maintaining full productivity." "It is no coincidence," he said, "that our present [economic] troubles parallel and are proportionate to the intervention and intrusion in our lives that result from unnecessary and excessive growth of government." As a solution, he proposed "removing the roadblocks that have slowed our economy and reduced productivity," specifically by "lighten[ing] our punitive tax burden" and, continuing the first-principles theme of federalism, "restoring the balance between the various levels of government."

In a speech to the United Kingdom Parliament on June 8, 1982, President Reagan highlighted the importance of these principles by contrasting them to the competing principles of the Soviet Union. However bad the circumstances in the United States might have been in the early 1980s, they paled before the human catastrophe wrought by communism. As Reagan noted, the world's great revolutionary crisis was "happening not in the free, non-Marxist West, but in the home of Marxist-Leninism, the Soviet Union. It is the Soviet Union that runs against the tide of history by denying human freedom and human dignity to its citizens." "The dimensions of this failure," he continued, "are astounding: A country which employs one-fifth of its population in agriculture is unable to feed its own people." This was a direct result of "a society where productive forces are hampered by political ones."

By 1984, to the astonishment of numerous so-called "experts," the United States economy was roaring. As President Reagan quipped in 1983, "We knew the program was a success when they stopped calling it 'Reaganomics.'" President Reagan won reelection—this time by a 512-electoral-vote margin, losing only Walter Mondale's home state of Minnesota and (of course) the District of Columbia. The vision driving the Reagan economic policy was captured in a May 16, 1984, speech to the American Retail Association: "There was only one way to go, and that was [to] use three simple words as our guide: Trust the people. Lasting economic recovery had to be built on the solid rock of the American free enterprise system."

President Reagan's Farewell Address in 1989 summarized the principles underlying the solutions implemented during his two terms. He explained that "when you put a big tax on something, the people will produce less of it. So, we cut the people's tax rates, and the people produced more than ever before," generating "the longest peacetime expansion in our history [with] real family income up, the poverty rate down, entrepreneurship booming, and an explosion in research and new technology." One anecdote related in that speech says it all:

It was back in 1981, and I was attending my first big economic summit. ... I sat there like the new kid in school and listened, and it was all Francois this and Helmut that. They dropped titles and spoke to one another on a first-name basis. Well, at one point I sort of leaned in and said, "My name's Ron." Well, in that same year, we began the actions we felt would ignite an economic comeback—cut taxes and regulation, started to cut spending. And soon the recovery began.

Two years later, another economic summit with pretty much the same cast. At the big opening meeting we all got together, and all of a sudden, just for a moment, I saw that everyone was just sitting there looking at me. And then one of them broke the silence. "Tell us about the American miracle," he said.

Foreign Policy and the Rolling Back of Communism

A THIRD KEY ELEMENT in the Reagan Revolution was a sharp break with the conventional, establishment, and almost wholly bipartisan consensus on foreign policy. For decades, the establishment view, across administrations and congressional delegations of both parties, was to try to contain to some extent the international spread of communism while engaging in an uneasy détente with the Soviet Union and communist China, undergirded by the notion of "mutually assured destruction" in the event that anyone was provoked into nuclear war. Ronald Reagan had other ideas.

President Ronald Reagan changed America's foreign policy from one of containing communism to one of rolling it back. This was a momentous shift, which led to the fall of the Berlin Wall, freedom in Eastern Europe, and the collapse of the former Soviet Union.

Reagan first announced this shift in American foreign policy in his June 8, 1982, speech to the Parliament of the United Kingdom, when Margaret Thatcher was prime minister. In this speech President Reagan referred to "The Berlin Wall" as "that dreadful gray gash across the city, [which] is in its third decade. It is the fitting signature of the regime that built it." Reagan added, "We're approaching the end of a bloody century plagued by a terrible political invention—totalitarianism." Reagan was not content to contain the spread of totalitarianism. Instead, he had "a plan and a hope for the long term—the march of freedom and democracy which will leave Marxism-Leninism on the ash-heap of history as it has left other tyrannies which stifle the freedom and muzzle the self-expression of the people."

When President Reagan gave this speech about leaving Marxism-Leninism on the ash-heap of history, he was berated by many in the foreign policy establishment for dangerous saber-rattling. The collapse of communism in 1989 and of the Soviet Union in 1991 suggests that Ronald Reagan was wiser than the establishment.

The establishment that was so unsettled by President Reagan's unabashed defense of freedom found even more occasion for pearl-clutching when President Reagan spoke to the National Association of Evangelicals on March 8, 1983. In warning against a "nuclear freeze" movement that equally blamed the United States and the Soviet Union for world tensions, President Reagan said of our communist adversaries, "[L]et us be aware that while they preach the supremacy of the state, declare its omnipotence over individual man, and predict its eventual domination of all peoples on the Earth, they are the focus of evil in the modern world." He warned against "the temptation of blithely declaring yourselves above it to all and label both sides equally at fault, to ignore the facts of history and the aggressive impulses of an evil empire, to simply call the arms race a giant misunderstanding and thereby remove yourself from the struggle between right and wrong and good and evil."

In this speech, President Ronald Reagan called the Soviet Union "the focus of evil in the modern world" and an "evil empire." No prior American president had ever challenged communism in this way, and President Reagan's speech brought moral clarity as to what was at issue in the Cold War. He added that "I believe that communism is another sad, bizarre chapter in human history whose last pages even now are being written."

Perhaps the most important statement of Reaganism's foreign policy principles was President Reagan's historic speech on June 12, 1987, at the Brandenburg Gate. The gate was located right at the Berlin Wall, which for decades had separated communist-ruled East Berlin from free West Berlin. The gate had stood for several centuries, but from the end of World War II until 1989, it was closed off, serving as a symbol of the communist tyranny that controlled both entry into and exit from East

Berlin. President Reagan explained that "[b]ehind me stands a wall that encircles the free sectors of this city, part of a vast system of barriers that divides the entire continent of Europe. From the Baltic south, those barriers cut across Germany in a gash of barbed wire, concrete, dog runs, and guard towers. ... Standing before the Brandenburg Gate, every man is a German, separated from his fellow men. Every man is a Berliner, forced to look upon a scar." In response to then-recent moves in the Soviet Union ostensibly moving toward a marginally more open society, President Reagan made perhaps his most momentous statement: "There is one sign the Soviets can make that would be unmistakable, that would advance dramatically the cause of freedom and peace. General Secretary Gorbachev, if you seek peace, if you seek prosperity for the Soviet Union and Eastern Europe, if you seek liberalization: Come here to this gate! Mr. Gorbachev, open this gate! Mr. Gorbachev, tear down this wall!"

The Brandenburg Gate speech was a stroke of genius on President Ronald Reagan's part, though some of his timid foreign service employees thought he should not have given it because it was provocative and might jeopardize détente and arms control. Ed Meese aide John Richardson recalls: "The Reagan mindset of tear down the wall ... [the] State [Department] fought to the last minute before the speech was given, State fought to strike that." These advisors believed in the Truman Doctrine of containing but accepting Soviet communism in Eastern Europe while militarily protecting Western Europe. President Reagan did not believe that communism should merely be contained. He thought it should be rolled back and overthrown. He knew that the only things holding communism together, in 1987, were military troops at the borders of all of the communist nations of Eastern Europe, facing inward with guns to shoot their fellow countrymen for seeking freedom in Western Europe.

Reagan's demand for freedom resonated deeply with the people of Eastern Europe, and the first crack in the wall came when Hungary began allowing its citizens, and East Germans, to cross the border into Western Europe. What began as a trickle of people fleeing Eastern Europe rapidly became an unstoppable flood. On November 9, 1989, two and a half years after President Reagan demanded that President Gorbachev tear down the Berlin Wall, and ten months after President

Reagan left office, the people of East Berlin stormed the wall, the Brandenburg Gate was opened permanently on December 22, 1989, and on October 3, 1990, East and West Germany merged together into one united Federal Republic of Germany. On December 26, 1991, the Soviet Union dissolved into fifteen new nation-states.

Ed Meese explained to us that when President Reagan was asked by a top aide what his policy toward the Soviet Union would be, Reagan replied by saying, "It is really very simple. We will win, and they will lose." And that is precisely what happened—without a single shot (much less a nuclear weapon) being fired! President Reagan understood economics so well, and so intuitively, that he knew a command-and-control economy could never stand the test of time. By launching an arms race with the Soviet Union and getting Saudi Arabia to flood the oil markets and thereby reduce the value of the Soviet Union's oil production, President Reagan forced the Soviets into bankruptcy, and the Soviet Union and its entire Eastern European and Russian empire collapsed.

It takes a lot, even for a president, to stand up to the entire foreign policy establishment of both parties. But President Reagan did not come to his views casually. As Ed Meese explains,

Ronald Reagan won the Cold War largely because he had been thinking about this a long time. He got introduced to communism way back in the 1940s, when he was president of the Screen Actors Guild, and the Communist Party tried to take over the movie industry so they [could] use it for propaganda purposes.... And from that experience he had a great knowledge of and studied co mmunism. Ronald Reagan was always [a] great student.... He was a[n] avid reader and a person who remembered what he read.... And so he studied communism. And that led him to ... study international communism because one of his close friends was an author of books on communism. [H]e was very knowledgeable about the subject of communism both domestically and internationally way before he [became] president and even ... as governor. [H]e brought those ideas into the presidency, but he also brought in with him people who would carry out [Reagan's core] idea that [the] communists were not unbeatable.

[Ronald Reagan] felt that the totalitarian ideas that were the

- 49 -

foundation [of] communism [were the] ...means of [its] own destruction and that people could not be oppressed and held captive for long periods of time. ... [T]hen beyond that he felt it was important to engage the communists on a moral plane, and that is why he [gave] speeches [explaining] that communism essentially was the face of evil in the world. [Ronald Reagan] felt that the oppressed peoples, the people in the prisons, in the various captured countries and so on could be roused up to again work for freedom. And when he talked about communism as being an evil force, we learned later from people who had been in prison at that time, how much this stoked the sense of freedom in the people who were in the captive nations. And then ...the third thing that was very important, was [Reagan's willingness] to support freedom fighters around the world. Whether it was in Nicaragua, whether it was in Angola, whether it was in Poland, wh[er]ever it happened to be. And so a combination of this [Reagan Doctrine that we could roll back communism, and not simply contain it,] and the implementation of that doctrine [along with the creation by the United States of] the best and the strongest military force that any the world had ever seen [resulted in our winning the Cold War].

Restoration of Constitutionalism and the Rule of Law

A FOURTH ELEMENT of Reaganism, which occupies much of this book, is the restoration of constitutionalism and the rule of law. Ronald Reagan was not a constitutional theorist, but he grasped at a very basic level the key tenets of originalism. Unlike Richard Nixon, he did not explicitly run against the Supreme Court, but he understood that much of the court's work product bore little relation to the country's governing document. On September 26, 1986, after Antonin Scalia was sworn in as an associate justice and William Rehnquist was sworn in as chief justice, President Reagan noted that the Framers "settled on a judiciary that would be independent and strong, but one whose power would also, they believed, be confined within the boundaries of a written Constitution and laws. ... The judicial branch interprets the laws, while the power to make and execute those laws is balanced in the two elected branches." He invoked Thomas Jefferson's warning against making the

Constitution "a blank paper by construction" and James Madison's injunction that if "the sense in which the Constitution was accepted and ratified by the nation is not the guide to expounding it, there can be no security for a faithful exercise of its powers."

For reasons that we explain in a subsequent chapter, President Reagan in 1986 could not yet draw on an established vocabulary for originalism. That vocabulary was still being developed—primarily in the Meese Justice Department, as we will soon see. Accordingly, he couched his praise for Justice Scalia and Chief Justice Rehnquist in terms of their support for "judicial restraint," a term he used multiple times. A few years later, he might have used different language. Intuitively, however, he understood that the Constitution is a written text with an ascertainable meaning and the task of constitutional interpretation is to uncover and articulate that meaning.

He also understood something that is missed by too many constitutional actors even today. President Reagan observed "that the Founding Fathers designed a system of checks and balances, and of limited government, because they knew that the great preserver of our freedoms would never be the courts or either of the other branches alone. It would always be the totality of our constitutional system, with no one part getting the upper hand." The courts thus play an important role in enforcing the Constitution, but they do not play an exclusive role. This "departmentalist" obligation of all three departments of the federal government to interpret, apply, and act in accordance with the Constitution is made clear by the overall structure of the document, which contains no express "Interpretation Clause" for any particular actor and specifically charges the president to swear an oath to "preserve, protect, and defend the Constitution of the United States." President Reagan understood that it was our Madisonian system of checks and balances; our separation of legislative, executive, and judicial power; our holding of midterm elections; and our federal division into fifty states that make our 235-year-old Constitution work. Yes, the Supreme Court plays a vitally important role in protecting the liberties secured by the Constitution, the federal Bill of Rights, the three transformative post–Civil War constitutional amendments, and the other amendments thus far ratified. But many other actors play vital roles as well. The Constitution means what it says, not what any particular person, group of persons, or coalition of judges says it says.

These four ideas of Reaganism may seem banal to some and anathema to others. In either case, in the 1980s they reflected a genuine revolution in thinking about government, economics, communism, and law—even, and perhaps especially, within a Republican Party establishment that was comfortable with big government, accommodating communism, and policymaking courts that relieved political actors of responsibility for big decisions. Indeed, Martin Anderson's invaluable 1988 account of the Reagan years is titled simply: *Revolution*.

REAGANITES

A REVOLUTION, of course, needs revolutionaries. Ronald Reagan, even with Ed Meese at his side, could not transform the operations of government, much less the basic ideas that had driven policy and law for decades. Some of those revolutionaries were relatively low-level actors whose participation was nonetheless crucial to the success of Reaganism. People at the top can give instructions, but people in the middle and bottom of the governmental hierarchies are the ones who can either follow those instructions or thwart them. President Reagan was not only on a wartime footing with communism; he was also on a wartime footing with what former president Donald Trump, quite rightly, called "the deep state." There are more than four million human beings who work as either federal officials or in the U.S. armed services. While the army is loyal to the president, the deep state is not. Each president gets only around four thousand political loyalists who serve in his administration and who try to supervise the three million civilian employees of the deep state. They compete in doing this with twenty-four thousand congressional staffers whose congressional bosses serve in office far longer than the two-year average for cabinet secretaries, the four years of one presidential term, or even the eight years of two presidential terms. Twenty-three senators in Steve Calabresi's and Gary Lawson's lifetimes have served for thirty-six years or longer.

But having good people at the top is essential, and Ronald Reagan had some of the best at his side. Ed Meese, of course, stands out. There were other vital actors in the Department of Justice whom we will discuss at some length in subsequent chapters. A number of other key figures in the Reagan Revolution, however, deserve a brief mention here, and we present them as seen through the eyes and words of Ed Meese.

Vice President George Herbert Walker Bush

VICE PRESIDENT BUSH had been President Reagan's most formidable opponent in the Republican primaries in 1980, and he served for one term as President Reagan's successor. When asked how he would describe Vice President Bush as a person, Ed Meese immediately said that "Vice President Bush was one of the best and most loyal vice presidents and, subsequently, one of the best presidents we have had in the history of the country." As vice president, "[h]e was fully supportive of the president's policies and his positions on issues... [and] an excellent representative of the president...in foreign policy matters." Importantly, Vice President Bush was careful never to overstep. For example, "when the president was shot and was in the hospital, the vice president was en route [back to Washington, D.C., from] Texas. ... And, when he came back, there was a suggestion made... by his staff or someone... that when he landed in Andrews Air Force Base, he should [fly directly by helicopter to] the White House lawn. [Vice President Bush] indicated that would not be appropriate. He did not want anybody to think that he was trying to take over from the president and [to] land [on the White House lawn] in the president's landing spot there. Instead, the helicopter took him to his residence which is the Naval Observatory, and then he came in my car to meet with the cabinet and so on. [This is a perfect] example of [the exemplary way in which he handled the job of being vice president.]"

William J. Casey

ONE OF THE leading Reagan Revolutionaries, according to Ed Meese in his wonderful book *With Reagan: The Inside Story*, was William J. Casey, who became Ronald Reagan's campaign manager in 1980 after the firing of John Sears and went on to serve as director of central intelligence from 1981 to 1987. Ed Meese describes Mr. Casey as "a great patriot [and] a real[ly] devoted follower of the president. He was a great person in terms of being a member of the Reagan team." Indeed, Ed Meese said that "it was really I [who] brought him aboard [the 1980

Reagan campaign]. I recommended to the president that he come aboard even before the president made the decision to remove Sears, and [that he] help with the issues which is what I was in charge of. And then that led ultimately to when Sears and his team [were] fired, the president asked Bill and me together to head the campaign [in] February of 1981."

Given Mr. Casey's experience, explained Mr. Meese, "he was a natural person for the job [of Director of Central Intelligence]. [T]he president needed someone of absolute integrity [and] someone who had his confidence completely.... And that was Bill Casey. So it was as a result of that, that [President Reagan] also then made Bill ... a member of the cabinet. Bill was a great contributor there. So, he was just a fine man, one of the finest people and also one of the most unforgettable people that I've ever met."

Caspar Weinberger

DEFENSE SECRETARY Casper Weinberger was obviously a big player in the Reagan Revolution. Ed Meese calls him "a person of great intelligence, great integrity, and [an] outstanding person as an individual.... [H]e had a bright sense of initiative, imagination, and innovation. [S]o he was the ideal person [to serve as secretary of defense]. He also had experience in Washington [where he had been] chairman of the Federal Trade Commission under President Nixon, as well as being [] first the Deputy Director and then Director of the Office of Management and Budget and finally being Secretary of Health[, Education] and Welfare. So he [had lots of prior] government [experience] as [well] as being... a fine lawyer.... A very good friend and, just an outstanding person in every aspect of his life."

William P. Clark Jr.

BILL CLARK served as deputy secretary of state from 1981 to 1982, as U.S. national security advisor from 1982 to 1983, and as secretary of the interior from 1983 to 1985. Mr. Meese called him "a tireless worker [and] a man of outstanding abilities and integrity. Bill was a good friend both to the governor and certainly to me as well... [and] was just an invaluable member of the Reagan team." Ed Meese emphasizes Mr. Clark's service as secretary of the interior, "where it was particularly in that role, [with] his love of the outdoors and love of rural America[, which] was pronounced, that he made a difference."

Lyn Nofziger

WE KNEW from reading Ed Meese's book *With Reagan: The Inside Story* that Lyn Nofziger, who had been Ronald Reagan's press secretary when he was governor of California, was also a key member of the Reagan Revolution. When asked, Ed Meese confirmed that "Lyn Nofziger was a very unique figure. [H]e was a newsman, or a journalist, [but] also quite a political strategist in his own way from having been involved in political activity going way back to the 1950s and 1960s." At the start of the Reagan presidency, Mr. Nofziger "was head of our political office, the Office of Political Affairs as it was known at the time. [This office] was basically the liaison between the White House and [the] various political supporters of the president on national issues." As did President Reagan, "Lyn [had] a great sense of humor.... And, he was a great person just to be around [and] also a very close and good friend of mine over the years, right [up] to the point of his unfortunate death from cancer. Absolutely I would say [that] of all the people who were really essential to Ronald Reagan and his career [Lyn Nofziger] was certainly one of them."

Jeane Kirkpatrick

JEANE KIRKPATRICK was a key member of the Reagan foreign policy team, serving as United Nations ambassador from 1981 to 1985. She was a Democrat, but, as Ed Meese explains, " [s]he was not partisan in the usual sense.... She was a staunch anti-communist, [and] she was a great promoter of freedom of the individual, political freedom. [She wrote a book in] which she bemoaned the Marxism of the Soviet Union and its satellites.... Ronald Reagan was very impressed with her book. It was one of the many books he had read on communism, and which made him such an expert on the subject."

Margaret Thatcher

MARGARET THATCHER, the longtime Conservative Party prime minister of the United Kingdom, was obviously a key ally of Ronald

Reagan's in winning the Cold War. She not only shared President Reagan's foreign policy goal of rolling back communism but also believed in a smaller and more limited role for government in the UK. Ed Meese says of her:

"[S]he was just exactly the right person [at] the time to be…a partner with Ronald Reagan, and [Margaret Thatcher was able to give him valuable information because] she had been in office a couple of years before he became president. And so she had a wealth of information to share with him from her vantage point, and that solidified and strengthened the relationship, the special relationship between the United Kingdom and the United States. But also, when [Ronald Reagan] went to his first [G-7] Summit, he and she were the only non-socialists there. [B]y the time [Ronald Reagan] left office and [Margaret Thatcher] left office, almost every one of those countries almost without exception had [a] right-of-center and more conservative government."

Other Key Figures

THIS LIST of important Reagan Revolutionaries, of course, is wildly underinclusive. Ed Meese mentions Malcolm Baldrige, the secretary of commerce, who "took his managerial, leadership capabilities to run the Department of Commerce but also to be an important advisor…to the president," and Secretary of State George Shultz, who "without a question also [contributed immensely to the Reagan Revolution]…in foreign policy matters." Ed Meese also praised Martin Anderson, an economist who wrote important books on welfare policy and Reaganism, and who "as a member of the campaign staff and then as a member of the White House staff the first couple of years was extremely important.…[B]y bringing him to the campaign and then into the White House, his knowledge having worked for most of the Nixon era [was harnessed by Ronald Reagan's White House on the domestic and economic policy side of things]."

The list could go on, but since this is a book about Ed Meese, we stop here. Excellent accounts of the Reagan Revolution and the people behind it are available in Martin Anderson, *Revolution: The Reagan Legacy* (1988), Lou Cannon, *President Reagan: The Role of a Lifetime* (1991), Steven F. Hayward, *The Age of Reagan: The Conservative Counterrevolution*

1980–1989 (2009), and William Inboden's, *The Peacemaker: Ronald Reagan, the Cold War, and the World on the Brink* (2022).

REAGANISM REDUX

WE END THIS much-too-brief chapter with some parting words from Ronald Reagan in his 1989 Farewell Address. Those words draw on a 1630 sermon delivered by John Winthrop to the Massachusetts Bay Colony settlers before they disembarked from their ships to found the cities of Boston and Salem. Winthrop famously said that the new world about to be built by Americans-to-be "shall be as a city upon a hill. The eyes of all people are upon us."[8] President Reagan's words in response speak for themselves, so we present them without embellishment or commentary:

> The past few days ... I've thought a bit of the "shining city upon a hill." The phrase comes from John Winthrop, who wrote it to describe the America he imagined. What he imagined was important because he was an early Pilgrim, an early freedom man. He journeyed here on what today we'd call a little wooden boat; and like the other Pilgrims, he was looking for a home that would be free.
>
> I've spoken of the shining city all my political life, but I don't know if I ever quite communicated what I saw when I said it. But in my mind it was a tall, proud city built on rocks stronger than oceans, wind-swept, God-blessed, and teeming with people of all kinds living in harmony and peace; a city with free ports that hummed with commerce and creativity. And if there had to be city walls, the walls had doors and the doors were open to anyone with the will and the heart to get here. That's how I saw it, and see it still.
>
> And how stands the city on this winter night? More prosperous, more secure, and happier than it was eight years ago. But more than that: after 200 years, two centuries, she still stands strong and true on the granite ridge, and her glow has held steady no matter what storm. And she's still a beacon, still a magnet for all who must have freedom, for all the pilgrims from all the lost places who are hurtling through the darkness, toward home.
>
> We've done our part. And as I walk off into the city streets, a final word to the men and women of the Reagan revolution, the

men and women across America who for eight years did the work that brought America back. My friends: we did it. We weren't just marking time. We made a difference. We made the city stronger, we made the city freer, and we left her in good hands. All in all, not bad, not bad at all.

And so, goodbye, God bless you, and God bless the United States of America.

All right, one bit of commentary: it should be noted that even the supporters of the "shining city on a hill" idea have accepted the Left's derisive name for it, which is "American exceptionalism." This is not a term that President Ronald Reagan would have *ever* used. President Reagan did not think that Americans were inherently better than the peoples of other countries. He thought that the United States was a beacon of liberty and democracy to the whole world—hence a "shining city on a hill"—because of the ideas that it represented. Reaganism and the Reagan Revolution were not about whether the U.S. was better than France, Germany, Iran, or China. It was about a universal human goal of all people, in all cultures, all over the world for freedom, equality, prosperity, and human dignity.

CHAPTER THREE
COUNSELLOR TO THE PRESIDENT

COORDINATING POLICYMAKING

PRESIDENT RONALD REAGAN organized his first-term White
House staff in an unusual but very productive way. To ensure the
foreign and domestic policy success of the Reagan Revolution, President Reagan put Ed Meese, "his most trusted general policy adviser,"[1]
in the top spot as counsellor to the president. Ed Meese's office was on
the 1st floor of the West Wing of the White House, in the northeast
corner, where Henry Kissinger's office had been in the Nixon-Ford
days. Meese was thus just a stone's throw away from the Oval Office,
facilitating unlimited contact with the president about any foreign or
domestic policy topic.

Ed Meese was made a member of the cabinet, and he was empowered always to summarize, at the end of almost every cabinet meeting,
what had been discussed, what action items had been decided, and
what remained pending. The ability to summarize the action items
that come out of a cabinet meeting is significant in the decision-making process.

Ed Meese was also a member of the National Security Council (NSC)
both as counsellor to the president and as attorney general of the United
States. It is not standard practice for the attorney general to be a member
of the National Security Council, and Ed Meese was the principal player
on the council. Whenever there was a disagreement between Meese and
Secretary of State Alexander Haig or George P. Schulz, Reagan always
sided with Ed Meese. Reagan's first national security advisor, Richard
Allen, was a very close ally of Ed Meese's. The second national security
advisor, Bill Clark, reported directly to the president, but he was such a
close friend and ally of Ed Meese's that this changed nothing. Ed Meese
also rebuffed an attempt by White House chief of staff James A. Baker
III to become chairman of the Reagan National Security Council.

Ed Meese was thus effectively in charge of coordinating policymaking below the presidential level in both foreign and domestic affairs. Meese reported only to President Reagan himself, whose revolutionary ideas he completely shared. By appointing Ed Meese to be the chairman of the Domestic Policy Council, President Reagan deliberately empowered Ed Meese, whose loyalty he knew he could always count on. Ken Cribb, who worked side by side with Meese throughout the Reagan administration, says that "Meese...was the most powerful man in the government at that point."

President Reagan freed up Ed Meese to act as Reagan's right-hand man (with the humble title of counsellor) by naming James A. Baker III, a George H. W. Bush campaign staff person, to be chief of staff in the Reagan White House. This put Jim Baker in charge of President Reagan's schedule, paper flow into and out of the Oval Office, the White House staff, and congressional and media relations. Reagan's idea was that he, Ronald Reagan, would make all of the important policy decisions, that Ed Meese would advise the president on policymaking and see that those policies were reflected throughout the executive branch, and that Jim Baker would then help implement the Reagan-Meese policy decisions as liaison to Congress and the very hostile press. (Baker, unlike Ed Meese, did not have cabinet rank.) Michael Deaver, who had been Governor Reagan's deputy chief of staff in California, was named deputy chief of staff to Jim Baker. Deaver handled the incredible staging of Ronald Reagan's public events, like his magnificent speech commemorating D-Day on the 40th anniversary of that event on the cliffs of Normandy. Jim Baker also put Mike Deaver in charge of making Nancy Reagan, the First Lady, happy. This was a considerable task, which Deaver was quite good at.

Reagan, Meese, Baker, and Deaver referred to "the Troika" of the latter three as co-running the operations of the Reagan White House. In practice, however, Ed Meese was the only member of the Troika with policy coordination power, since he knew best what Ronald Reagan would have wanted to get done. At President Reagan's request, in November 1980, Ed Meese and Jim Baker drew up a written document specifying their relationship, with Meese as the policy adviser and Baker as the policy implementer, although as chairman of the Domestic Policy Council and a permanent member of the National Security Council,

Meese implemented a lot of policy directly through talks with cabinet secretaries. As Ed Meese described it in 1992, "My realm was policy co-ordination on behalf of the President; since I had a strong interest in policy matters and knew the President's views quite well, this was a natural role for me.... Jim Baker, by his own admission, didn't have such an intense interest in policy matters. On the other hand, he knew Washington and the ways of government very well.... Mike Deaver ... had a well-honed sense of public relations and knew how best the President should be presented...."[2]

People who see government as a process of logrolling, public relations, media battles, and congressional debates would naturally conclude that James Baker was the central player in the Reagan administration and "Reagan's closest adviser,"[3] because Baker was the Reagan administration's point man for the "inside-the-Beltway" dramas that fill up news cycles. Thus, journalist Chris Whipple describes the Meese-Baker power-sharing arrangement by saying, "Baker had cleverly seized the levers of power. While Meese was technically in charge of 'policy,' Baker was in charge of executing it."[4] Baker agreed with this assessment: "I worked it out in a way that Ed could handle—and I was still in a position to run everything."[5] This starkly illustrates the difference between the mindsets of ordinary Washington insiders and revolutionary thinkers like Ed Meese. Ed Meese, like Ronald Reagan, was a man with revolutionary ideas. Reagan and Meese's goal was not just to get things done. It was to get done those things that would change the world in an enduring way that would resonate far beyond the current (or next) session of Congress. For that purpose, controlling "policy" (we find Whipple's quotation marks around that term telling) is the key enterprise. And as Meese aide John Richardson explained to us, Ed Meese had all the policymaking entities in the administration "reporting to him," while Baker controlled the "operational" side. Richardson added that what many journalists and insiders "missed is [that] Reagan had this unique ... structure for the chief of staff where the [chief of staff] didn't hold the kind of authority under Reagan in the first term that historically the chiefs of staff did [because of] the Meese policy operation." Legislative bargains—and James Baker unquestionably and crucially excelled at securing them—are important, but legislative bargains come and go while "policy" ideas live on. Ronald Reagan and Ed Meese understood this even as many around them did not.

With regard to policy formulation, one cannot understand the functioning of the Reagan administration without understanding the functioning of Reagan's cabinet council system. It all starts, of course, with the cabinet. The "cabinet" is just the name we give to a group of the president's top advisers. The composition of the cabinet typically changes a bit from one administration to another, but it is built around the heads of certain key government departments and is fleshed out with whoever the president wants to include in the core advisory group. Because there are more than a dozen key agencies and plenty of other important actors, such as the United Nations ambassador and the president's chief of staff, the cabinet is typically large; President Reagan's cabinet had nineteen members, and more recent cabinets have grown into the mid-twenties. (President Biden's cabinet in 2024 has twenty-five members.) The cabinet, in whatever manner it is constituted at any given moment, has no formal legal power. Meese's close aide and friend Ken Cribb explains, "[I]t's completely up to the president of the United States, whether ... [the cabinet] does anything or not." President Reagan, like President Dwight Eisenhower before him, made extensive use of his cabinet because, as Cribb put it, he "liked to hear the advice of his principal officers, not just the narrow set of political operatives in the West Wing, right? [He thought it] helped him make [good] decisions."

Anyone who has attended meetings, however, knows that there are both benefits and costs to making policy through groups the size of a modern cabinet. Ed Meese figured out how to get the benefits of cabinet policy work without an avalanche of unwieldy large-group meetings. He devised a system of "cabinet councils" that would break out issues for the agencies and officers that had the most direct interest and expertise in them. In retrospect, that may seem obvious. At the time, it was entirely novel, and it was vital to the Reagan administration's success.

One can find a detailed account of the cabinet council system—which probably should be required reading for students of government—in Martin Anderson's *Revolution*.[6] The short version is that the councils—"an idea that Ed Meese came up with"[7]—were "designed to deal with certain specific issues of national policy. ... The members of the cabinet councils were selected primarily on the basis that the departments they headed were deeply involved in the specific issues that would be discussed."[8] The councils became the chief policymaking vehicles in the Reagan administration (apart from the president himself) "because only the cabinet councils could deal effectively with national issues that cut across two or more departments, and that included most of the issues."[9] As Ed Meese put it, "[T]he councils weren't simply boxes on an organizational chart, but working groups of manageable size that insured a focused effort by people who had knowledge and jurisdiction over policy."[10]

At the outset of the Reagan administration, there were cabinet councils on economics, the environment, trade, human resources, and agriculture. The cabinet councils were crucial because, as Ken Cribb relates, "issues were actually brought to the president, not by the White House staff like Jim Baker or Mike Deaver, but by the cabinet councilors." By the time matters reached full cabinet consideration, "a hell of a lot of policy development has been done through one of the five cabinet councils that Meese devised." And "Meese was a member of all five cabinet councils as well as being on the National Security Council. He played a role in every policymaking entity." As Martin Anderson described it, "The administrative support for the cabinet councils came out of the Office of Cabinet Administration in Ed Meese's office,"[11] and the staff "reported all administrative matters to ...Meese's office."[12]

This system placed Ed Meese at the center of the administration's policymaking web across virtually all fields. It also made sure that policymaking conformed to the administration's overall agenda rather than the parochial agendas of individual cabinet officers. As Cribb explains, "Usually in the typical administration, the cabinet secretary for commerce is in there lobbying the president against his fellow cabinet members for special treatment for the Commerce Department issues. The Reagan cabinet council system had the opposite effect. The Reagan system had the cabinet working together as a body on behalf of the president and coordinating therefore the operation of the cabinet agencies under the president's agenda. ... The things that Reagan and Meese were interested in moved the world, and they made sure that the cabinet was working for President Reagan on issue after issue, and not the other way around."

While this system may seem simple and intuitive, it ran so contrary to the standard affairs of government that "[t]he operations of the cabinet councils were largely unnoticed by the media, and of those who cared about them at all, few ever understood their true purpose and function. In fact, most members of the White House staff did not seem to understand them...."[13] Ken Cribb agrees: "If you asked [Jim] Baker about [the policymaking role of the cabinet councils]..., he wouldn't know what you were talking about—never mind [Michael] Deaver."

This does not mean that people like Baker and Deaver were unimportant to the Reagan administration. Far from it. President Reagan wanted to receive as much information as he could before making decisions, so he preferred to hear from three people daily—Meese, Baker, and Deaver—rather than having an H. R. Haldeman–like, all-powerful White House chief of staff, the way President Richard M. Nixon had done. Reagan's White House during the first term had a three-spokes-to-the-wheel form of organization, much like President Franklin D. Roosevelt's White House did in the 1930s and 1940s. Jim Baker probably performed a useful "canary in the mine shaft" function in that he predictably signaled to the president and to Ed Meese what the establishment and the press were up to on any given day, and he was very effective in dealing with a hostile Congress. Michael Deaver was probably the best person ever to do advance work for a president; his staging of President Reagan's speech on the 40th anniversary of the D-Day invasion of Nazi-occupied France was a work of genius. These were functions vital to the success of the Reagan Revolution. But Ed Meese was the central actor on matters of policy coordination. He simply did not boast about it to his colleagues or the press. Instead, Ed Meese played a discrete role as counsellor to President Reagan similar to General Dwight David Eisenhower's role when he was president of the United States, as Meese's son Michael pointed out to us in an interview. Eisenhower was always perceived as being apolitical and above the fray even when silently he was controlling what was going on.[14] Ed Meese was a "hidden-hand" counsellor to President Reagan, a role he continued to play as attorney general. And, as a person with a deep religious faith, Ed Meese was raised to be, always was, and still is, completely humble. He was content to be, and to be seen as, part of a White House Troika, along with Baker and Deaver, even though it was Ed Meese who was involved in all of Reagan's most important decisions and got them implemented.

POLICIES MADE

THE POINT OF a policymaking process, of course, is to make policy. There were several major policy initiatives—one secret—which were the highlights of President Ronald Reagan's first year in office. Ed Meese played a major role in all of them because they were at the core of President Reagan's agenda, to which Ed Meese was fiercely loyal.

First, President Reagan proposed a radical tax cut, which slashed marginal income tax rates sharply. This proposal was largely developed by the transition team, with help from Martin Anderson and the economist Arthur Laffer. Ed Meese ran the transition team, and this proposed legislation was ready to go to Capitol Hill as soon as Ronald Reagan took the oath of office on January 20, 1981. The Economic Recovery Tax Act of 1981 cleared Congress in August 1981 and was signed into law by President Ronald Reagan on August 13, 1981. The passage of this legislation set off an economic boom that has gone on with a few interruptions for the last forty-three years. It also helped the Reagan goals of "repositioning the role of the national government" and promoting "free markets and free labor," which were discussed in chapter 2. The details of the Reagan tax plan are beyond the scope of this book; for those interested in the details, Martin Anderson's lengthy inside account of them is essential reading.[15]

Second, in August 1981, the Professional Air Traffic Controllers Organization (PATCO), the only labor union that had supported Ronald Reagan over Jimmy Carter, announced that it was going to strike to get a wage increase. President Reagan had no doubt about what his response to such a strike would be. In a meeting with Transportation Secretary Drew Lewis and Counsellor Ed Meese, President Reagan said that he would give striking air traffic controllers forty-eight hours to go back to work, after which they would be fired for breaking the law. Ed Meese's involvement in this matter with Drew Lewis showed the Reagan cabinet council system at its best. Meese asked the White House Office of Cabinet Affairs under Craig Fuller and Ken Cribb to remain in constant communication with the Department of Transportation until this critical matter was resolved.

The illegal strike began at 7:00 a.m. on August 3, 1981, and on August 5, 1981, President Reagan fired the 11,345 striking air traffic controllers who had refused to return to work and banned them for life from ever again holding any federal government job. The vacant positions were filled with a mix of non-striking air traffic controllers, supervisors, staff personnel, some non-rated personnel, military air traffic controllers, and controllers transferred temporarily from other facilities. PATCO was decertified by the Federal Labor Relations Authority on October 22, 1981. New air traffic controllers were trained, and life went on as normal.

The firing of the 11,345 air traffic controllers by President Reagan showed the leaders of the Soviet Union that Ronald Reagan, unlike some other presidents, was as tough as nails.[16] The fact that President Reagan would bust a GOP-friendly union for an illegal strike put the Soviet leadership on notice that they faced a hard and determined foe who was not afraid to resort to strong measures. The action also reassured ordinary Americans who had experienced years of feckless presidential leadership. Some sources have suggested to us that President Reagan's action may also have emboldened private-sector employers to be more aggressive in resisting unreasonable unionization demands. Although demonstrating that kind of cause-effect relationship on a topic as complex as workplace economics is tricky business and beyond our capacity, we note that in 1981, 18.7 percent of the American workforce was unionized, while by 2024 only 12 percent was unionized, and private-sector union membership was at 6.3 percent. The limited role of private-sector unions, coupled with the drastic cut in marginal tax rates and new government regulations, set off an economic boom, which has lasted for forty-three years.

Third, Ed Meese was a critical member of the Reagan White House Committee on Federal Judicial Selection, chaired by White House counsel Fred Fielding. Others on the committee in 1981 were Attorney General William French Smith; Pendelton James, White House personnel director and a close Meese ally; Assistant Attorney General Jonathan Rose of the Office of Legal Policy; and Ken Cribb (when he became Meese's deputy). The membership of this committee was somewhat fluid in that Lyn Nofziger attended sometimes, as did people from legislative affairs. In any event, the committee made decisions by consensus and not by taking votes. In 1981–1982, President Reagan stunned legal academia by nominating nineteen federal circuit court of appeals judges, including Yale Law School professors Robert H. Bork to the D.C. Circuit and Ralph K. Winter to the Second Circuit, University of Chicago Law School professors Richard Posner to the Seventh Circuit and Antonin Scalia to the D.C. Circuit, Texas Supreme Court justice William Garwood to the Fifth Circuit, and distinguished federal district judges Edward R. Becker to the Third Circuit and Patrick Higginbotham to the Fifth Circuit. In 1983–1984, seventeen more court of appeals judges were confirmed, including many distinguished jurists well known to the legal community even today (such as Joel Flaum, Ken Starr, and Juan Torruella) and a number of bona fide conservative icons, such as Pasco Bowman on the Eighth Circuit and J. Harvie Wilkinson on the Fourth Circuit. At the end of his first term, President Reagan nominated two enduring giants in conservative legal thought—University of Chicago Law professor Frank Easterbrook to the Seventh Circuit and Texas lawyer Edith Jones to the Fifth Circuit—who were confirmed early in 1985. Richard Posner turned out to be a disappointment to rule-of-law advocates, but the others were brilliant conservative radicals who would go on to help reshape U.S. constitutional law and statutory interpretation.

Ed Meese was thus centrally involved in judicial selection during President Reagan's first term even before he became attorney general in 1985. This was the beginning of the Reagan Revolution in the courts that would come to full fruition when Ed Meese became attorney general. It was also the mechanism, detailed in much of this book, by which Ronald Reagan effectuated his fourth goal mentioned in chapter 2 of promoting "constitutionalism and the rule of law."

Fourth, and quite secretly, on September 14, 1981, Ed Meese held a meeting in the White House on developing a missile defense program, the Strategic Defense Initiative (SDI), to intercept incoming intercontinental nuclear ballistic missiles (ICBMs). Patriot air missile defense systems, which in 2024 are making such a difference on the battlefields of Ukraine and in defending Israel from terrorist attacks, are directly descended from President Reagan's Strategic Defense Initiative (SDI), which the left in the 1980s derided as being a "Star Wars" fantasy.

The idea of developing a Strategic Defense Initiative had long been a passion of Ronald Reagan's going back to when he was governor of California and had paid a visit to the Lawrence Livermore National Laboratory in Livermore, California.[17] Lawrence Livermore specializes in the research and development of science and technology applied to national defense. Ed Meese's September 14, 1981, meeting was the first formal discussion in the Reagan White House of Ronald Reagan's dream that one day the United States could cover itself, as Israel has now done, with an iron dome missile defense system.

After a follow-up meeting on October 12, 1981, Ed Meese decided it was time to go directly to the President with a proposal to implement SDI, and on January 8, 1982, the informal missile defense group met secretly with Reagan in the Roosevelt Room."[18] Suffice it to say that President Reagan was thrilled with the group's briefing, and advocacy of the Strategic Defense Initiative became a major Reagan priority for the rest of his term in office.

Implementing those systems was complicated by the Anti-Ballistic Missile Defense Treaty (ABM Treaty), which had been signed by President Richard M. Nixon and Soviet leader Leonid Brezhnev in Moscow on May 26, 1972. Under that treaty, both the United States and the Soviet Union were limited to building only two complexes with one hundred anti-ballistic missiles each, so as to forestall an arms race. President Reagan and his foreign policy defense team concluded that the ABM Treaty could not be allowed to stand in the way of the full development and deployment of the Strategic Defense Initiative but that for the moment there was no plan to build more than two missile sites with one hundred missiles each.

The ABM Treaty capped the number of sites and missiles that could be developed to protect against ICBMs, but it did not apply to more limited theater missile defense systems like the Patriot system. The Patriot missile system began to replace the older Nike-Hercules U.S. missile defense system starting in 1984. In 1991, these systems received battlefield testing during the first Gulf War, which was won by the United States and its allies in six weeks.

As the technology improved for developing an SDI system that would defend successfully against incoming ICBMs, the administration of President George W. Bush gave Russia six months' notice that the

United States was withdrawing from the ABM Treaty altogether, which we did on June 13, 2002. The United States then created a Missile Defense Agency that might guard against nuclear attacks by rogue nations like North Korea and Iran, although not necessarily against a nuclear fusillade from Russia or China. Russian dictator Vladimir Putin and Chinese dictator Xi Jinping have now developed hypersonic missiles to elude the United States' Reaganite SDI system. So far Russia has used seven of its so-called hypersonic missiles with non-nuclear payloads in the Russo-Ukrainian War. In all seven instances, U.S. batteries of Patriot missiles have successfully shot down the Russian hypersonic missiles. Meanwhile the United States is building its own hypersonic ICBMs, and neither the Russians nor the Chinese have very effective missile defense systems yet.

Just as birds are thought to be descended from dinosaurs, Ronald Reagan's SDI program led to both the development and the deployment, as early as the first Gulf War, of the highly successful Patriot missile defense systems. Ronald Reagan was the great architect and founder of all of this, and, characteristically, it was Ed Meese who helped him along the way. Together, they have revolutionized modern warfare. Citizens in Kiev and Tel Aviv sleep better at night thanks to Ronald Reagan and Ed Meese.

SDI was a major part of Ronald Reagan's goal of "rolling back communism" instead of merely "containing it" discussed in chapter 2. The Strategic Defense Initiative was a huge threat to the Soviet Union because that country lacked the scientific and technological ability to match the U.S. by building a Strategic Defense Initiative or missile defense system of its own. Just as importantly, the Soviet Union was in the process of slowly going bankrupt, so that even if it had been able to build a missile defense system, it could not have afforded to do so. President Reagan's advocacy of the Strategic Defense Initiative was thus another key factor in driving the Soviet Union to the bargaining table under its new leader Mikhail Gorbachev. Once Gorbachev finally came to the bargaining table, Ronald Reagan made clear to him what price Gorbachev would have to pay for peace.

On October 11 and 12, 1986, President Reagan and Soviet leader Mikhail Gorbachev held a summit in Reykjavík, Iceland. The talks stalled, and Reagan famously walked away with no deal with Gorbachev. Half a year later, on June 12, 1987, standing in front of the closed Brandenburg Gate and the Berlin Wall, Reagan finally made it clear what his terms were for peace with the bankrupt Soviet Union. Ronald Reagan said, as we have already seen, "General Secretary Gorbachev, if you seek peace, if you seek prosperity for the Soviet Union and Eastern Europe, if you seek liberalization: come here to this gate! Mr. Gorbachev, open this gate! Mr. Gorbachev tear down this wall!"

Those were Ronald Reagan's terms for peace, and when Gorbachev accepted them, reluctantly, communism, the Cold War, the Warsaw Pact, and the Soviet Union itself came to an end without so much as a shot being fired.

A fifth accomplishment of the first year of Ronald Reagan's historic presidency was the beginning of a sustained campaign of deregulation spearheaded by Reagan's Executive Order 12291, which instructed the greatly empowered Office of Information and Regulatory Affairs (OIRA) within the Office of Management and Budget to do cost-benefit analysis of economically significant regulations. During the Reagan and first Bush administrations, OIRA reviewed between two thousand and three thousand regulations a year. Vice President Bush was President Reagan's deregulation czar, and so this was one area of domestic policy that fell outside of Ed Meese's portfolio. In September 1993, President Clinton cut the number of regulations reviewed by OIRA from between two thousand and three thousand back to between five hundred and seven hundred annually. While actual deregulation proved difficult during the Reagan years, in part because of resistance from hostile holdover judges, the president's sustained efforts at least forestalled new versions of costly and intrusive measures characteristic of the modern administrative state. No major regulatory initiatives came out of the Reagan administration's first term.[19] Ronald Reagan's efforts at deregulation, coupled with his tax cuts and the reduction in private-sector unions, did more than anything else to spur the enormous wave of economic growth we have seen in the last forty-three years. Deregulation is, at the end of the day, simply another way of cutting taxes. This furthered Reagan's goal of reforming the economy by stimulating free markets and free labor discussed in chapter 2.

To summarize, the five great achievements of Ronald Reagan's first year as president were a massive tax cut that slashed marginal income tax rates; the breaking of a public employee union, which scared the daylights out of Soviet leaders; the use of the White House Judicial Selection Committee to transform the federal courts with brilliant conservative judges; the secret move to start development of a Strategic Defense Initiative, which would force the Soviet Union to ultimately tear down the Berlin Wall; and the moves toward avoiding or eliminating costly and needless regulations.

Ed Meese was centrally involved in furthering all five of these initiatives. In doing so, Ed Meese knew that he was implementing Ronald Reagan's policy preferences. Ed Meese was modest, and he gave all the credit for these accomplishments to President Reagan and others, but he was obviously a major policy player.

POLICYMAKERS

OF COURSE, Ed Meese did not work alone, as we noted in the previous chapter. He was an integral part of a team, whose coach and general manager was President Reagan. Our point is only that Ed Meese was first among equals when it came to formulating, developing, and implementing the policies championed by President Reagan.

James Baker, we have noted, was not focused on policy development. But he excelled at the day-to-day politics needed to turn policy ideas into law. As secretary of the Treasury during President Reagan's second term, Jim Baker was able to get congressional Democrats to cut the marginal tax rate to as low as 28 percent! This victory for supply-side economics was won by Jim Baker, and before him by Donald Regan, and it was one of the most momentous policy victories of the Reagan era. It greatly furthered both Reagan's goals of "reorienting the role of the national government" and of promoting free markets and free minds discussed in chapter 2. And securing the agreement of a hostile Congress on something like tax cuts was not something that Ed Meese could accomplish. As he explained to us, he did not himself have contact with Congress because "part of the division of responsibility was that I had the responsibility for the cabinet and working through them with the various departments of the government and the executive branch. Whereas Jim had the responsibility for the administration of the White House, and dealing with the press, and the legislature." Even with that division, Ed Meese was, along with Baker and Dick Darman, part of the Legislative Strategy Group, a body chaired by Baker to "decide what was doable and what was not on Capitol Hill,"[20] which Meese described as "a good way to coordinate what was going on in Congress with Ronald Reagan's priorities. And the fact that I was a part of it, meant that [it] bridged the gap between the legislative activity, and the policy work being done in the departments." The underlying policies were developed by people like Meese, Martin Anderson, and, of course, President Reagan.

Despite some differences in outlook, Ed Meese worked very amicably with Jim Baker. Family and faith had made Ed Meese totally comfortable in his own skin, and he is by nature and faith a deeply humble man. Meese told us, "Well, my idea was not aggrandizing power to myself, my idea was to serve the president, and that was all. So, I had no particular desire for individual, political, or other power."

President Reagan's foreign policy team initially included Meese's closest ally from the campaign, William J. Casey, as director of the Central Intelligence Agency (CIA), who was also made a member of the National Security Council, unlike some other CIA directors; Casper Weinberger as secretary of defense; and Dick Allen as national security advisor who reported to the president. Every one of these individuals was committed to Ronald Reagan's view that the Soviet Union was "an evil empire" and that Marxism-Leninism would be consigned to "the ash heap of history." The only weak links in that loop were Secretary of State Alexander Haig, from 1981 to 1982, and to a much lesser degree Secretary of State George Schulz, from 1982 to 1989. Haig and Schulz pursued arms control agreements with the Soviet Union, which Ronald Reagan did or did not sign based on his own best judgment after running them by Meese, Casey, Weinberger, and whoever was the national security advisor at the time.

The president's inclusion of Ed Meese, along with Bill Casey, Bill Clark, and Casper Weinberger, as key foreign policy and national defense advisors would likely seem strange to many observers. They "had no foreign policy experience whatsoever. They had no significant military experience, no diplomatic experience, and no intelligence experience."[21] Bill Clark was perhaps "the least-qualified national security advisor in history."[22] "What they had instead," Martin Anderson noted with characteristic insight, "was political brilliance, a sense of strategy, common sense and, above all, a long record of loyal service to Ronald Reagan."[23] Ronald Reagan did not need careerists or academic experts to know that communism had to be defeated.

There was tension initially between Secretary of State Alexander Haig and Jim Baker, as well as with Ed Meese and the national security team. Haig wanted to play the same role for Ronald Reagan that Henry Kissinger had played in Richard M. Nixon's presidency; he "saw himself literally as the vicar of foreign policy....[He] was incredulous that President Reagan might consult anyone else on any element of foreign policy, no matter how small."[24] Haig's hubris became publicly visible on March 30, 1981, when President Reagan experienced an assassination attempt. Ed Meese, Jim Baker, and Mike Deaver all rushed to the hospital to be with the president. At the time, Vice President Bush was on a plane coming back from Texas. The White House press secretary Larry Speakes was asked on national television who was in charge, and he said he really did not know. Shortly, Al Haig came bursting into the press room out of breath and looking not very reassuring, and he blurted out: "As of now, I am in control here, in the White House, pending the return of the vice president and in close touch with him. If something came up, I would check with him, of course."

Ed Meese said he has always thought that Al Haig got a bum rap for this event because "Haig....was afraid one of our opponents, the Russians or somebody else, the Soviets would try to take advantage of an apparent gap in authority. And so he went pounding up the stairs, and he had had a heart problem at that time. And he got up there all out of breath, and that's when he said, 'As of now, I'm in charge,' or words to that effect, which was constitutionally inaccurate, but he was trying to stave off [a crisis] and meant well."

President Reagan did, however, replace Haig with George P. Shultz, who served admirably in Meese's view as secretary of state from July 16, 1982, to the end of the Reagan administration. Shultz worked well with the Meese-Casey-Weinberger national security team, but it was

Meese, Casey, and Weinberger who called the shots on foreign and defense policy.[25]

A meaningless "scandal," fueled by anonymous leaks from within the Reagan administration, forced National Security Advisor Richard Allen, a Meese ally, to retire.[26] The choice to succeed Allen was William Clark, at the time deputy secretary of state, whose views on foreign and defense policy were identical to Meese's. Since Bill Clark had been Governor Reagan's chief of staff when Meese was legal affairs secretary, Clark's ties to Reagan were as deep as Meese's.[27] The net effect of this was to turn the so-called "Troika" into a four-person "Quad" with Ed Meese getting an extra vote! As Ken Cribb described it, "[Bill Clark ended every day he was in the White House] up on the big blue couch in Ed Meese's corner office. They reviewed the day's activities and planned the next day's activities."

Cribb added, "The bottom line of the maneuver that got Richard Allen fired as national security advisor is [that squishy moderates in the White House] successfully removed a [junior] Meese aide, and they elevated Clark into the role. ... The White House moderates were such smart power operatives that they maneuvered Bill Clark, Meese's best ally ..., into the Oval Office itself."

There is tension within any administration, and tension on foreign policy in the Reagan administration was inevitable—though the collateral damage to people like Richard Allen should not lightly be dismissed. In any event, at least some of that tension arose from Jim Baker's desire for foreign policy credentials, perhaps to build a resume for a future presidential run. The occasion arose when Bill Clark was appointed to succeed James Watt as secretary of the interior. Clark was a rancher who loved the wide-open spaces of the American West. He loved to ride horseback, and when President Reagan rode horseback it was usually with Bill Clark. Jim Baker came up with the idea that he should be Reagan's third national security advisor, with Mike Deaver replacing him as White House chief of staff. He got the backing of Secretary of State George P. Shultz and Nancy Reagan and persuaded the president to announce his new appointment the day Bill Clark left the White House, while keeping Ed Meese, Bill Casey, and Cap Weinberger in the dark. A news release was actually drafted and printed to announce the change. But President Reagan wanted to consult the National Security Council first in person, without Jim Baker being present. Ed Meese, Bill Clark, Bill Casey, and Cap Weinberger objected strenuously to the idea, with Bill Casey saying to President Reagan, "Mr. President, you can't have the biggest leaker in Washington as your National Security advisor!"[28] Reagan went back upstairs and told Mike Deaver and Jim Baker that the plan was off.

The president was on good ground in withdrawing his offer to make Jim Baker national security advisor, apart from the strong perception that Baker's White House office was a prominent source of leaks. Baker had evidently told the president that, in Ken Cribb's words, "the 'fellows' had all approved of it." Ed Meese was among the "fellows," and it was not true.

Conservatives like Cribb then wanted Jeane Kirkpatrick, who was departing as U.S. ambassador to the United Nations, to be the new national security advisor, but Ed Meese and Bill Clark unfortunately never considered her. Ed Meese and Bill Clark together persuaded Reagan to appoint Robert McFarlane, Bill Clark's low-key deputy, to be Clark's replacement. So ended Jim Baker's attempt to get into foreign and military policy. Later on, he switched places with Don Regan to become Treasury secretary and, according to Baker's biography, began thinking about leaving the government altogether to become the Major League Baseball commissioner.

THE POLICYMAKER

THE CHIEF POLICYMAKER in the Reagan administration was, of course, Ronald Reagan. Many pundits may recoil from this notion, having bought the line that President Reagan was a disengaged "grandfather whom one humors but does not take very seriously."[29] The truth, according to Ed Meese, "is that many pundits tried to create the impression that Ronald Reagan disliked the work of the presidency.... [W]hile he did not get involved in the minutiae of bureaucracy..., he was definitely the one who had the vision and made the decisions, all the key decisions." Ed Meese was standing behind him all the way. Ed Meese was the leading voice in the administration for conservative, Reaganite principles. Whenever there were gatherings of President Reagan's political appointees, Ed Meese always got the loudest and longest standing ovations of anyone other than President Reagan himself. The four thousand Reagan political appointees all knew that Ed Meese was Ronald Reagan's indispensable right-hand man. Of course, whenever Ed Meese was praised for doing anything, he always said the credit went to President Reagan and not to himself.

Ed Meese was unlike anyone Washington, D.C., insiders had ever seen before. He did not care about money, personal power, fame, sex, or getting good press. There was no way Washington insiders could corrupt him because he was not vain, greedy, lazy, angry, envious, lustful, or a glutton. Nor, contrary to some reports, was he disorganized. Ed Meese's portfolio within the Reagan administration was so vast that some people who hoped for certain outcomes from him were sure to be disappointed. It is sometimes easier to think that your ideas were misplaced rather than to think that they were rejected or ranked lower than others on the priority list. In any event, the myth somehow arose that Ed Meese was "disorganized under the best of circumstances,"[30] "famously disorganized,"[31] and that Meese's briefcase was a "black hole because it was reputed that anything that disappeared inside it never came out."[32] Both of us have seen Ed Meese in action for nearly four decades, and he may well have the most orderly mind either of us has encountered. Meese's White House aide John Richardson confirms our impression, saying that Meese "had his list of what he was working on and [his] priorities. He kept everything backed up in his mind.... [H]e moved a lot of business in person instead of in paper. But he was very efficient." On the briefcase myth, Richardson retorts, "Oh, that's absolutely not true. It did not happen. Meese was highly organized personally and professionally."

Ed Meese understood brilliantly that there is no limit to the good one can accomplish in Washington, D.C., so long as you let other people take the credit for it. All Ed Meese cared about was helping President Ronald Reagan achieve his policy agenda, which coincided completely with Ed Meese's own personal agenda in every way. It is for this reason that the press vilified Ed Meese, and it created the fake news scandals about Meese, which we shall discuss and dismiss in a chapter that follows.

One more note: before swapping roles with Don Regan to become Treasury secretary, "[l]ooking for [a] cabinet position… [Jim] Baker set his sights on the Justice Department. But when William French Smith prepared to step down, Baker again found himself at odds with Ed Meese, who [Baker thought] had his hopes on becoming attorney general. Meese had been fascinated with law enforcement for years and Reagan accommodated him by nominating him to be Attorney General in January 1984. 'This is his lifelong dream,' Reagan wrote in his diary."[33]

We asked Ed Meese if serving as attorney general was his lifelong dream. He quite honestly said, "No." Ed Meese said that he just wanted to serve Ronald Reagan in the way that Ronald Reagan wanted him to do. And we fully believe that.

CHAPTER FOUR

ED MEESE AND PRESIDENT REAGAN'S SECOND TERM

DURING PRESIDENT RONALD Reagan's second term from 1985 to 1988, Ed Meese not only served as attorney general of the United States but also continued to play many of the same roles that he had played as counsellor to the president during Ronald Reagan's first term. Three of those roles deserve special mention.

First, Ed Meese served as a member of the National Security Council until his resignation as attorney general on August 12, 1988. By then, hardline CIA director Bill Casey had died, Defense Secretary Caspar Weinberger had retired, and Ed Meese was left as the last of the Cold War hawks on the National Security Council during the crucial time when President Reagan was negotiating with the new leader of the Soviet Union, Mikhail Gorbachev.

Second, Ed Meese served as chairman of the Domestic Policy Council during President Reagan's second term, and he coordinated the work of many of the cabinet departments. The Domestic Policy Council helped produce a hardline Federalism Executive Order issued by President Reagan, and it accomplished a shift in power back from the federal government to the states. Ed Meese was staffed for the Domestic Policy Council by the exceptionally able Becky Norton Dunlop who had previously served as special assistant to the president and director of the Cabinet Office.

Finally, Ed Meese helped President Reagan survive the political fallout from the Iran-Contra Affair, which is discussed in detail in a subsequent chapter. Ed Meese investigated the scandal, fired those responsible for it, defended the administration on Capitol Hill, and helped President Reagan find and work with his third White House chief of staff, former Senate majority leader Howard Baker, a liberal Republican with deep reservoirs of trust in both parties on Capitol Hill. We have no doubt that Ed Meese not only staved off the possible impeachment of President Reagan because of the Iran-Contra scandal, but also left Ronald Reagan so popular that, after two terms, he was succeeded by his own Republican vice president George H. W. Bush. This was the first time one party controlled the White House for more than eight years since 1933–1953 among Democratic presidents and since 1921–1933 among Republican presidents. Neither political party has controlled the White House for more than eight years in the thirty-one years since the Reagan–Bush I era ended in 1993.

The bottom line is that Ed Meese lost only the title of "Counsellor to the President" when he became attorney general. He continued to do all the things he had been doing during the first term *in addition to running the Justice Department!* Meese's brilliant intellect, fierce work ethic, organized mind, and total humility made him a wonder to behold. A full treatment of Ed Meese's second-term duties apart from being attorney general would require another book; we touch here only on a few highlights.

Member of the National Security Council

IN 1947, Congress created the National Security Council (NSC) in order to "(1) advise the President with respect to the integration of domestic, foreign, and military policies relating to the national security…, (2) assess and appraise the objectives, commitments, and risks of the United States…, (3) make recommendations to the President concerning policies on matters of common interest to the departments and agencies of the United States Government concerned with the national security; and (4) coordinate, without assuming operational authority, the United States Government response to malign foreign influence operations and campaigns."[1] The NSC is thus the principal advisory body for coordinating the country's security policies. The law creating the agency names as members of the NSC "the President, the Vice President, the Secretary of State, the Secretary of Defense, the Secretary of Energy, the Secretary of the Treasury, [and] the Director of the Office of Pandemic Preparedness and Response Policy."[2] The council does not automatically include the attorney general, but it may include "such other officers of the United States Government as the President may designate."[3] To no one's surprise, President Reagan included Ed

Meese on his National Security Council during Reagan's second term.

There is, alas, relatively little that we can concretely say about Ed Meese's work on the NSC and his resulting role in national security policy. Ed Meese himself could tell us little because of his humility, penchant for attributing credit to others (he described the council to us as "it was a matter of, just everybody giving their best thinking"), and, most importantly, vigilance about not breaking confidences or discussing anything that might still be classified information to which he had access in those days. His top NSC staffer, Commander Ann Rondeau, similarly could not responsibly provide many details. (She could only say, "You can imagine all the issues.") Even George Shultz's encyclopedic (more than 1,100 pages) account of his days as secretary of state[4] says—entirely appropriately—very little about the inner workings of the NSC. We can safely assume, however, that the role was significant given the challenges presented during President Reagan's second term.

The dominant national security challenge was relations with the Soviet Union, which posed perils but also the promise of a great victory in the Cold War. As we noted in an earlier chapter, Soviet leader Mikhail Gorbachev first tried to rope President Reagan into an arms control treaty that would have been bad for the United States at the Reykjavík Summit from October 11 to October 12, 1986, but when Reagan flat out rejected it and literally walked away from the negotiating table, Gorbachev sued for peace, and in 1987 the Intermediate-Range Nuclear Forces Treaty was adopted between the United States and the Soviet Union. Soon thereafter, the Brandenburg Gate was opened, and with that communism collapsed, Germany reunified, the Warsaw Pact dissolved with its members becoming members of NATO, and the Soviet Union dissolved into fifteen separate, independent, and free nations. While these events occurred after President Reagan left office, they were the inevitable consequence of eight years of the Reagan foreign policy. As Ken Cribb aptly put it, "I do not think of the fall of the wall and the freedom of the captive nations as the first act of the Bush administration. That's right. It was the last act of Reagan."

Several Reagan administration actions led to victory in the Cold War. One, as we have noted, was the strong push toward missile defense, which the Soviet Union's communist economy could not match. Another was supporting the freedom fighters in Afghanistan, Angola, and Nicaragua, which bled the Soviet Union on many fronts until it died without putting any American troops on the ground anywhere. A third, reported in the press but not officially confirmed, was to encourage Islamic Saudi Arabia and the Gulf state nations to lower petroleum prices by pumping a lot of oil in the wake of the Soviet invasion of Islamic Afghanistan because lowering the U.S.S.R.'s oil and gas revenues would drive the U.S.S.R. into bankruptcy. All three of these moves put so much strain on the Soviet economy that Mikhail Gorbachev sued for peace.

Ed Meese unsurprisingly credits only President Reagan with devising the strategies that won the Cold War: "[M]uch of the policies were things that the president himself had initiated after thinking about it over a long period of time, before he ever became president." The NSC members, he said, "gave their advice to the president, but.... [t]here was only one vote that mattered—President Reagan's." We do find it hard to believe that the NSC did not play some role in the development of these strategies (Calabresi observed Ann Rondeau working extraordinarily long hours on behalf of Ed Meese at the NSC), but we cannot document it. When specifically asked about encouraging Saudi Arabia to help bankrupt the Soviet Union, Ed Meese told us only, "That's something that I cannot talk about."

Ann Rondeau, who went on to become one of the few women to serve as a three-star admiral in the United States Navy, was able to tell us, however, that Ed Meese and President Reagan were receiving much intelligence concerning the weakness of the Soviet economy, which indicated that a strong push to defeat rather than simply contain international communism might be successful. The possibility became more real in 1985 during Reagan's second term once Mikhail Gorbachev assumed the reins in the Soviet Union. Margaret Thatcher famously said that when she met Gorbachev in 1984, she knew that "this was a man with whom I could do business."[5] Ed Meese and Ann Rondeau both confirm that President Reagan respected Prime Minister Thatcher's judgment on this score, which encouraged the president to pursue a serious but firm negotiation approach. Compared to other Soviet leaders, Ed Meese said, "Gorbachev was much more knowledgeable about the Western world. And, also, he seemed to be more agreeable to at least discussion and sometimes agreement."[6]

Of course, even the likes of Ronald Reagan, Margaret Thatcher, and Ed Meese needed help to secure peace, even from a Soviet leader open to the prospect. Ann Rondeau points out that Pope John Paul II and Lech Wałęsa and the Solidarity labor union in Poland were adding to the pressure on the Soviet Union. She explains that many important people "came together and formed a campaign to bring down the Soviet Union. And it happened to be the Pope was helpful to this a lot. And I did not know what was going on in the Vatican, but you know that things were.... And I just think it was great leaders coming up to the great moment."

So, we are not going to credit Ed Meese with winning the Cold War. But we are going to suggest that he helped. And even a small role in an event of that magnitude is worth noting.

Apart from the ongoing problems posed by Soviet communism, the other major national security event in President Reagan's second term was Operation El Dorado Canyon, which was an April 15, 1986, airstrike against Libya, in retaliation for Muammar Gaddafi's longstanding support of terrorism and his specific role in a Berlin nightclub bombing that killed two American military personnel and injured seventy-nine other Americans. Ed Meese is sure that the National Security Council would have approved this operation, but he missed the meeting because he was in Mexico at that time meeting with the president and attorney general of Mexico about the drug situation. Ed Meese thought the air strikes on Libya were a proportionate response saying, "Yes, I feel it was a success. It did what it was intended to do, and that was to show there was retaliation for the bombing of the La Belle Disco." Military aviation expert Walter J. Boyne concurred, noting that "[t]he crushing [air] strikes caused a remarkable reduction in Libyan-sponsored terrorist activity."[7]

We asked Ann Rondeau if she could tell us anything more about the work of the NSC during Ed Meese's tenure within the bounds of confidentiality and national security. She replied: "Pakistan was always an issue. India was, like it is today, this promising country that... didn't want to be aligned.... And so we were working a number of issues with India, Pakistan, and... nuclear weapons issues.... We worked... a lot with DEA in Mexico, DEA Columbia, DEA in Latin America, as well as frankly some of the DEA issues over in Europe."

It is no great secret that conservatives have often not seen eye to eye on national security policy with whomever is in the State Department at any given moment, and that was to some extent true as well with Secretary of State George Shultz, though Shultz must be credited with "engineering the nuclear arms reduction agreements with the Soviet Union that Reagan searched for so long."[8] Ed Meese, with his characteristic diplomacy and unfailing good will, says only that Shultz "and Cap Weinberger had frequent policy exchanges that reflected the differing viewpoints of the Defense and State departments."[9] Because Ed Meese and Cap Weinberger were, as Ann Rondeau puts it, "very close politically, philosophically, and personally," Meese "oftentimes would side with Weinberger" and "often did not see eye to eye" with Shultz, leading to "an interesting dynamic in the NSC meetings." But she adds that "they were all men who felt as though they were serving the nation the best way they could." In the end, however, CIA director Bill Casey and the various men who served as national security advisors were always on Ed Meese's side of any disagreement between Ed Meese and Secretary of State George Shultz, and President Reagan was always on Ed Meese's side in any disagreement as well. As Ann Rondeau put it, "When Meese went into the president with something, he came out with what he needed, and he always won the case."

Having said that, we have never heard Ed Meese speak critically of George Shultz, who ably served President Reagan in several important capacities, both foreign and domestic, even though he "had not been a great fan of Ronald Reagan, and he supported Ford against Reagan during the primaries in 1976."[10] Shultz, in turn, had little public criticism of Ed Meese, praising Meese for his staunch protection of the president's interests[11] and observing of the first-term Troika of Meese, Baker, and Deaver that "[a]ll three had...developed the antennae of sensitivity and subtlety so keenly needed around any president."[12] His harshest criticism—which is notably mild by the standards of Washington politics—was to say that he saw Meese "as a kind of unfathomable St. Patrick, talking the snakes out of their holes; what he would do with those snakes afterward, I was never sure."[13] All of which shows that people can disagree about policies, even life-and-death policies, while still remaining gentlemen. That is a lesson for the ages.

One more note on national security: We observed at the end of chapter 3 that in the wake of President Reagan's administration, some really remarkable things happened beyond the collapse of international communism, which is now on "the ash heap" of human history, which is where President Reagan wanted it to go. President Reagan left office on January 20, 1989. And in mid-May 1989, hundreds of thousands of people began gathering in Tiananmen Square, in Beijing, China, demanding freedom. And they created a Goddess of Liberty, which looked like the Statue of Liberty. They held demonstrations for two months, until on June 4, the Communist Chinese army rolled out the tanks and shot everybody and put the demonstrations down. But it seems as if that uprising for freedom was very much inspired by the uprisings for freedom that President Reagan had urged in Eastern Europe and the Soviet Union. The Chinese people saw and admired Ronald Reagan's "Shining City on a Hill." The Communist Chinese government that slaughtered the demonstrators no doubt saw that same city, understood it, and feared it. Moreover, the Berlin Wall fell on November 9, 1989; West and East Germany were reunified on October 3, 1990; the Warsaw Pact was dissolved on July 1, 1991; and the Soviet Union dissolved into fifteen successor nations on December 26, 1991. As President Reagan said on January 11, 1989, in his "Shining City on a Hill" Farewell Speech, "We did it. We weren't just marking time. We made a difference. We made the city stronger, we made the city freer, and we left her in good hands. All in all, not bad, not bad at all."

CHAIRMAN OF THE
DOMESTIC POLICY COUNCIL

ED MEESE's formal role during President Reagan's second term, in addition to being attorney general, was serving as the chairman of the Domestic Policy Council (DPC). The DPC was created by Richard Nixon in 1970 to serve as a clearinghouse and coordinating body for the president's domestic policy agenda and to "provide policy advice to the President on domestic issues."[14] It has membership as large as the cabinet (and much overlap with it), and in President Reagan's second term, it replaced the cabinet councils as the chief formal tool for domestic policymaking. Ed Meese ran it.

He was staffed in performing this role by a brilliant, conservative woman, Becky Norton Dunlop, who had previously been a special assistant to the president and director of his Cabinet Office. Becky admired Ed Meese for his total loyalty to President Reagan and to conservative principles. "He was always seeking to advance conservative principles given the political arena that we were operating in, which was sometimes difficult. He was a great boss, great to work for, expected the best, and was always wonderful to deal with."

Becky Norton Dunlop helped Ed Meese's Domestic Policy Council prepare significant reports to President Ronald Reagan on matters ranging from adoption to outdoor recreation to families. Two of those reports bear special mention.

In his February 4, 1986, State of the Union Address, President Reagan observed that "[a]fter hundreds of billions of dollars in poverty programs, the plight of the poor grows more painful." Accordingly, he announced, "I am charging the White House Domestic Council to present me by December 1, 1986, an evaluation of programs and a strategy for immediate action.... I'm talking about real and lasting emancipation, because the success of welfare should be judged by how many of its recipients become independent of welfare." The DPC accordingly convened the Low Income Opportunity Working Group, consisting of participants from more than a dozen agencies (including eight cabinet agencies), supplemented by fifteen White House staffers, including future White House chief of staff Andrew Card. The group produced a report, entitled "Up from Dependency: A New National Public Assistance Strategy," which has shaped debate about welfare policy for most of the last forty years.

After hearings in seven cities, twenty-two discussion groups, and extensive conversations with present and former welfare recipients, welfare workers, and nearly half the country's governors, the report called for "a basic change in public assistance policy."[15] The welfare report concluded that the existing welfare system fostered dependence, harmed families, misdirected resources, discouraged innovation, and wasted money on duplicative and inefficient programs.[16] It proposed radical decentralization to "create the proper climate for innovation by giving states the broadest latitude to design and implement experiments in welfare policy,"[17] such as work requirements[18] and programs to promote self-reliance and family unity.[19] This focus away from bigger and more expensive handouts from Washington and toward programs tailored to local conditions and designed to generate self-sufficiency proved to be a blueprint for welfare reform proposals for decades to come, including major reforms in the 1990s during the Clinton administration.

The welfare report extolled "[t]he virtue of the federal system ... [and] its ability to foster state experimentation and to promote political activity within diverse communities."[20] This focus on federalism dovetailed with a parallel report from the DPC's Working Group on Federalism entitled *The Status of Federalism in America*. This remarkable document sets forth the essentials of one important component of the Meese Revolution in constitutional thinking that will occupy part II of this book.

Taking the lead role in producing the federalism report was Charles J. ("Chuck") Cooper, the brilliant young assistant attorney general for the Office of Legal Counsel (OLC) and today one of the nation's leading constitutional lawyers. Gary Lawson, as a staff attorney in OLC, wrote a significant portion of the document relating to constitutional theory. The federalism report was, in essence, a law review article, though an article that no law journal would have published in 1986.

Constitutional doctrine circa 1986 placed essentially no federalism constraints on action by the national government. Congress was treated as though it had effectively unlimited legislative authority. No federal statute regulating private conduct, even in matters that seemed entirely within the control of the states, had been found to exceed Congress's powers since 1936. One case in 1976 had held that Congress could not subject state governments to federal labor laws, such as minimum wage laws, but that decision had been overruled in 1985. Combined with decades of case law imposing novel and textually dubious judge-made constraints on state authority, detailed strings attached to federal grants, and broad federal preemption of state authority, the federalism report aptly observed:

> The last 200 years have witnessed the evisceration of federalism as
> a constitutional and political principle for allocating governmental
> power between the States and Washington. The Founding Fathers'
> vision of a limited national government of enumerated powers
> has gradually given way to an expansive, intrusive, and virtually

omnipotent national government. States, once the hub of political activity and the very source of our political tradition, have been reduced—in a significant part—to administrative units of the national government, their independent political power usurped by almost two centuries of centralization.[21]

The federalism report discussed, from the standpoint of original meaning rather than current court doctrine, the constitutional design for federalism, with detailed analyses of each area of federal encroachment on state prerogatives, from broad expansion of federal power "[t]o regulate Commerce...among the several States"[22] to Congress's use of spending conditions to control state action.[23] Most intriguing to us (since one of us wrote it) was the section entitled "Miscellaneous Judicial Decisions Eroding Federalism." The central thesis of this section was that "*any* judicial decision that departs from the original meaning of the Constitution does serious damage to the structure of constitutional federalism, regardless of the subject of the decision,"[24] because such decisions amount to constitutional amendments without going through the process specified in Article V, in which states are key actors. "Article V provides the States with a say—and any thirteen States with an absolute veto—over changes in the nation's governing document. Accordingly, when judges, openly or tacitly, claim the power to amend the Constitution, they are infringing on important prerogatives of the States."[25] This kind of thinking was unprecedented in modern executive documents. It infused the entire federalism report.

Reports, of course, are fine things—especially, as we shall see in part II of this book, when they lay down broad principles that can lead to action years or even decades down the road. At least some action from the DPC, however, also had significant near-term effects in President Reagan's second term. In particular, the federalism report, under the umbrella of the DPC, helped secure from President Ronald Reagan a 1987 executive order that surely stands as the strongest presidential declaration of principles of constitutional federalism in modern times.

Executive orders are instructions from the president to executive officials about how to carry out their duties. This particular set of instructions, drafted by Chuck Cooper and his staff in the OLC, sought to "restore the division of governmental responsibilities between the national government and the States that was intended by the Framers of the Constitution and to ensure that the principles of federalism established by the Framers guide the Executive departments and agencies in the formulation and implementation of policies. ...."[26] For that purpose, it declared certain "Fundamental Federalism Principles":

(A) Federalism is rooted in the knowledge that our political liberties are best assured by limiting the size and scope of the national government.

(B) The people of the States created the national government when they delegated to it those enumerated governmental powers relating to matters beyond the competence of the individual States. All other sovereign powers, save those expressly prohibited the States by the Constitution, are reserved to the States or to the people.

(C) The constitutional relationship among sovereign governments, State and national, is formalized in and protected by the Tenth Amendment to the Constitution.

(D) The people of the States are free, subject only to restrictions in the Constitution itself or in constitutionally authorized Acts of Congress, to define the moral, political, and legal character of their lives.

(E) In most areas of governmental concern, the States uniquely possess the constitutional authority, the resources, and the competence to discern the sentiments of the people and to govern accordingly. In Thomas Jefferson's words, the States are "the most competent administrations for our domestic concerns and the surest bulwarks against antirepublican tendencies."

(F) The nature of our constitutional system encourages a healthy diversity in the public policies adopted by the people of the several States according to their own conditions, needs, and desires. In the search for enlightened public policy, individual States and communities are free to experiment with a variety of approaches to public issues.

(G) Acts of the national government—whether legislative, executive, or judicial in nature—that exceed the enumerated powers of that government under the Constitution violate the principle of federalism established by the Framers.

(H) Policies of the national government should recognize the responsibility of—and should encourage opportunities for—individuals, families, neighborhoods, local governments, and private associations to achieve their personal, social, and economic objectives through cooperative effort.

(I) In the absence of clear constitutional or statutory authority, the presumption of sovereignty should rest with the individual States. Uncertainties regarding the legitimate authority of the national government should be resolved against regulation at the national level.[27]

In an era of constantly expanding federal governmental power, this was an extraordinary statement. The order then instructed all executive departments and agencies to engage in "strict adherence to constitutional principles. Executive departments and agencies should closely examine the constitutional and statutory authority supporting any Federal action that would limit the policymaking discretion of the States, and should ... grant the States the maximum administrative discretion possible."[28] The order also counseled that federal regulatory preemption of state authority be "restricted to the minimum level necessary to achieve the objectives of the statute pursuant to which the regulations are promulgated,"[29] and it mandated a "Federalism Assessment" of any proposed policies.[30]

As we said in chapter 2, Ronald Reagan sought to reorient our understanding of the relationship between the federal government and the states. Ed Meese's Domestic Policy Council was an important part of that reorientation.

Formal structures are an important aspect of policymaking, but they are not the only mechanisms for formulating and implementing ideas. As the old saying goes, personnel is policy.

When Howard Baker, at Ed Meese's urging, became President Reagan's chief of staff in 1987, conservative Republicans were more than a little concerned that a liberal Republican was now running Ronald Reagan's White House. Ed Meese assuaged them by persuading Baker to hire Ed Meese's counsellor, T. Kenneth Cribb Jr., to be the assistant to the president for domestic affairs, serving as President Reagan's chief advisor on matters of domestic policy. Cribb was also the director of the Domestic Policy Council.

As it happened, Ken Cribb and Steve Calabresi were both in Ed Meese's office at the Justice Department when Ed Meese came back from the Oval Office and happily said that he had just saved Ronald Reagan's presidency from disaster by helping Reagan to hire Baker. Ken immediately told Ed Meese that it was essential that he capitalize on his current goodwill with Howard Baker by getting himself, Ken Cribb, appointed to Howard Baker's transition team. Ed Meese immediately agreed. Howard Baker took over as White House chief of staff from Donald Regan on February 27, 1987. On March 4, 1987, the White House announced that "Kenneth Cribb, Counsellor to Attorney General Edwin Meese, has joined the Chief of Staff's transition team. Mr. Cribb will join Tom Griscom and James Cannon for the period of the transition, concentrating on domestic programs, policies, and personnel matters." UPI immediately ran a story written by Ira R. Allen under the headline "Conservative Added to Baker's Staff." The story said that "[b]owing to conservative pressure, White House Chief of staff Howard Baker added a protégé of Attorney General Edwin Meese to his new team at the White House, spokesman Marlin Fitzwater said Wednesday. Kenneth Cribb ... will ... 'concentrate on domestic programs, policies and personnel matters,' Fitzwater said, acknowledging his appointment should ease conservative fears about Baker. ... He said Cribb, 38, will stay 'an indefinite period—a month or two.'" Cribb's role in the transition was a success, and President Reagan and Howard Baker asked Cribb to stay on as assistant to the president for domestic affairs. The appointment was formalized on March 30, 1987; a White House press release said that Cribb "will be responsible for implementing the domestic agenda for the White House. He will have direct liaison with the Office of Cabinet Affairs, the Public Liaison Office, and the Office of Policy Development." The *New York Times* noted the next day that Cribb's appointment "was promoted by many members of the conservative movement who feared that Mr. Baker, considered to be more of a moderate, might cause Mr. Reagan to stray from his ideological roots."

Ken Cribb had been Ed Meese's right-hand man during Reagan's first term as president and then as counsellor to the attorney general, where he played a major role in judicial appointments, all staffing decisions, and more generally in running the Justice Department. Ken

Cribb was the obvious man for this job in Howard Baker's administration of the Reagan White House given his prior five-year experience in the White House and given his tremendous political and interpersonal political abilities. Ken could be Ed Meese's eyes and ears in the White House, ensuring that Ed Meese would have President Reagan's back should anything problematic happen. It was a measure of Ed Meese's enormous reservoirs of trust with Ronald Reagan that President Reagan hired Howard Baker and Ken Cribb for these two key White House jobs. Ed Meese should get credit for all the good conservative things that Ken did while he was working for eighteen months for Howard Baker—and Ken heartily agrees with that assessment.

While Ed Meese and Ken Cribb both knew this change was the right thing to do for Ronald Reagan and the Reagan Revolution, the need to go their separate ways after working together for seven years side by side was truly wrenching. They both teared up, and Ed Meese said, "Ken, losing you will be like amputating my right arm," and there was only one person he would do that for, and that person's name was Ronald Reagan. They both gave each other heartfelt hugs. Ken Cribb, in turn, served dutifully on the 2nd floor of the West Wing of the Reagan White House. Steve Calabresi was his only aide until the end of June 1987, when David McIntosh replaced Steve—and ultimately became special assistant to the president for domestic affairs.

Ken and Howard Baker got along very well, but it was a bit frustrating for Ken to "babysit" Baker after the heady days of Ronald Reagan's first term and then the joy of running the Justice Department as a law school of which Ken was effectively the dean! Ken did enjoy working with Steve Calabresi for four months and then with David McIntosh for a year and a half, but he had never craved a West Wing White House office or White House mess privileges. Ken is as pure an intellectual as either of us has ever met, and his passion during his previous seven years at Ed Meese's side was for fomenting a real intellectual revolution.

Steve Calabresi, for his part, spent four wonderful months in 1987 working for Ken Cribb and his secretary, Debbie, with all three of us crowded in one very small 2nd-floor West Wing office—later used by Hillary Clinton for the eight years of her husband's presidency. Luckily for Calabresi, Ken did not have enough clout with Howard Baker to assign Steve to an office in the old Executive Office Building. Steve greatly enjoyed eating in the White House mess and watching President Reagan up close in the West Wing. It was truly a thrill and an honor for him to have this job.

There were four signature accomplishments of Cribb's nearly two years in Ronald Reagan's White House. We think they are really Ed Meese's accomplishments, because it was Meese who put Ken Cribb, Steve Calabresi, and David McIntosh in the West Wing of Howard Baker's White House in the first place, and all three saw themselves as Meese's agents.

First, Calabresi and McIntosh worked together to draft a document entitled "America's Economic Bill of Rights," which was issued on July 3, 1987. This was designed as a classical-liberal alternative to Franklin D. Roosevelt's famous call for a socialist "second Bill of Rights," delivered in a State of the Union speech on January 11, 1944. The actual rights enshrined in the Constitution, "our rights to life and liberty," had, said Roosevelt, "proved inadequate to assure us equality in the pursuit of happiness." Thus, Roosevelt spoke of government (meaning taxpayer) guarantees of "rights" to jobs, income, housing, and the like.[31] President Reagan, by contrast, spoke on a beautiful summer day at the Jefferson Memorial of "[t]he freedom to work. The freedom to enjoy the fruits of one's labor. The freedom to own and control one's property. The freedom to participate in a free market." He observed that "[t]his country was built by people seeking to support themselves and their families by their own labor, people who treasured the right to work and dispose of their earnings as they saw fit, people who were willing to take economic risks."

Second, in May of 1987, a draft of President Reagan's proposed Brandenburg Gate speech was circulated to Ken Cribb, along with fifteen other top White House aides, for comment on whether Reagan should offer to end the Cold War if Gorbachev would open the Brandenburg Gate and tear down the Berlin Wall. The State Department was fiercely against this "provocative" rhetoric, and some conservatives got Ken worried that maybe Gorbachev would take Reagan up on his offer and that the Germans might then demand the removal of U.S. nuclear cruise missiles from German soil. Ken asked Calabresi for his advice.

Steve Calabresi told Ken that he thought that if Gorbachev tore down the Berlin Wall, communism and the Warsaw Pact would collapse and that we would win the Cold War. Calabresi noted that Soviet troops along the Berlin Wall all faced east with their machine guns to shoot anyone who sought to go to Western Europe in search of freedom. Eliminating those Soviet troops facing east would unleash a floodgate of humanity into Western Europe. With some misgivings, Ken signed off in front of Steve Calabresi that he favored Reagan giving the Berlin Wall speech.

In retrospect, it did not matter at all whether Ken Cribb and Steve Calabresi favored Reagan giving the Berlin Wall speech on June 12, 1987. Ronald Reagan had long ago resolved to give this speech, and nothing his advisors said or did was going to change his mind. Still, it was thrilling to be there and weigh in on the matter. On June 12, 1987, Ronald Reagan gave the speech, and on November 9, 1989, the Berlin Wall was torn down!

Third, President Ronald Reagan's Federal Communications Commission (FCC) in 1987 was slowly trying to get rid of a policy called the Fairness Doctrine, which President Lyndon Johnson had foisted on the FCC as a way to shut down politically critical speech on talk radio and television.[32] The Fairness Doctrine obligated radio and television stations to give equal time to opponents of anything controversial, including anything controversial said by talk radio hosts,[33] and to provide "public interest programming," with inveterately leftist bureaucrats deciding what counts as "public interest." In 1985, the FCC, under the extraordinary leadership of Chairman Mark Fowler, took steps toward repealing the doctrine,[34] and the Democratic Congress, in 1987, passed a bill to head off repeal by codifying the Fairness Doctrine into federal statutory law. President Reagan planned to veto the bill, but Steve Calabresi, acting as an Ed Meese agent, came up with a specific message that he wanted in President Reagan's veto message.

The Supreme Court had quite wrongly upheld the constitutionality of the Fairness Doctrine in the 1969 Warren Court *Red Lion Co. v. FCC* opinion.[35] Steve Calabresi, following Ed Meese's Tulane speech on departmentalism, which we discuss in chapter 7, wanted President Ronald Reagan to say that he, as a co-equal interpreter of the Constitution to the Supreme Court, thought that the Fairness Doctrine was in fact unconstitutional and that the *Red Lion* case from 1969 was wrongly decided. Calabresi persuaded his law school and Yale College roommate Peter Keisler,[36] who had landed a job working for Howard Baker's White House counsel, A. B. Culvahouse, to say this in drafting President Reagan's veto message of the Fairness Doctrine bill. Doing so might embolden the FCC to scrap the Fairness Doctrine sooner, and totally, and it would preclude Solicitor General Charles Fried from defending the Fairness Doctrine in the federal courts based on settled Supreme Court precedent.

On June 19, 1987, President Reagan vetoed the Fairness Doctrine, with a message that included the following robust defense of the Constitution:

TO THE SENATE OF THE UNITED STATES:

I am returning herewith without my approval S. 742, the "Fairness in Broadcasting Act of 1987," which would codify the so-called "fairness doctrine." This doctrine, which has evolved through the decisional process of the Federal Communications Commission (FCC), requires Federal officials to supervise the editorial practices of broadcasters in an effort to ensure that they provide coverage of controversial issues and a reasonable opportunity for the airing of contrasting viewpoints on those issues. This type of content-based regulation by the Federal Government is, in my judgment, antagonistic to the freedom of expression guaranteed by the First Amendment.

In any other medium besides broadcasting, such Federal policing of the editorial judgment of journalists would be unthinkable. The framers of the First Amendment, confident that public debate would be freer and healthier without the kind of interference represented by the "fairness doctrine," chose to forbid such regulations in the clearest terms: "Congress shall make no law ... abridging the freedom of speech, or of the press." More recently, the United States Supreme Court, in striking down a right-of-access statute that applied to newspapers, spoke of the statute's intrusion into the function of the editorial process and concluded that "[i]t has yet to be demonstrated how governmental regulation of this crucial process can be exercised consistent with First Amendment guarantees of a free press as they have evolved to this time." *Miami Herald Publishing Co. v. Tornillo*, 418 U.S. 241, 258 (1974).

I recognize that 18 years ago the Supreme Court indicated that the fairness doctrine as then applied to a far less technologically advanced broadcast industry did not contravene the First Amendment. *Red Lion Broadcasting Co. v. FCC*, 395 U.S. 367 (1969)....

Quite apart from ... technological advances, we must not ignore the obvious intent of the First Amendment, which is to promote vigorous public debate and a diversity of viewpoints in the public forum *as a whole*, not in any particular medium, let alone in any particular journalistic outlet. History has shown that the dangers of an overly timid or biased press cannot be averted through bureaucratic regulation, but only through the freedom and competition that the First Amendment sought to guarantee. ...

S. 742 simply cannot be reconciled with the freedom of speech and the press secured by our Constitution. It is, in my judgment, unconstitutional. Well-intentioned as S. 742 may be, it would be inconsistent with the First Amendment and with the American tradition of independent journalism. Accordingly, I am compelled to disapprove this measure.

RONALD REAGAN
The White House
June 19, 1987

THIS POWERFUL MESSAGE set the stage for the Federal Communications Commission's August 4, 1987, decision abolishing the Fairness Doctrine altogether on a 4–0 vote, led by Chairman Dennis Patrick.[37] The Reagan veto message was prescient and timely. In the wake of the abolition of the Fairness Doctrine, conservative talk radio, which had previously been censored, took off with people like Rush Limbaugh and eventually former Meese aide Mark Levin. Conservative talk radio, and indeed Fox News, would never have been possible had the Fairness Doctrine not been abolished. This was indeed one of the greatest domestic policy and constitutional law accomplishments of the Reagan administration.

Calabresi and McIntosh's fourth Ed Meese–inspired project during their brief tenure at the White House was to have President Reagan set up and appoint the members of a Margaret Thatcher–inspired

Commission on Privatization, which was publicly announced on September 4, 1987. The president's stated goal was to "help fulfill the commitment I made in my Economic Bill of Rights to end unfair government competition and return government programs and assets to the American people. Privatization follows in the great tradition of free enterprise and private ownership of property that has long been a part of American history...."[38] The commission succeeded in privatizing Conrail, the national freight rail system, and it was able to shrink thirty-eight thousand federal government jobs by turning them over to government contractors instead of conducting activities in-house. The commission urged Congress to sell Amtrak and certain federal oil reserves, but Congress unfortunately refused to do this.

The Commission on Privatization, during its brief tenure, only scratched the surface of what is possible. The United States never nationalized as much industry as did the United Kingdom, so there was not as much industry to privatize in the United States as in the U.K. The main assets the U.S. government ought to privatize are the huge federally owned land stakes in western states like Nevada, Oregon, Idaho, Montana, Wyoming, California, Washington State, and especially Alaska. These should be opened up by a new federal Homestead Act.

The original Homestead Acts were 19th-century laws by which an individual could acquire property, which he would then occupy or sell to someone else.[39] An 1862 law signed by President Lincoln opened millions of acres of federally owned land to anyone, of any race, who would cultivate it. Nearly 10 percent of the total area of the United States was privatized through Homestead Acts. The general rule was that an individual could get five acres to homestead. He had to then live on that land for five years, after which he owned it and could sell it to somebody else. It fulfilled President Abraham Lincoln's ambition to make property owners out of as many Americans as possible. Homesteading might have gone further, especially with the newly free Black Americans who had been enslaved, had President Lincoln not been assassinated.

Of course, no one wants to homestead the many national parks created since 1872, when Congress and President Ulysses S. Grant established Yellowstone National Park.[40] But those parks represent only a small percentage of the enormous federal landholdings. How many people know that the federal government currently owns 27.4 percent of all of the land in the United States? Is the federal government likely to be an effective owner or manager of this land? National parkland covers 52.2 million acres, while the federal domain contains more than 600 million acres. We could keep all of our great national parks and forests and still privatize millions of acres of federal land—about half of all the federally owned land. And anyone worried about the environmental effects of privatization—and we mean *truly* worried and not virtue-signaling worried—should take a good hard look at government land management in practice. Communist countries are environmental cesspools, as any competent economist could readily predict. Communist-lite government management is unlikely to fare much better.

It should also be said that, apart from specific projects mentioned above, Ken Cribb always worked on reforming judicial selection, whatever his specific portfolio. Consequently, when he was appointed assistant to the president for domestic affairs, the only thing he asked in return was to be placed on the Judicial Selection Committee, which met in the Roosevelt Room, just outside the Oval Office. He thus worked on the importance of a judiciary faithful to the Constitution for the entire nine years of his service with Ronald Reagan: from the 1980 campaign, where he was deputy to Chief Counsel Loren Smith; to the 1980 Presidential Transition, where Smith and Cribb were responsible for the Department of Justice and all regulatory and administrative agencies; to the first term as assistant counsellor to the president, where he staffed Ed Meese's work on the Judicial Selection Committee; to the second term as counsellor to the attorney general, where he helped coordinate the Department of Justice's work on judicial selection; and finally, as assistant to the president for domestic affairs, where he worked with the speechwriters so that the president would use the word "text" or "written" whenever he used the word "Constitution." In every one of these jobs, his highest personal priority was to help restore fidelity to the Constitution, or as he would always insist, "to the text of the Constitution as ratified."

RONALD REAGAN'S RIGHT-HAND MAN

ED MEESE was also of critical help to President Reagan in enabling him to survive the political fallout from the Iran-Contra Affair, which is discussed in a subsequent chapter. Ed Meese investigated the scandal, fired those responsible for it, defended the administration on Capitol Hill and before the national press corps, and helped President Reagan find and work with his third White House chief of staff, former Senate majority leader Howard Baker, a liberal Republican with deep reservoirs of trust in both parties on Capitol Hill.

The Iran-Contra Affair was a major political scandal, which consumed a lot of time and attention in the United States during President Ronald Reagan's last two years in office. The scandal grew out of the fact that top Reagan administration officials at the National Security Council, without the president's or the National Security Council's permission, secretly facilitated the sale of military equipment to the Islamic Republic of Iran even though that country was subject to an arms embargo. These transfers were made to elicit Iranian aid in securing the release of Americans held hostage in Lebanon and the Middle East. Oliver North, a National Security Council official, used the proceeds from these sales to help fund the anti-communist Contras in Nicaragua. The Contras were engaged in a decades-long fight against the communist Sandinista government of Nicaragua. At the time, a statute known as the Boland Amendment was adopted as a rider to an appropriations bill forbidding the use of the appropriated money by the Defense Department, the CIA, or any other agency or entity of the United States involved in intelligence activities to fund the Contras. The amendment did not actually apply to the National Security Council, but Colonel Oliver North's use of the proceeds of the arms sales to fund the Contras infuriated congressional Democrats who had just won control of both houses of Congress in the 1986 midterm elections.

A Lebanese magazine exposed the arrangement to exchange arms with Iran for help in securing the release of hostages on November 3, 1986. President Reagan defended his administration's actions in a nationally televised address on November 13, 1986. Afterward, Ed Meese suggested to President Reagan that he should be deputized by the president to conduct a thorough internal investigation into the arms-for-hostages matter, so that the administration would be the first to know exactly what had happened. Conducting such an investigation was a thankless task that earned Ed Meese no small amount of grief, but Meese characteristically volunteered to do this to protect his good friend Ronald Reagan by finding out exactly what had happened. As it turned out, North destroyed or hid pertinent documents between November 21 and November 25, 1986, while Attorney General Ed Meese conducted his thorough five-day internal Reagan administration investigation into the Iran-Contra Affair, during the same time period. Meese disclosed on November 25, 1986, that profits from the Iranian arms sales had been diverted by Col. Oliver North to aid the Contras without the knowledge or approval of either President Reagan or of the National Security Council itself. That same day North was fired from his position at the National Security Council, and President Reagan also forced his national security advisor, Vice Admiral John Poindexter, to resign. Subsequent investigations by Special Prosecutor Lawrence Walsh and by a special joint Senate-House Committee charged with investigating the Iran-Contra Affair consumed the final two years of the Reagan administration.

Attorney General Ed Meese publicly defended President Reagan throughout this period of time. The affair was investigated to death by the Joint Committee of the U.S. Congress; by the Tower Commission, established on December 1, 1986, by President Reagan to conduct another even more thorough internal executive branch review; and by an independent counsel named Lawrence Walsh. The Walsh investigation, in particular, was a partisan witch hunt because Walsh hired a team of ultra-left-wing lawyers who viscerally hated Ronald Reagan to work for him. All of the people indicted by Walsh or convicted in trials he supervised either had their convictions overturned on appeal or were among six individuals pardoned by President George H. W. Bush on December 24, 1992, when most of the country was celebrating Christmas or Hanukkah. Those pardoned included former defense secretary Caspar Weinberger, former national security advisor Robert McFarlane, former assistant secretary of state Elliott Abrams, and three other officials. Presidents Reagan and Bush both denied ever having had any knowledge of the Iran-Contra Affair.

While White House chief of staff Donald Regan had no knowledge of the Iran-Contra Affair, his control over and supervision of the White House staff was called into question by the whole matter. Regan obviously did not know what the National Security Council in his own

White House was doing. As a result, Regan was the target of many at-tacks, and by February of 1987, Regan informed President Ronald Reagan that he wanted to resign. As we explained in the introduction to this book, President Reagan then asked Attorney General Ed Meese to help him in finding a new White House chief of staff. This illustrates the extent to which Ed Meese was de facto counsellor to the president during President Ronald Reagan's second term. In fact, probably one of the most important decisions Ronald Reagan made during his second term was a Paul Laxalt—and Ed Meese—inspired selection of a new White House chief of staff Howard Baker. The stakes could not have been higher. Congressional Democrats were already muttering about impeachment, while major foreign policy decisions involving Mikhail Gorbachev and the Soviet Union had to be made.

As we mentioned in the introduction, Ed Meese helped President Reagan hire Howard Baker as his third White House chief of staff, and the appointment had exactly the calming effect on Capitol Hill that Ed Meese had hoped it would have. The Iran-Contra investigations went on and on, but they were drained of the hatred that had previously been voiced. No more whisperings about impeachment were heard, and the Howard Baker appointment so thoroughly saved Ronald Reagan's pres-idency that Reagan was successful in his efforts to help elect his own vice president, George H. W. Bush, as his successor in the Oval Office in the 1988 presidential election. Ed Meese did the president and the country a huge service by enabling the appointment of Howard Baker as Ronald Reagan's third White House chief of staff. The result, as Rea-gan historian Steven Hayward put it, was that "Reagan helped create the political environment that made it possible for his party to achieve the rarity of winning the White House for a third straight election in 1988."[41] We give due credit to Howard Baker, but due credit must also be given to Ed Meese.

PART II

THE MOST SIGNIFICANT
ATTORNEY GENERAL IN U.S. HISTORY

Ed with his grandmother, Cornelia Meese, and his younger brother Myron in 1934.

She instilled in Ed a life-long love of reading.

Ed and his three younger brothers admiring a police car. The future attorney general was fascinated by law enforcement at an early age.

As a Boy Scout in 1941.

As a student at age 17.

Yale Debating Association

Ed at Yale College.

*Ed, front row center,
with the Yale Debating Association.*

Yale yearbook photo.

*1959 wedding photographs of
Ed and Ursula.*

Wedding photograph with their parents.

From left to right:
Charles Herrick,
Lillian Herrick,
Ursula Herrick Meese,
Edwin Meese III,
Leone Meese, and
Edwin Meese Jr.

1981 in the residential wing of the White House.

From left to right:
Scott Meese,
Ursula Meese,
Ronald Reagan,
Ed Meese,
Dana Meese,
and Mike Meese.

1982 at the Reagan Ranch.
Mike Meese, Dana Meese,
Ed Meese, and President Reagan.

It happened to be the exact day
that Ed's son Mike was promoted to
1st Lieutenant in the Army so the
president was congratulating him.

Ed and Ursula at their son Mike's wedding in 1983, along with Ed's parents Leone Meese and Edwin Meese Jr.

Ed and Ursula at their daughter Dana's wedding in 1999.

50th wedding anniversary; renewing vows, 2009.

With Louetta Erlin (Ursula's maid of honor at the wedding), Ursula, Judge Lois Herrington, and George Meese.

50th wedding anniversary cake cutting.

Ed and Ursula, Jim Herrick (Ursula's brother), John and Marge Minnie, and Lee Knudsen (all but Lee Knudsen were there 50 years ago).

Ed and Ursula on their 50th wedding anniversary.

Thanksgiving 2023.

Ed and Ursula with their two children, Mike and Dana, their spouses, and their five grandchildren and nine great-grandchildren.

Presidential candidate Ronald Reagan, Ed Meese, and Bill Casey working on the 1980 campaign.

President Ronald Reagan seated in the Oval Office after his inauguration, with Deputy Chief of Staff Mike Deaver, Chief of Staff Jim Baker, Counsellor to the President Ed Meese, Press Secretary Mike Brady, and National Security Director Dick Allen standing behind the president.

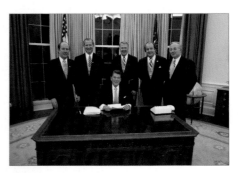

White House Chief of Staff Jim Baker, Counsellor to the President Ed Meese, and Deputy White House Chief of Staff Michael Deaver ("the Troika").

Counsellor to the President Ed Meese, CIA Director Bill Casey, and President Ronald Reagan.

President Reagan and Counsellor to the President Ed Meese at work together in the Oval Office.

President Reagan with two future attorneys general: Ed Meese and Bill Barr. Reagan and Meese self-consciously cultivated young talent on their farm team in the hopes of projecting their influence to future presidencies.

The first person Ronald Reagan would turn to, if he had trouble, was Ed Meese.

Michael Deaver, Ed Meese, and President Ronald Reagan.

Ed Meese speaking to the press as counsellor to the president at the White House.

*Meese and
Ken Cribb,
Meese's right-hand
man, wearing
Adam Smith neckties.*

*President Reagan,
Ken Cribb, and
Ed Meese share a
humorous moment in
the Oval Office.*

Dear Ed- I told everyone you could do Bills job & here is proof. Ron

*William French Smith
and Ed Meese asleep
in 1985, with a note
from Ronald Reagan
saying:*

*Dear Ed- I told every-
one you could do Bill
Smith's job & here is
proof. Ron.*

CHAPTER FIVE
PROLOGUE: THE LEGAL WORLD
BEFORE ED MEESE

To APPRECIATE ED Meese's accomplishments as the 75th attorney general of the United States, one needs to know something about the Reagan Revolution, about Ed Meese's role during President Ronald Reagan's first term as counsellor to the president, and about Ed Meese's humility, character, boundless energy, and rock-ribbed conservatism. But it is equally critical that one know something about the legal world that Ed Meese inherited when he was sworn in as attorney general on February 25, 1985. We hinted at that world in the introduction, but there is a much deeper story to be told that puts the rest of this book in proper context.

Many parts of the story that concern world events, economic affairs, and national politics in the years leading up to the Reagan presidency are largely known to those who lived through them and to honest historians, though they are perhaps less well known to people born in the past four decades. We have already said a lot about the failings of President Jimmy Carter's foreign and economic policies, and we have alluded to President Reagan's and Ed Meese's rejection of the foreign policy of détente and containment of communism and their embrace of a foreign policy advocating the rolling back and eventual defeat of communism. The Reagan Revolution was a strong repudiation of the foreign and economic policies of the Nixon, Ford, and Carter years. It was also an equally strong repudiation of the legal orthodoxy of the day. Accordingly, we focus in this chapter on a portion of the story, involving constitutional law, that was not broadly understood even forty years ago when it happened and that definitely is not broadly understood today, including among constitutional law scholars. In order to see how thoroughly Attorney General Ed Meese shaped constitutional law, and accordingly to understand the constitutional world of the 21st century that he helped build, one has to see the world of constitutional law through Ed Meese's eyes in the early 1980s.

When one thinks about the concerns of constitutional law in the early 1980s, one naturally thinks about court decisions, primarily or even exclusively decisions of the United States Supreme Court. As we will explain in subsequent chapters, that account is incomplete even on its own terms: Congress, the president, and the federal executive branch in general are also important contributors to the making of constitutional law, and Ed Meese played a vital role in making those contributions more transparent and thought-provoking. But constitutional law is also shaped by forces subtler and less visible than formal legal decisions made by government agents of any kind, and to understand constitutional law, one must understand those forces. Consider some of the forces that reigned unchallenged in the early 1980s before Ed Meese became attorney general of the United States.

By tradition, even though not by legal command, all federal judges have been lawyers, as are most (not all, but most) important legal actors in the executive department[1] and a good many members of Congress.[2] The attorneys general of the United States have all been lawyers, and as a result they have been trained to have a particular mindset. In the early 1980s, lawyers were trained in law schools, where they learned the methods and techniques that legal academics thought were deserving of attention. Early 1980s constitutional law classes wove together the fifty or so most important policy decisions of the Supreme Court, and then reasoned analogically, and with an eye on good public policy from an early 1980s (and typically leftist) perspective, to a solution to the then current case before the Supreme Court.

The message to law students and to future attorneys general and Supreme Court justices in the early 1980s was that constitutional law is basically a realm of judge-made common law that evolves over time, always toward PROGRESS, in which doctrinal case law is everything and attention to the text of the Constitution or its original public meaning is just weird. Justice Robert Jackson eloquently explains this view in his famous—and today still widely celebrated in the academy—1952 concurring opinion in *Youngstown Sheet and Tube Co. v. Sawyer*:

> Just what our forefathers did envision, or would have envisioned had they foreseen modern conditions, must be divined from

materials as enigmatic as the dreams Joseph was called upon to interpret for Pharaoh. A century and a half of partisan debate and scholarly speculation yields no net result but only supplies more or less apt quotations from respected sources on each side of any question. They largely cancel each other.[3]

Justice Jackson made the above remarks with respect to the line between presidential and congressional power, but he might as well have been talking about any other area of constitutional law. New Deal attorneys general and Supreme Court justices believed that the whole text of the Constitution was meaningless. All of its key provisions, they believed, contain materials as enigmatic as the dreams Joseph was called upon to interpret for Pharaoh. Constitutional law was about court decisions, and court decisions were about wise policy choices.

This was not a new idea. Half a century before Justice Jackson, Harvard law professor James Bradley Thayer, of whom we will hear more shortly, wrote in perhaps the most influential law review article of all time that the fundamental error in constitutional law was to treat it as a legal rather than political discipline. As he put it in 1893, having courts think about texts and interpretation "easily results in the wrong kind of disregard of legislative considerations; not merely in refusing to let them directly operate as grounds of judgment, but in refusing to consider them at all. Instead of taking them into account and allowing for them as furnishing possible grounds of legislative action, there takes place a pedantic and academic treatment of the texts of the constitution and the laws. And so we miss that combination of a lawyer's rigor with a statesman's breadth of view...."[4] Even before Thayer, judges and attorneys general, who were trained in the common-law method by reading law with successful practitioners, learned to rely on Supreme Court, legislative, and executive precedents rather than the constitutional text. This surfaced as early as 1803, when the Supreme Court said that "practice and acquiescence under it for a period of several years, commencing with the organization of the judicial system, afford an irresistible answer and have indeed fixed the construction. It is a contemporary interpretation of the most forcible nature. This practical exposition is too strong and obstinate to be shaken or controlled."[5]

It is thus no surprise that constitutional law classes in the early 1980s wove together the fifty or so most important policy decisions of the Supreme Court. Law professors, especially if they mostly agreed with the court's policy decisions, reinforced this anti-textual method. Those academics, in addition to providing classroom training to budding lawyers, wrote books and articles, some of which were directed at their peers, some of which (like this one) were directed at a broader public, and some of which were aimed squarely at real-world governmental decision-makers. Those academic writings played an important, and too often unacknowledged, role in shaping the decisions that constituted binding law in the early 1980s. They provided material that judges and other actors could directly rely upon in framing their decisions, and, perhaps more importantly, they both defined and reflected the milieu in which judges and others were trained and operated.

Among the most important "others" were the judges' law clerks. Law clerks are often hired right out of law school, or occasionally with a few years' experience after law school. The clerks are thus a transmission belt carrying current academic thought to the bench. In some instances, depending on the judges, clerks are the principal drafters of judicial opinions—and in extreme cases the clerks function effectively as the judges. The clerks, typically with little practical experience in either law or life, naturally bring their academic training to their tasks.

Thus, before we look at the hard doctrines of constitutional law that governed the legal world of the early 1980s, we must first look at the academic world that spawned, maintained, and reinforced those doctrines. As Robert Bork put it in 1985, if we "discern what is being taught in the law schools," we will also discern "what may be the views of the profession and the judges of the next generation."[6] Neither Ed Meese nor anyone else could change the hard doctrines of an out-of-control Supreme Court without understanding and confronting their seemingly arcane academic foundations.

In chapter 13, we will see how things have—and in some respects have not—changed as a result of Ed Meese's legacy. For now, however, we look back four decades to the beginning of Ed Meese's service as attorney general of the United States.

The Constitution in the Classroom before Ed Meese

HOW DO COURTS (and legislators and executive officials who must make constitutional decisions) actually decide cases? How *should* courts (and other actors) actually decide cases in an ideal world? These are the kinds of questions one would expect a law school course in constitutional law, or any other subject, to address and that one would expect legal academics to explore in their scholarly enterprises.

As it happens, the first question often becomes the province of political scientists more than law professors, because it involves tricky empirical questions that might require sophisticated analytical tools that many law professors, possessing only law degrees, may not have.[7] Law professors, to be sure, spend much of their time describing what courts do, but it is one thing to describe particular court decisions or lines of decisions and quite another to theorize at a general empirical level about the broad paths and mechanisms of judicial behavior. On the other hand, ask almost any law professor how cases *should* come out, and you will probably get a mouthful. A staple, perhaps *the* staple, of legal scholarship is a work explaining how the academic author thinks that the courts have failed to shape the law the way that the author favors.

It would not be surprising if these academic biases find their way into the classroom. Anyone who goes to law school usually comes away with a decent sense of how his or her professors, or at least most of them, believe that cases should be decided. That may be less true in certain technical areas of legal doctrine, but it is especially true in constitutional law. Importantly, the focus in constitutional law is often less on how specific cases ought to come out than on the broader methods used to reach those decisions. To be sure, academic choices of method can be and often are driven by the kinds of results that academics think those methods will reach, but the methods have lives of their own that transcend even the most hot-button cases. Constitutional law is a subject that is concerned as much with *how* decisions are reached as with the decisions themselves. Thus, to appreciate what Ed Meese accomplished, one has to have some sense of the academic debate about methods as that debate stood when he took office as attorney general.

Partly as a result of Ed Meese's influence that we describe throughout this book, the modern world of constitutional theory is much more diverse, complex, and sophisticated than it was forty years ago. Today, one sees not only debates between originalists and non-originalists but also vibrant debates within the contending camps that are often quite fundamental. There are enough variants of originalism, for example, to fill up entire academic conferences. In the 1980s, however, the menu of available options for constitutional interpretation was very thin and relatively simple. The basic question was whether the Constitution had any relevance for constitutional law. As Justice Jackson put it, were the textual, historical, and case law issues in every case "as enigmatic as the dreams Joseph was called upon to interpret for Pharaoh"? And if by some chance one could ascertain the meaning of the Constitution's text, would it make a difference in how a case should come out?

One possible approach to deciding constitutional cases that a lawyer might have learned about in the early 1980s, before the "Meese Revolution," is something resembling what today we would call *originalism*, though it had no generally employed name in those days. In its broadest sense, this approach urges courts to decide cases in accordance with the Constitution's *original meaning*—referring to the document's meaning at the time of its enactment. For the United States Constitution, the time of enactment would be 1788 for the bulk of the document, 1791 for the first ten amendments, 1865 for the Thirteenth Amendment, 1868 for the Fourteenth Amendment, 1870 for the Fifteenth Amendment, and so on. This approach decidedly rejects Justice Jackson's skepticism about the ability to ascertain constitutional meaning using text, structure, and history, at least over a large range of cases. It maintains that seemingly "open-ended" constitutional clauses, if examined carefully and honestly, often turn out to be terms of art with relatively clear original meanings. Even when clear meanings do not emerge, the Domestic Policy Council's 1986 federalism report pointed out that "what we do know about the original meaning of the document will provide guideposts and set boundaries. ... In other words, one can know that a particular answer to a constitutional question is wrong without knowing precisely which answer is right."[8] Importantly, if words found in the Constitution change meaning over time—if, for example, "due process of law" meant one thing in 1791, another thing in 1868, and still another thing in 2024—a theory of *original meaning* would instruct courts to use the meaning in place at the time of enactment rather than a modern meaning that has supplanted the older one in either popular or technical discourse. That is why this "Meesian" approach has come to be called *originalism*. This approach today has many variants that give differing weights to things like the concrete intentions of particular historical figures, the early practices of governmental actors, the inferred intentions of various Framers or ratifiers of the Constitution, hypothetical intentions of fictitious actors like "We the People," and so forth, but those variants were not theoretically developed circa 1980 when Ed Meese was about to enter federal service. All one could have at that time was a vague sense that constitutional law should have the Constitution at its center and that the Constitution's meaning traced back in time to some important constitutional moments when texts came into existence. But even that vague and untheorized sense, if one had it, set one far apart from the herd. Indeed, in the academy, one would be nearly alone.

One countervailing academic approach in the pre-Meese era was to urge courts to prefer modern meanings to original ones. Those modern meanings might be shaped by expectations and practices far removed from original meaning. This is one form of what is often called *living constitutionalism*—the key ideas being that the Constitution must adapt to changing social preferences rather than vice versa and that federal judges and other federal governmental actors, rather than the people or the states acting through Article V's amendment process, are appropriate persons to update the document to fit their perceptions of modern conditions. There is also an implicit assumption that adapting to changing social preferences is always progress, and that societies always progress (however progress is defined). They never rot. This assumption is fundamentally false, though that would be the subject of a very different book.

A third approach commonplace in the early 1980s rejected altogether the idea of trying to attach meaning, either original or modern, to the Constitution's words. The focus instead was on deciding cases in accordance with specified moral theories, economic theories, or political programs untethered to the actual Constitution. This approach was often called, including by its advocates, *noninterpretivism*, which reflects the idea that one is not really trying to interpret the Constitution in any linguistic sense; instead, one is trying to manage and shape a political and social order using constitutional cases as a handy vehicle. *Noninterpretivism* was the overwhelmingly popular approach to constitutional interpretation before Ed Meese became attorney general. Assuming that the desired shaping changes over time, this would be another form of *living constitutionalism*.

If this were a book on constitutional theory, we would do a much longer and more thorough job of describing the full range of approaches that have developed over the past half century, including the many variants within each of the larger categories, and including some prominent approaches that we have not mentioned here.[9] For present purposes, however, this crude sketch of constitutional methods circa 1980 is sufficient.[10] And within the terms of this sketch, the dominant view circa 1980 was some form of *noninterpretivism*, under which the Constitution itself is essentially irrelevant to constitutional law.

To a large extent, the academy took seriously the aphorism from former (and, at the time he made the comment, future) chief justice Charles Evans Hughes that "[w]e are under a Constitution, but the Constitution is what the judges say it is…."[11] At least, they took it seriously when it looked like the judges would mostly agree with the academy. At a minimum, the academic consensus sided with Justice Jackson's skepticism about finding constitutional meaning. As Judge Bork put in 1985, "Today, the reigning theory is that interpretation may be impossible, and is certainly inadequate."[12]

If one finds it hard to believe that there could have been serious debate about whether the Constitution is relevant to constitutional law, much less a consensus that it is not actually relevant, consider the words of by all rights the leading constitutional theorist of that era: John Hart Ely. Professor Ely taught, among other places, at Yale Law School (1968–1973), Harvard Law School (1973–1982), and Stanford Law School (1982–1996), serving as dean of the latter from 1982 to 1987. His 1980 book *Democracy and Distrust*, published by Harvard University Press, is among the most influential books on constitutional theory ever written—and certainly was the most influential book of its time. To paraphrase the old commercial, when John Hart Ely spoke, people listened.

Ely's own approach questioned whether one should bother with the text of the Constitution. Ely's book essentially concluded that the text of the Constitution was meaningless over a large range of cases because it had so many open-ended clauses, i.e., clauses for which he did not have the patience or the desire to find the original public meaning.[13] Ely proposed his own "participation-oriented, representation-reinforcing"[14] theory of judicial review that amounted to a paean to the main lines of the Supreme Court's post-1937 jurisprudence, with the notable exception of *Roe v. Wade*, the famous 1973 case, which created out of constitutional thin air a woman's right to have an abortion. Ely dedicated his book to former chief justice Earl Warren, and he sought to defend the Warren Court's decisions, especially those getting rid of Jim Crow race discrimination and its one-person, one-vote decisions requiring that legislative districts be as nearly equal in population as possible. For our purposes, what matters most is not Professor Ely's own views (some of which might be right) but rather his description of the state of constitutional theory, about which he said this in 1978: "Today we are likely to call the contending sides 'interpretivism' and 'noninterpretivism'—the former indicating that judges deciding constitutional issues should confine themselves to enforcing values or norms that are stated or very clearly implicit in the written Constitution, the latter indicating the contrary view that courts should go beyond that set of references and enforce values or norms that cannot be discovered within the four corners of the document."[15] And again: "What distinguishes interpretivism from its opposite is its insistence that the work of the political branches is to be invalidated only in accord with an inference whose starting point, whose underlying premise, is fairly discoverable in the Constitution."[16]

Thus, in the 1970s and early 1980s, before Ed Meese served as attorney general, the big academic debate was whether or not to read the Constitution when doing constitutional law. The most common answer was no, and the academics argued mostly about what kinds of values or preferences to put in place of the Constitution. Another prominent (and today still prominent) constitutional scholar wrote in 1982 that "interpretivism has been thoroughly discredited."[17] Indeed, as one approached the 1980s, those who dared advocate limiting judicial review to things actually in the Constitution would be "dismissed as unsophisticates or out-of-date legal primitives."[18] In a subtle but important reflection of these trends, the leading constitutional law casebook of that era, written by Stanford professor Gerald Gunther, listed the justices who had served in each Supreme Court seat as appendix 1 and the text of the Constitution and its amendments as appendix 2.[19] Professor Gunther eventually corrected this after Ed Meese made fun of him in a speech.

Today, almost half a century later, in a post–Ed Meese world, there is a vibrant debate in the courts and the academy regarding these broad approaches to constitutional decision-making. One crude but useful measure of the academic debate is a simple word search of the Westlaw database of law reviews, which as of May 2023 shows more than 9,000 references to "originalism" and more than 8,400 references to "originalist" in legal scholarship since the year 2000 and more than 8,000 references to "original meaning" during that post-2000 period. If one includes years before 2000, one gets the dreaded "10,000" response to these terms, meaning that there are more than 10,000 such references—perhaps many more—and the search engine is urging use of a narrower set of terms to allow for manageable research. These numbers would surely be considerably larger if one included books and popular-press articles in addition to articles in scholarly journals. Most of those references are sharply critical of originalism, originalists, and original meaning, but the sheer number of those references is a good indication that originalism is currently taken seriously as a mode of constitutional decision-making.

The data shows that this was not the case when Ed Meese entered the federal government.

We both went to law school in 1980, on the eve of the presidential election, and graduated in 1983, two years before Ed Meese became attorney general. The number of references to "originalism" in the Westlaw law review database just mentioned for the entire period of recorded history before 1984 was *nine*—and one of those references involved contract interpretation rather than constitutional interpretation. All eight of the references to originalism as a constitutional method were critical of the concept, and half of them are attributable to two figures (Paul Brest and Sanford Levinson).

More significantly, all eight of those references occurred in the period from 1980 to 1983. That is correct: prior to 1980, when the two of us entered law school and Ronald Reagan was elected president, there were exactly *zero* references to "originalism" in American law reviews that are included in the Westlaw database.[20] Zero.

If one goes instead to the HeinOnline database of law reviews, which is somewhat larger than the Westlaw database, the number of 1980–1983 references to "originalism" jumps to a still-paltry twenty-seven. The pre-1980 number, however, stays at zero. The same is true for "originalist," which shows up eight times in the Westlaw database and twenty-two times in the HeinOnline database between 1980 and 1983 and zero times in either database before 1980.

The term "original meaning," for its part, showed up in a constitutional context in roughly one hundred Westlaw references and a more robust eight-hundred-plus HeinOnline references pre-1984, but a good percentage of those references involve a narrow discussion about the constitutionality of the death penalty (of which we will say more later). More importantly, these references to the Constitution's "original meaning" are simply references, without elaborate explanation, definition, or defense. To our knowledge, there was *no* extended explication or defense of the idea of originalism or original meaning in a law review article before we graduated from law school. (There was a modest defense in a book in 1977 and another in a book in 1980, which we will address shortly.)

Of course, this kind of computerized search looks only for words, not concepts, so it might well miss some things that were originalist in substance but did not use the term. But even a Westlaw search for the broad term "interpretivism" before 1984 yields fewer than one hundred references (eighty-four, to be exact), with "interpretivist" yielding slightly more than fifty. All but seven of the mentions of "interpretivism" and all but five mentions of "interpretivist" came after 1980. Again, the numbers are higher if one looks at a broader database such as HeinOnline, but even then one can find only sixteen references to "interpretivist" before 1980.

This crude data confirms our qualitative judgment about the state of constitutional theory in the legal academy circa 1980. When we left law school in 1983, there were about 170 law schools in the United States. To our knowledge, there were perhaps *six* full-time tenure-track law professors anywhere in the country doing significant work that could fairly be described as primarily originalist or interpretivist in orientation.

Joseph Grano at Wayne State University Law School was a giant in the field of criminal law, and while he wrote little about constitutional law in general, in 1981 he wrote an article powerfully applying a form of interpretivism.[21] Lillian BeVier at the University of Virginia has long been a leading scholar on First Amendment issues, and her first major publication in 1978 identified her as an originalist.[22] Earl Maltz, first at Arkansas Little-Rock and for many decades since at Rutgers-Camden, was a prodigious writer of legal history, primarily on the Fourteenth Amendment, with an explicit focus on original meaning. Robert Nagel at Colorado Law would later become an important voice in constitutional theory, arguing more for judicial restraint than for originalism, and by 1983 he had written a book review reflecting skepticism about the noninterpretivist academic consensus.[23] Grover Rees was an assistant professor at the University of Texas School of Law in the early 1980s and was an interpretivist of sorts who was denied tenure.[24] Bernard Siegan, Ed Meese's colleague at the University of San Diego, wrote a book robustly defending judicial protection of economic liberty as consistent with the original intentions of the Framers.[25] As far as we can tell, that is all.

Perhaps the number of originalists/interpretivists rises past a half dozen if one counts either Professor Ely because he believed that judicial review had to be based on a "value the Constitution marks as special"[26] or Professor Henry Monaghan of Columbia University because he said that "any theory of constitutional interpretation which renders unimportant or irrelevant questions as to original intent, *so far as that intent can be fairly discerned*, is not, given our traditions, politically or intellectually defensible."[27] But given their overall bodies of academic work, calling them originalists is pushing things pretty far,[28] and we doubt whether either scholar would have chosen to be put in the originalist camp. The same is true of David Currie at the University of Chicago. In the early 1980s, Professor Currie produced a flurry of articles on the Supreme Court's first hundred years, later collected into an indispensable book.[29] Professor Currie did not expressly associate himself with any particular interpretative theory, but he took the Constitution seriously, and his work has always been a valued reference for originalists. The same can be said of Professor Currie's longtime colleague

Philip Kurland. Professor Kurland was an academic curmudgeon who had nice things to say about almost nothing or no one, but he was a particular critic of the Warren Court.[30] In 1987, along with Straussian political theorist Ralph Lerner, he produced a five-volume set of founding-era materials, called *The Founders' Constitution*, which remains a leading resource for originalist scholars. But neither Professor Currie nor Professor Kurland set forth a clear account of constitutional interpretation. And there were surely a few devotees of originalism on law faculties who never came to our attention because they stayed in the closet and wrote on other matters. But even on the most optimistic assumptions, the academic originalist cupboard in the 1970s and early 1980s was basically bare.

Crucially, *none* of the foregoing scholars who would associate themselves in some fashion with originalism or interpretivism saw themselves as an interpretative *theorist* in the way that Ed Meese was to become an interpretative theorist. That is, they swore allegiance to interpreting the Constitution, but it was not part of any of their scholarly projects to put forth a developed *theory* of interpretation that would discuss the nature of original meaning; the roles of intentions, history, or concepts in interpretation; the distinction between interpretation and adjudication; the relationship between original meaning and precedent; or the many other things necessary to develop a full-blown interpretative theory.[31] The closest anyone came even to attempting a justification for originalism was perhaps Bernie Siegan, but he never got beyond "examining the intentions of those who formulated the words,"[32] given that "[t]he interpreter's great task is fulfilling the will of the authors of the fundamental document and of its amendments without damaging the fabric of the society."[33]

To be sure, there were several professors in the academy at that time who would subsequently do important work on originalist theory—Larry Alexander at the University of San Diego,[34] Richard Kay at the University of Connecticut, John Baker at Louisiana State University,[35] and Stephen Presser first at Rutgers and then at Northwestern—but that theoretical work did not emerge until the late 1980s and afterward.

Antonin Scalia, if one is wondering about him, had been appointed to the federal bench in 1982 and so was not a full-time academic in 1983. But even as an academic before 1982, Justice Scalia did not produce anything that could be called originalist scholarship. His academic focus was on doctrinal administrative law, which helps explain why his confirmation hearings in 1986 were so dry (he was confirmed by a 98–0 vote in the Senate, however difficult that is to grasp in the current environment). All of his voluminous "academic" writings on constitutional theory came *after* he was a judge. Robert Bork was also appointed to the federal bench in 1982 and thus was no longer a full-time academic as of 1983; we will say more about Judge Bork and his role in originalism in a moment.

Thus, in American law schools in 1983, one was hard-pressed to find *any* voices on behalf of a straightforward interpretation of the United States Constitution. At something like 95 percent of American law schools, one would find no one. Originalism—and even the more modest "interpretivism," which suggested that interpreting the Constitution was perhaps a good idea—was a theoretical option, but not one that had any sustained academic support, defense, or development.

So, when living constitutionalists or noninterpretivists of that era criticized originalism or interpretivism, about whom and what they were complaining?

With regard to the whom: to a large extent, their target was someone who by 1980 had been dead for nearly a decade: Supreme Court justice Hugo Black. Black was an iconoclastic jurist who served on the Supreme Court from 1937 to 1971. He was erudite but not academic; he was a senator for ten years before serving on the court. President Roosevelt appointed him, in the wake of Supreme Court decisions invalidating some key provisions of the New Deal, because he was a faithful New Dealer who would reliably vote to uphold those programs. But when the Warren Court's focus shifted in the 1960s from upholding the New Deal to imposing a leftist social, political, and economic agenda by judicial fiat, Justice Black sometimes broke with his Warren Court colleagues, and he did so by appeal to things that could loosely be called originalist or interpretivist.

Perhaps his most famous departure from leftist legal orthodoxy was his 1965 dissenting opinion in *Griswold v. Connecticut*,[36] in which the court laid the groundwork for numerous future cases, including *Roe v. Wade*,[37] by invalidating an archaic and unenforced Connecticut law forbidding contraception. The court's rationale for finding the law

unconstitutional amounted to generating a new "right of privacy" out
of several more concrete and limited constitutional provisions that provided calibrated protection to various aspects of privacy. While not all
justices subscribed to this reasoning, Justice Black and Potter Stewart
were the only dissenters. Justice Black's lengthy dissent, spanning twen-
ty-one pages in the Supreme Court Reports, included the following
memorable passage:

> [T]here is no provision of the Constitution which either express-
> ly or impliedly vests power in this Court to sit as a supervisory
> agency over acts of duly constituted legislative bodies and set aside
> their laws because of the Court's belief that the legislative policies
> adopted are unreasonable, unwise, arbitrary, capricious or irratio-
> nal. The adoption of such a loose, flexible, uncontrolled standard
> for holding laws unconstitutional, if ever it is finally achieved, will
> amount to a great unconstitutional shift of power to the courts
> which I believe and am constrained to say will be bad for the
> courts and worse for the country. Subjecting federal and state laws
> to such an unrestrained and unrestrainable judicial control as to
> the wisdom of legislative enactments would, I fear, jeopardize the
> separation of governmental powers that the Framers set up and at
> the same time threaten to take away much of the power of States
> to govern themselves which the Constitution plainly intended
> them to have.
>
> I realize that many good and able men have eloquently spoken
> and written, sometimes in rhapsodical strains, about the duty of
> this Court to keep the Constitution in tune with the times. The
> idea is that the Constitution must be changed from time to time
> and that this Court is charged with a duty to make those changes.
> For myself, I must with all deference reject that philosophy. The
> Constitution makers knew the need for change and provided for
> it. Amendments suggested by the people's elected representatives
> can be submitted to the people or their selected agents for ratifica-
> tion. That method of change was good for our Fathers, and being
> somewhat old-fashioned I must add it is good enough for me.[38]

The Warren Court gave Justice Black plenty of material for more salvos.
As the lone dissenter in a 1967 case holding that government wiretapping

of a public phone booth is subject to the Fourth Amendment's prohibition of "unreasonable searches and seizures,"[39] Justice Black wrote:

I do not believe that the words of the Amendment will bear the meaning given them by today's decision, and ...I do not believe that it is the proper role of this Court to rewrite the Amendment in order "to bring it into harmony with the times" and thus reach a result that many people believe to be desirable. While I realize that an argument based on the meaning of words lacks the scope, and no doubt the appeal, of broad policy discussions and philosophical discourses on such nebulous subjects as privacy, for me the language of the Amendment is the crucial place to look in construing a written document such as our Constitution.[40]

In 1967, this was a radical view on the Supreme Court. Three years later, on the eve of his death, Justice Black dissented from a decision holding that defendants in juvenile courts could be convicted only by proof beyond a reasonable doubt:

[N]owhere in ... [the Constitution] is there any statement that conviction of crime requires proof of guilt beyond a reasonable doubt. The Constitution thus goes into some detail to spell out what kind of trial a defendant charged with crime should have, and I believe the Court has no power to add to or subtract from the procedures set forth by the Founders. I realize that it is far easier to substitute individual judges' ideas of "fairness" for the fairness prescribed by the Constitution, but I shall not at any time surrender my belief that that document itself should be our guide, not our own concept of what is fair, decent, and right.[41]

Statements such as these explain why many leading constitutional theorists call Justice Black "the 20th century's greatest originalist"[42] and "[t]he most influential originalist judge of the last hundred years."[43] One should be clear that modern originalists do not necessarily claim Justice Black as one of their own, much less agree with all of his conclusions about constitutional meaning,[44] but in the pre-Meese milieu of the 1970s and early 1980s, his stray comments about taking the Constitution seriously were enough to set off the academy.

A secondary target was then-justice, and later chief justice, William Rehnquist, who in 1976 published a speech in which he sharply criticized strong forms of living constitutionalism that maintained that "nonelected members of the federal judiciary may address themselves to a social problem simply because other branches of government have failed or refused to do so."[45] To be sure, Justice Rehnquist did not offer originalism as his alternative to this freewheeling approach, beyond an offhand reference to "values...which may be derived from the language and intent of the framers"[46] and the observation that "a mere change in public opinion since the adoption of the Constitution, unaccompanied by a constitutional amendment, should not change the meaning of the Constitution."[47] Justice Rehnquist's position was institutional: he agreed with the academic mainstream that the Constitution contained "majestic generalities"[48] that could be broadly construed, but he thought that Congress and the president were better suited than courts to provide those broad constructions.[49] His position was judicial restraint (about which we will say more shortly), not a thought-out theory of textual interpretation. As with Justice Black, however, these modest remarks coming from a Supreme Court justice were anathema to the mainstream legal academy.

Apart from these random and untheorized comments from a few Supreme Court justices, the academic works taken to represent "originalism," "interpretivism," or anything in that family were essentially twofold.[50] For all practical purposes, the entire corpus of originalist/interpretivist academic scholarship when we were in law school and Ed Meese took federal office was one book and one article.

The book was Raoul Berger's *Government by Judiciary: The Transformation of the Fourteenth Amendment*, published in 1977.[51] Berger was seventy-six years old when the book came out. Two decades later, at the ripe young age of ninety-six, he issued a revised second edition, with *considerable* additions that could have constituted a book in themselves.[52] While Berger spent a few years in the early 1960s as a law professor at Berkeley, for the thirty-plus years during which he produced prodigious and influential legal scholarship,[53] he never had a tenure-track appointment, much less tenure, at an American law school. He wrote *Government by Judiciary* at Harvard as the Charles Warren Senior Fellow in American Legal History. The book was a sustained assault on the Warren Court's jurisprudence involving the Fourteenth Amendment. It was *not* a general book on constitutional theory or any topic beyond the Fourteenth Amendment, though in other books Berger addressed topics ranging from separation of powers[54] to federalism.[55] Berger saw himself first and foremost as a historian. His focus was on describing the concrete intentions and expected original applications of specific historical figures who principally drafted and then proposed to the states the Fourteenth Amendment. That is a form of originalism, though hardly the only form, and today it finds very few (though a few, to be sure) adherents among self-described originalists, who tend to focus on more abstract public meanings rather than historically concrete intentions. Berger said relatively little about the text of the Fourteenth Amendment. His strict intentionalism and commitment to original expected applications (i.e., to identifying which specific practices of the time important people thought were and were not covered by a provision) led him, for example, to conclude that the Supreme Court was wrong in *Brown v. Board of Education*[56] to hold that segregated public schools violated the Fourteenth Amendment; we strongly disagree with Berger on that point as a matter of a more textually grounded original public meaning.[57]

Berger's influence in the 1970s and 1980s cannot be overstated. To a large degree, he *was* interpretivism to the legal academy for many years; one scholar in 1980 said of interpretivism, "[t]he beleaguered Raoul Berger is perhaps its sole prominent exponent."[58] "Beleaguered" indeed. Criticism of Berger was "a cottage industry in constitutional scholarship."[59]

Berger defended his strict intentionalism until his death in 2000, just months shy of his 100th birthday, but he saw that defense as incidental to his historical enterprise rather than central to it. As he explained in a 1983 response to critics, "I have never attempted to formulate a general theory of interpretivism; my goal has been more modest and quite narrow.... I was content to leave it to future legal scholars to fashion a general theory of interpretivism."[60] Berger never wanted to be the standard-bearer for originalism or interpretivism; he simply wanted to follow the historical materials where he thought they led. He came to represent originalism simply because there was no one else writing about it. As Larry Alexander aptly put it in 1981, "Berger has forced all serious constitutional theorists to deal with questions regarding proper principles of constitutional interpretation and the proper role of the courts, questions that many theorists, basking in the warm glow of Warren Court decisions on individual rights, felt content to ignore."[61] It is thus no criticism of Berger to point out that his writings left original-ism seriously undertheorized.

The other academic work sometimes taken as representative of origi-nalism or interpretivism before Ed Meese became attorney general was Robert Bork's 1971 article "Neutral Principles and Some First Amend-ment Problems."[62] The article is a modern classic; it has been cited by more than two thousand scholarly articles, and it featured prominently in some serious discussions of interpretivism in the 1970s and 1980s.

As with Raoul Berger, Robert Bork was both an unlikely and an un-willing standard-bearer for originalism. Just as Berger was a historian rather than an interpretative theorist, Bork's principal field was anti-trust law. His major academic work was *The Antitrust Paradox: A Policy at War with Itself*, published in 1978, which stands today as perhaps the most important and influential book yet written on antitrust law. Of his twenty-five scholarly and popular press articles before his appoint-ment to the federal bench in 1982, more than twenty were on antitrust law. His academic work in constitutional law was episodic at best. In addition to the "Neutral Principles" article, his only other constitution-al piece was a seven-page comment criticizing a Harvard professor's argument for a constitutional right to welfare.[63]

As did Raoul Berger, Bork openly disclaimed any intention of provid-ing a comprehensive interpretative theory. Bork began his 1971 article by saying, "The remarks that follow do not, of course, offer a general theory of constitutional law. They are more properly viewed as ranging shots...."[64] Lest one miss it, he said it again: "At the outset I warned that I did not offer a complete theory of constitutional interpretation. My concern has been to attack a few points that may be regarded as salient in order to clear the way for such a theory."[65] Those "few points" concerned the need for courts to be able to explain the bases for their decisions and to apply them consistently in future cases, both features which he saw lacking in many decisions of the court that were (and still are) favorites of the political left. Along the way, he emphasized that "[t]he judge must stick close to the text and the history, and their fair im-plications, and not construct new rights"[66] and that concrete intentions trump general language.[67] Neither claim was developed any further than we have just set out here. Bork's article staked out a position, but it made no real effort to explain or defend it from the standpoint of interpretative theory. Indeed, when Bork took a more serious swing at interpretative theory in his 1990 book *The Tempting of America: The Political Seduction of the Law*, he modified his position to bring it more in accord with the then emerging originalist consensus in favor of objective public meaning of legal texts rather than particularized historical intentions.[68] Bork did argue that court opinions construing the Constitution had to do more than state a neutral principal—such opinions also had to be neutrally derived from some neutral principal completely independent of a judge's own personal policy preferences. This was a foundational cornerstone for the edifice that became modern-day originalism, but it was only one stone.

Thus, someone in 1983 looking for a theoretically sophisticated explication or defense of originalism in a pre–Ed Meese world would find nothing. Literally nothing. The academic works taken to define the idea of originalism looked to and catalogued specific intentions of historically concrete actors, without serious investigations of the nature of interpretation or possible alternative accounts of original meaning. Originalism was floating out there as a possible interpretative method, but it was a method without either a descriptive or normative theory behind it.

That addresses the "who" that noninterpretivists thought they were contesting in the 1970s and 1980s. The "what" was occasionally interpretivism or originalism, but more often it was something even more amorphous called "judicial restraint" or "strict construction." This was the position staked out by Justice Rehnquist in 1976, and to a large extent it drove the positions of Oliver Wendell Holmes, Felix Frankfurter, Hugo Black, Raoul Berger, Attorney General William French Smith, Robert Bork, Antonin Scalia, and others as much or more than the primitive versions of originalism that we have sketched in this chapter did.

We cannot in this volume describe the constitutional revolution wrought by the Warren Court, though we will say a few more words about it shortly, but it rivaled in magnitude even the constitutional revolution of the post-1937 New Deal Court. The Warren Court, among other things, remade criminal law, secularized as much of American public life as it could, and fundamentally transformed American politics by making courts key actors in shaping election law and policy. Virtually all of these moves were celebrated by the academic and cultural left, which found getting five votes on the Supreme Court a relatively easy way to implement its agenda, especially in what today we would call "red" states where the left's views would find little popular support. Unsurprisingly, there was political and cultural backlash to at least some of the Warren Court's boldest actions, including proposed constitutional amendments to undo the Court's decisions banning prayer in public schools and ordering legislative districting on the basis of population rather than geography, interest, or history.

Richard Nixon campaigned for president in 1968 largely against the Warren Court, promising to appoint justices who would follow "strict construction" of the Constitution.[69] It was not at all clear what that term meant; President Nixon, in his memoir, said only that he thought "the Court should interpret the Constitution rather than amend it by judicial fiat"[70] and that he sought nominees who "shared my conservative judicial philosophy."[71]

A *conservative* judicial philosophy, however, is not necessarily the same thing as an *originalist* judicial philosophy. Originalism describes an approach toward ascertaining the meaning of the Constitution's text. Conservatism, in the judicial context, might mean or include some version of originalism, but it might not. It might mean favoring policy outcomes that conform to a "conservative" rather than "liberal" platform, such as being tough on violent crime. Or it might describe an attitude toward the institutional role of the court. for President Nixon and the judges that he ultimately appointed, was the principal problem with the Warren Court that it misinterpreted the Constitution or that it did "too much" and was "too active"? Those are not necessarily the same things; it is possible to misinterpret the Constitution by having the court do *too little* and letting legislatures and executives (and lower court judges) get away with objectively unconstitutional action. As it happened, most criticism of the Warren Court took the latter form of a complaint about "judicial activism" and a call for "judicial restraint."

The academy that sought to defend, consolidate, and expand the Warren Court's jurisprudence generally took the enemy to be "judicial restraint" rather than "originalism." To go back to the Westlaw database of law journals: the term "judicial restraint" prior to 1984 shows up more than 450 times, and while "originalism" and "originalist" had literally no presence in the scholarly debate before 1980, "judicial restraint" appeared nearly 300 times in that period. The much broader HeinOnline database shows more than 4,000 uses of "judicial restraint" before 1983 and more than 3,000 before 1980.

More significantly, the idea of judicial restraint, unlike the idea of originalism, was deeply theorized long before Ed Meese came on the scene. The most important work in the history of American constitutional law was an article published in 1893 that was also issued as a slim book: James Bradley Thayer's "The Origin and Scope of the American Doctrine of Constitutional Law."[72] Thayer proposed, as both a description of and prescription for judicial practice, that federal courts only overturn acts of Congress or the president "when those who have the right to make laws have not merely made a mistake, but have made a very clear one,—so clear that it is not open to rational question."[73] Thayer's rationale for this rule of clear mistake, as it is sometimes called, is that such a rule

> recognizes that, having regard to the great, complex, ever-unfolding exigencies of government, much which will seem unconstitutional to one man, or body of men, may reasonably not seem so to another; that the constitution often admits of different interpretations; that there is often a range of choice and judgment; that in such cases the constitution does not impose upon the legislature any one specific opinion, but leaves open this range of choice; and that whatever choice is rational is constitutional.[74]

Both of us are longtime critics of this hyper-deferential judicial approach, which we do not think is prescribed by the Constitution,[75] but we cannot deny that it has found implicit and explicit expression in court decisions that have often spoken of—or applied without directly speaking of—a "presumption of constitutionality."[76] Thayer was describing a real phenomenon, and he elevated it to a theorized principle in which the presumption was virtually as strong as the "beyond a reasonable doubt" presumption in favor of defendants in criminal trials. While Thayer's article is not frequently cited by the Supreme Court, its reasoning underlay much of the development of post-1937 constitutional law, in which the court generally showed great deference to Congress and administrative agencies, even in the construction of those entities' own powers. Justices Oliver Wendell Holmes and Felix Frankfurter were friends with and students of Professor Thayer at Harvard Law School, and their Supreme Court decisions were Thayerian as well. Justices Warren Burger, William Rehnquist, Byron White, and Antonin Scalia were also all deeply influenced by Thayerian ideas. When the Warren Court began more freely remaking institutions in the 1950s and 1960s, a natural "conservative" response was to invoke the seemingly settled Thayerian view of judicial deference or passivity; hence the emphasis on "judicial restraint." To be "conservative" in the Warren Court and early Burger Court era was not necessarily to be *originalist*.

Thus, a glance at the academy in the early 1980s reveals a robust debate about "judicial restraint" versus "judicial activism," but almost no serious debate about "originalism" and its interpretative alternatives. The debate about restraint and activism sounded in policy, not in attempts to ascertain the meaning of the Constitution.

The Constitution in the Courts Circa 1980

IN THE INTRODUCTION, we saw a bit of how Ed Meese viewed the work product of the Supreme Court in 1985 when he spoke to the American Bar Association. To what extent did the courts share the academy's attitude toward the Constitution and constitutional interpretation?

In one sense the courts differed sharply from the academy. Much of the academy openly called for, and celebrated, constitutional law divorced from the Constitution. Whatever their actual practices may have been, courts were seldom that open about abandoning the enterprise of interpretation. As Judge Bork said in 1971, "The Supreme Court regularly insists that its results, and most particularly its controversial results, do not spring from the mere will of the Justices in the majority but are supported, indeed compelled, by a proper understanding of the Constitution of the United States. Value choices are attributed to the Founding Fathers, not to the Court."[77] Modern scholars sometimes sound similar themes about judicial practice.[78] To some extent, that account of judicial practice has always been accurate. Even when the court obviously and blatantly implemented its own policy views in the name of the Constitution, as in *Dred Scott v. Sandford*,[79] it typically tried to couch its analysis in the language of constitutionalism.[80] Even the Warren Court produced a number of key decisions that seem strikingly originalist in orientation, containing extensive discussions of founding-era history.[81] In that sense, originalism and interpretivism have always been an important part of constitutional law, regardless of the academy's views.

On the other hand, Ed Meese was obviously right, from an originalist perspective, to take issue with a good portion of the Supreme Court's work product. Numerous decisions, throughout the court's history, have not only flown in the face of seemingly clear constitutional commands but have shown little or no interest in uncovering the original meaning of those commands.

One obvious example from the New Deal era is *Home Building & Loan Ass'n v. Blaisdell*.[82] The Constitution declares that "[n]o State shall…pass any…Law impairing the Obligation of Contracts."[83] The obvious meaning and purpose of this provision, known as the Contracts Clause, is to prevent states from enacting debtor-relief legislation—something that was very popular in a few states, such as Rhode Island, in the founding era. During the Great Depression, when deflation raised the value of money and hence the burdens on mortgage borrowers, Minnesota forbade mortgage lenders from foreclosing on mortgages when debtors defaulted. Although this law, rewriting mortgage contracts within the state, seemed squarely within the clear prohibition of the Contracts Clause, the Supreme Court upheld the law by a 5–4 vote, employing one of the court's most explicit expressions of living constitutionalism:

> [T]here has been a growing appreciation of public needs and of
> the necessity of finding ground for a rational compromise between
> individual rights and public welfare. … It is no answer to say that
> this public need was not apprehended a century ago, or to insist
> that what the provision of the Constitution meant to the vision of
> that day it must mean to the vision of our time. … With a growing
> recognition of public needs and the relation of individual right to
> public security, the court has sought to prevent the perversion of

the clause through its use as an instrument to throttle the capacity of the states to protect their fundamental interests.[84]

That was just the beginning. A catalogue of non-originalist decisions after the New Deal would fill a lengthy book. Perhaps the most notorious example was Roe v. Wade,[85] which invalidated the abortion laws of all fifty states without even identifying which provision of the Constitution supposedly dictated this result. Two decades after Roe, a majority of the court settled on the Fourteenth Amendment's Due Process of Law Clause as the source of this right,[86] but Roe offered nothing more specific than "the Fourteenth Amendment's concept of personal liberty and restrictions upon state action...or...the Ninth Amendment's reservation of rights to the people."[87]

Right after Roe was decided, Professor Ely, who agreed with Roe's result on policy grounds, described it as "bad constitutional law...because it is not constitutional law and gives almost no sense of an obligation to try to be."[88] Roe was overruled by the Supreme Court after half a century.[89] But while Roe for many people and for many years came to symbolize disrespect for the Constitution, it was only the tip of a huge iceberg.

In 1978, the court's cases involving government and religion departed so radically from any plausible interpretation of the Constitution that they inspired Philip Kurland to write an article entitled "The Irrelevance of the Constitution: The Religion Clauses of the First Amendment and the Supreme Court."[90] He added a companion piece with a similar title on the court's free speech cases,[91] and he made clear that "my allegation regarding the irrelevance of the Constitution is not limited to the interpretation of the so-called religion clauses of the first amendment. The cases decided under that rubric are but examples, and not the most egregious examples at that, of the Court's substitution of its judgment for those of the founding fathers."[92] Professor Kurland did not exaggerate. Especially with regard to the so-called Establishment Clause, which provides that "Congress shall make no law respecting an establishment of religion,"[93] the court has taken a provision obviously designed to prevent Congress either from declaring a particular sect to be the national religion or to interfere (either positively or negatively) with state efforts to establish religion within their own boundaries and transformed it into a vehicle for imposing the court's own vision of secularism on both the federal and state governments—to the point of crafting detailed judicial rules for public Christmas displays or voluntary school prayer activities. Those doctrines might or might not reflect wise legislative policy, but they have no colorable foundation in the Constitution's original meaning.

Some of the Supreme Court's caseload over the past half century has concerned the death penalty, and the key cases were decided in the 1970s, a decade before Ed Meese was about to enter the Department of Justice. The Constitution's original meaning played only a trivial role in those cases.

The death penalty sparks enormous controversy on policy grounds, but as a constitutional matter, if one takes seriously any variant of originalism, there is no intellectually plausible case for the categorical unconstitutionality of capital punishment. The first criminal statute enacted by the 1st Congress in 1790 prescribed the death penalty for half a dozen offenses,[94] including counterfeiting,[95] and even specified the mode of execution as hanging.[96] The opening words of the Fifth Amendment, ratified in 1791, require indictment by grand jury "for a capital, or otherwise infamous crime,"[97] which rather clearly assumes that there will be "capital" crimes. The amendment then provides that the federal government may not deprive a person of "life, liberty, or property, without due process of law"[98]—language which was repeated seventy-seven years later in the Fourteenth Amendment for state governments[99] and which rather clearly contemplates the occasional execution. The Eighth Amendment forbids "cruel and unusual punishments,"[100] which surely prevents use of the death penalty in some circumstances, such as to punish jaywalking (or counterfeiting?), but to "read" the Eighth Amendment to prohibit *all* capital punishment is beyond absurd.

Nonetheless, in 1972, drawing on language from a 1958 plurality opinion by Chief Justice Earl Warren in a non-capital case saying that the Eighth Amendment "must draw its meaning from the evolving standards of decency that mark the progress of a maturing society,"[101] a 5–4 majority in *Furman v. Georgia*,[102] in five separate opinions, invalidated all existing death penalty statutes. In the wake of that decision, thirty-five states—almost the three-quarters needed to ratify a constitutional amendment—enacted or re-enacted statutes prescribing a death penalty. Faced with that immediate response, the court four years later in *Gregg v. Georgia*,[103] a case briefed and argued by then solicitor general Robert H. Bork, backed down from the strong implications of *Furman* and allowed the death penalty in some situations, subject to court-specified procedures and limitations.[104] The reasoning of *Gregg*, however, was far from originalist.

As we noted, an originalist opinion rejecting a broad constitutional challenge to the death penalty could have been a few sentences long.[105] The court's plurality opinion did contain those few sentences pointing out the Constitution's obvious approval of the death penalty,[106] but those sentences were sandwiched between a lengthy discussion of why original meaning is not conclusive[107] and an even longer discussion of the policy consequences of the death penalty and the specific mechanics of the Georgia statute at issue.[108] The Constitution's actual meaning was something of an afterthought (or perhaps a middle thought) in this discussion. A three-justice concurring opinion added some flavor to the plurality opinion but made no additional reliance on original meaning,[109] nor did a lengthy dissent in a companion case that declared unconstitutional statutes that made the death penalty *mandatory* for certain crimes.[110] Justice White's dissenting opinion in that case discussed factors bearing on original meaning in less than one paragraph.[111]

Another body of constitutional thought facing Ed Meese circa 1980 threatened to create a constitutional right to welfare. From an originalist constitutional standpoint, this is an absurd idea, but in the 1960s and 1970s it gained a measure of traction on the Supreme Court, and it still has a vibrant life in law school scholarship and classrooms.

In the founding era, there was serious debate about whether Congress had *power* to hand out welfare even in the face of disasters like a fire that destroyed Savannah.[112] The notion that it was *obligated* to do so by the Constitution is laughable. Similarly, the Fourteenth Amendment might forbid states from invidiously *discriminating* in the administration of some welfare programs if they have them, but there is nothing that remotely requires them to have such programs in the first place.

Nonetheless, making the welfare state a constitutional requirement has been an academic project for some time. As a starting point, legal realists in the early 20th century worked hard to undermine the notion of private property as a natural right, insisting that property itself was a kind of welfare or gift from the government.[113] In 1980, Stanford law professor Thomas Grey famously summarized the academic consensus on the idea of "property" when he wrote: "It seems fair to conclude from a glance at the range of current usages that the specialists who design and manipulate the legal structures of the advanced capitalist economies could easily do without using the term 'property' at all."[114]

Yale Law School professor Charles Reich, by far the most influential person in the doctrinal development of constitutionalized welfare rights, openly announced in 1964 that "[p]roperty is not a natural right"[115] and that traditional property and welfare were conceptually indistinguishable; as he put it, "all property might be described as government largess."[116] Because, according to Professor Reich, "[i]t is necessary, then, that largess begin to do the work of property,"[117] the next logical step was to insist that largess—welfare—be treated as itself a protected constitutional right:

> Eventually those forms of largess which are closely linked to status must be deemed to be held as of right. … The presumption should be that the professional man will keep his license, and the welfare recipient his pension. These interests should be "vested." If revocation is necessary, not by reason of the fault of the individual holder, but by reason of overriding demands of public policy, perhaps payment of just compensation would be appropriate. …
>
> The concept of right is most urgently needed with respect to benefits like unemployment compensation, public assistance, and old age insurance. … Only by making such benefits into rights can the welfare state achieve its goal of providing a secure minimum basis for individual well-being and dignity in a society where each man cannot be wholly the master of his own destiny.[118]

It is impossible to overstate the importance of Professor Reich's 1964 article. A 2012 survey identified it as the 7th most cited law review article of all time.[119] A 2013 article in a major law review made explicit what was implicit in Reich's argument: the elimination of welfare programs might be an unconstitutional "taking" of property without just compensation, in violation of the Fifth Amendment's Takings Clause,[120] which says, "nor shall private property be taken for public use without just compensation."[121]

Parallel to Reich's argument was another set of arguments grounded in 20th-century academic political philosophy. Perhaps the most prestigious law review placement in the United States is the invitation to write the *Harvard Law Review*'s annual Supreme Court foreword. In 1969, the foreword was written by Harvard professor Frank Michelman, entitled "On Protecting the Poor through the Fourteenth Amendment,"[122] which argued for a constitutionalized government obligation to provide minimum benefits to everyone. Professor Michelman, who is one of the most distinguished legal theorists of the past several generations, elaborated on the idea in subsequent articles throughout the 1970s,[123] and in 1979 he could accurately report: "Some years ago I speculated that persons in our country might have not only moral but constitutional rights to provision for certain basic ingredients of individual welfare, such as food, shelter, health care, and education. That suggestion, which we might call the welfare-rights thesis, has found some strong support. ...."[124] The concept of constitutionalized welfare rights, in which welfare stands on the same constitutional footing as land, gold, and cars, is very much still on the academic agenda today.

The idea gained some traction in the courts between 1951 and 1970. For most of the country's history, government benefits, including even government jobs, were not considered "life, liberty, or property" for purposes of the Constitution's Due Process of Law clauses, much less "property" for purposes of the Takings Clause.[125] That started to change in the 1950s, as the court began protecting employees from anti-communist purges. The protection was procedural only; the court began requiring due process of law, meaning fair hearings, for anyone who, in the words of Justice Felix Frankfurter, would "suffer grievous loss of any kind,"[126] whether or not the thing lost (such as a government job) would have counted as a property interest protected by due process of law before 1951. frankfurter's broad formulation of what counts as constitutionally protected property quickly became settled law; by 1961, it clearly commanded a majority of the court.[127]

The court took a big step toward Professor Reich's world in 1969 in *Shapiro v. Thompson*,[128] which struck down one-year residency requirements for welfare in several states and the District of Columbia. The rationale was an odd combination of "equal protection of the laws" and the unenumerated "right to travel," and the case did not say (because the issue was not presented) that a state or the District of Columbia must have a welfare system at all. But treating welfare recipients as a constitutionally cognizable class was a potential building block for a larger holding. Even Chief Justice (and former state governor) Earl Warren—joined by Justice Black and, in a separate opinion, Justice Harlan—dissented.

In 1970, the court raised and then dashed the hopes of the welfare rights crowd in the span of about a month. In March 1970, in *Goldberg v. Kelly*,[129] it held (over yet another dissent from Justice Black) that states could not terminate welfare recipients from the rolls without first holding an administrative proceeding so robust that it closely resembled a trial. By 1970, it was obvious that the court's post-1951 cases required treating welfare benefits as a kind of "property" entitled to protection under due process of law (though not yet "property" for purposes of the Takings Clause). If the constitutional inquiry truly was whether the loss of something was "grievous," welfare was an obvious candidate. And, indeed, when the case was argued in the late 1960s, the state of New York did not even bother trying to argue that welfare could not count as constitutional "property," because that conclusion was too clear for argument under then governing law.[130] New York did not even dispute that it needed to provide a trial-type hearing to make sure that welfare terminations were justified. It was only arguing that it did not need to provide all of that procedural machinery *before* terminating benefits rather than afterward. The issue was not whether to give welfare rights robust protection. The issue was only when to do so.

Nonetheless, even though no one in the case was arguing about whether welfare benefits were constitutional "property," the court went out of its way to lay the groundwork for broader future holdings. It first announced that "[i]t may be realistic today to regard welfare entitlements as more like 'property' than a 'gratuity,'"[131] pointedly citing Professor Reich's article. It continued:

> From its founding the Nation's basic commitment has been to foster the dignity and well-being of all persons within its borders. We have come to recognize that forces not within the control of the poor contribute to their poverty. This perception, against the

background of our traditions, has significantly influenced the development of the contemporary public assistance system. Welfare, by meeting the basic demands of subsistence, can help bring within the reach of the poor the same opportunities that are available to others to participate meaningfully in the life of the community. At the same time, welfare guards against the societal malaise that may flow from a widespread sense of unjustified frustration and insecurity. Public assistance, then, is not mere charity, but a means to "promote the general Welfare, and secure the Blessings of Liberty to ourselves and our Posterity." The same governmental interests that counsel the provision of welfare, counsel as well its uninterrupted provision to those eligible to receive it; pre-termination evidentiary hearings are indispensable to that end.[132]

By tying welfare to the Constitution's preamble (as well as to another footnoted citation to Professor Reich), it was not a stretch to imagine the next step being a holding that welfare was a constitutional requirement.

A month after *Goldberg*, however, the court backed down from these broader implications by holding that Maryland did not violate the Constitution by placing a cap on how much welfare any family could receive.[133] The fact that such a case even got to the Supreme Court, that the court had to overturn a lower court ruling that Maryland indeed had violated the Constitution by limiting welfare payments,[134] and that two justices dissented on constitutional grounds[135] is a good sign of how little in those days the Constitution had to do with constitutional law.[136]

We could easily fill chapters on Supreme Court decisions or doctrines that flagrantly fly in the face of any plausible conception of original meaning. Those departures are so pervasive that they have spawned an entire theory of constitutionalism grounded in the seeming irrelevance of the Constitution to judicial decision-making.[137] And the departures were by no means confined to "hot-button" issues with obvious political and ideological valence. Indeed, perhaps the best illustrations of the vanishing role of the Constitution in the courts circa 1980 come from mundane rather than notorious cases.

A classic illustration is *Ohio v. Roberts*,[138] a relatively obscure case decided in 1980, just as Ed Meese was about to enter federal service. The case does not involve any hot-button issues but only some technical (though, as it happens, spectacularly consequential) matters regarding the admissibility in criminal trials of certain evidence. The case was overruled in 2004 in perhaps the most consistently originalist decision in modern times,[139] which itself is part of Ed Meese's legacy. Back in 1980, however, the decision was joined by all of the so-called "conservative" justices on the court at that time. It beautifully exemplifies how far the courts that Ed Meese was about to face as attorney general had strayed from anything resembling attention, much less fidelity, to the Constitution.

The story begins in 1791 with ratification of the Bill of Rights. Much of the Bill of Rights deals with technical questions of criminal procedure. The Sixth Amendment alone contains more than half a dozen prescriptions about the conduct of federal criminal trials,[140] all of which today are deemed to apply to state trials as well by virtue of the Fourteenth Amendment. One of those prescriptions, which today we call the Confrontation Clause, guarantees a criminal defendant (but not a civil defendant) the right "to be confronted with the witnesses against him." Much of the time, that constitutional right is protected by non-constitutional evidence law, which excludes from trials a lot of "hearsay," meaning statements that are related secondhand ("I heard John say that Joan robbed the bank," "Heard it from a friend who heard it from a friend who heard it from another you've been messin' around") or through documents rather than firsthand by live witnesses describing their own experiences under oath and subject to cross-examination. But non-constitutional evidence law has a *lot* of exceptions to this general rule against hearsay, some of which vary from state to state, so sometimes criminal defendants can be convicted by evidence that does not come from the observations of live witnesses testifying in their trials. The issue then becomes whether use of that non-live evidence violates the Sixth Amendment right to confront witnesses.

If one looks at the Constitution, there are two sets of questions that obviously call out for answers: who counts as "witnesses" against a defendant and what does it mean to "confront" those witnesses? The questions are obvious from the text of the Sixth Amendment, but the answers are far from obvious. "Witnesses" might include only people who actually show up in court, meaning the Confrontation Clause says nothing at all about the use against a criminal defendant of hearsay statements by non-testifying persons. The term might instead refer to anyone whose statements constitute any kind of evidence, in which case the clause would address *all* uses of out-of-court statements against defendants in criminal trials. Or the term might include only a subset of persons whose statements are used by the prosecution—perhaps only those persons who make their statements with the *expectation* that they will eventually be used in court, as opposed to people who make statements in casual conversations. Similarly, in order to "confront" a witness (once one has figured out that someone really is a "witness" within the meaning of the Constitution), must that witness actually be in court? Is it good enough that one had a chance to "confront" them in an earlier proceeding? If so, what kind of earlier proceedings count? Does it matter whether the "witnesses" whose out-of-court statements are introduced are still available to be brought into court rather than dead or off the grid?

If the object of constitutional adjudication is to ascertain and then apply the meaning of the Constitution, these are precisely the difficult questions that one would need to address. An originalist approach would try to determine what those terms—"witnesses" and "confront"—meant in 1791 (or perhaps in 1868 if one thinks that the Sixth Amendment was "incorporated" against the states by the Fourteenth Amendment[141]).

In 1980, the Supreme Court asked none of these questions. Instead of trying to ascertain the meaning of the Constitution, the court tried to identify and balance "competing interests,"[142] including the government's "strong interest in effective law enforcement, and ... precise formulation of the rules of evidence applicable in criminal proceedings"[143] and, on the defendant's side, "the integrity of the fact-finding process"[144] and the Sixth Amendment's "preference for face-to-face confrontation at trial."[145] As the *Roberts* decision put it, "This Court, in a series of cases, has sought to accommodate these competing interests. True to the common-law tradition, the process has been gradual, building on past decisions, drawing on new experience, and responding to changing conditions."[146] Notably absent from this litany of relevant considerations is the original meaning of the Constitution.

The court's resolution of this conflict of interests is almost anticlimactic.

It held—correctly, as it happens—that out-of-court statements can only be used against defendants when the speaker is unavailable to testify in person.[147] That conclusion is well supported by the history and context of the confrontation right and is repeated in Justice Scalia's originalist decision for the court in 2004.[148] Less plausibly, the court then allowed use of an out-of-court statement by an unavailable person "if it bears adequate 'indicia of reliability.' Reliability can be inferred without more in a case where the evidence falls within a firmly rooted hearsay exception. In other cases, the evidence must be excluded, at least absent a showing of particularized guarantees of trustworthiness."[149]

What is wrong with using only reliable evidence? As a matter of policy, there is nothing wrong with it. As a matter of constitutional meaning, the Sixth Amendment does not prescribe "reliability" in general. Instead, it chooses a *specific means for measuring and obtaining reliability*—namely, confrontation of witnesses in court. As Justice Scalia wrote for the court in 2004 when it overruled *Roberts*, "Admitting statements deemed reliable by a judge is fundamentally at odds with the right of confrontation. To be sure, the [Confrontation] Clause's ultimate goal is to ensure reliability of evidence, but it is a procedural rather than a substantive guarantee. It commands, not that evidence be reliable, but that reliability be assessed in a particular manner: by testing in the crucible of cross-examination. The Clause thus reflects a judgment, not only about the desirability of reliable evidence (a point on which there could be little dissent), but about how reliability can best be determined."[150] Even farther removed from the Constitution, the court in *Roberts* chose as a proxy for reliability "firmly rooted hearsay exception[s]." "In other words: If evidence was admitted by virtue of a hearsay exception that the justices on the Court circa 1980 would have learned about in law school half a century earlier, it automatically counts as 'reliable' and its admission therefore does not violate the Confrontation Clause. If it is admitted pursuant to some newfangled hearsay exception…, then the Court will decide case by case whether the evidence is sufficiently reliable to be admitted over a Confrontation Clause exception."[151]

The *Roberts* opinion was written by Nixon appointee Justice Blackmun and joined by Justices Rehnquist and Powell and Chief Justice Burger, all of the court's so-called "conservatives." The only dissenting voices objected, with some force, only to the court's decidedly hasty conclusion that the relevant witness in the *Roberts* case had been shown to be unavailable to testify in court. No one objected in 1980 to the court's account of the Sixth Amendment—which was not really an account of the Sixth Amendment at all but rather an account of the court's view of wise policy.

To paraphrase Professor Ely's description of *Roe*: the problem with *Roberts* was not so much that it was bad constitutional law as that it was not really constitutional law at all.

Roberts, however, was typical of the court's approach to constitutional cases in the decades leading up to Ed Meese's tenure in the federal government. Constitutional cases were not really occasions for ascertaining the meaning of the Constitution. Rather, they were occasions for judicial policymaking. Sometimes those judicial policies had a "conservative" valence, as in some criminal cases in the Burger Court era. (*Roberts*, for example, can be seen as "conservative" because it leaves fewer occasions than would an honest application of the Sixth Amendment for guilty criminals to walk on evidentiary technicalities.) More often those judicial policies had a "liberal" valence. But almost never were the courts actually interpreting the Constitution.

That was the legal world facing Attorney General Ed Meese when he took office on February 25, 1985.

CHAPTER SIX
ATTORNEY GENERAL OF
THE UNITED STATES

E D MEESE BECAME the 75th attorney general of the United States on February 25, 1985, serving until August 12, 1988. Perhaps the most intellectually consequential and powerful of any of the now eighty-four people who have served as attorney general of the United States, Meese put the full weight of Ronald Reagan's transformative eight-year presidency behind the principle that laws and the Constitution had to be interpreted in accordance with the original public meaning of their texts. In his July 9, 1985, speech to the American Bar Association, he declared that this doctrine, soon to become known as "originalism," would be the official policy of the Reagan-Meese Justice Department.

Before then, originalism had been largely unknown to the bench, bar, and academy. Ed Meese popularized and institutionalized it, most effectively by persuading Reagan to nominate originalists Antonin Scalia and Robert H. Bork to the Supreme Court. Though defeated in his nomination to the court, Bork remained a popular and outspoken exponent of originalist jurisprudence from his perch in academe and in think tanks. Perhaps just as significantly, Ed Meese helped make possible the academic careers of several generations of originalist law professors. His Department of Justice served as the incubator and bully pulpit for ideas that at that point in time had little voice in the legal academy.

It is vital that we note at the outset that the history of the Meese Justice Department that follows addresses almost exclusively the civil law and constitutional law side of the Justice Department, not the criminal law side of the department, which Ed Meese essentially ran himself. To describe Ed Meese's running of the criminal law side of the Justice Department, and his accomplishments in doing that, would require writing a second book, which we would not be competent to write. Suffice it to say that Ed Meese's running of the criminal law side of the department was at least as transformative as was his running of the civil side of the department.

Ed Meese gave more than thirty important speeches as attorney general that criticized the U.S. Supreme Court and its precedents as no other attorney general had done before. He advanced originalism as a positive alternative to the seat-of-the pants common-law and policy approach to constitutional law of earlier decades. As a result, originalism became a key part of Republican Party legal orthodoxy. Today, six out of the nine Supreme Court justices and roughly half of the federal lower court judges are originalists to one degree or another. There are perhaps a hundred originalist law professors today compared to fewer than half a dozen forty years ago.

Finally, Ed Meese and Ronald Reagan made a concerted effort to constitutionalize their charisma in the Federalist Society, which Meese empowered and legitimated as a permanent institutional proponent of originalism. The Federalist Society has over seventy thousand members today, chapters in all two hundred American law schools, and lawyer's chapters in almost every major American city. Yale Sterling Professor of Law Bruce Ackerman has written an important book called *Revolutionary Constitutions: Charismatic Leadership and the Rule of Law* (2019), which explores how certain leaders use their charisma to help other institutions rather than enhance their own power. Just as Mahatma Gandhi constitutionalized his legitimacy in the Indian Congress Party (which has now out lived him for seventy-six years), so too did President Reagan and Attorney General Meese constitutionalize their charisma in the Federalist Society, which aspires to be a permanent player in the American legal world.

The Meese Department of Justice in Action

ED MEESE'S MISSION reflected that of President Ronald Reagan. Ronald Reagan's two ironclad commands to Meese when he began service as attorney general were to help appoint justices, judges, and lawyers who would restore reverence for and obedience to the words of the Constitution, as it was originally understood, and to have the Justice Department operate according to the rule of law and to apply the law fairly without favor or prejudice toward anyone. Reagan particularly insisted that the law be administered by the department non-politically. For that reason, there was a strict rule that no one in the White House was to contact the Justice Department or any person in the Justice Department on any case.

Ed Meese more than lived up to these two directives from President Reagan. He helped President Reagan appoint spectacular federal judges, and his Justice Department's operational divisions, including but not limited to the Criminal Division, the Civil Division, the Civil Rights Division, the Lands Division, the Antitrust Division, and the Tax Division, all took their leads with respect to an originalist understanding of the law from Ed Meese. Meese pursued at least six major initiatives in his three and a half years as attorney general, which we discuss in more detail in subsequent chapters. In the order of importance in which he (not necessarily we) viewed them:

First, as will be explored in chapter 11, he transformed criminal justice policy by cracking down hard on recidivists, drugs, and the distribution of obscene material, as well as supervising the implementation of the Sentencing Commission's Sentencing Guidelines and asset forfeiture laws. With his good friend Lois Herrington, the assistant attorney general for the Office of Justice Programs from 1983 to 1986, he also took unprecedented steps to aid the victims of crime.

Second, described in detail in chapter 9, he helped President Reagan transform the federal judiciary by appointing brilliant originalist lawyers, jurists, and legal academics to fill half of all federal judgeships. The Department of Justice was the key actor in judicial selection during Ed Meese's tenure as attorney general.

Third, as seen in the next chapter, Ed Meese as attorney general gave more than thirty profound, provocative, and, at the time, highly controversial speeches, which helped turn originalism from a fringe academic viewpoint into the guiding theory of constitutional interpretation used in 2024 by a majority of Supreme Court justices and by half of the lower court federal judiciary. We are unaware of any instance in American history in which the speeches of a non-presidential executive figure had this kind of impact.

Fourth, as detailed in chapter 8, Ed Meese created an incubator for originalist ideas by holding major academic conferences at the Justice

Department, with esteemed legal academics, on such topics as federalism, the separation of powers, and economic liberties. This "academy in exile" not only helped develop and theorize originalism in a way that the mainstream legal academy would never countenance, it was the training ground for a generation of academics-to-be who acquired the credentials, skills, and knowledge to break through academic walls and bring originalist ideas into faculty lounges, classrooms, and law journals.

Fifth, elaborated in chapter 11, Ed Meese hired a brilliant assistant attorney general for the Office of Legal Counsel (OLC), Charles J. Cooper, who put originalism into real-world practice by issuing a stunning series of originalist OLC opinions from 1985 to 1988, proving that originalism was a workable legal theory even before Justices Scalia and Thomas started doing it on the Supreme Court. The OLC speaks with the voice of the attorney general on legal matters within the executive branch,[1] so these unprecedented OLC opinions reflected the official legal positions of the Reagan administration.

Sixth, as told in chapter 10, Meese and his likable and intellectual solicitor general, Charles Fried, worked together to craft a series of briefs that led to some stunning victories at a Supreme Court that was quite far from being originalist in 1985–1988. There were significant defeats as well, as we shall see, but even those losses sometimes set the stage for later moves in originalist directions.

These initiatives were all driven by Ed Meese's commitment to certain core principles. The first was that recidivists commit most new crimes and so therefore they needed to be locked up far longer in prison than was typical at the time. The second was that a full-fledged war had to be waged against drug abuse, and that the assets of those involved in drug crimes, and in other crimes, should be forfeited to the government. The third was a staunch belief that the Constitution and laws should be construed according to the original public meaning of their texts. The fourth was an unwavering commitment to a legal principle of color-blindness and opposition on legal grounds to all forms of affirmative action, which is to say institutionalized favoritisms, as contrary to both constitutional and statutory law. The fifth was the attorney general's staunch belief that criminal trials ought to be a search for truth, taking into account all available evidence, and that the exclusionary rule, which forbids prosecutors from using relevant evidence, ought to be overturned by the Supreme Court. The sixth was a staunch commitment to both federalism and the separation of powers. And the seventh was a belief that the courts should protect economic liberties more robustly by restoring the original meanings of the clauses in the Constitution that forbid the taking of property without just compensation or the impairment of contractual obligations by state governments. With respect to the latter principle, throughout the 20th century, those clauses had been construed by courts so narrowly as to be nearly meaningless in a large range of cases—in contrast to the wildly expansive interpretations of clauses (or in some cases emanations from penumbras of clauses) to yield results more in accord with the political and cultural values of the academic left. Ed Meese simply did not accept the New Deal Supreme Court's decision in *United States v. Carolene Products*,[2] whose famous fourth footnote[3] said that laws restricting economic liberties should get only rational basis scrutiny while those affecting so-called personal privacy rights got strict scrutiny.

Moreover, Ed Meese did all of these things while playing a major role in President Reagan's domestic policy, foreign policy, and national defense policy. He also fended off special prosecutors and the Iran-Contra scandal, as is detailed in chapter 12.

The bottom line is that Attorney General Ed Meese was an exceptionally busy man. His typical workday began with his ride to the office at 6:30 in the morning reading the President's Daily Briefing, then a 7:00 a.m. meeting with the FBI director, often relating to issues of drug abuse and drug trafficking or the crisis of the week. On Tuesdays he would attend a morning fellowship meeting, and then at or shortly after 8:00 a.m. he would meet with his leadership group "for some of the critical things that we had to decide among ourselves or for them to discuss with me confidentially": his counsellor, Ken Cribb, later Brad Reynolds after Ken left to go to the White House; the deputy attorney general, who was initially Lowell Jensen; and his chief of staff, John Richardson, who was later replaced by Mark Levin.

From 8:30 a.m. to 9:00 a.m. would be the morning executive staff meeting. "This was attended by several of the heads of different components, like the director of the FBI, the head of the Civil Division, some of the other division heads. There might be about fifteen people there. We'd go through all the issues of the day and make decisions, or make assignments. All of the assistant attorneys general, as well as Solicitor General Charles Fried, attended this key decision-making meeting. That'd be done by 9:00 a.m., and then we would start the day," which "depending on what was hot that day," might mean going to the White House for meetings with the cabinet or other kinds of events.

Afternoons, the attorney general might address disputes within the department—say, if the solicitor general held a different view of the law from that of a functional division such as the tax, civil, or criminal divisions—or travel to other cabinet departments like the Pentagon. If he had any time to spare, he might meet with individuals inside or outside the DOJ, often until 8:00 p.m., or catch up with the paperwork that's "necessarily a part of the job."

Counting it all up Ed Meese typically worked a sixteen-hour day when not traveling on government business. Despite this schedule, Mr. Meese called the attorney general position "the job of a lifetime. I regard it as the happiest job I've ever held at any point in my life, and the greatest privilege."

Those who worked in the department under Mr. Meese enjoyed it too. Steve Calabresi has told Ed Meese that he ran the most interesting law school faculty Steve had ever been privileged to be a part of. It was far more intellectually lively than the Northwestern Pritzker School of Law, Harvard Law School, the Brown University Political Science Department, and Yale Law School, where he had taught. Meese not only ran the DOJ and got its work done, he fostered an intellectual exchange of ideas and discussion and a depth of discussion and debate that is frankly absent from most top law schools today.

THE MEESE JUSTICE DEPARTMENT'S "FACULTY"

EVEN WITH HIS sixteen-hour days, Meese couldn't run a federal department or engineer a legal revolution single-handedly. Just as Ronald Reagan needed Reaganites, Ed Meese needed Meesians. Ed Meese assembled a cast of characters to help him run the DOJ that we immodestly, somewhat self-interestedly, but honestly believe is unrivaled in

American legal history for erudition, energy, and commitment to the rule of the law. No story of the Meese Department of Justice is complete or even mildly informative without discussing the extraordinary legal minds that helped spark and implement the Meese Revolution.

Ken Cribb: The Indispensable Man

KEN CRIBB deserves his own section—arguably his own chapter—as having played *the* critical role in making the Meese Justice Department an intellectual hotbed. Cribb was indispensable in the appointing of excellent originalist judges to the Supreme Court, the federal circuit courts of appeals, and to the federal district courts. Brilliant and politically savvy, Ken Cribb was like the dean of a conservative-libertarian law school that made up the civil side of the Meese DOJ. He is probably the most important person to serve in the Reagan administration that most people have never heard of.[4]

When he was nominated to be attorney general, Ed Meese asked Ken to head the transition. That work had to proceed quietly, since it was customary that a presidential nominee take no overt steps regarding the proposed position until confirmation by the Senate. Ken quietly interviewed the key DOJ officials and took advice from outside experts and scholars. Briefing books were prepared regarding all important aspects of the job. When the nomination was assured, a delighted Ed Feulner, president of the Heritage Foundation, asked what help was needed. Ken asked that Heritage host a retreat so that all of the officials, experts, and scholars who had been consulted could brainstorm their final recommendations. They gathered at a country inn in West Virginia and prepared their ideas for the attorney general designate. Ed Meese used these recommendations to supplement his own well-shaped plans for the Department of Justice. The result was that the new AG hit the ground running.

Ken helped Ed Meese hire everyone on the civil side of the Department of Justice. Ed Meese did not need any help hiring good intellectual policymakers on the criminal side of the department because of his extensive, career-long involvement in criminal law enforcement. Ed Meese and Ken Cribb understood that personnel is policy, and Cribb was the key to creating the Meese Justice Department's intellectual environment.

It is Ken who more than anyone else helped to make Ed Meese the most intellectually influential attorney general in the nation's history.

T. Kenneth Cribb was born on August 7, 1948, in Spartanburg, South Carolina. A loyal son of the educated and intellectual South, he was the quintessential example of "a Southern Gentleman," a remarkable breed of person that has unfortunately died out. Like Ed Meese, Ken was wise, brave, just, temperate (most of the time), and full of love for his fellow human beings. He was and is an utterly delightful human being.

Ken graduated from Washington and Lee in 1970, and from 1971 to 1977 he served as the national director of the Intercollegiate Schools Institute (ISI), which promotes conservative intellectual thought and debate on college campuses. It lists as its core beliefs: 1) limited government; 2) individual liberty; 3) personal responsibility; 4) the rule of law; 5) the free-market economy; and 6) traditional values.[5]

From 1977 to 1980, Ken attended the University of Virginia School of Law, one of the very best law schools in the country, then signed on as deputy to the chief counsel of the Reagan campaign, Loren A. Smith, where he caught Ed Meese's attention. Ken served as Ed Meese's principal deputy during President Ronald Reagan's first term while Ed Meese was serving as counsellor to President Reagan. Ken was as indispensable to Ed Meese as Ed Meese was to President Reagan. He played a vital role in all the good work that was done in President Reagan's first term as president, assisted by John Richardson, a key aide who was brought over to the Justice Department when Ken followed Mr. Meese to the DOJ in 1985.

At the Justice Department, Ken continued to play the role of Ed Meese's right-hand man and de facto chief of staff under the title of counsellor to the Attorney General, managing the flow of paper and people into and out of Mr. Meese's office, and always pushing things in a more conservative direction whenever possible. Ken was also smart and funny, the social glue that held the Justice Department together. He loved to party and drink in moderation after hours, and he always attended a White Tie Optional Viennese Waltz Ball around Valentine's Day; when his Southern belle of a mother (Dicksie Cribb) was visiting, she added to the fun. Ken's associates from those days particularly remember that he co-hosted the annual white tie affair replete with full orchestra for an evening of Viennese waltzing. On occasions such as this, he would often have on his arm the world-famous Clare Boothe Luce. Ken was a confirmed bachelor, and he was thirty-eight and thirty-nine years old when Steve Calabresi worked for him at the ages of twenty-eight and twenty-nine as a special assistant to Ed Meese.

More than anyone else other than Ed Meese, it was Ken who turned the Department of Justice into functionally a law school between June 1985 and February 1987, when Steve Calabresi worked there. Ken was exceptionally well read and a true intellectual. He hired as many fellow intellectuals as he could manage and was always pushing, with great success, for the hiring of younger intellectual conservatives over more moderate forty-year-olds with long resumes. Ken's love of ideas and debate animated everything he did.

Meese told us that Ken was "just an outstanding friend, a marvelously loyal person. He did a great job. He had the facility of bringing people together and working out problems—personality problems, political problems, almost any kind of problem, with his sense of humor and his great personality. He promoted the kind of team effort I hope was the hallmark of my staff." When Ken left DOJ to work for Howard Baker in the White House, Ed Meese told him that it was like losing his right arm, and that the only man he'd cut off his right arm for was Ronald Reagan. Here is why Ken Cribb was Meese's indispensable man.

It begins with staffing. Ken Cribb firmly believed that hiring "excellent personnel leads to excellent policy." He had an Aristotelian passion for intellectual and lawyerly excellence, and no patience for political hacks out for themselves rather than the Reagan and Meese revolutions. It was he who staffed the civil, constitutional law side of the Department of Justice and deserves credit, along with Ed Meese, for all which that side of the Meese Justice Department accomplished.

Ken's first hire was to cause the nomination of William Bradford ("Brad") Reynolds, a former assistant to the solicitor general under Robert H. Bork in the Nixon administration, to be the associate attorney general, who was the head of the civil, constitutional law side of the Justice Department. Meese and Cribb had worked with Reynolds for years in opposition to affirmative action. Ed Meese and Ken Cribb knew Brad was smart, deep, and a fellow revolutionary. That, coupled with four years of experience as an assistant attorney general under William French Smith, made Brad a natural pick to be associate attorney general.

Unfortunately, the Senate refused to confirm Brad Reynolds due to opposition from so-called civil rights groups who opposed his stance on affirmative action. Ed Meese and Ken Cribb were furious over this but made him de facto associate attorney general regardless of his formal title, the role Brad played throughout Mr. Meese's term as attorney general.

The next appointment decision was harder—assistant attorney general for the Office of Legal Counsel (OLC), the prestigious post once held by Supreme Court justices William H. Rehnquist and Antonin Scalia. It is the job of the Office of Legal Counsel to serve as the president's and the attorney general's lawyer. It is imperative to have someone exceptional in that job. Ken Cribb also wanted a movement conservative at OLC because that office had, during Attorney General William French Smith's time in office, been filled by the outstanding but more conventional Washington super-lawyer Ted Olson.

Ken wanted to appoint a brilliant, rock-solid conservative: the thirty-three-year-old Chuck Cooper, a former William Rehnquist law clerk. During President Reagan's first term, Chuck had been the deputy assistant attorney general to William Bradford Reynolds in the Civil Rights Division. Brad loved Chuck and favored appointing him to be head of OLC, but Mr. Meese understandably paused in hesitation over the fact that this was a really major appointment, and Chuck Cooper was only thirty-three years old.

Meese told Ken to find assistant attorneys general who were at least forty years old and had some gray hair. Ken pointed out that he was only thirty-seven years old and had no gray hair, to which Ed Meese replied, "Ken, you're bald. You have no hair at all!" (This was true: Ken Cribb has been bald for as long as either of us has known him.) Ken responded that Republicans forty years old or older were all establishment, country-club Republicans who did not come out of the conservative movement. It was vital, he said, to have a brilliant, energetic, movement conservative as OLC head. Meese thought the matter over. He then persuaded President Reagan to appoint Chuck Cooper to run OLC. The appointment was a spectacular success. Chuck emerged as an intellectual heavyweight unafraid to take on Solicitor General Charles

Fried and who critically, along with Ed Meese, saved Ronald Reagan's presidency and made possible the 1988 election of President George Herbert Walker Bush by dealing with the Iran-Contra scandal effectively. We will say more about all of these things later.

Next Ken persuaded Ed Meese to hire Steve Markman, a thirty-two-year-old former staffer to Senator Orrin Hatch, Ed Meese's closest ally in the Senate, to be the assistant attorney general for the Office of Legal Policy (OLP). The OLP is a little-known unit within the Department of Justice responsible for assisting the attorney general in recommending candidates for federal judgeships.[6] Mr. Meese complained again about the absence of gray hair but ultimately agreed to the appointment because of Ken's urging and Senator Hatch's advocacy. Markman and his staff went on to produce thirty scholarly working papers that were the equivalents of *Harvard Law Review* articles on various topics, and to hold three major conferences with distinguished legal academics and judges. Markman contributed mightily to the intellectual vibrancy of the Meese Justice Department and in the identification and screening of judicial candidates.

Another great hire supported by Ken Cribb was the appointment in 1985, at the start of Ed Meese's tenure, of Harvard Law School professor Douglas H. Ginsburg to be assistant attorney general for the Antitrust Division. Ginsburg was thirty-nine, and he so impressed Ed Meese, Ken Cribb, and Brad Reynolds that after little more than a year in the Department of Justice he was appointed to a prestigious judgeship on the United States Court of Appeals for the District of Columbia Circuit, where he continues to serve with great distinction as a senior judge while also teaching at the Antonin Scalia Law School at George Mason University. In 1987, after the Senate rejected Robert Bork's nomination to the Supreme Court, President Reagan nominated Ginsburg in Bork's place. A UPI story at the time characterized the nomination as "an apparent triumph for Meese, who urged Reagan to choose someone who, like Bork, believes in the judicial philosophy of 'original intent.'"[7] Indeed, Doug Ginsburg would have been a historically great Supreme Court justice, but he pulled his nomination after only a week because of pearl-clutching among establishment Republican senators about some prior marijuana use in the 1960s and 1970s. Ed Meese said of Ginsburg at the time that "his action taken during his younger days was a mistake. It certainly does not affect his qualifications to sit on the Supreme Court and he should be confirmed expeditiously."[8] But in the wake of doubts about confirmability, Ginsburg withdrew from consideration on November 7, 1987, paving the way for Anthony Kennedy's appointment to the Supreme Court.

Following his move to the court of appeals, Ginsburg was replaced at the Antitrust Division by another strong Reaganite intellectual, Charles Rule. It goes without saying that having Harvard Law School professor Doug Ginsburg running the Antitrust Division during most of Steve Calabresi's tenure at the Justice Department contributed to making the Meese Justice Department feel like a superb law school.

John Bolton was yet another stellar hire, entirely the work of Ken Cribb. Bolton, thirty-seven, was appointed assistant attorney general for the Office of Legislative Affairs (OLS), which, according to its handbook, has "responsibility for the development and implementation of strategies to advance the Department's legislative initiatives and other interests relating to Congress.... [and] also articulates the Department's position on legislation proposed by Congress."[9] Bolton is a brilliant, acerbic, movement conservative and originalist, but he is and was a substance guy, not a get-along-better-with-Congress guy, which was what OLA was supposed to do. In 1988, Bolton was appointed to be the head of the Civil Division, replacing Richard Willard, which was a job for which he was much more temperamentally suited. Bolton went on to a legendary career in the second Bush administration, where he served at one time or another as undersecretary of state for Arms Control and International Security Affairs, the 25th U.S. ambassador to the United Nations, and the 27th U.S. national security advisor. Bolton later served as national security advisor to President Donald Trump. (When that did not work out, President Trump was quoted as saying that if he had followed John Bolton's advice, the United States would be in four wars right now.[10])

Ken Cribb knew in recommending John Bolton for OLA that Bolton was hard to get along with and thus a poor fit for OLA but got him hired anyway because Bolton would be another loud voice at the 8:30 a.m. decision-making staff meetings of the assistant attorneys general for a bold Reaganite agenda—which indeed he was.

Ken Cribb wisely recommended that Meese retain two of William French Smith's best assistant attorneys general: thirty-seven-year-old Richard K. Willard, who was the head of the Civil Division, and F. Henry Habicht II, who was only thirty-two and the head of what is now called the Environment and Natural Resources Division (then known as the Lands and Natural Resources Division). Both were brilliant lawyers. Richard Willard was a movement conservative who used his perch at the Civil Division in three effective ways. First, he promoted an agenda of federal tort reform which often clashed with the more "states' rights" positions of people like Chuck Cooper in OLC. Second, Willard (with Steve Calabresi's support) generally prevailed, as the Reagan administration implemented what to many was a surprisingly broad view of federal preemption of state authority,[11] notwithstanding complaints about such policies in Chuck Cooper's report on federalism for the Domestic Policy Council and some strong statements in President Reagan's executive order on federalism urging a limited view of federal preemption. Calabresi believed in dual federalism: the idea that either Congress or the fifty states have power over an issue but that there are no concurrent powers held by both the federal and the state governments other than the powers of taxation. The idea that there were such concurrent powers was a legacy of the New Deal, which called its approach "marble-cake-federalism." This meant that if one level of government decided not to take away your liberty or property, the other level of government still could. Third, Willard often sparred with Solicitor General Charles Fried over civil cases in the federal court pipeline on their way to the Supreme Court, which helped to sharpen the issues for them both.

In keeping with the Cribb-inspired theme of hiring, Richard was a true intellectual who contributed significantly to making the Meese Justice Department feel like a great law school. Richard Willard's deputy assistant attorneys general, Lee Liberman Otis and Brent Hatch, were also highly intelligent, energetic key players in much of what the Meese Justice Department did.

Hank Habicht, for his part, was a strong and articulate voice for more significant protection for economic liberties, which was an important theme running through Ed Meese's tenure as attorney general.

Steve A. Matthews, a brilliant movement conservative who had graduated from law school in 1980, served as the deputy to Assistant Attorney General Stephen J. Markman. He had exclusive authority from Ed Meese to run judicial selection of originalists for lower federal court judgeships for the Meese Justice Department, despite not being forty with gray hair. A former roommate of Ken Cribb's, the two were close allies. Steve is an extremely able and intelligent lawyer, and so another Ken Cribb triumph. Steve is also a rock-ribbed conservative intellectual.

Ken Cribb also wisely recommended keeping Terry Eastland on as director of the Office of Public Affairs, which is the Justice Department's chief speechwriting unit, and that Eastland hire movement conservatives Gary McDowell and Blair Dorminey, a law school classmate of Steve Calabresi and Gary Lawson. This turned out to be an excellent move. The three of them drafted fine speeches for Attorney General Meese, some of which we discuss in the next chapter, and those speeches often drew front-page news coverage and helped spawn contemporary debates about originalism.

Finally, Ken Cribb hired Attorney General Meese's outstanding personal staff, which he supervised as counsellor to the attorney general. John Richardson had worked with Meese and Cribb at the White House in the first Reagan term, then succeeded Ken Cribb as chief of staff for Ed Meese after Ken Cribb went back to work at the White House in February 1987. Richardson was followed by Mark Levin, who has had a phenomenal post-government career as a best-selling author and the host of one of the most popular call-in radio shows in the country as well as a television show on Fox News. Steve Calabresi and John Harrison, along with Ken Cribb, covered constitutional law matters and judicial interviews for Ed Meese. Another invaluable Meese special assistant was David M. McIntosh, who went on to become the director of Ronald Reagan's Domestic Policy Council from December 2, 1987, to September 8, 1988, a congressman from Indiana for six years, and is now the president of the Club for Growth.

The key players on the civil side of the Justice Department all got along well, but they sometimes jockeyed for power, as one would expect in any cabinet-level department. But many deep friendships were formed at Justice between June 1985 and February 1987. The Meese Justice Department gathered some of the best and the brightest libertarian and conservative legal minds in the country, and as such it was unlike any other Justice Department in American history.

This was only the civil side of the department. The criminal law side was headed up during Steve Calabresi's tenure by the extraordinarily able Deputy Attorney General D. Lowell Jensen from 1985 to 1986 and later by Assistant Attorney General Stephen Trott, now a judge on the U.S. Court of Appeals for the Ninth Circuit.

Thus, thanks in large measure to both Ed Meese and Ken Cribb, the Meese DOJ was staffed with intellectually oriented people who were Reagan conservatives or libertarians. As Ed Meese said, "One of the things we did was assemble an outstanding group of lawyers, who not only understood the law, and were able practitioners of the law, but also had a sense of the Constitution. [My staff] understood our objective of reviving constitutionalism, and [they] effectively implement[ed] the philosophy that Ronald Reagan [laid out in his speeches]."

"We were looking for people who'd be both good lawyers in the administration and to credential young people for future offices in the executive branch and in the judiciary," Meese added. Among those so credentialed were future associate justice Samuel Alito and many future law professors amounting to a "who's who" of scholars: Steve Calabresi (Northwestern Pritzker), John Harrison (University of Virginia), Gary Lawson (University of Florida), John McGinnis (Northwestern Pritzker), Michael Stokes Paulsen (St. Thomas), and Mike Rappaport (University of San Diego). Other Reagan administration alumni who were credentialed in the Reagan era but not directly under Ed Meese included future Supreme Court chief justice John Roberts, future Supreme Court justice Clarence Thomas, and future attorney general (on two separate occasions) Bill Barr. Future Harvard Law School dean, and now interim provost at Harvard University, John Manning, an ardent textualist, worked as a line attorney for Chuck Cooper in the Office of Legal Counsel.

This is the legacy of Ken Cribb.

William Bradford Reynolds

AFTER KEN CRIBB, the next most important player on the civil side of the Meese Justice Department was William Bradford Reynolds. A 1964 graduate of Yale College and a 1967 graduate of Vanderbilt Law School, Brad Reynolds was born on June 21, 1942, and unfortunately died on September 14, 2019, well before this book could be published. We did, however, conduct two one-hour interviews with Brad long before he died, so his perspective on the Meese Justice Department is reflected in this book. Brad Reynolds's formal title was Assistant Attorney General for the Civil Rights Division, but his actual role was much broader.

Reynolds essentially functioned as associate attorney general despite never being confirmed to that position by the Senate. A brilliant lawyer with more legal experience than Ken, Brad chaired a Litigation Strategy Working Group that set policy for the assistant attorneys general on the civil side of the Justice Department. He also ran the investigation of Supreme Court candidates for the Meese Justice Department—fifteen during his time there. He read the federal court of appeals opinions of Judges Antonin Scalia, Robert H. Bork, and Anthony M. Kennedy with a lawyerly thoroughness and attention to detail honed from his work in the solicitor general's office under Nixon and Solicitor General Robert H. Bork, where he met and became a close personal friend of Assistant Attorney General for the Office of Legal Counsel William H. Rehnquist. Reynolds and Rehnquist had offices next door to each other in the 1970s before President Nixon appointed Rehnquist to the U.S. Supreme Court.

Brad presided over Rehnquist's promotion process from associate to chief justice in 1986 and over the appointment of Antonin Scalia, then fifty, to fill Rehnquist's associate justice seat. In early June 1986, Meese met with President Reagan to urge the nomination of Rehnquist as chief justice and Scalia as associate justice. Meese returned to Ken and Brad waiting eagerly in his office for news of how it went. Thumbs up on both appointments. Ken characteristically broke out the sherry to propose a toast, despite its being only 10:00 a.m. Brad hadn't had a drink in years but made an exception that day.

Brad Reynolds also chaired an important Litigation Strategy Working Group that set policy for the assistant attorneys general on the civil side of the Justice Department. After Ken Cribb left the Department of Justice with Steve Calabresi in February 1987, Brad, John Richardson, and Mark Levin became Ed Meese's principal advisors.

While Ken Cribb was a warm, funny, Falstaffian figure, Reynolds was, like his namesake, William Bradford, the department's Puritan—ascetic, thin, driven, usually somewhat somber and serious. Cribb was a great foil because he knew how to make Reynolds laugh. Ken loved Brad as a brother and brought out the best in him, his intelligence, work ethic, his commitment to libertarian conservatism, and his opposition to a racial spoils system. Together, Ken and Brad were a formidable team.

Brad was, according to Ed Meese, "absolutely instrumental in the Justice Department, both for Bill Smith, my predecessor, and for me. So, when Ronald Reagan stole Ken Cribb away from me to work in the White House as head of Domestic Affairs, I asked Brad, in addition to his duties as assistant attorney general in charge of the Civil Division, to become my principal advisor—counsellor to the attorney general. By that time, he had organized the civil division so well and had such good people working for him, he could carry the additional duty."

Charles Fried

LIKE MANY of his predecessors and successors in the solicitor general's role (such as now justice Elena Kagan), Charles Fried had been a very distinguished law professor at Harvard Law School. A solicitor general supervises litigation involving the United States in the Supreme Court and in the federal courts of appeals. Fried was thus in charge of conducting arguments before the Supreme Court, including personally arguing important cases and overseeing the writing of all of the government's appellate briefs. This is an indescribably important job.

A Czech-born Harvard Law School professor, Charles Fried was a European classical liberal who was born in 1935 and who sadly died as this book was going to the publisher on January 23, 2024, but well after we had interviewed him. Charles Fried's jurisprudence resembled that of Justice John Marshall Harlan the younger, for whom he had clerked, whose judicial philosophy of balancing, prudence, and evolving traditionalism was in conflict with Meese's judicial philosophy of originalism. Brad Reynolds would often haul Charles into the AG's office to get him "talked to" by Meese, but it was a hopeless endeavor. While Charles could be moved by Brad and Ken Cribb, he was stubborn. Nor did Meese care to strong-arm his solicitor general, as Fried himself has repeatedly noted.[12] Meese would lobby Charles, but never tell him what to do or make any effort to fire him. Charles served as solicitor general from June 1, 1985, to noon on January 20, 1989, leaving office at the exact same moment as Ronald Reagan left the presidency.

Fried considered originalism to be "out of line with how the Court has always worked" and "a method that does not deliver what it promises."[13] He advocated a common-law constitutionalism that argued from analogy and precedent, and that adapted the Constitution to changing circumstances.[14] "I used to tease the lawyers in my office that the ideal SG's brief would have not one word that is not in quotation marks and attributed to some prior Supreme Court opinion."[15] We believe that he was the principal author in his youth of Justice John Marshall Harlan's brilliant—but wrong—dissenting opinion in *Poe v. Ullman*,[16] where the Supreme Court declined to decide whether a 19th-century Connecticut statute that limited birth control use violated the constitutional rights of married persons. The majority concluded that no live case was actually presented because no one was being prosecuted under the statute. Justice Harlan thought the court should decide the case anyway and that the law was unconstitutional. The dissenting opinion's key methodology endorsed so-called "substantive due process":

> Due process has not been reduced to any formula; its content
> cannot be determined by reference to any code. The best that can
> be said is that, through the course of this Court's decisions, it has
> represented the balance which our Nation, built upon postulates
> of respect for the liberty of the individual, has struck between that
> liberty and the demands of organized society. If the supplying
> of content to this constitutional concept has of necessity been
> a rational process, it certainly has not been one where judges
> have felt free to roam where unguided speculation might take
> them. The balance of which I speak is the balance struck by this
> country, having regard to what history teaches are the traditions
> from which it developed as well as the traditions from which it
> broke. That tradition is a living thing. A decision of this Court
> which radically departs from it could not long survive, while a
> decision which builds on what has survived is likely to be sound.
> No formula could serve as a substitute, in this area, for judgment
> and restraint.[17]

This passage, and the whole Harlan opinion, is elegantly written, in a style in which only Charles Fried could write. And Justice Harlan was hospitalized at the time the opinion was written. In any event, this dissenting opinion became the foundation for the Supreme Court's 1965 decision in *Griswold v. Connecticut,*[18] which invalidated the old Connecticut law banning the use of contraceptives by married couples, and *Griswold,* in turn, led to *Roe v. Wade,*[19] in which a 7–2 majority of the Supreme Court fabricated a right of women to abort their babies for no reason at all until twenty-seven weeks of pregnancy.[20] We doubt Ed Meese, Ken Cribb, and Brad Reynolds were aware of the fact that Charles Fried had played a key role as a law clerk in causing *Griswold v. Connecticut* to occur when they convinced President Reagan to appoint Charles as solicitor general. But then again, perhaps it's too attenuated a chain of causation to assume.

Charles became solicitor general somewhat by accident. Attorney General William French Smith's two finalists for Ronald Reagan's first solicitor general in 1981 were Rex Lee, an establishment conservative who had lots of friends, and Antonin Scalia, a much more conservative and pugnacious young law professor at the University of Chicago Law School who had served as assistant attorney general for the Office of Legal Counsel under Presidents Nixon and Ford. Since Bill Smith was in some respects a country-club Republican who had spent his life practicing law, Smith picked Rex Lee over Antonin Scalia, despite Scalia being much brighter than Lee, much more conservative, and despite his having prior Justice Department experience. When Smith called Scalia to tell him he had picked Rex Lee, Scalia *hung up* the phone on him. It's not usually a good career move to hang up on the sitting attorney general of the United States if you want any other legal job in that attorney general's administration. Notwithstanding this episode, Scalia's expertise in administrative law earned him Ronald Reagan's second appointment to the highly influential U.S. Court of Appeals for the District of Columbia Circuit on August 17, 1982.

Scalia served on the D.C. Circuit with great distinction until 1986, where he became famous for sending around what his colleagues called "Nino-grams." These were brilliantly argued, pithy legal memos identifying flaws in a colleague's legal opinions. Ed Meese was able, in 1986, to get Scalia to be appointed to the Supreme Court. Suffice it to say that if William French Smith hadn't resigned as attorney general to retire in California, Justice Scalia probably wouldn't have been picked over the more senior D.C. Circuit judge Robert H. Bork for an early Supreme Court nomination. On that matter, as on so many others, all things turned on the timing of Ed Meese's becoming attorney general during President Reagan's second term.

Rex Lee resigned as solicitor general on June 1, 1985. His principal deputy solicitor general from 1982 to 1983 had been moderate conservative former Harvard Law School professor Paul M. Bator, who, upon his return to Harvard Law School, persuaded his friend and colleague Charles Fried to replace him as principal deputy solicitor general. Thus, when Lee left the Justice Department, Charles Fried became acting solicitor general for the Meese Justice Department. Meese's first major decision thus was to hire a new solicitor general, which turned out to be quite hard to do. Steve Calabresi arrived at DOJ as a special assistant to Ed Meese at this time, in late June 1985, with a focus on constitutional law.

Brad Reynolds had served as an assistant solicitor general in the Nixon administration under Robert Bork and was highest on Meese's list, but he had just been denied Senate confirmation for associate attorney general, so we knew he could never be confirmed for solicitor general.

Ken Cribb and Brad Reynolds huddled and came up with offering the solicitor general's office to D.C. Circuit Court of Appeals judge Antonin Scalia, who had so badly wanted the job back in 1981. Scalia's then clerk Lawson, at the ripe old age of twenty-seven and with no political experience or interest, brazenly advised Scalia to seek the solicitor general job, suggesting that it would not only help the country but might also strengthen his claim to a future Supreme Court appointment. Judge Scalia declined, correctly pointing out that if he gave up his court of appeals judgeship—which, as an administrative law nerd, he truly loved—for a few years as solicitor general on the off chance that he *might* get a spectacularly rare Supreme Court appointment, he'd have nowhere to go after the Reagan administration except back to the academy or private practice. So, Judge Scalia took himself off the board, heartily thanking Brad and Ken for the feeler. Meese does not recall sounding Scalia out to be solicitor general, which is not surprising because the possible candidacy died at such an early point in the process that it would never even have been proposed to him.

In the meantime, Charles Fried who was, and remained until his death, a flatterer par excellence, was hard at work persuading Brad Reynolds that he was "sound" on affirmative action, which was mostly true. He also impressed Ken Cribb, who appreciated the fact that Charles was, and remained for his whole life, a true intellectual who was widely read and who, like Ken Cribb, was a superb and often hilarious conversationalist. Charles talked his way into Brad Reynolds's and Ken Cribb's confidence, and Steve Calabresi's first effort at influencing politics, two weeks into his job as special assistant to Attorney General Meese, failed totally when he couldn't persuade Ken that hiring Charles to be solicitor general was a bad idea. To be sure, Calabresi greatly enjoyed Charles Fried's company and respected (and continued to respect) his prodigious intellect. He just doubted whether Charles Fried was truly at heart the man who should be in charge of defending the Reagan Revolution in the U.S. Supreme Court.

Those doubts sprang from two encounters Calabresi had had with Fried in the early 1980s when Fried was a Harvard Law School professor and Calabresi was a Yale Law student, serving as the first president of the Yale Law School Federalist Society. On April 24 and 25, 1982, at the Federalist Society's first national student conference, held at Yale Law School on the topic of federalism, Professor Fried took up the role of institutional contrarian. The speakers mostly advanced the proposition that the federal government was too big, per President Reagan and D.C. Circuit Court of Appeals judge Robert H. Bork's keynote address to the conference. Fried noted the danger of village tyrants and pointed to the confiscatory rent control ordinances of the City of Santa Monica, California, on rental housing. Professor Fried then took up saying, "Remember Santa Monica" to anyone arguing that the federal government was too big. Calabresi thought Fried had a valid point that village tyrants were threats to liberty, for reasons James Madison gave back in 1788 in the 10th *Federalist Paper*,[21] but Fried was generally seen as being off the Reagan reservation on federalism and was a good, provocative law professor but not someone you would hire to represent specifically Ronald Reagan before the U.S. Supreme Court.[22]

Then at the 3rd annual Federalist Society national law students' conference held at Harvard Law School, on a panel with University of Texas School of Law professor Lino Graglia discussing the legality and wisdom of affirmative action, Fried took issue with Professor Graglia, who characteristically came out swinging hard against affirmative action by saying that none of his Italian ancestors were complicit in slavery, so he didn't see why it was fair to penalize his kids in university admissions processes or job searches. Professor Fried disagreed and advanced what he thought was a "middle ground" position: Harvard Law School could use affirmative action in student admissions, but not in faculty hiring. The Harvard Law School faculty, said Fried, was like the Boston Symphony Orchestra, which should be picked solely based on merit, while the Harvard Law School student body was like the audience "listening" to the beautiful music that the faculty played. Calabresi and all the other conservative-libertarian law students in the room considered this to be an elitist, condescending double-standard. In July of 1985, twenty days into his job working as a special assistant to Ed Meese, he went to Ken Cribb with his opinion that Fried's views were disqualifying from the job of Ronald Reagan's solicitor general.

Ken Cribb laughed off Calabresi's concerns. Ken loved having a staff that was to his right, he said, but he had a really good gut feeling about Charles, and he was going to go with his instinct. Steve Calabresi literally got down on his knees and begged Ken not to make this appointment, but Ken Cribb was unmoved. On October 23, 1985, Charles Fried was appointed solicitor general, having been unanimously confirmed by the Senate.

It must be said of Fried that he was, and remained until his death in 2024, a true intellectual—an academic's academic and a real gentleman. He added greatly to the intellectual atmosphere of the Meese Justice Department. In the end, Calabresi came around to the view that Meese, Reynolds, and Cribb had made the right choice by appointing Fried as solicitor general over a movement hardliner. The department, after all, needed to be heard by many different audiences, including the general public and future generations. Meese's speeches, Office of Legal Policy working papers, Office of Legal Counsel opinions, and executive orders and conservative-libertarian judicial appointments were pathbreaking and were addressed to the general public and to future generations, but Meese also needed to win the federal government's cases from 1985 to 1989 before a totally non-originalist Supreme Court that mostly swung the other way. Former John Marshall Harlan law clerk Charles Fried was someone Lewis Powell, Sandra Day O'Connor, and Anthony M. Kennedy might actually find persuasive.

An establishmentarian solicitor general made perfect sense to Ed Meese. Moving the public and the courts was a complex endeavor that meant having different aides with different political philosophies would only help. And Charles Fried did have what Ed Meese wanted in asking for appointees with grey hair. Bottom line, Charles Fried was a great law professor and a good man. He was simply right for the job of solicitor general in the Reagan administration given the composition of the Supreme Court at that time. Meese said later that Fried was a great team player and that he had done a great job of representing what the department decided, even when Meese didn't necessarily personally agree with that decision, exclaiming, "I have very high regard for Charles Fried!"

Charles J. Cooper

CHARLES J. ("CHUCK") COOPER was among the most powerful of the assistant attorneys general on the civil law side of the Meese Department of Justice, second only to Brad Reynolds. As head of the Office of Legal Counsel (OLC), he was essentially "general counsel" to the executive branch. Much of the authority of an attorney general is exercised by OLC in the form of opinions on constitutional and statutory matters. Former heads of the office include former chief justice William H. Rehnquist, former associate justice Antonin Scalia, and William P. Barr, who served as attorney general under Presidents George H. W. Bush and Donald Trump. The OLC's staff attorney positions are a noted breeding ground for law professors.

OLC's job is to give the attorney general and the president in-house legal advice on matters of constitutional and statutory law. It is the executive branch's equivalent of the Supreme Court on matters that may not be justiciable in court. Apart from the president, it has the last word within the executive branch on all constitutional and statutory questions. OLC is monumentally important and powerful, and Chuck Cooper was a highly active head of OLC, even though he took office at the young age of thirty-three. Chuck received his B.A. and J.D. from the University of Alabama and clerked for then associate justice William Rehnquist on the U.S. Supreme Court. He was proud of accentuating his Alabama southern drawl. Prior to becoming head of OLC, Chuck had been the deputy assistant attorney general for Civil Rights under Brad Reynolds. He was also close with Ken Cribb, with whom he had worked when Ed Meese and Ken were still in the White House.

Chuck was a brilliant intellectual who wasn't particularly fond of intellectuals as a class. He was funny, aggressive, energetic, and active. If he saw a void in the policymaking sphere, he immediately filled it. Chuck replaced William French Smith's head of OLC, Ted Olson, who was thought by some to have been too much of an establishment, country-club Republican. No one would ever have said of Chuck Cooper that he was "squishy." An ardent defender of states' rights and federalism, he was also a committed constitutional originalist. Charles Fried admitted being pulled over by "the federalism police"[23] a few times in his memoir, by which he meant Chuck and Steve Calabresi.

Chuck assembled a very able and talented staff of young lawyers, including future Supreme Court justice Sam Alito, whom Chuck plucked out of the solicitor general's office to be his deputy. He also employed as career lawyers Gary Lawson, who went on to be (says Calabresi) a talented academic, and John Manning, who went on to become the current dean of the Harvard Law School and as of this writing the interim provost of Harvard University, all after joining the Democratic Party. Chuck's office thus contributed mightily to the feeling that the Meese Justice Department was a right-of-center law faculty. That being said, Chuck's brilliant lawyers, including outstanding holdovers from prior administrations who didn't share Chuck's views, were very professional in the OLC opinions they wrote. Chuck wouldn't have tolerated anything else.

Between 1985 and 1988, Chuck issued a blizzard of originalist OLC opinions on almost every subject under the sun, some of which we explore in chapter 11. This was long before Justices Antonin Scalia and Clarence Thomas issued their originalist Supreme Court opinions. Chuck had a huge influence on the Department of Justice and was a key player in the Supreme Court selection committee headed by Brad Reynolds. Chuck also played a huge role in the investigation of the Iran-Contra scandal. Meese considered Chuck Cooper's role "vital" at OLC and particularly on Iran-Contra. He considered him a "loyal friend" who "did a great job" in a key position at DOJ.

Richard Willard

RICHARD WILLARD was a holdover from William French Smith's Justice Department. He proved to be an enormously important figure in the running of the Meese Justice Department. Richard was the assistant attorney general for the Civil Division, in charge of all the civil litigation of the United States in the federal district courts and circuit courts of appeals. He had hundreds of lawyers working for him and managed them well. A committed libertarian-conservative, he was more likely than Chuck Cooper to side with the Chamber of Commerce rather than the states on federalism issues, and he strongly pushed for national tort reform. Richard also regularly interviewed judicial candidates, and he played a key role in interacting with Charles Fried on solicitor general approvals over federal appeals. Richard was a conservative whose urbane and intellectual manner made him well suited to be a conservative influence on Charles Fried.

Richard Willard was, along with Deputy Solicitor General Carolyn Kuhl, a former law clerk to then Ninth Circuit judge Anthony M. Kennedy. Willard and Kuhl were both on the Supreme Court Search Committee chaired by Brad Reynolds, which also included Ken Cribb, Steve Calabresi, John Harrison, Lee Liberman Otis, Chuck Cooper, and Steve Matthews, but *not* Solicitor General Charles Fried. Calabresi and Harrison were both former Robert H. Bork law clerks, Lee Liberman Otis was a former Antonin Scalia D.C. Circuit law clerk, and Willard and Kuhl were, as we just said, former Kennedy clerks. Everyone on the Supreme Court Search Committee advocated the appointment of the federal court of appeals judge for whom they had clerked. John Harrison wrote the legal memo making the case for Bork, Lee Liberman Otis wrote the memo making the case for Scalia, but Ken Cribb insisted that his former roommate Steve Matthews write the memo on Kennedy. Matthews concluded that Kennedy was an originalist on all matters except those involving sexual orientation, as to which he was a libertarian. Kennedy's two former law clerks on the Search Committee, Willard and Kuhl, were both libertarians too. Part of the reason Kennedy made it onto the Supreme Court was because of Willard's and Kuhl's ardent support for him in the Meese Justice Department.

Along with his two superb deputy assistant attorneys general, Lee Liberman Otis and Brent Hatch, Richard Willard contributed mightily to making the Meese Justice Department a fun and intellectual working environment.

Stephen J. Markman

STEPHEN MARKMAN served as the assistant attorney general for the Office of Legal Policy. Steve took over a division of the DOJ that had no clear portfolio and turned it into a powerhouse for converting Meese's originalist ideas into the law of the land. Markman's office organized Meese's academic conferences with law faculty on subjects ranging from federalism to economic liberty to the separation of powers. It also produced blue-covered mini-law-review articles, of which there may have been as many as thirty, on subjects ranging from the original meaning of the Fourteenth Amendment's Privileges or Immunities Clause to the merits and demerits of the exclusionary rule—a work of scholarship Yale Sterling Professor of Law Akhil Amar has praised as being one of the best in print. Markman's office was also the central administrative body in the Department of Justice for judicial selection. Not bad for a minister without a portfolio.

Markman came to the Justice Department from Senator Orrin Hatch's office as an avowed, across-the-board conservative originalist on everything. Calabresi can't remember ever disagreeing with Markman on anything. He was quite mild-mannered and slightly shy. As he did with everyone, Ken Cribb liked to tease him and make him laugh. Steve had an excellent sense of humor and was an energetic and effective manager who got a lot of work done. After leaving the Justice Department, Steve Markman went on to an illustrious career as a Michigan State Supreme Court justice, including a tenure as its chief justice.

Meese said that Markman "couldn't have done a better job, not only at the research and vetting of the candidates for the federal judiciary but in developing concepts of legal policy and in finding the answers to many difficult legal questions... [including] knotty problems that would come up in the future."

Terry Eastland, Gary McDowell, and Blair Dorminey

MEESE'S SPEECHES epitomized his revolution. Chief speechwriter Terry Eastland was head of the DOJ Public Affairs Office from June 1985 to February 1988, the office responsible for writing speeches and publicizing them. His team included distinguished academic and writer Gary McDowell, who had worked with Raoul Berger at Harvard, and Blair Dorminey, a Yale Law School classmate of Steve Calabresi and Gary Lawson. Terry, Gary, and Blair were key parts of the team, all witty, well-read, and fun-loving intellectuals who transformed what might otherwise have been a morose bureaucracy.

Terry left Justice in 1988 for the *Weekly Standard* magazine. Gary McDowell went on to academic appointments in London, England, and at the University of Richmond and continued to write about originalism until his death in 2021. We were able to interview Gary before his death. We regret hugely that he did not live to read this book.

Meese raved about this team's sense of Ronald Reagan, its understanding of the direction of the administration and of constitutional law, and its ability to crystallize ideas, concepts, and legal research into recommendations for his speeches.

Attorney General Meese's Personal Staff

MEESE HAD A LARGE personal staff of special assistants under Ken Cribb's supervision.

Ken Cribb's deputy in 1985 was Steve Calabresi's friend from working on Ronald Reagan's 1980 campaign, Steve Galebach, a brilliant lawyer, ardent pro-lifer, and deeply conservative evangelical Christian. He managed the AG's huge incoming paper flow until putting John Richardson and Steve Calabresi in charge as he went on to do more policy. John Richardson had worked at the White House with Cribb and Meese and was deeply loyal to both. Conservative, hard-working, and very able, he eventually became Ed Meese's chief of staff. Steve Galebach eventually left politics altogether because he found it to be inconsistent with the demands of his very deep faith. This left Steve Calabresi as Ken Cribb's right-hand man on policy and DOJ oversight.

Steve Calabresi was initially hired in part on the advice of Steve Galebach, a friend from the 1980 Reagan campaign, but he also got a big boost from Judge Robert H. Bork, for whom Calabresi worked as a law clerk. Judge Bork had taught Steve Calabresi at Yale Law School and strongly recommended him to Ken Cribb. Ken was intrigued by the Federalist Society, which Calabresi had co-founded. He correctly saw it as a law school version of the Intercollegiate Studies Institute (ISI) at which Ken had previously worked (and eventually headed as president from 1989 to 2011).

Calabresi was so nervous about his job interview with Ken Cribb that he went to his friend Lee Liberman Otis's office in the Civil Division for a last-minute pep talk and to be walked up the stairs to Ken's 5th-floor office. Lee's parting words to him were to say positive things about Russell Kirk, a socially conservative intellectual whom Ken admired. Calabresi, a Hayekian libertarian-conservative, took that advice, and the lunch with Ken went swimmingly. Ken was funny, intellectual, interesting, charming, and put Steve at ease. He got the job offer. Judge Bork let him out of his clerkship a month early for what he describes as the happiest nineteen months of his career, starting at the end of June 1985.

Steve Calabresi got a seat on Brad Reynolds's twenty-member team to identify Supreme Court nominees, he planned speeches, and he interviewed dozens of federal courts of appeals candidates. He spent a lot of time with the attorney general, who was unfailingly kind, appreciative, considerate, and a pleasure to talk to in every way. Cribb, however, was his immediate boss, and Steve became his right-hand man. Cribb being Meese's right-hand man, and Meese President Reagan's, meant that Steve felt deeply honored by the trust being placed in him, and a duty to live up to an experience so extraordinary that even clerking for Justice Scalia on the Supreme Court paled by comparison.

In the executive branch, unlike the courts, you can set your working agenda rather than having to handle problems litigants bring through the door. Calabresi set his mind to how to accomplish the Reagan-Meese agenda. One of his first ideas, in the summer of 1985, was for the attorney general to write the West Publishing Company to ask them to publish presidential signing statements—often issued when the president signs a bill into law—along with the congressional legislative history of a law, in the *United States Code Congressional and Administrative News* (U.S.C.C.A.N.). This would allow presidents to explain how they construed a law. This did three things: it countered congressional legislative history, alerted the executive branch to parts of a law the executive regarded as unconstitutional, and directed the executive branch not to enforce that part of the law and how to exercise any discretion in a new law.[24]

The West Publishing Company agreed to this proposal, which greatly augmented presidential power in the field of statutory interpretation, as well as effectuating the president's constitutionally granted control over the executive branch to take care that the laws be faithfully executed.[25] All subsequent White House Counsel's offices have used this tool to shape the way executive branch inferior officers and courts construe federal law. The signing statement initiative had a permanent and transformative effect in augmenting presidential power. This initiative, along with conducting dozens of interviews of U.S. circuit courts of appeals candidates, was Steve Calabresi's biggest accomplishment as a special assistant to Attorney General Meese. Calabresi also provided Ed Meese with key guidance on constitutional law speeches and kept a wary eye on what Charles Fried's solicitor general's office was up to.

John Harrison, who is currently the James Madison Distinguished Professor of Law at the University of Virginia School of Law, was another of Mr. Meese's special assistants. John was, and remains, a true intellectual who is very widely read. He analyzes issues with rigorous, almost mathematical logic. John was and is a genius, and he and Steve Calabresi worked together very closely as the two Yale Law School–trained constitutional law experts on Mr. Meese's personal staff. They were also both former law clerks to Judge Robert H. Bork. John Harrison and Steve Calabresi so liked talking about constitutional law that they may have spent too much work time discussing it. These discussions later became handy, however, when they both ended up as chaired law professors. John Harrison also did judicial interviews and, together with Steve Calabresi, gave guidance to Mr. Meese's speechwriters. John was another key figure in creating the very academic, law school–like atmosphere of the Meese Justice Department.

David McIntosh worked as a special assistant to Meese for two years from 1986 to 1988. He took charge of managing the paper flow into and out of Meese's office. In June 1988, David replaced Steve Calabresi as Ken Cribb's lone staffer at the White House on domestic policy issues when Steve left the White House in June of 1987 to begin his much less fun Supreme Court clerkship with Justice Antonin Scalia. David finished the work Steve began on issuing a Ronald Reagan Economic Bill of Rights on July 3, 1987, and in setting up the President's Privatization Committee in September 1988.

David and Steve Calabresi had been close friends since Yale College, where they had both served, like Meese, as president of the Yale Political Union. They were co-founders with Lee Liberman Otis of the Federalist Society for Law and Public Policy Studies, an organization to which Meese gave some of his most famous speeches.

David's projects involved better protecting property rights, in what was then called the Lands Division and is now called the Environment Division, addressing the overreaching of much of the environmental regulation. Attorney General Meese wanted him to monitor and report back to him on a number of cases winding through the circuit courts, with guidance to the division on how to defend private property rights. He also found the cases on abortion memorable, monitoring what was going on in the solicitor general's office. "I worked a lot with Ken. I also prepared the attorney general for trips. One trip that the attorney general made was to China to discuss the rule of law in the National Chinese Congressional Hall, and we did a lot of background briefings for him on that."

We asked him if the atmosphere of the Meese Justice Department as being a brilliant national law school faculty changed after Ken Cribb left DOJ to go the White House in March 1987, taking Steve Calabresi with him. He said it did. When Brad Reynolds replaced Ken Cribb as counsellor to Attorney General Meese, the atmosphere of the Justice Department changed from being that of a brilliant law faculty to being that of a large law firm. This further shows what an enormous role Ken Cribb played in causing the Meese Revolution to happen, which is part of the reason why Steve Calabresi has dedicated his work on this book to Ken Cribb.

Working together, McIntosh and Calabresi created the first Federalist Society neckties, featuring small heads of James Madison. One morning Attorney General Meese noticed some of his assistant attorneys general wearing these Federalist Society neckties and asked admiringly where he could get one. He was told that his special assistants Steve Calabresi and David McIntosh were selling them. Pausing for a moment, he smiled firmly, and said, "Well, OK, so long as the profits are not going to the Contras."

Mark Levin was Ed Meese's chief of staff after Ken Cribb and John Richardson left the Justice Department. As a critic of judicial activism, Mark is brilliant and exceptionally well read, as well as very articulate, passionately conservative, and a true believer in the Reagan Revolution. Mark could be bitingly funny, and he kept the Justice Department running in a conservative intellectual direction long after Ken Cribb and Steve Calabresi had gone. Steve Calabresi's and Mark Levin's tenures at the Meese Justice Department barely overlapped, so there is not much more we can say about him from firsthand experience, but his post-government books, radio show, and Fox television show have made him one of the most successful alumni of the Meese Justice Department. Ed Meese had nothing but admiring things to say about Mark Levin:

Mark Levin was a great supporter of Ronald Reagan from the start, and he had worked in various parts of the administration. Through friends in other departments, I heard about him. When I came over to the Department of Justice from the White House, I created a new position in my own office, my own staff, called management analyst, because I felt I needed someone to work on the organizational and managerial functions of the department. And I said to Mark, "What I'd like you to do is work on the things I would do myself if I had the time, but I don't, because of my other duties."

We did a number of things along [the] lines of improving the management organization and operational functions of the Justice Department, with Mark's help, including for the first time creating a Justice Command Center—so that we had a twenty-four-hour command center—which we found we needed one time when there was an uprising in one of the penitentiaries. When my excellent chief of staff John Richardson, who had done a great job in that role, went off to go to business school, I asked Mark to take over as chief of staff, and he did an outstanding job, just totally loyal, and a great organizer, a person who could take on complex responsibilities and do them very well.

Mark is now one of the most prominent commentators in the journalistic world. He's had an astonishing career. When I was leaving the Mayflower Hotel this morning, a woman walked up to me and said, "I just want to shake your hand. I heard you on Mark Levin's radio show once, and it's such an honor to meet you." That's evidence of how ubiquitous Mark's work is!

* * *

Overall, the Meese Justice Department was a cast of characters worthy of a Shakespearian play—Ken Cribb, Brad Reynolds, Chuck Cooper, Steve Markman, Doug Ginsburg, John Bolton, Richard Willard, Lee Liberman Otis, Brent Hatch, Hank Habicht, Steve Matthews, Terry Eastland, Gary McDowell, Blair Dorminey, and countless others, such as Carolyn Kuhl, Roger and Nancie Marzulla, and Mike Carvin. This was no surprise since all were card-carrying members of the Reagan Revolution. Revolutions, by their nature, attract intellectuals, and intellectuals tend to be an unusual, even eccentric, group of players. This was as true of the Reagan Revolution as it was of George Washington's and Abraham Lincoln's revolutionary cabinets and administrations. Ken Cribb alone could carry several acts of a Shakespearian play. He was, in part, King Henry V, but with a dash of Falstaff mixed in just to keep life funny, interesting, and unpredictable.

But in the end, of course, the central actor in the Meese DOJ was Attorney General Meese. Steve Calabresi remembers asking Ed Meese in 1986 whether he'd ever be interested in serving on the U.S. Supreme Court, as some former attorney generals have gone on to do. It was probably a cheeky question for a twenty-eight-year-old special assistant to ask of Ronald Reagan's best friend and the attorney general of the United States, in retrospect. Calabresi still remembers Ed Meese's laugh and the twinkle in his eyes as he said, "No. Not under any circumstances."

When interviewed for this book decades later, Meese answered the same question of what he would have done if Ronald Reagan had asked to appoint him to the Supreme Court: "Well, first of all, that opportunity did not arise," he replied, "so I didn't have to make that decision, and it would've been a tough one only if President Reagan had asked me to do it. But I never wanted to be a judge. I think have expressed before [that] to me it would be like being sentenced to law school for the rest of your life. And I never was that fond of law school, quite frankly."

Meese added, "I actually had a chance at one point in my life to be a judge, in a way. It was during my time in the army serving on court-martial boards, as a member of the court, and I can remember sitting there, and, and having to restrain myself from jumping over the bench and telling the lawyer who was then an advocate, this is the way you do it. So, it was then that I knew that being a judge wasn't really one of the things that suited my personality or my wishes.'"

We agree. Being attorney general suited him much better.

CHAPTER SEVEN
ATTORNEY GENERAL ED MEESE'S SPEECHES

O<small>NE MIGHT EXPECT</small> an account of a Department of Justice's accomplishments to begin with its court victories, litigation strategies, enforcement practices, or perhaps its role in judicial selection. The attorney general's public speeches seem like an unlikely starting point.

But the Meese Justice Department was unlike anything that came before it or has come afterward. Ed Meese's speeches as attorney general were actually the most important part of his legacy, as they laid the foundation for everything else that happened within the Justice Department. Those speeches made headlines and shaped both public and academic debate in ways that are unprecedented for any executive official below the level of president (and well beyond most presidents). Ed Meese's speeches were the manifesto of the Meese Revolution, and anyone who wants to understand modern law forty years later needs to understand those speeches' contents, goals, and enduring impact on American law. He well understood the gravity of the decision whether or not to embark on this public strategy, and Ed Meese called in Ken Cribb and Brad Reynolds for a go or no-go decision on whether to go forward with the speeches. All three thought it was the right thing to do, and so it was.

Ed Meese's speeches were a hallmark of his tenure in office. The speeches argued for originalism in constitutional and statutory interpretation, directly challenging the jurisprudence of all nine justices on the Supreme Court at that time. When Ed Meese delivered the first bombshell, at the annual conference of the American Bar Association on July 9, 1985, less than six months into his tenure as attorney general, even the two Supreme Court justices who were conservatives—Chief Justice Warren Burger and Justice William Rehnquist—were not originalists. They were *conservative*, in the sense that they decided cases in accordance with political values (like "tough on crime") that would likely be associated with conservative politicians, but they were not *constitutionalists*. They had little to no interest in figuring out what the Constitution objectively means. In that respect, they were children of the early 20th-century "legal realist"[1] revolution, which denied that law could or should consist of even-handed application of objectively determinable rules but instead was just ordinary politics in another guise.[2] In arguing for originalism, Ed Meese was arguing for the autonomy of law.

This chapter focuses on four of Ed Meese's most important speeches, addressing originalism, departmentalism, federalism, and the separation of powers—all subjects that are at the very core of U.S. constitutional law. Ed Meese also gave important speeches while he was attorney general on numerous other topics, such as the costs of the exclusionary rule, the importance of the traditional concept of the family, religion, terrorism, criminal justice and law enforcement, the war on drugs, and pornography. We simply do not have space to discuss all of those speeches here; we concentrate on the ones that have had the most defining impact on law over the past forty years. Readers who are interested in reading the other speeches given by Ed Meese can find them at the Justice Department's website.[3]

CONSTITUTIONAL INTERPRETATION

IN THE INTRODUCTION, we mentioned Ed Meese's famous July 9, 1985, speech to the American Bar Association. Such speeches to the ABA by attorneys general are typically anodyne praises for the rule of law, an independent judiciary, and the platitudes and administration policies of the moment. Ed Meese had something else in mind.

Ed Meese criticized the Supreme Court's then recent rulings on federalism and religious liberty while generally praising its decisions on criminal procedure, which expanded the ability of police to gather and use evidence in criminal cases. That detailed critique of Supreme Court decisions was itself noteworthy. But there was a much deeper theme behind Attorney General Meese's speech. "[I]t is important," he told the assembled lawyers, "to take a moment and reflect upon the proper role of the Supreme Court in our constitutional system." This was not going to be a speech about the Reagan administration's criminal, antitrust, or government contracting enforcement priorities. This was going to be a speech about first principles.

The biggest problem with the court circa 1985, said Attorney General Meese, was not necessarily the results that it reached but the way that it reached them:

As has been generally true in recent years, the 1984 term did not yield a coherent set of decisions. Rather, it seemed to produce what one commentator has called a "jurisprudence of idiosyncrasy." Taken as a whole, the work of the term defies analysis by any strict standard. It is neither simply liberal nor simply conservative; neither simply activist nor simply restrained; neither simply principled nor simply partisan. The Court this term continued to roam at large in a veritable constitutional forest.

More specifically, he argued, "it seems fair to conclude that far too many of the Court's opinions were, on the whole, more policy choices than articulations of constitutional principle. The voting blocs, the arguments, all reveal a greater allegiance to what the Court thinks constitutes sound public policy than a deference to what the Constitution—its text and intention—may demand." The problem was not that the court was making bad policy. The problem was that the court was making policy at all rather than ascertaining and applying the meaning of the Constitution.

Attorney General Meese did not merely offer a critique of existing practice. He had an alternative as well:

What, then, should a constitutional jurisprudence actually be? It should be a Jurisprudence of Original Intention. By seeking to judge policies in light of principles, rather than remold principles in light of policies, the Court could avoid both the charge of incoherence and the charge of being either too conservative or too liberal.

A jurisprudence seriously aimed at the explication of original intention would produce defensible principles of government that would not be tainted by ideological predilection.

This belief in a Jurisprudence of Original Intention also reflects a deeply rooted commitment to the idea of democracy. ... To allow the courts to govern simply by what it views at the time as fair and decent, is a scheme of government no longer popular; the idea of democracy has suffered. The permanence of the Constitution has been weakened. A Constitution that is viewed as only what the judges say it is, is no longer a constitution in the true sense.

Recall from chapter 5 the primitive, and even nonexistent, state of originalism in the courts and the academy in the early 1980s. Ed Meese in 1985 was proposing an interpretative revolution.

The proposed revolution was in nascent form in mid-1985; there was much in the attorney general's comments that needed more development. Throughout the rest of this book, we talk about the evolution of these ideas in Ed Meese's July 1985 speech into modern originalism, including the fleshing out of the idea of "original intention" into a focus on applying the objective original public meanings of legal texts to problems that have arisen in the modern world. But here is where the process of evolution really began. It did not begin in a law school or an academic article. It began in an attorney general's speech.

Perhaps anticipating the revival of Justice Robert Jackson's objection that materials used to ascertain original meaning are "as enigmatic as the dreams Joseph was called upon to interpret for Pharaoh," Attorney General Meese added: "Those who framed the Constitution chose their words carefully; they debated at great length the most minute points. The language they chose meant something. It is incumbent upon the Court to determine what that meaning was."

The most powerful part of the speech was brief and to the point: "It has been and will continue to be the policy of this administration to press for a Jurisprudence of Original Intention. In the cases we file and those we join as amicus, we will endeavor to resurrect the original meaning of constitutional provisions and statutes as the only reliable guide to judgment. ... Any other standard suffers the defect of pouring new meaning into old words, thus creating new powers and new rights totally at odds with the logic of our Constitution and its commitment to the rule of law." Originalism was not simply an academic theory. It was the right way to do law, and it was how the Meese Department of Justice would do law.

If anyone doubted whether Ed Meese meant what he said, he used his theory of originalism to call into question one of the foundational features of modern Supreme Court doctrine: the "incorporation" of the

Bill of Rights into the Fourteenth Amendment. A bit of background might be helpful for non-lawyers:

The Bill of Rights is the name we today give to the Constitution's first ten amendments, ratified in 1791.[4] Those amendments, including such things as the First Amendment free speech and religion clauses, the Second Amendment right to keep and bear arms, and various protections for criminal defendants, apply *only* to the federal government, not to state or local governments. In 1833, the Supreme Court made it clear that the Fifth Amendment's prohibition on takings of property without just compensation applied only to federal action.[5]

Thirty-five years later, the Fourteenth Amendment was ratified. That 1868 amendment says nothing explicitly about the first ten amendments, but it says that states cannot "abridge the privileges or immunities of citizens of the United States" or "deprive any person of life, liberty, or property, without due process of law." Does that mean that states, after 1868, must also obey the 1791 Bill of Rights?

In a story too complicated to tell here, the Supreme Court slowly found that compliance by states with at least some Bill of Rights provisions is part of "due process of law." Starting in the 1960s and continuing today, the court has issued piecemeal rulings making almost all (not quite all, but almost all) of the provisions of the Bill of Rights applicable to the fifty states as well as to the federal government. When Ed Meese gave his speech in 1985, that process of "incorporating" the Bill of Rights into the Fourteenth Amendment had been largely complete for more than fifteen years and had included all provisions of the First Amendment, including for nearly forty years the part saying that "Congress shall make no law respecting an establishment of religion."

Ed Meese said that "nothing can be done to shore up the intellectually shaky foundation upon which the doctrine [of incorporation] rests." Challenging this doctrine, he recognized, involved challenging "a good portion of constitutional adjudication [since 1925, which] has been aimed at extending the scope of the doctrine of incorporation." But such a challenge was overdue, as "nowhere else has the principle of federalism been dealt so politically violent and constitutionally suspect a blow as by the theory of incorporation."

This was resort to first principles with a vengeance.

Scholars today still debate whether, how, and to what extent the Fourteenth Amendment, as a matter of original meaning, "incorporates" the Bill of Rights against the states.[6] Our aim here is not to resolve that question, or even to say that we agree with Ed Meese about incorporation,[7] but only to show that Ed Meese in 1985 was putting things into dialogue that would have been inconceivable as serious topics of conversation just a day earlier.

To give credit where credit is due, Ed Meese asked his two speechwriters on his July 9, 1985, speech, Gary McDowell and Blair Dorminey, to frame it as a commentary on the Supreme Court term and to argue for originalism. It is fair to say that they succeeded in their mission on both counts.

The success of many ideas can be measured by the criticism that they bring. Criticism of Ed Meese's call for a Jurisprudence of Original Intention was not long in coming, and it came from a sitting Supreme Court justice. On October 12, 1985, Justice William J. Brennan Jr., the ideological and political leader of the U.S. Supreme Court's left wing, responded to Ed Meese in a speech to the Text and Teaching Symposium at the Georgetown University Law Center in Washington, D.C.

Justice Brennan began with two remarks that seemed indirectly aimed at Ed Meese. The first declared that "the Constitution embodies the aspiration to social justice, brotherhood, and human dignity that brought this nation into being." At one level, this is uncontroversial to the point of being trite—who could be against justice, brotherhood, and dignity? At a deeper level, however, this statement by Justice Brennan was a reaffirmation of the pre-Meese conventional wisdom that constitutional adjudication is not about the meaning of *texts* but about judicial imposition of *political programs*. Surely Ed Meese and William Brennan would not have the same things in mind if they spoke of "social justice" or "dignity." The founding-era conception of those terms, for example, was probably best captured by the Massachusetts Constitution of 1780 (which is still in force) when it declared that "All men are born free, and equal and have certain natural, essential, and unalienable rights; among which may be reckoned the right of enjoying and defending their lives and liberties; that of acquiring, possessing, and protecting property; in fine that of seeking and obtaining their safety and happiness." Twenty-four out of thirty-seven states had such "born free and equal" clauses in their state bills of rights in 1868 when the Fourteenth Amendment was ratified, and thirty-nine out of fifty states have such clauses in their state bills of rights today. Justice Brennan presumably was not talking about armed self-defense of persons and property when he spoke of "dignity"; he was asserting that the Constitution is a font into which *his* values—*his* conceptions of "social justice, brotherhood, and dignity," such as welfare rights and opposition to capital punishment—could be poured.

Justice Brennan's second introductory point made that clear when he spoke of the Constitution's "broad" phrasing and "majestic generalities and ennobling pronouncements," which he called "both luminous and obscure." The ghost of Justice Robert Jackson smiled.

Of course, Justice Brennan did not say that the Constitution means whatever he thought it meant: "Justices are not platonic guardians appointed to wield authority according to their personal moral predilections." Rather, he said, "the debate is really a debate about how to read the text, about constraints on what is legitimate interpretation."

To what "debate" was Justice Brennan referring? The answer is: the "debate" begun by Ed Meese just months beforehand—and which did not exist until Ed Meese began it. Justice Brennan was directly responding to Ed Meese's challenge to the policy-oriented conventional wisdom regarding constitutional adjudication:

There are those who find legitimacy in fidelity to what they call "the intentions of the Framers." In its most doctrinaire incarnation, this view demands that Justices discern exactly what the Framers thought about the question under consideration and simply follow that intention in resolving the case before them. It is a view that feigns self-effacing deference to the specific judgments of those who forged our original social compact. But in truth it is little more than arrogance cloaked as humility. It is arrogant to pretend that from our vantage we can gauge accurately the intent of the Framers on application of principle to specific, contemporary questions. All too often, sources of potential enlightenment such as records of the ratification debates provide sparse or ambiguous evidence of the original intention. ...

Perhaps most importantly, while proponents of this facile historicism justify it as a depoliticization of the judiciary, the political underpinnings of such a choice should not escape notice.... Those who would restrict claims of right to the values of 1789 specifically articulated in the Constitution turn a blind eye to social progress and eschew adaptation of overarching principles to changes of social circumstance....

... [T]he genius of the Constitution rests not in any static meaning it might have had in a world that is dead and gone, but in the adaptability of its great principles to cope with current problems and current needs. What the constitutional fundamentals meant to the wisdom of other times cannot be their measure to the vision of our time.

This was a powerful statement (and the speech contains much more that is well worth a complete reading) of the "living constitution" model, in which the Constitution must be updated by judicial decisions to conform to "the demands of human dignity [which] will never cease to evolve."

Justice Brennan in 1985 raised several intellectually serious challenges to Ed Meese's speech. First, Attorney General Meese's July 1985 speech emphasized original *intentions*. As Justice Brennan correctly pointed out, that raises the question of *whose intentions* are important. The Constitution's literal authors—which was mostly five people on a Committee of Detail as part of a larger Constitutional Convention? The Constitution's expressly declared author, which is "We the People"? The state ratifying conventions that gave the Constitution legal effect? The larger public whose acquiescence gave the Constitution practical effect? What if those intentions conflicted? What about opponents of the Constitution? Do their intentions count, and if so in what fashion? These are all legitimate, and indeed essential, questions to pose.

Second, looking to intentions (of whomever) requires answering the more basic question: intentions with respect to *what*? Is the goal to ask how specific persons from a specific time period would have addressed a precise question? Does something fall outside the compass of the Constitution if it involves subject matter, such as electronic communications or air travel, beyond the 18th-century experience? Or is the relevant intention the intended *abstract meaning of a concept*, such as "unreasonable searches and seizures," whose content could adapt to modern conditions? And if a jurisprudence of original intention means the latter, how is that any different from Justice Brennan's "living constitutionalism"?

If a Jurisprudence of Original Intention had been studied carefully in law schools for decades prior to 1985, there would have been extensive discussions of these questions and possibly some consensus among advocates of such a jurisprudence about how to operationalize that theory into judicial practice. For reasons described in chapter 5, that had not happened in the academy in 1985. But if a Jurisprudence of Original Intention was going to be the official policy of the Department of Justice, and indeed of the Reagan administration more broadly, real-world answers to these kinds of questions had to be worked out.

Justice Brennan may or may not have known this when he gave his speech, but the very questions he was asking were already being asked internally in the Department of Justice by those who were crafting the Jurisprudence of Original Intention. Accordingly, when Justice Brennan gave his speech, it did not take long for Attorney General Meese to respond. He did so on November 15, 1985, barely a month after Justice Brennan's speech, in an address to the District of Columbia chapter of the Federalist Society's Lawyers Division.[8] This address was very far from the last word in the development of originalism, but it represents a vital landmark. And it is a key example of Ed Meese institutionalizing his and Ronald Reagan's charisma in the then infant Federalist Society.

Attorney General Meese began with a paean to spirited constitutional debate (which perhaps should be posted today in law school faculty lounges):

A large part of American history has been the history of Constitutional debate. From the Federalists and the Anti-Federalists, to Webster and Calhoun, to Lincoln and Douglas, we find many examples. Now, as we approach the bicentennial of the framing of the Constitution, we are witnessing another debate concerning our fundamental law. It is not simply a ceremonial debate, but one that promises to have a profound impact on the future of our Republic.

The current debate is a sign of a healthy nation. Unlike people of many other countries, we are free both to discover the defects of our laws, and our government through open discussion and to correct them through our political system.

The speech's substantive object was "to discuss further the meaning of constitutional fidelity [and] ... [i]n particular ... to describe in more detail this administration's approach."

Ed Meese's November 1985 speech further developed several themes regarding the mechanics of originalism that he had raised four months earlier. One theme concerned the claimed unknowability of original meanings, à la Justice Jackson and the dreams of Pharaoh. Ed Meese had responded to that claim briefly in July 1985, but he had much more to say this time around:

> The period surrounding the creation of the Constitution is not a dark and mythical realm. The young America of the 1780's and 90's was a vibrant place, alive with pamphlets, newspapers and books chronicling and commenting upon the great issues of the day. We know how the Founding Fathers lived, and much of what they read, thought, and believed. The disputes and compromises of the Constitutional Convention were carefully recorded. The minutes of the Convention are a matter of public record. Several of the most important participants—including James Madison, the "father" of the Constitution—wrote comprehensive accounts of the convention. Others, Federalists and Anti-Federalists alike, committed their arguments for and against ratification, as well as their understandings of the Constitution, to paper, so that their ideas and conclusions could be widely circulated, read, and understood.

> In short, the Constitution is not buried in the mists of time. We know a tremendous amount of the history of its genesis. The Bicentennial is encouraging even more scholarship about its origins. We know who did what, when, and many times why. One can talk intelligently about a "founding generation."

A second theme responded to Justice Brennan's claim, which Ed Meese characterized as "misunderstanding," "[c]aricatures," and "straw men," that originalism locked itself into the events of the 18th century and could not deal with changed conditions. Not true, said Attorney General

Meese: "Our approach does not view the Constitution as some kind of super-municipal code, designed to address merely the problems of a particular era—whether those of 1787, 1789, or 1868. ... [T]he Framers were not clairvoyants—they could not foresee every issue that would be submitted for judicial review." This answers one of the key questions about the mechanics of originalism: it is not seeking *concrete answers* that would have been provided at a specific moment in time by specific people, but rather is searching for the abstract *meaning of words and phrases*. The Framers "addressed *commerce*, not simply shipping or barter," and described "'unreasonable searches and seizures,' not merely the regulation of specific of specific law enforcement practices of 1789."

Moreover, all the Framers knew that, as Judge Robert H. Bork wrote in 1990: "The world changes in which unchanging values find their application."[9] Better phrasing would be: "The world changes in which unchanging *legal texts* find their application." Meanings are fixed, but the range of circumstances to which those meanings can apply changes over time. The founding generation understood that there could arise new means of searching, new forms of communication or commerce, and even new religions like the Church of Jesus Christ of Latter-day Saints.

So what is the "original" part of originalism? Here is where Attorney General Meese started to flesh out the mechanics of originalism. "Our approach to constitutional interpretation," he declared, "begins with the document itself." Founding-era actors "chose their words carefully. They debated at great length the most minute points. ... They proposed, they substituted, they edited, and they carefully revised. Their words were studied with equal care by state ratifying conventions." Everyone at the time assumed that "the meaning of the Constitution can be known." Otherwise, the entire enterprise of constitutionalism made no sense.

The central inquiry focuses on the constitutional *text*. The "meaning" of that text that can be "known," of course, varies with context. "In places [the Constitution] is exactingly specific. Where it says the Presidents of the United States must be at least 35 years of age it means exactly that. (I have not heard of any claim that 35 means 30 or 25 or 20.)"[10] On other occasions, the Constitution is less precise, expressing "particular principles," such as "the right to be free of an unreasonable search or seizure," "religious liberty," or "the right to equal protection of the laws." But even in those less specific instances, "[t]hose who framed these principles meant something by them. And the meanings can be found." The meanings will be broader or narrower in different instances, but the meanings are there.

Thus, concluded Attorney General Meese, "[t]he approach this administration advocates is rooted in the text of the Constitution as illuminated by those who drafted, proposed, and ratified it. ...Our approach understands the significance of a written document and seeks to discern the particular and general principles it expresses. It recognizes that there may be debate at times over the application of these principles. But it does not mean these principles cannot be identified." Thus, "[w]here the language of the Constitution is specific, it must be obeyed. Where there is a demonstrable consensus among the framers and ratifiers as to a principle stated or implied by the Constitution, it should be followed. Where there is ambiguity as to the precise meaning or reach of a constitutional provision, it should be interpreted and applied in a manner so as to at least not contradict the text of the Constitution itself."

With this speech, one sees a move toward a focus on the public meaning of the text, with the intentions of particular actors serving as evidence of that meaning but not the meaning itself. We will hear more about that move later.

The speech points out that some constitutional provisions take the form of very specific rules (for example, the minimum age to be president) while others take the form of general standards whose application will vary with circumstances (such as the Fourth Amendment's ban on "unreasonable searches and seizures"). In either case, one has to read the text to see whether one is dealing with a specific rule or a general standard. And if one is dealing with a standard, that does not mean that anything goes. The standard has an original meaning, even if that meaning just sets boundaries rather than yielding a single defined result.

These are the sorts of issues about constitutional interpretation that one would expect academic scholars to wrestle with daily. But the academy had no use for the Constitution's original meaning. Ed Meese had to do the academy's job for it.

In 1985, the move from a focus on specific intentions of particular founding-era figures to a more abstract conception of public meaning was still nascent. The November 1985 speech to the Federalist Society contains the seeds for that account of originalism, but the account had not yet fully developed. That raises this rather profound question: if originalism was not fully theorized in 1985, how could the Department of Justice make it official policy, as Ed Meese announced in July 1985? Don't you need to know what you are doing before you try to do it?

At one level, the answer is yes, which is why even in 2024, after four decades of theorizing, self-described and sophisticated originalists like Clarence Thomas and Neil Gorsuch (not to mention the present authors) frequently disagree with each other about the outcomes prescribed by originalism. At another level, however, the question is something of a red herring. One does not need to have a theory or method fully operationalized in order to know that it points in the right direction. People knew enough in 1985 to get the ball rolling, even as they knew refinements were inevitable. Several important things were clear enough in 1985 to justify, and indeed mandate, the Reagan Justice Department's move toward originalism. A full defense of originalism would require a separate book (which we are contemplating), but hopefully a few thoughts will do for now.

First, while there are some important matters for which a Jurisprudence of Original Subjective Intentions and a Jurisprudence of Original Public Meanings point in different directions, there is an enormous range of cases in which all plausible originalist methods converge on the same point. Whether one looks to the objective public meaning of the words of the Fourteenth Amendment or the subjective expectations of actors in 1868, there is no straight-faced way to derive a constitutional right to abortion, as Justice Alito's extremely thorough opinion in *Dobbs v. Jackson Women's Health Organization* shows.[11] The same is true of numerous key questions of constitutional power, structure, and right. In 1985, there was a target-rich environment for which the details of originalism did not matter. Any variant of originalism would do.

Second, and perhaps more importantly, it was clear in 1985—as it is today—that originalism of some kind was (and is) the right way to argue and decide constitutional cases. Waiting for a perfected originalist theory would let the perfect be the enemy of the good—and essentially assure the triumph of the bad. Even a partially formed originalism was a huge step upward from the policymaking incoherence that was constitutional law at the time.

Originalism is the standard way to ascertain the meaning of any document or communication. It is how one understands ordinary conversation. It is how one understands law review articles criticizing originalism. It is how one understands Supreme Court opinions (for decades, the "original meaning" of *Roe v. Wade* was gospel for the academic left). It is how one would try to understand the Code of Hammurabi or the 1663 Rhode Island Charter if one wanted to read them. As originalist scholar Saikrishna Prakash has put it, originalism is a "Default Rule"[12] of communication. There are some contexts, such as reading poetry, in which that default rule might not apply, but the Constitution is obviously not a poem. It is a legal document. One would not read end-of-life instructions in a living will looking for metaphors or evolving social values.

Any alternative to originalism empowers interpreters over the text. To be sure, there are traditions of textual reading that do indeed elevate the words of interpreters above the words being interpreted. But it is noteworthy that the mostly Protestant founders, schooled in "*sola scriptura*," did not include an "interpretation clause" in the Constitution. Nothing in the Constitution designates a "supreme interpreter." The document speaks for itself.

More specifically, the text of the Constitution says that the only way in which the Constitution can be altered is by following the amendment process set out in Article V, and not by a 5–4 decision of the Supreme Court saying what five elite lawyers think is the latest embodiment of "human dignity." The text of the Constitution tells us the only way in which it can be legally changed, and it simply does not allow for constitutional changes by Supreme Court precedents or changes in public opinion. Article V would be pointless if the Constitution did not have a determinate original meaning.

Furthermore, the Constitution says in Article VI, clause 2: "This Constitution, and the Laws of the United States which shall be made in Pursuance thereof; and all Treaties made, or which shall be made, under the Authority of the United States, shall be the supreme Law of the Land; and the Judges in every State shall be bound thereby, any Thing in the Constitution or Laws of any State to the Contrary notwithstanding."

If federal law binds "the Judges in every State" then surely it binds the supreme and inferior judges of the federal government to follow the law. Again, this provision takes for granted that there is law to follow.

All of these considerations explain why originalism is the best (and only) way to ascertain the Constitution's meaning. They do not explain, however, why ascertaining the Constitution's meaning is a good thing. Today, it is commonplace to hear open calls to abandon the Constitution.[13] In 1985, the call was typically subtler, coming in the form of "living constitutionalism" that would essentially replace the actual Constitution with a new version more in accord with leftist elite opinion. The bottom line is the same in each case: a lot of people really dislike the Constitution and would much prefer something else in its place.

To some extent, that dislike is understandable. The Constitution is a document that runs on consensus. To get laws passed, one needs majorities in two separate houses of Congress elected in widely varying regions and states, plus the signature of a president elected by an electoral college process that also requires support across a broad swath of the country. Changing the Constitution through Article V requires a three-quarters supermajority of disparate states. The constitutional process is deliberately constructed to make sure that national rules on anything come only when a lot of people from different backgrounds and with different interests agree that it is a good idea. This scheme is extremely frustrating to people who think they know better than others—much less to people who think they know The Truth. Why should people who "know better" (or know The Truth) have to convince those ignorant non-believers to go along? In 1913, a Columbia professor complained that the Constitution establishes a system in which "the ignorant rule the enlightened and the vulgar rule the refined."[14] It is not surprising that some today who consider themselves enlightened and refined recoil at the prospect that they might not get their way.

James Madison responded to this phenomenon more than two centuries ago in perhaps the most important passage in the history of political science:

> But what is government itself, but the greatest of all reflections on human nature? If men were angels, no government would be necessary. If angels were to govern men, neither external nor internal

controls on government would be necessary. In framing a government which is to be administered by men over men, the great difficulty lies in this: you must first enable the government to control the governed; and in the next place oblige it to control itself.[15]

The United States Constitution is a document designed with human nature in mind. In constructing a governmental structure, there are two kinds of risks. One is that bad people will be able to use the power of government to do bad things. The other is that good people will find it too difficult to use the power of government to do good things. The Constitution to some extent errs on the side of minimizing the first risk: The requirements of consensus make it harder—far from impossible, but harder—for power to be abused. The cost of that consensus requirement is that some ideas that some people think are good, and possibly even some ideas that are objectively good, will not get implemented. Those who think that the Constitution strikes the wrong balance between these risks will not be persuaded that following the Constitution is the right way to go.

With all due respect to those latter people, the entire sweep of human history shows the wisdom of the Constitution. Hence, the third, and in the end the most basic, reason why originalism is the right way to run a country is that the United States Constitution, as amended twenty-seven times, strikes that balance between risk and reward better than any document yet created by human hands. The Constitution, and the governmental structure that it puts in place, has led Americans to be the freest, most equal, wealthiest, most technologically advanced, and happiest people in the world. We have the highest GDP per capita of any of the G-20 democracies, the best universities in the world (to which people from other countries flock), a technology sector that has placed men on the moon and discovered in six months the best vaccines in the world against the coronavirus, and far and away the strongest and most technologically sophisticated military in the world. If we fully opened our borders, millions of people would come to live in the United States from Asia, Latin America, Africa, China, Russia, and all across the world. In contrast, in 2021, only 1,800 people renounced their American citizenship out of a population of 331,893,745 people, and most of them did it to avoid paying taxes. In 2019, there were 2,094,000 people of sub-Saharan

African ancestry who had left their native lands to come to a country that the American Left often derides as being fundamentally racist.

The modern academy, in which both of us are embedded, typically speaks only of the wrongs committed in this country's history. Those wrongs, some of which were sanctioned by the original Constitution of 1788, are undeniably real—often tragically so. But the country's enormous accomplishments, including the formal amendment of the Constitution to rid it of slavery, are equally real. One of us has co-authored a casebook comparing the G-20 constitutional democracies to one another.[16] We submit to you that we could prove that the United States has a more just history and a better Constitution today than do *any* of the other seventeen G-20 nations which are constitutional democracies. The United States, because of its amended Constitution, is still the Shining City on a Hill about which President Ronald Reagan spoke so eloquently in his Farewell Address to the American people. Ed Meese fully shares the view that the United States is a Shining City on a Hill and a beacon of liberty to oppressed people everywhere, from the Russian Federation to Iran and to the Communist Chinese empire.[17]

To be sure, the people who wrote, ratified, amended, and applied the Constitution were not all good people. The founding generation was full of slave owners, misogynists, and imperialists. So is all of recorded (and surely unrecorded) human history. That is the point that the Constitution understands so well. The world is, and always will be, full of bad people—and, perhaps even more dangerously, good people who think they know more than they actually know. Any governmental structure that does not accommodate that basic fact is a blueprint for disaster.

The Constitution's merit does not depend on the personal merit of its Framers. To think so is to commit the ad hominem fallacy of attacking an arguer rather than an argument. The Constitution, once framed, does not care who framed it. It does not care whether the Framers were good people, bad people, or simply people. The real question is whether the Constitution creates a political structure that responds well to the realities of human nature. For the reasons noted above, the answer is obvious.

Originalism is the right way to ascertain the Constitution's meaning. Following the Constitution is the right way to run a government. That is all that Ed Meese needed to know in 1985, and he knew that much. His 1985 speeches do not fully define originalism, but they do mark its formal public birth. We will say more about its continuing growth in later chapters.

DEPARTMENTALISM

THE CONSTITUTION does not contain an "interpretation clause" that designates someone as the document's supreme interpreter. But isn't that the job of the Supreme Court? Didn't the Supreme Court say so in 1803 in the great case of *Marbury v. Madison*?[18]

Two of the great myths in American law are that the Constitution gives the Supreme Court a unique and superior role in constitutional interpretation and that *Marbury v. Madison* settled that matter if anyone cared to question it. Both claims are not just wrong but obviously wrong.

The Constitution never mentions the word "interpretation." It never expressly grants any actor a power of interpretation and does not expressly grant courts a power of judicial review. The only powers granted by the Constitution are legislative powers, executive powers, and judicial powers. All of those powers require those who exercise them to engage in interpretation to ascertain the scope and limits of their powers (and the powers of other actors), but those powers of interpretation are *incidental* to the exercise of those powers. And they are incidental to the exercise of *all* of those powers. Members of Congress, presidents, and judges all have exactly the same powers of interpretation, because those powers all come from the same source: the need of all governmental actors to conform their actions to the Constitution.

This position seems strange only because congresses and presidents have found it convenient to punt their interpretative responsibilities over to courts, and courts have been willing to field the punts.[19] None of that is mandated, or even permitted, by the Constitution.[20]

As for the Supreme Court: in 1803 the big question was whether courts were even *permitted* to disagree with Congress and the president when those actors got together to pass a statute and considered it constitutional. *Marbury* correctly said yes, the courts can reach their own judgment about the meaning of the Constitution as an incident to their "judicial Power" to decide "cases" or "controversies." But that simply establishes interpretative *equality* of the three branches of the federal government. It does not purport to give the courts interpretative *superiority*.[21]

Over the course of many decades, however, congresses and presidents ceded so much responsibility to the courts that it came to seem natural to equate the Constitution with what courts said about the Constitution. To a large extent that is still true today; the vast bulk of constitutional law cases do not actually involve interpretation of the Constitution; they involve interpretation of prior Supreme Court opinions. Obviously, to the extent that those court decisions deviate from the Constitution's original meaning, they form a kind of "shadow constitution" that displaces the real one.

On October 21, 1986, almost a year after his speeches announcing and developing originalism, Attorney General Meese gave a speech at Tulane University entitled "The Law of the Constitution." This speech—known colloquially as "the Tulane speech"—reinforced Attorney General Meese's call for originalism by drawing attention to "a distinction that is essential to maintaining our limited form of government. That is the necessary distinction between the Constitution and constitutional law. The two are not synonymous."

The distinction between the Constitution and constitutional law is basic but often overlooked. "The Constitution," Ed Meese explained, "is—to put it simply but, one hopes, not simplistically—the Constitution. It is a document of our most fundamental law. ... [A]s such it is, in its own words, 'the supreme Law of the Land.'" "Constitutional law," Attorney General Meese contrasted, "is that body of law which has resulted from the Supreme Court's adjudications involving disputes over constitutional provisions or doctrines. To put it a bit more simply, constitutional law is what the Supreme Court says about the Constitution in its decisions resolving the cases and controversies that come before it." In terms of volume, constitutional law dwarfs the Constitution. The court "has produced nearly 500 [now 600] volumes of reports of cases. ... This stands in marked contrast to the few, slim paragraphs that have been added to the original Constitution as amendments. So, in terms of sheer bulk, constitutional law greatly overwhelms the Constitution."

Constitutional law, Ed Meese continued, is certainly a kind of law. "It binds the parties in a case and also the executive branch for whatever enforcement is necessary." But there is a difference between being a kind of law and being "a 'supreme Law of the Land.'" Statutes enacted by Congress and signed by the president are law; the Constitution expressly says so.[22] But if those statutes—those laws—conflict with the Constitution, the statutes must give way. The Constitution is also law, and it is hierarchically superior to other forms of law such as statutes. Attorney General Meese was saying the same thing about the relationship between court decisions and the Constitution. Court decisions are a kind of law, just as statutes are a kind of law. The Constitution, however, sits at the top of the law heap, and the Constitution is not equivalent to the court decisions regarding it.

On reflection, "[t]he point should seem so obvious as not to need elaboration." Nonetheless, Attorney General Meese pointed out, "there have been those down through our history—and especially, it seems, in our own time—who have denied the distinction between the Constitution and constitutional law." That is not surprising; if people think that constitutional law better suits their preferences than does the Constitution, one might expect them to elevate the former over the latter. A good example used by Ed Meese in his speech was the 1857 decision in *Dred Scott v. Sandford*,[23] which helped precipitate the Civil War by denying Congress the ability, which it obviously possesses by virtue of Article IV's Territory Clause,[24] to ban slavery in federally owned territory. In his senatorial race against Stephen Douglas in 1858, Abraham Lincoln vigorously challenged the court's absurd misreading of the Constitution. Douglas responded that when the court decides a constitutional question, that decision becomes "the law of the land." "Lincoln," Meese noted, "disagreed," and Lincoln's view "makes most sense in a constitutional democracy like ours." The court's decision in *Dred Scott* was binding on the parties to that case, but it was not a conversation-stopping declaration of constitutional Truth. If it was, the court could never even overrule itself.

Thus, "constitutional interpretation is not the business of the Court only, but also, and properly, the business of all branches of government. ... Each of the three coordinate branches of government created and empowered by the Constitution—the executive and legislative no less than the judicial—has a duty to interpret the Constitution in the performance of its official functions."

This position, which has come to be known as "departmentalism" (because every government department, legislative, executive, or judicial, must be a constitutional interpreter), is an obvious corollary of originalism. The Constitution means what it means, not what anyone says that it means—not the president, the Congress, or the courts. The Constitution's meaning is accessible to all:

> For the same reason that the Constitution cannot be reduced to
> constitutional law, the Constitution cannot simply be reduced to
> what Congress or the President say it is either. Quite the contrary.
> The Constitution, the original document of 1787 plus its amend-
> ments, is and must be understood to be the standard against which
> all laws, policies and interpretations must be measured.

Nothing that Ed Meese said in his Tulane speech should be remotely controversial. Something like it was said by Thomas Jefferson, James Madison, Andrew Jackson, Abraham Lincoln, and Franklin Roosevelt, among others. But anyone who lived through 1986 recalls the firestorm that erupted when Ed Meese suggested that Supreme Court decisions might sometimes be wrong and that the Constitution is higher law than the court's opinions. A contemporaneous summary of the acerbic commentary from the academic and cultural left was provided in 1987 by Sanford Levinson, a brilliant left-leaning law professor and political scientist who carried no water for Ed Meese:

> Eugene C. Thomas, the president of the American Bar Association,
> asserted that Supreme Court decisions are indeed the law of the
> land and that "public officials and private citizens alike are not free
> simply to disregard" their status as law. The implication of such
> disregard is to "shake the foundations" of our system." Ira Glasser,
> executive director of the American Civil Liberties Union, de-
> scribed Meese's speech as an "invitation to lawlessness" and "a call
> to defiance and to undermining the legitimacy of abiding by deci-
> sions that you disagree with." Laurence Tribe, the Tyler Professor
> of Constitutional Law at Harvard University, said Meese's position
> "represents a grave threat to the rule of law because it proposes a
> regime in which every lawmaker and every government agency

becomes a law unto itself, and the civilizing hand of a uniform interpretation of the Constitution crumbles."

In The New York Times, Anthony Lewis accused the Attorney General of "making a calculated assault on the idea of law in this country: on the role of judges as the balance wheel in the American system." Lewis described Meese's position as "invit[ing] anarchy," and he quoted Benno Schmidt, former Dean of the Columbia University Law School and President of Yale University, who denounced Meese as "a man of power, not a man of law," who is taking the country on a "disastrous" course. The following Sunday The New York Times gave its most important Op-Ed space to an essay by Paul Brest, of the Stanford University Law School, headlined Meese, the Lawman, Calls for Anarchy.[25]

Levinson was virtually alone on the academic left in thinking the critique misguided; his backhanded endorsement of Ed Meese's defense of departmentalism was that "[j]ust as a stopped clock is right twice a day, so Attorney General Meese can be a source of insight."[26]

Of course, the left was desperate to preserve Roe v. Wade, which for half a century was proclaimed "the law of the land" so many times that the phrase was like a mantra. And perhaps the left just liked the Supreme Court's case law in general more than it liked the Constitution. In any event, Attorney General Meese's speech sparked academic discussion that continues to this day. We have both defended departmentalism at length in our scholarship. We doubt whether the issue would have been taken seriously but for Ed Meese's headline-making speech.

There is an interesting backstory to the Tulane speech. Ed Meese and Steve Calabresi only received it from the speechwriters as the two were boarding the attorney general's private jet, which would take the attorney general first to a lunch meeting with the U.S. attorney's office in Chicago and second to Tulane, Louisiana, where he would deliver the speech at dinner time. Steve Calabresi read the speech, which he had urged the speechwriters to compose, and he discovered that the original draft urged the general public, litigators, and lower court judges to disobey Roe v. Wade until the Supreme Court overruled it! Steve Calabresi could picture the banner headlines to which this would have led, such as "Attorney General Ed Meese Urges Everyone to Disobey Roe v. Wade!"

Calabresi rewrote the Tulane speech in a frenzy, while Ed Meese was visiting with the Chicago U.S. attorney's office, to eliminate any reference to *Roe v. Wade* and also to improve and tighten the argument. When Meese reboarded his private jet to fly to Louisiana, Steve Calabresi explained what he had done to the speech's text and why he had done it. Meese then asked if Calabresi thought he should even give the speech at all, and Calabresi said, "Yes, because it states such an important overlooked foundational principle—Departmentalism." But Calabresi warned Meese that the speech would generate bad press when he gave it, although it would become a key part of his legacy. Calabresi told Meese that the departmentalist argument of his Tulane speech would put him in the company of Thomas Jefferson, James Madison, Andrew Jackson, Abraham Lincoln, and Franklin D. Roosevelt, and that the speech would enter the history books with the remarks of those illustrious presidents. Meese then edited the draft as Steve Calabresi had rewritten it. The two arrived in Tulane, Meese gave the speech, and the two returned that night to Washington. A few days later, all hell broke loose about the speech in the *New York Times* and the *Washington Post*. Ken Cribb sternly admonished Steve Calabresi, saying, "We have to do a better job with these speeches in protecting Ed Meese." The speech went on to become canonical, as Calabresi had predicted it would.

FEDERALISM

FEW SUBJECTS were more important to Ronald Reagan and Ed Meese than federalism. A central theme of President Reagan's first inaugural address was that the states had created the federal government and not the other way around. In his July 1985 ABA speech on originalism, Ed Meese made the need to revitalize federalism a central part of his remarks. Just a few months later, on September 6, 1985, in a speech to the American Enterprise Institute, Attorney General Meese turned to federalism once again.

The speech was a deep primer on the value of federalism—"a vital if controversial and often misunderstood part of our public discourse." According to Attorney General Meese, the Supreme Court had failed to adequately protect the states as political entities from congressional overreach because of "a general confusion—often public as well as judicial—over precisely what political advantages federalism brings to our constitutional order. In short, we no longer seem sure why federalism matters." Thus, he said, it was important "to move away from the narrower legal issues raised by particular court cases and dwell on ... the more fundamental political issues of federalism."

The Constitution embodies federalism by enumerating the specific powers of federal institutions "to resist the tendency toward a single, centralized, and all-powerful national government." "The institutional design," he said, "was to divide sovereignty between two different levels of political entities, the nation and the states. This would avoid an unhealthy concentration of power in a single government." But while this division of authority would be part of "the basic principled matrix of American constitutional liberty," there is also "a deeper understanding—in fact, a far richer understanding" of the value of federalism that "is too often lost in our judicial shuffles and legal squabbles."

Dealing with issues at a local rather than national level, said Attorney General Meese, "can contribute to a sense of political community and hence to a kind of public spirit, that is too often ignored in our public discussions about federalism." The essence of popular government is the opportunity for people "to give full vent to their moral sentiments. Through deliberation, debate, and compromise a public consensus can be formed as to what constitutes the public good." But over a large range of cases, that consensus is more achievable at a local than at a national level. Thus, "there is something lacking in the traditional progressive liberal notion that a grand sense of community can be developed at the national level as a result of big, intrusive governmental programs. ...An essential sense of community is far more likely to develop at the local level, through state and local politics, and through voluntary private associations." The strength of the constitutional system is that it fosters "a community of communities."

Much of the speech focused specifically on abortion and *Roe v. Wade*, as the Department of Justice had recently filed a brief asking the Supreme Court to overrule the decision. But the principle emphasized in Meese's speech—that community is often best achieved at a local rather than national level—is generalizable, and it resonates even more soundly today, in our highly polarized times. When people sharply disagree on matters such as abortion, capital punishment, and the very nature of justice, nationalizing those issues in a winner-take-all fashion is a blueprint for conflict. Federalism, as Ed Meese explained, "was designed to allow us to be self-governing in the truest, the deepest sense."

Ed Meese's and Ronald Reagan's determination to resuscitate federalism, through the idea that the federal government is one of limited and enumerated powers, partially explains why they chose William Rehnquist rather than Robert Bork or Antonin Scalia to be chief justice of the United States in 1986 when Warren Burger retired. Judges Bork and Scalia thought that the constitutionality of the New Deal federalism rulings that expanded federal power essentially without limit was settled by precedent, and as law professors neither seriously explored federalism as a scholarly interest. Chief Justice Rehnquist, however, cared passionately about federalism, and he could persuade Sandra Day O'Connor, his law school friend, and later Justice Anthony M. Kennedy to reinvigorate constitutional federalism. In 1995, a decade after Attorney General Meese's ABA speech, Justice Rehnquist wrote the opinion for the Court in *United States v. Lopez*,[27] which for the first time in half a century found limits on the constitutionally enumerated powers of Congress. On the heels of another decision limiting Congress's ability to order state legislatures to act,[28] this spawned a revival of constitutional federalism that is still in its early stages today and was utterly unthinkable before 1985.[29]

As with many of the ideas that came out of the Meese DOJ, it would require a separate book even to scratch the surface of a doctrinal or normative account of federalism. But Steve Calabresi has developed the case for federalism at length,[30] and so a few words on the subject are appropriate.

The United States is the world's 3rd most populous and 4th largest country. There are many subcultures of a regional sort in the United States, which, as Meese's speech emphasized, makes at least some decentralization of power essential. The trick is to figure out which powers need to be nationalized and which are best left to people or other levels of government. Those decisions need to be made with a presumption—a rebuttable presumption, but a presumption nonetheless—against centralizing power. There are at least four good arguments for leaving decision-making power presumptively at the state level.

First, tastes, cultures, and geographical conditions differ among the fifty states, which means that oftentimes deciding things with one national rule makes everyone unhappy. When Jimmy Carter was president, Congress imposed a national speed limit of 55 miles per hour by denying federal highway funds to any state that had a higher speed limit. Reagan got the law modified in 1987 to allow speeds on rural highways to reach 65 miles per hour, and after some additional piecemeal modifications, the law was fully repealed in 1995, leaving setting speed limits up to the states. Montana, which is a very low population density state, for a time opted for no speed limit at all (it now caps at 80 miles per hour), while New Jersey, which is the highest population density state, opted for a speed limit of 65 miles per hour. More people were happy as a result of leaving this matter up to the states than would have been the case had the national speed limit of 55 miles per hour been retained. Driving from Los Angeles to Helena is not the same as driving from Boston to New York City.

A second argument for federalism is that the states can compete with one another in offering different bundles of public goods to lure citizens and businesses in other states to move. Just as competition in the free market generates optimal outcomes, so too does competition among states as to the bundle of public goods they provide to their citizens lead to optimal outcomes. State governments in California and Florida offer very different packages of taxes and services. It is easier for people to change states than to change countries.

A third argument for presumptive state power is that when the states are in competition with one another, they will have an incentive to experiment, and some of these experiments will prove to be successful and will become national models. States right now have very different primary school curriculums. Self-described experts may think they know which one is definitively "best," but surely the best way to find out is to try out various options and see what results actually occur. If teaching that math is racist really leads to better engineers, we should be able to see those results if states such as California try it.

Fourth, and finally, concentrating some power in the states allows them to act as a check on national power. This is especially so since the party in power in the White House tends to lose midterm elections and state elections held in odd-numbered years. This means that the party in power in the White House loses power in the thirty-nine of the fifty states that elect their governors and state legislatures in the midterm election or in odd-numbered-year elections. As a result, the president usually is counterbalanced by a situation in which a majority of the state governors are from the opposing political party. This guards against presidential dictatorship.[31]

There are four counterbalancing situations in which national power is desirable. First, there are some major activities, like running NASA's space program or maintaining a nuclear arsenal, for which there are economies of scale, which make it more sensible to centralize the activity. Second, the states may face collective action problems in coming together to enact needed rules, such as those banning interstate crimes. The Constitution anticipated this by granting Congress power over "Commerce … among the several States." Third, the states may, through their policies, generate negative external effects on other states which only a national rule can solve. The classic example is air and water pollution, which may originate in one state and greatly burden another state into which the polluted air or water may flow. Fourth, and finally, for reasons predicted by James Madison in *The Federalist* more than two centuries ago, the federal government might be more protective of the rights of small, discrete. and insular minorities than are the states.

All of these ideas were implicit in Ed Meese's speech back in 1985. While federalism today hardly reflects the constitutional model, it is closer than it was four decades ago. This is yet another development that surely would not have happened without the conversation started by Ed Meese.

As a sign of how vital it was to start that conversation, Meese, in a speech that we are about to describe on another subject, related how just before his speech on federalism "a member of the media called to ask what the nature of my remarks would be. 'Federalism,' he was told. 'Federalism? What's that?' he replied."

Separation of Powers

ED MEESE cared just as passionately about the separation of powers as he did about federalism, as shown in an address that he gave at the University of Dallas on February 27, 1986.

The speech was about much more than separation of powers. A large portion of it reiterated the Department of Justice's commitment to originalism. Much of it summarized the state of constitutional law doctrine regarding separation of powers circa 1986. At that time, there were two recent Supreme Court decisions finding that congressional statutes violated the constitutional separation of powers: a 1976 decision regarding the appointment of members of the Federal Election Commission[32] and a 1983 case invalidating "legislative vetoes," in which Congress tries to enact laws without using the procedures specified in Article I.[33] That is two more decisions than one could have found in the previous four decades. From 1936 to 1976, there were exactly *zero* congressional statutes found to violate the constitutional separation of powers. The case law was so out of sorts with the Constitution that Congress thought (and it won in the court of appeals before the Supreme Court said otherwise) that it could appoint Federal Election Commission officers even in the face of a constitutional provision saying that all federal officers must be appointed by the president with the advice and consent of the Senate or, in the case of lesser officers, by the president, executive department heads, or federal courts on their own. A congressional power to appoint those officers, or to have both houses of Congress approve their appointments (the statute did that as well) is as obviously unconstitutional as a twenty-five-year-old president or eight senators from Wyoming. The same is true of Congress trying to make laws without going through the bicameralism (both houses of Congress approving) and presentment (giving the president a chance to veto) procedures required by the Constitution for lawmaking. But in the post–New Deal era, Congress thought, with considerable reason, that it had been given a free hand to remake the constitutional structure as it pleased. The two decisions in 1976 and 1983 drew lines at some wildly extreme departures from the constitutional text, but in 1986 it was not clear how far those lines might extend.

Ed Meese urged the court to reconsider other aspects of the separation of powers, including constitutional problems with insulating government agencies from control by the president. Case law dating back to the 1930s allows Congress to create what amounts to autonomous bureaucrats with tenure—something nowhere contemplated by the

Constitution. Meese specifically called for the overruling of *Humphrey's Executor*,[34] a 1935 case that allowed Congress to shield agency officials from presidential removal, and an end to the so-called headless fourth branch of government with its agencies independent of presidential powers of command and control. Modern law has begun the reconsideration suggested by Meese, and sought by the Department of Justice, nearly forty years ago, and cases concerning control of the administrative state continue to reach a Supreme Court that is now markedly more interested in the Constitution's original meaning than was true in early 1986, when the court did not even have a lone Justice Scalia to raise the alarm bells.

But the real substance of Ed Meese's speech on separation of powers was its profound observations on the importance and value of the Constitution's structural provisions. As he did with originalism, departmentalism, and federalism, Ed Meese called for a return to first principles:

> Returning to fundamentals is not always easy. Nor is it always accepted as appropriate. You see, quite often fundamental constitutional principles prove to be stumbling blocks to the many groups always pushing for different policies and programs. These fundamental principles frequently rub lawyers the wrong way, too. For a due regard for the Constitution tends to get in the way of those who seek to transform that document by interpretation, those who seek, as Jefferson said, to make it a blank paper through construction. But as I said, the Constitution is and must be understood to be more than a litigator's brief or a judge's decision. Our substantive fundamental constitutional values have a shape and content that transcend the crucible of litigation.

First principles of constitutionalism, of course, means originalism: "As we begin to celebrate our Constitution and the durable political order it spawned, we need to return to the founding period with an enthusiasm for learning. We need to look upon the Founders as more than historical curiosities and to consider their theories of politics as more than intellectual artifacts of a long-gone age. We need to return to that time, read what they wrote, and recall what they said with a fresh interest."

Anticipating the objection that the founders were ignorant primitives whose views are unworthy of attention, Attorney General Meese observed that "we first have to free ourselves of the all-too-common notion that our generation is somehow more enlightened or more theoretically sophisticated than theirs." There are obvious respects in which the current generation knows much more than did people two centuries ago—more about science, technology, and (alas) warfare. But none of those disciplines inform the constitutional structure. That structure reflects a view of human nature that is timeless. Ed Meese spoke of those timeless truths:

> Our technological accomplishments over the past two hundred
> years have been awesome. But the fact is political life remains
> much the same. For all our technological advances, and all our
> sophisticated scientific analyses, the world is still plagued by wars,
> by tyranny, by ignorance, and by poverty. And, still, freedom is
> too often the exception rather than the rule throughout much of
> the world. Yet we, we Americans, have endured in both comfort
> and freedom. Our system has proved different. Our Constitution
> remains, as Abraham Lincoln once said, the last best hope of earth.
> Often imitated, never completely equaled, our Constitution is
> unique. By returning to our roots, by engaging in a dialogue with
> the best minds of that generation, we can learn why we have suc-
> ceeded—and, I submit, how we may most successfully perpetuate
> our political institutions.

"[W]e find ourselves ... obligated," Meese continued, "... to recover the theoretical underpinnings of our Constitution's provisions for separation of powers," which requires us "to open ourselves to the Founders' teachings. For in this area of constitutional concern as in so many others, our political problems are not in principle different from the ones the Founders faced. Though the problems may come to us in new and novel guises, at bottom they are pretty much the same. And the Founders' thinking can serve us well as a theoretical beacon as we pass through churning political waters similar to those they successfully navigated so long ago."

There were things the founders did not know, and some things about which they were tragically wrong, but they understood the science of government better than do the denizens of modern university political science departments. They constructed "a science of politics that sought to erect hurdles to the various passions and interests that are found in human nature." They constructed an "institutional scheme" including "such devices as representation, bicameralism, independent courts of law, and the [quoting Alexander Hamilton] 'regular distribution of powers into distinct departments.'"

This "idea of separation of powers along with the idea of federalism constituted for the Framers the principled matrix of American constitutionalism." How do these structures secure liberty? We see no alternative to quoting Ed Meese at greater length than our editors will probably like:

What this means, in the simplest possible terms, is that the Constitution does not make our liberties dependent upon the good will or the benevolence of those who wield power. The Constitution's Framers did not mistakenly assume that this nation was to be governed by that "philosophical race of kings wished for by Plato." No, they knew, as Hamilton said in *The Federalist* No. 6, that they were "yet remote from the happy empire of perfect wisdom and perfect virtue." Sound institutions were thus meant to offset the defects of human reason and virtue.

Recognizing that human nature was marred by man's "fallible" reason and the influence upon that reason by his passions and his interests, the Framers sought to construct institutions that would "refine and enlarge" public opinion. These institutional contrivances—representation, a bicameral legislature, an independent judiciary, and an energetic executive—would serve (in Madison's words) as "successive filtrations" through which popular opinion would be forced to pass before being translated into public law and policy. The purpose was not to thwart popular will but only to slow down popular passions and give the people "time and opportunity for more cool and sedate reflection."

By hedging against this natural tendency of popular institutions "to yield to the impulse of sudden and violent passions, and to be seduced by factious leaders into intemperate and pernicious resolutions," the Constitution seeks to check popular passions and elevate public reason. As Madison put it, "it is the reason of the public alone that ought to controul and regulate the government.

The passions ought to be controuled and regulated by the government."...

... [T]he security and happiness and liberty of the people depends upon the entire constitutional design, not just a single part of it. ... The substantive rights sought by the Constitution's Framers were understood to be best secured through orderly and nonarbitrary procedures that would be clearly defined by the entire constitutional system. ...

This emphasis on "sound procedure...[as] a necessary means to achieving substantive justice" does not find universal assent. As Meese noted, some will say that "[t]he true substance of American justice... depends less upon adherence to procedure than upon the evolutionary moral vision of public officials. The ends, they argue, justify the means—any means—necessary to achieve them." "This view," he said, "we must simply reject." We agree, and we end with Attorney General Meese's explanation:

The greatest strength of the American Constitution is its design to replace the rule of men by the rule of law. The alleged benevolence of public officials in any branch is not to be trusted as the basis for our constitutional safety and political progress. This goes for "conservatives" and "liberals" alike. The imposition of a conservative ideology through a disregard for the institutional arrangements of the Constitution is no more politically palatable or constitutionally legitimate than the imposition of a liberal ideology... .

... [T]rue constitutional freedom presupposes a popular commitment to the law and a respect for legal institutions. Such a public attachment is the "strongest bulwark" a government such as ours has against the erosion of public order and private rights. That is what a young Abraham Lincoln meant when he argued in 1838 that "reverence for the laws" must "become the *political religion* of the nation." He knew the danger to liberty posed by false prophets who would, by their words and deeds, seek to supplant the Constitution and the laws of the nation in their ambitious quest to refound the republic in their own image. That is what keeps our Constitution and this republic what it has been for nearly two hundred years: "the last best hope of earth" to the cause of freedom.

CHAPTER EIGHT

DOJ UNIVERSITY SCHOOL OF LAW: ACADEMIC CONFERENCES AND THE OFFICE OF LEGAL POLICY MONOGRAPH SERIES

I N AN INTERVIEW with a political scientist, one of us described the Department of Justice under Attorney General Ed Meese as "the academy in exile."[1] Much of this book explains why.

The Meese Department of Justice was not simply the government's litigating and legal policymaking office. It was also a hotbed of ideas, dialogue, contest, discussion, debate, and even formal academic conferences. We have been in the legal academy for nearly a combined seventy years, and the level and consistency of intellectualism that we experienced in the mid-1980s remains unmatched in our lifetimes. The Meese Department of Justice incubated thoughts regarding originalism, separation of powers, federalism, religious liberty, criminal law theory, and a host of other topics that continue to drive legal discourse and practice decades later. To paraphrase the late Judge Bork, it was an intellectual feast.

That intellectual atmosphere was a function of the personnel, many of whom we have already discussed in this book. The Meese Department of Justice contained some of the most brilliant and interesting legal minds of the past several generations—people like law professors and then professors-to-be John Harrison, Mike Rappaport, John McGinnis, and Charles Fried (in addition to the two of us); future jurists like Sam Alito, Stephen Markman, and Carolyn Kuhl; top-notch advocates like Chuck Cooper, Richard Willard, Mike Carvin, and Steve Matthews; and even world-class political scientists like Gary McDowell. Importantly, these people all shared a commitment to dialogue, open exploration of ideas, discussion, and disagreement, even on fundamental issues like abortion. Dialogue took place in offices, over coffee or tea, and even at home after work. This meant that some of the most important developments in legal theory during that time came through casual conversations rather than formal legal structures or recorded documents. The "faculty lounge" in the Meese Justice Department was a better forum for serious discussion than any law school faculty lounge that we have encountered as academics. Political scientist Paul Baumgardner put it well in an important article in 2019: "Meese designed a professional environment that mirrored the legal academy in meaningful ways."[2]

None of this was an accident. As we detailed in chapter 6, the Department of Justice was assembled by Ed Meese and his right arm Ken Cribb with the express purpose of promoting intellectualism over traditional staffing criteria like age, experience, or demonstrated party loyalty. Former law professor Meese set the tone, and Cribb, the consummate intellectual, orchestrated the construction of the most productive surrogate law faculty the country has ever seen.

This chapter explains a few of the formal manifestations of this overt intellectual focus of Ed Meese's DOJ. But nothing can fully convey the day-to-day development and discussion of ideas or the sense of excitement, engagement, collegiality, and mutual respect that permeated the Justice Department in those heady days.

While the driving force behind the DOJ University School of Law (as we sometimes call it) was unquestionably Ken Cribb, the counsellor to the attorney general and the "school's" unofficial "dean," the formal programming in Meese's Justice Department ran through the Office of Legal Policy (OLP). The OLP is a little-known unit, dating only from 1981 when it was created under William French Smith, with the stated mission "to develop and implement the [Justice] Department's significant policy initiatives, handle special projects that implicate the interests of multiple Department components, coordinate with other interested Department components and other Executive Branch agencies, and serve as the primary policy advisor to the Attorney General and the Deputy Attorney General." If that sounds vague, it is because it is vague. The OLP has little formal authority. We doubt whether anyone can name more than two or three people who have ever headed the office. (We can't.) In the Meese Justice Department, however, the office was indispensable.

The head of the office was Assistant Attorney General Stephen Markman, who had previously been a top aide to Utah senator Orrin Hatch and who went on to become a long-serving, and highly influential, chief justice of the Supreme Court of Michigan. Steve is a brilliant, unassuming lawyer who has a terrific sense of humor and is a great public speaker. He served as the first president of the Washington, D.C., Lawyers Chapter of the Federalist Society while he worked for Ed Meese. Markman's equally brilliant deputy, Steve Matthews, led the judicial selection effort for the Meese Justice Department, but Markman's shop also employed a team of young Federalist Society lawyers, which included Betsy Dorminey, the wife of Blair Dorminey (who was a chief Meese speechwriter). As a result, OLP worked, together with Terry Eastland and Gary McDowell at DOJ's Office of Public Affairs, to promote an academic-style atmosphere.

One of the key topics of discussion, of course, was constitutionalism. Once Ed Meese declared that originalism was the official policy of the Department of Justice, it fell to OLP to help flesh out what that meant concretely for litigation strategy, enforcement priorities, legislative initiatives, and clear thinking. OLP did many other things during that time as well, some of which we will touch upon shortly, but our first focus is the development of constitutional theory.

If the Department of Justice was a "real" law school, one would expect its "faculty" to produce cutting-edge publications and hold academic conferences. The Meese DOJ, through the OLP, delivered on both counts. It hosted three academic conferences devoted to federalism, separation of powers, and economic liberties. In addition, OLP, working together with other lawyers in the DOJ, produced a series of monographs that were essentially law review articles or university press books. These monographs are an extraordinary public record of Ed Meese's desire to have his Justice Department win the constitutional law war of ideas. Taken together, the monographs and conferences illustrate the extent to which the Meese DOJ functioned in some ways as a national law school.

The result is that almost everything we know today as constitutional originalism traces back to the Meese Department of Justice.

Academic Conferences

THE DOJ HELD three major academic conferences during Ed Meese's tenure as attorney general: one on federalism, one on the separation of powers, and one on "the Constitution, Economic Liberties, and the Extended Commercial Republic." The first two topics are unsurprising for a Republican attorney general, but the idea of holding a Department of Justice conference on economic liberties was a marked break from Republican constitutional orthodoxy during the half century from the New Deal constitutional revolution of 1937 to the holding of this conference in 1986.

Although economic freedom is obviously a central theme of the Constitution, the Supreme Court in the 1930s and thereafter effectively ceded control of economic life to governments—to the federal Congress through expansive interpretations of the power to regulate "Commerce...among the several States," to administrative agencies through an abandonment of constitutional limits on Congress's ability to subdelegate its expansive power to the executive, to state legislatures through effective elimination of the constitutional prohibition on state laws "impairing the Obligation of Contracts," and to all government bodies by making it difficult to challenge government action as a taking of "private property...for public use, without just compensation." Conservative theorists more concerned about "judicial activism" than about correctly interpreting and applying the Constitution generally applauded these developments; criticism of judicial decisions expanding "rights" near and dear to the left typically went hand in hand with encomia for the New Deal decisions expanding government power over so-called economic matters. A famous Supreme Court footnote from 1938[3] setting out this duality of rights (with economic rights at the bottom) became the mantra for left and right alike to give government at all levels a free hand to, as a 1976 Supreme Court decision put it, "adjust the burdens and benefits of economic life."[4]

Ed Meese, as a constitutionalist and originalist, was willing to challenge this bipartisan orthodoxy. His former colleague at the University of San Diego Law School, Bernard Siegan, wrote extensively about economic liberty until his death in 2006,[5] including an iconoclastic work published in 1980 called *Economic Liberties and the Constitution*, which was a full-throated defense of "judicial activism," grounded in a commitment to original meaning,[6] in enforcing protections actually found in the Constitution. In his welcoming remarks to the conference, Meese described Professor Siegan as someone "whom I revere as a former University of San Diego Law School colleague and to whom many of us owe a great deal for stimulating interest in this subject … [by chronicling] the dangerous impingement of the modern regulatory state upon economic liberty." Attorney General Meese so admired Professor Siegan that he persuaded President Reagan to nominate him to the U.S. Court of Appeals for the Ninth Circuit in 1987. Regrettably, the Senate did not confirm this nomination.

Ed Meese's principal theme in his opening remarks was (paraphrasing John Adams) "that the moment the idea is admitted into society that property is not as sacred as the laws of God, anarchy and tyranny commence." In 1986, "under what might be called the levelling pressures of contemporary liberalism, the legacy of liberty in regard to property has been somewhat dimmed in the public mind." This was not just a problem of policy; it was a problem of constitutionalism. "We must recognize," he continued, "that certain economic rights do exist and are central to the American constitutional order. They are well supported in both the text and history of the Constitution, and they deserve full and fair consideration."

To the inevitable cry of "judicial activism," Attorney General Meese countered that "judicial deletion of economic rights from the Constitution is a species of activism every bit as deplorable as the unwarranted manufacture of new, so-called civil rights." He noted that the conference attendees surely were not "fans of unfettered and arrogant judicial power." But neither should they endorse "raw, unbridled majoritarianism. Both excesses are equally to be feared, for either one, when allowed to go un-reined, will lead to the end of the rule of law and the loss of liberty."

The substantive content of the conference addressed the Takings Clause, the Contracts Clause, and the Commerce Clause. A highlight was a presentation by Richard Epstein, who in 1985 had written a book calling for a broad application of the Constitution's Takings Clause that would treat a large number of regulatory actions as takings requiring just compensation to persons whose property values were adversely affected by government action.[7] Professor Epstein, one of the smartest human beings ever to walk the planet, devoted his talk at the conference instead to Congress's power to regulate interstate commerce, which post-1937 case law had interpreted as giving Congress essentially unlimited power. (From 1937 to 1995, a period of explosive growth in both the kind and quantity of federal economic regulation, not a single congressional law controlling private conduct was found by the Supreme Court to exceed Congress's constitutionally enumerated powers.) Professor Epstein did not begin his extraordinary academic career as an advocate of originalism, but his talk at the Meese conference turned into the first major law review article in decades to call for a return to the original meaning of the Constitution's Commerce Clause.[8]

The conference proceedings were not published, but nearly two years later, on March 16, 1988, the OLP produced a lengthy monograph on "Economic Liberties Protected by the Constitution." The report explored many of the themes addressed at the 1986 conference, along with several others, such as the Constitution's technical rules on taxation and bankruptcy. As Meese said in his introductory comments to the report, the 1986 conference "served as a catalyst for increased discussion of these issues both within the Department and outside it." The report, he noted, "examines both the original meaning of constitutional provisions which address economic freedoms and current scholarly literature on the topic," "does not purport to establish ultimate conclusions on the issues presented," "will generate considerable thought on a topic of great national importance, and will be of interest to anyone concerned about a provocative and informative examination of the issues." In other words, it conformed to the ideal of academic scholarship.

This monograph could easily have been a law review article or a university press book. We would need a book of our own to analyze its conclusions and to explore how case law since 1988 has to some extent evolved in the direction of the report's conclusions, which urged more vigorous enforcement of the express constitutional rules against state laws impairing the obligation of contract and government action that takes private property without just compensation. Our purpose here, however, is simply to highlight the academic character of the Meese DOJ, and for that purpose one paragraph from the report's Executive Summary describing its aims is enough:

> This Report examines the original meaning and surveys the case
> law development of those constitutional provisions that have been

invoked in defense of economic liberties, evaluates scholarly analyses of economic liberties issues, and proposes possible standards that might be applied in analyzing two important constitutional provisions that protect economic liberties: the just compensation clause and the contract clause. The analysis set forth herein is merely tentative. The standards developed in this Report reflect our best assessment of the economic liberty clauses' original meaning; we do not attempt to achieve "desirable public policy results" at any cost. Furthermore, we take no position on the desirability from a public policy standpoint of the results we derive. This Report should be read with the knowledge that principled interpretivists differ (and may well continue to differ) as to the scope of constitutional protection afforded individual economic liberties. Principled analysis of the Constitution's "economic liberties" provisions generates no easy answers. Further discussion and debate is necessary, however.[9]

Seven years after the report and nearly a decade after the conference, in 1995, the Supreme Court for the first time in more than half a century found that a congressional law regulating private conduct—in this case forbidding possession of a gun in a school zone—exceeded Congress's constitutional power, because holding a gun is not plausibly "Commerce … among the several States." Subsequent cases over the past three decades have very modestly extended that decision, and nothing has seriously undercut it. The Takings Clause is enforced with slightly more vigor in 2024 than in 1986,[10] though the Supreme Court has yet to revive the Contracts Clause against state governments.

The most important event at the Meese Justice Department's economics liberties conference in the summer of 1986, however, did not directly involve the conference's topic. It was perhaps the single most important moment in the history of originalism subsequent to Ed Meese's 1985 ABA speech.

The keynote address at the conference was delivered by then judge Antonin Scalia on June 14, 1986. Judge Scalia may have seemed to some a strange person to keynote a conference on economic liberties. In October 1984, Judge Scalia had debated Richard Epstein at a Cato Institute program on "Economic Liberties and the Judiciary," with Judge Scalia taking the "judicial restraint" position against Professor Epstein's advocacy of aggressive judicial protection of economic freedom.[11] Moreover, Judge Scalia gave this keynote lunch speech knowing he was going to be interviewed by President Ronald Reagan on Monday, June 16, 1986, for possible appointment to the Supreme Court. Scalia did not know that a vacancy was about to open up on the Supreme Court, because Chief Justice Warren Burger had secretly told President Reagan nine months in advance that he would retire at the end of June 1986. The secret that Chief Justice Burger was going to retire stayed a secret because only five people knew about it: President Reagan, White House chief of staff Donald Regan, Attorney General Meese, Ken Cribb, and Brad Reynolds, and none of them leaked. The knowledge on the part of Meese, Cribb, and Reynolds added to the suspense in the room for these three people—all of whom did know about the pending vacancy. Scalia's speech was in some ways an audition for a Supreme Court appointment. He could not have performed better had he known what was at stake. It is the most important speech on originalism ever given that was not delivered by Ed Meese. We both consider ourselves privileged to have seen it.

Judge Scalia, unsurprisingly to those who knew him, opened by saying that as a professor he liked "'teaching against the class'—that is, taking positions that the students were almost certain to disagree with, in order to generate some discussion, if not productive thought." He did the same with public talks: "It is neither any fun nor any use preaching to the choir." In this case, he cracked, "I was initially at a loss to think of a subject that would be sufficiently obnoxious." Then, he said, "[a]s I was musing in my chambers…, the room was filled with the sound of a voice—loud, though it was in a whisper—which seemed to be coming from the picture of Mount Sinai that we have in the D.C. Circuit's conference room (I always wondered what it was doing there, by the way). It said: CRITICIZE THE DOCTRINE OF ORIGINAL INTENT." And the game was on.

Judge Scalia was already famous in 1986 for his critique of the use of "legislative history"—which primarily consists of reports of congressional committees prepared by staff members—in interpreting statutes. The statutes enacted by Congress, Scalia maintained, meant what they said, not what any particular members of Congress, much less their staffers, thought they said or wanted them to say. Statutory meaning was a public affair, not a private one.[12] When he gave speeches on that subject, he noted, he would often get questions that "go something like this: 'From what you say, Judge Scalia, I presume you disagree with Attorney General Meese concerning original intent as the correct criterion for interpreting the Constitution.'" After all, evidence of original intentions, such as writings in 18th-century newspapers or the records of the Constitutional Convention, is essentially "legislative history" for the Constitution. Isn't sauce for the goose also good for the gander?

Judge Scalia said yes: "The burden of my brief remarks today is that it seems to me that [participants in the debate about original intent] ... should mean not 'original intent of the Framers' but 'original intent of the Constitution.'" This might be the most important sentence in the history of originalism. Judge Scalia was saying that the Constitution's meaning, like the meaning of statutes, is a public rather than private matter. "What was the most plausible meaning of the words of the Constitution to the society that adopted it—regardless of what the Framers might secretly have intended?" Subjective intentions of particular Framers might be "strong indications of what the most knowledgeable people of the time understood the words to mean," but they are simply one piece of evidence for the ultimate inquiry into the Constitution's objective meaning. Moreover, "[e]ven if you believe in original intent in the literal sense, you must end up believing in original meaning, because it is perfectly clear that the original intent was that the Constitution would be interpreted according to its original meaning."[13] After all, James Madison, the father of the Constitution, deliberately kept his notes on the proceedings at the Philadelphia Constitutional Convention secret until they were published after Madison's death in 1836. Madison believed, and the other Framers agreed with him, that the Constitution should be construed to have the original public meaning it had to the state ratifying conventions, which made the Constitution the supreme law of the land. Thus, said Scalia, "'original intent' would more accurately be expressed [as] 'original meaning.'" Hence, "I suppose I ought to campaign to change the label from the Doctrine of Original Intent to the Doctrine of Original Meaning. As I often tell my law clerks, terminology is destiny."

Judge Scalia had no way to know this, but precisely the issue he raised had been roiling inside the DOJ for a year beforehand. Looking back in

2018 on Meese's ABA speech, Terry Eastland recalls presenting to the attorney general the original draft of the speech focusing on a Jurisprudence of Original Intention. "[Gary] McDowell had come up with the phrase, and Meese was ready to use it."[14] But, noted Eastland, "[w]ithin the department, there was almost immediate disagreement about original intention. According to some, not original intention but original meaning was the jurisprudence needed; it was the original meaning of the words at issue in a case that is the law and not the intentions of those who wrote them."[15] Ed Meese himself "was not dogmatic" about original meaning versus original intent; "[i]n his speeches, he used both terms."[16] Eastland's account is dead-on accurate—as we can attest, being two of the people arguing internally for a Jurisprudence of Original Meaning.

Immediately after Judge Scalia had finished his luncheon speech, Ken Cribb, who was counsellor to the attorney general, wrote the word "stipulated" on a piece of paper and taped it to the lectern from which Judge Scalia had delivered his remarks. From that day forward, Attorney General Meese always argued for a Jurisprudence of Original Public Meaning instead of original intent. For example, the November 1986 report of the Domestic Policy Council's Federalism Working Group, discussed in chapter 4, said that originalism "does not require that one know precisely how the Framers of the Constitution would have decided particular cases. As Justice Antonin Scalia put it, the focus is on discovering the 'original meaning' of the language found in the Constitution, not the original subjective intent of specific historical figures. See Address to Attorney General's Conference on Economic Liberties (June 1986)."[17] Scalia's speech marked the official transition from a Jurisprudence of Original Intention to a Jurisprudence of Original Meaning.

This episode reveals some important things about both Ed Meese and Antonin Scalia. Meese showed himself, as Terry Eastland noted, to be open to changing his mind, or informing his remarks, as a result of academic and intellectual criticism. Not everyone is as humble and willing to concede prior errors as is Ed Meese. Meese's willingness to respond to constructive criticism is a huge and unusual virtue. He could, after all, have decided not to support Scalia for the Supreme Court vacancy that was then pending, but he never even considered doing that.

The episode is also revealing about Antonin Scalia. Scalia was willing to risk his chance at a Supreme Court appointment in the interest of persuading his allies of some academic truths. This was a gutsy thing to do. It also responded to the most powerful liberal objections to originalism, which focused on (genuine) problems with using history, difficulties making sense of the "intentions" of collective bodies, and the framing generation's own focus on objective rather than subjective meaning. Scalia recast, and perhaps rescued, the whole originalist project with his speech.

In addition, Scalia distanced originalism from the limitations, and sometimes prejudices, of past actors, such as the many advocates of the Fourteenth Amendment in 1868 who did not subjectively intend to allow racial intermarriage or integrated public schools. Raoul Berger, a strict intentionalist, thought these 19th-century views decisive about the Fourteenth Amendment's meaning. But if one looks to text and original public meaning rather than subjective expectations or intentions, the results in cases like *Brown v. Board of Education*[18] and *Loving v. Virginia*[19] are obviously correct.[20] Virtually all subsequent originalist scholarship by the likes of Judge Robert H. Bork, Professor Randy Barnett, Professor Steven G. Calabresi, Professor Michael McConnell, Professor John Harrison, Professor Gary Lawson, Professor John McGinnis, Professor Michael Rappaport, Professor Larry Solum, Professor Akhil Reed Amar, Professor Jack Balkin, and many others has looked at the original public meaning of words and not at the intentions of those who wrote them.

Finally, Judge Scalia's extraordinary pre-nomination speech shows how much like a law school the Meese DOJ truly was. There were wonderful intellectual constitutional and policy debates, and the outcomes of those debates guided Ed Meese's hands as he exercised the high powers of his office as attorney general.

In early 1987, the triumph within the DOJ of a Jurisprudence of Original Meaning was formalized by issuance of a nearly 200-page (with appendices[21]) OLP document entitled *Original Meaning Jurisprudence: A Sourcebook*. If the title was not enough of a giveaway, Ed Meese's brief introduction talked about the debate between "those who believe that the Constitution must be interpreted in accordance with the original meaning of its terms, and…those who see the Constitution as a document whose meaning changes over time to accommodate the shifting values of each succeeding generation."[22] The OLP *Sourcebook* identified the relevant inquiry as "to construe the objective meaning of words as understood by those who adopted them."[23] It systematically addressed every extant objection to originalism, grounding answers in the premise that "[o]ur fundamental law is the text of the Constitution as ratified, not the subjective intent or purpose of any individual or group in adopting the provision at issue."[24] What to do with a multiplicity of founding-era intentions? "[T]his attack on interpretivism again confuses subjective intent with original meaning. All historical evidence of meaning is relevant, but no source is always controlling. ... [W]e should apply a constitutional provision according to the plain and natural import of its terms as understood by the ratifying society as a whole."[25] How to attach meaning to a jointly produced document? "In everyday discourse, people frequently communicate collective thoughts, consensus opinions, and common understandings through a single statement or group of statements. The notion of a collective understanding is also a common and legitimate legal concept used to describe the meaning of treaties, statutes, contracts, and other jointly drafted documents."[26] Originalism locks us into the specific practices of the past? "These criticisms rest on a fundamental confusion of the Constitution's *meaning*—which is fixed and permanent—with its *application* to modern issues."[27] We could go on.

The theory of originalism has progressed in many important ways over the past four decades. But the OLP in 1987, building out the foundation laid by Ed Meese, Antonin Scalia, Robert H. Bork, and the active minds collaborating in the Department of Justice, produced a work that, had it been written in narrative rather than Q&A form, could have been a top-flight law review article. Except that no top-flight law review would likely have published it.

THE OFFICE OF LEGAL POLICY MONOGRAPHS AND WORKING PAPERS

THE ORIGINALISM *Sourcebook* was hardly the only significant scholarly work to emerge from OLP. Far from it. The Meese OLP issued a blizzard of monographs and working papers, many of which were essentially short academic press books or long law review articles. They were, at a minimum, of the same quality as the law review articles published in top-ten law school law reviews (though that is perhaps damning with faint praise, given the contents of those journals). As such, they reveal the extent to which the civil side of the Meese DOJ functioned as a law school. A few of those works deserve special mention.

Report to the Attorney General on Wrong Turns on the Road to Judicial Activism: The Ninth Amendment and the Privileges or Immunities Clause, September 25, 1987

IF ONE SITS DOWN to read the Constitution straight through, it gets boring very quickly. Most of the document sets out structures for the selection and operation of the federal government's institutions, such as lengthy, tedious, and subsequently modified provisions for choosing the president and vice president. Even the amendments are largely technical matters primarily involving tweaks to the original institutional design features and matters of criminal procedure. It is difficult to read the Constitution and get the sense that one is looking at "a charter of aspirations,"[28] "a reflection of the tension between our understanding of our present state and our understanding of social ideals toward which progress is possible,"[29] or "that set of beliefs, or whatever, that has some hold on our behavior, our beliefs, and our collective and individual identity."[30] So how did scholars and judges manage to pull from this document cases like *Dred Scott* and *Roe v. Wade* or the idea that the Constitution contains welfare rights?

Aside from ignoring the Constitution altogether, the engines of a large portion of anti-constitutional doctrine and theory are a few stray sentences found in the amendments. The key ones are the provisions in the Fifth and Fourteenth Amendments saying that neither the federal nor state governments can deprive people of "life, liberty, or property, without due process of law"; the Ninth Amendment's declaration that "[t]he enumeration in the Constitution of certain rights shall not be construed to deny or disparage others retained by the people," and the portions of the Fourteenth Amendment saying that no state "shall make or enforce any law which shall abridge the privileges or immunities of citizens of the United States" or "deny to any person within its jurisdiction the equal protection of the laws." In 1943, Justice Robert Jackson described the Bill of Rights as a whole as "majestic generalities."[31] Four years later, he used the same phrase to describe the key provisions of the Fourteenth Amendment,[32] and we were off to the races.

In an August 1986 speech, Justice Brennan singled out the Due Process and Equal Protection Clauses as "particularly empty vessels" that are "adaptable to … changing conceptions of social justice." Justice Brennan, as did Donovan in *Indiana Jones and the Last Crusade*, chose poorly. Equal protection is about evenhanded enforcement of pre-existing rights by the police, state prosecutors, and state courts rather than the substance of those rights, while due process of law is primarily a separation of powers provision requiring executive and judicial actors to follow the law when depriving people of vested rights. Most interpreters overlook the fact that the noun in the Equal Protection Clause is "protection" and "equal" is only an adjective. The purpose of the Equal Protection Clause was to guarantee free enslaved people, and Northerners in the South, protection by Southern police officers, firefighters, and state prosecutors from deadly attacks by the Ku Klux Klan. The Fourteenth Amendment addresses the making and enforcing of laws that "abridge" or "shrink" the rights of Black people in the South by providing that "No state shall make or enforce any law which shall abridge the privileges or immunities of citizens of the United States."

Since the first sentence of the Fourteenth Amendment makes everyone born in the United States a citizen of both the federal government and "of the State wherein they reside," the Privileges or Immunities Clause originally protected both rights of national and of state citizenship, such as the common-law rights mentioned in the Civil Rights Act of 1866, which everyone agrees was constitutionalized by Section 1 of the Fourteenth Amendment. These state common-law rights, protected by the Privileges or Immunities Clause, include the rights "to make and enforce contracts, to sue, be parties, and give evidence, to inherit, purchase, lease, sell, hold, and convey real and personal property, and to full and equal benefit of all laws and proceedings for the security of person and property, as is enjoyed by white citizens, and shall be subject to like punishment, pains, and penalties, and to none other, any law, statute, ordinance, regulation, or custom, to the contrary notwithstanding."[33]

Many scholars and some judges, however, following the lead of John

Hart Ely,[34] were more attracted to the Ninth Amendment and the Fourteenth Amendment's Privileges or Immunities Clauses as the vehicles for finding favored interests in the Constitution. Those arguments were in full bloom in 1987—on all sides of the ideological spectrum, one should note. Leftists used them to try to argue for things like abortion rights, while some conservatives thought they could be used in support of robust protection of economic freedom. The nearly 100-page OLP monograph on *Wrong Turns on the Road to Judicial Activism: The Ninth Amendment and the Privileges or Immunities Clause*, published on September 25, 1987, was a response to both sides.

Attorney General Meese's introductory comments to the monograph reflect his own intellectual honesty and humility as well as the academic orientation of the Meese DOJ. He noted "increased discussion over whether the Ninth Amendment and the Privileges or Immunities Clause of the Fourteenth Amendment are sources of unenumerated rights." The monograph, he said, was "a contribution to that debate" which "will generate considerable thought on a topic of great national importance, a topic about which there are several reasonable points of view." Modern academics, who are not always noted for recognizing the reasonableness of competing points of view, could learn a thing or two about academic values from Ed Meese.

An assessment of the substantive arguments put forward in the monograph is beyond the scope of this book. (As with many issues dealt with by the Meese DOJ, it would require a book in itself.) Suffice it to say that we do not necessarily agree with all of those arguments, especially with regard to the Fourteenth Amendment's Privileges or Immunities Clause. The OLP analysis draws heavily on an 1873 Supreme Court decision in the *Slaughter-House Cases*,[35] which all modern originalist law professors think was profoundly mistaken about that clause's original meaning.[36] Academics on the Left and the Right are persuaded by the article by John Harrison, "Reconstructing the Privileges or Immunities Clause."[37] Thus, the Fourteenth Amendment may in fact sweep more broadly than the OLP believed in 1987, though no plausible account of original meaning can draw forth from that provision the bulk of the modern far-left agenda, welfare rights, and a racial spoils system. The monograph was on stronger ground with respect to the Ninth

Amendment, where it concluded "the unenumerated rights retained by the people are those aspects of the people's original sovereignty not delegated to the federal government. Accordingly, by definition, such unenumerated rights cannot conflict with or override the delegated powers." The truly striking thing about the 1987 OLP monograph's discussion of the Ninth Amendment in 1987 is how thoroughly it uses public meaning originalism to explain why the Ninth Amendment does not support at all the invention of an abstract "right to privacy" against *state* governments, much less the abortion rights invented in *Roe v. Wade.* Nothing published since 1987 successfully repudiates the OLP monograph's construction of the Ninth Amendment.

Modern originalist scholarship, as we noted, has fleshed out considerably the original understanding of the Fourteenth Amendment's Privileges or Immunities Clause—an understanding that Justice Clarence Thomas has forcefully brought to the Supreme Court.[38] In 1987, that scholarship was in its infancy. The monograph was state-of-the-art work for its time, making use of text, history, structure, and founding-era dictionaries in a sophisticated fashion. It is incredible that academic work of this quality was produced by young employees of Assistant Attorney General Stephen Markman in Ed Meese's Justice Department.

Seven-Paper Series Requested by Attorney General Ed Meese on "The Current Status of the Truth-Seeking Function of the Criminal Justice System"

CRIMINAL LAW was a central theme of the Meese DOJ. That is not surprising—not only is it a core function of the department in any administration, but it was a personal interest of Ed Meese, whose law career revolved almost wholly around criminal law. Much of the Warren Court revolution of the 1960s involved constraints on law enforcement, including restrictions on the ability of prosecutors to use evidence in court that was obtained in violation of the Supreme Court's decisions on searches, seizures, and confessions. Accordingly, the OLP produced a series of seven papers on criminal procedure, focusing largely on what kinds of evidence could be used in criminal trials. Not all of the issues raised by criminal procedure are constitutional. Some involve statutes or wise policy, and the OLP monographs covered this entire spectrum of criminal justice topics.

All seven of these OLP monographs begin with comments from Attorney General Meese explaining his reasons for asking the OLP to conduct the studies:

> Over the past thirty years ..., a variety of new rules have emerged that impede the discovery of reliable evidence at the investigative stages of the criminal justice process and that require the concealment of relevant facts at trial. This trend has been a cause of grave concern to many Americans, who perceive such rules as being at odds with the goals of the criminal justice system. Within the legal profession and the law enforcement community, debate over these rules has been complicated by disagreements about the extent to which constitutional principles or valid policy concerns require the subordination of the search for truth to other interests.
>
> This report is a contribution to that debate.

Perhaps the boldest of the monographs was a 127-page (single-spaced) *Report to the Attorney General on the Law of Pre-Trial Interrogation.* The context was the famous 1966 Supreme Court decision *Miranda v. Arizona,*[39] which said—over a vigorous dissent by Justices Harlan, Stewart, and White and a partial dissent by Justice Clark—that no statement made by a defendant while in police custody can be used in court unless the defendant was "warned that he has a right to remain silent, that any statement he does make may be used as evidence against him, and that he has a right to the presence of an attorney, either retained or appointed."[40] The use of such statements, said the court, violates the spirit, even if not the actual words, of the Fifth Amendment's guarantee that no person "shall be compelled in any criminal case to be a witness against himself." The decision laid out a detailed, legislative-like code for the conduct of police interrogations. The OLP monograph builds on Meese's many public speeches criticizing *Miranda* and a published law review article from Stephen Markman[41] and lays out a thorough case for the overruling of *Miranda.*

The monograph is an impressive piece of scholarship, discussing the right against compelled self-incrimination prior to the 17th century in England, the later development of the general right at common law, the

Fifth Amendment and the original meaning of that amendment as revealed in the state ratifying conventions, and Congress's effort to overturn *Miranda* by statute. (That statute was, quite wrongly we think, held unconstitutional by the Supreme Court in 2000,[42] over a dissent by Justices Scalia and Thomas, the only two originalists on the court at that time.) The monograph also pointed out how the Supreme Court's code of conduct was widely at variance with practices elsewhere in the world, such as England, Scotland, Canada, India, France, and Germany. That variance would be of no relevance if the Constitution actually commanded what the court required, but the Fifth Amendment only says that the accused shall not be "compelled" to testify against himself, meaning by torture, force, or subpoena. It is impossible to see how someone volunteering statements to police in the absence of the court's precise "*Miranda*" warning is compulsion within that term's original meaning.

The report accordingly presented several reasons why the Department of Justice should ask the Supreme Court to overrule *Miranda*:

First, the continued application of *Miranda* violates the constitutional separation of powers and basic principles of federalism. *Miranda's* promulgation of a code of procedure for interrogations constituted a usurpation of legislative and administrative powers, thinly disguised as an exercise in constitutional exegesis. . . .

Second, *Miranda*, by impeding the prosecution of crime, impairs the ability of government to protect the public. Compliance with *Miranda* markedly reduces the willingness of suspects to respond to questioning by the police. In a substantial proportion of criminal cases, confessions and other statements from the defendant are indispensable to a successful prosecution. When statements are not obtained in such cases through the operation of *Miranda's* system, criminals go free. . . .

Third, *Miranda's* system is a poorly conceived means of protecting suspects from coercion and overreaching in police interrogations. Its consequences are to divide suspects into two classes: those who "stand on their rights," and those who waive their rights and submit to questioning. . . .

Fourth, *Miranda* is damaging to public confidence in the law, and can result in gross injustices to crime victims. . . .

Fifth, the *Miranda* decision has petrified the law of pre-trial interrogation for the past twenty years, foreclosing the possibility of
developing and implementing alternatives that would be of greater
effectiveness both in protecting the public from crime and in
ensuring fair treatment of persons suspected of crime.[43]
This report is far and away the most comprehensive and intellectual critique of *Miranda* of which we are aware. It is entirely correct in its conclusion and recommendation. Pre-trial custodial interrogations should
be videotaped to protect against torture, and abusive law enforcement
agents should be civilly and criminally punished, but excluding relevant evidence from cases is not constitutionally required and makes
no sense. As Meese explained in his speech on this topic, the criminal
justice system should be a search for truth, not a game between the
prosecutor and the defendant's lawyer. Even if one thinks that *Miranda*
is good policy, it is not a policy found in the Constitution. *Miranda* is
a prime example of courts assuming to themselves a legislative role far
beyond their mission and competence, and the OLP paper still stands
today as an eloquent explanation of the legal and practical problems
posed by the doctrine.

Miranda is not the only judge-made doctrine that keeps relevant evidence out of court in criminal trials. The other is the so-called "exclusionary rule," which forbids the use at trial of evidence that results, even
indirectly, from an illegal search.

Here, unlike in *Miranda*, the doctrine is grounded in something
actually found in the Constitution. The Fourth Amendment prohibits
"unreasonable searches and seizures," and it requires warrants authorizing searches and seizures to be supported by "probable cause" and
to describe with particularity "the place to be searched, and the persons or things to be seized." The Constitution is very much concerned
with how law enforcement conducts its business. The Constitution does
not, however, specify the appropriate *remedy* for an illegal search. In
the founding era, the remedy would have been a lawsuit against the
government officials who violated the Fourth Amendment. Through
developments dating back to the 19th century, but formally taking hold
in doctrine only in the 20th century, the Supreme Court developed the
idea that the proper remedy for a Fourth Amendment violation was to

forbid the government from using the illegally seized evidence, even if it (and perhaps especially if it) conclusively demonstrated the defendant's guilt.[44] As future Supreme Court justice Benjamin Cardozo put it in 1926 while on the New York state court, "The criminal is to go free because the constable has blundered."[45]

On February 26, 1986, the OLP issued a monograph on *The Search and Seizure Exclusionary Rule*. The monograph is a comprehensive examination of the history of the Fourth Amendment and of the exclusionary rule. It explains the origins of the Fourth Amendment in the Framers' dislike of general warrant writs by British customs officials; the warrant clause and the search and seizure clause were both a response to those practices. The monograph notes that in the 19th century "the typical remedy for an illegal search was a civil action for damages against the transgressor." The Fourth Amendment exclusionary rule in federal criminal trials dates back only to *Weeks v. United States* in 1914[46]—or perhaps on a broader view of the doctrine to *Boyd v. United States* in 1886.[47]

As recently as 1949, the Supreme Court had declined to incorporate the exclusionary rule to apply to state criminal trials, which account for the overwhelming majority of all criminal trials.[48] Then, in *Mapp v. Ohio* in 1961,[49] the Supreme Court applied the exclusionary rule to the states. Subsequent law produced, and continues to produce, a dizzying array of exceptions and counter-exceptions to the baseline principle of exclusion. A substantial amount of Supreme Court case law over the past half century has involved the sometimes-minute mechanics of search-and-seizure practice.

The monograph argues for the replacement of the exclusionary rule with other mechanisms for protecting the Fourth Amendment's ban on unreasonable searches and seizures. The report's conclusions are shared by some of the country's leading constitutional thinkers, such as Akhil Amar, a Sterling Professor of Law at Yale University, whose magisterial book on constitutional criminal procedure[50] stands as one of the finest books on applied originalism yet written. Professor Amar praised the OLP Meese Justice Department series as being first-rate academic scholarship, in conversations with Steve Calabresi, and he opposes the exclusionary rule to this day because it gets in the way of the search for truth.[51]

Other OLP monographs covered *The Sixth Amendment Right to*

Counsel under the Massiah *Line of Cases*, dealing with Supreme Court–ordered exclusion from trial of certain incriminating statements of defendants made to informants; "The Admission of Criminal Histories at Trial," critiquing non-constitutional rules limiting the trial use of defendants' past criminal records; "The Judiciary's Use of Supervisory Power to Control Federal Law Enforcement Activity," addressing the Supreme Court's claimed power to exercise "supervisory authority over the administration of criminal justice in the federal courts";[52] "Double Jeopardy and Government Appeals of Acquittals," which is a measured look at whether government appeal of legal errors in cases tried without a jury would violate the Fifth Amendment's guarantee against any person being "for the same offense ... [being] twice put in jeopardy of life or limb"; and "Federal Habeas Corpus Review of State Judgments," under which "a state prisoner who has exhausted his avenues of appeal in the state court systems may continue to litigate the validity of his conviction or sentence by applying for habeas corpus in a federal district court."[53]

All of the topics covered in these reports are of major academic concern, and some, such as habeas corpus, are the subjects of distinct subspecialties in both the academy and legal practice and have undergone major statutory and doctrinal changes since 1987. It is not our mission, nor within our expertise, to opine on the constitutional and policy issues raised by these monographs. We mention them only as evidence of the academic and intellectual focus of the Meese DOJ. We have not read a single monograph that was not easily publishable in a major law review if the selection process were conducted honestly.[54] This was high-level work that easily meets and beats the standards of the legal academy. Steve Markman and his staff would merit tenure at any law school in the country.

Religious Liberty Under the Free Exercise Clause

RELIGIOUS LIBERTY has always been a priority for Ed Meese, as it has been for many Americans throughout history. Even today, Americans in general are more religious than people in Europe, Canada, and Australia. This difference goes back to colonial times, because Massachusetts, Connecticut, New Hampshire, Maine, and Vermont were settled originally by Puritan dissidents from the established Church of England (the forerunner of the Episcopal Church in the United States today). Rhode Island was settled by the Puritan dissident Roger Williams, who welcomed Jews and Quakers into his colony, which the other New England colonies would not do. William Penn founded Pennsylvania and Delaware as a haven for Quakers, and Lord Baltimore founded Maryland as a haven for English Catholics. New York was always a religious polyglot with members of the Protestant Dutch Reformed Church, Congregationalists, Episcopalians, and a small Jewish community. Every colony north of the Potomac River was founded either primarily or in part by religious dissidents seeking freedom of religion.

The southern colonies all established the Church of England as their established church. In the 1780s, Virginia opted for a separation of church and state. The Establishment Clause of the First Amendment was thus understood when it was ratified as only preventing the federal government from establishing a national church that would displace (disestablish) the state establishments of religion. As time went on, however, all the states disestablished their state religions and opted for protection for the free exercise of religion, which was also prominently protected from the federal government by the First Amendment. By 1868, when the Fourteenth Amendment was ratified, all thirty-seven states had free exercise of religion clauses in their state Bills of Rights, and two-thirds of the states had clauses in their state Bills of Rights forbidding the establishment of a religion.[55]

Americans today are much more likely than are U.K., European, or Canadian citizens to attend church services once a week, to say that they believe in God and in an afterlife, and to say that they believe in the Devil and heaven or hell. This is the case even though no U.S. state has an established church, whereas the U.K. has established the Church of England and one of the monarch's titles is "Defender of the Faith." As Judge Richard Posner, a self-described atheist, once told Steve Calabresi, "The United States privatized and deregulated religion, and as a result it has got a lot more of it!"

The self-described elites who become law professors and judges do not necessarily share to the same extent in this religiosity.[56] There are not, for example, a lot of Evangelicals on law faculties, though they constitute about a quarter of the country's population.[57] Indeed, a non-trivial cohort of the self-described elites is openly hostile to religious freedom, at least for people whose religious beliefs lead them to question elite orthodoxy on policy questions. In the 20th century, the Supreme Court turned downright hostile to religion in many contexts, using the Establishment Clause to squelch public expressions of religion ranging from prayers in schools to Christmas displays that had, in the court's view, too high a ratio of Jesus to reindeer. In other contexts, however, the court seemed protective, and to some (not us) perhaps even overprotective on occasion, of religious minorities like the Amish or Jehovah's Witnesses. Whether people agreed or disagreed with specific decisions, pretty much everyone in 1986 agreed that the case law on religious freedom was indecipherable and inconsistent.

In this context, the OLP produced a monograph on August 16, 1986, on *Religious Liberty under the Free Exercise Clause.* As with the other OLP reports, Ed Meese made clear in his introduction that the questions posed by the Free Exercise Clause are "difficult and perhaps intractable. ... But it is incumbent upon members of both the legal and the religious communities to work through the constitutional algorithms with diligence, tolerance, and good will." Characteristically, the hope was that the report "will spark new thought on a topic of considerable importance to the nation, a topic about which there are several reasonable points of view."

Once again, the resulting OLP monograph could easily have been a university press book. The monograph provides ten single-spaced pages of history. It construes—as no scholar had previously done—the textual meaning of "Congress," "prohibiting," "free exercise," and "religion" in thirty-five single-spaced pages.[58] It then offers an analysis of the belief/action dichotomy, a discussion of what "neutrality" means in the context of the Free Exercise Clause, and a theoretically sophisticated discussion of "balancing," which is frequently an essentially policy-laden judicial weighing of various interests that forms the basis of much judicial doctrine in many areas. The monograph carefully analyzes the pros and cons of balancing as a methodology for deciding cases and offers a measured and limited defense of cabined balancing in the free exercise context. Along the way, it contains a sophisticated discussion of originalist methodology, especially in circumstances where there is "ambiguity of the text standing alone" and where "the historical record may not give us sufficient guidance to eliminate conclusively all ambiguities in the text."[59] This was cutting-edge scholarship that would be the prize exhibit in the portfolio of almost any law professor.

Discrimination and Disparate Impact

EVERYONE IS AGAINST invidious discrimination on the basis of race, sex, religion, and the like. Congress has passed an array of statutes prohibiting such discrimination in various settings. The most famous is Title VII of the 1964 Civil Rights Act, which prohibits discrimination in employment "because of such individual's race, color, religion, sex, or national origin."[60] The key legal question is: what does it mean to act "because" of someone's characteristics? More broadly, what does it mean to discriminate?

The commonsense answer is that action occurs "because" of those characteristics when the characteristics are a *motivating force* behind the action. Legal liability on this understanding stems from basing action on statutorily forbidden *reasons*. That intent-based inquiry—which the law calls "disparate treatment"—is surely what most people understand discrimination to be about, and it is surely the conduct targeted by the 1964 Civil Rights Act.

In 1971, however, the Supreme Court followed the lead of activists within the federal government's Equal Employment Opportunity Commission and held that sometimes employers can violate Title VII of the 1964 Civil Rights Act even without intending to do so, if their actions have a "disparate impact" on favored groups.[61] This decision revolutionized civil rights law, and it was a crucial engine in the rise of numbers-based "affirmative action," as employers sought to stave off "disparate impact" liability through de facto quotas to make sure that their workforces contained the "right" number of members of various groups.

On November 4, 1987, the OLP produced a lengthy study on *Redefining Discrimination: "Disparate Impact" and the Institutionalization of Affirmative Action*. Unlike most of the OLP monographs, this was not a dispassionate or tentative exploration of ideas designed to promote discussion. It was a broadside attack on the doctrine, theory, and practice of disparate impact liability, notwithstanding Ed Meese's characteristic introduction that "[t]his study will generate considerable thought on a topic of great national importance, a topic about which there are several reasonable points of view."

The report itself claims to:

> demonstrate that "discrimination" was originally understood by members of Congress and others who supported the civil rights laws as a concept entailing intent or purpose, and argues that discrimination in this original sense is what we should be seeking to combat. The report describes the objective of the intent standard, equal treatment for individuals, and contrasts that with the objectives of the effects standard, proportional representation for groups, to be achieved inevitably by race-conscious decision-making.

Even more forcefully, the report summarized its findings in categorical terms:

> Discrimination, traditionally understood as a concept entailing purposeful or intentional conduct, has—through the guise of judicial construction and executive branch administrative interpretation...—been redefined into a concept of statistically disproportionate "effects" or "impact."
>
> As a result of this redefinition of discrimination, many of the nation's laws incorporating the non-discrimination principle of equal treatment have, in Orwellian fashion, been turned on their heads to effectively *require* the very behavior that they proscribe—the color- and gender-conscious treatment of individuals—so that statistically proportionate representation or results for groups might be achieved. In short, through this redefinition of discrimination, the rights of individuals to equal treatment have been subordinated to a new right of proportional representation for groups.[62]

This non-intentional conception of discrimination was described as "contrived," "revisionist," and "demonstrably inconsistent with the text and legislative history of all but one" of the federal civil rights laws.[63]

The report applies the methods of original understanding to statutory as well as constitutional interpretation, containing detailed studies of the original meaning of a wide range of federal antidiscrimination statutes, including Title VII and Title VI (prohibiting discrimination in federally funded activities) of the 1964 Civil Rights Act. As with other topics, it would require a book, and possibly several, to explore the full range of legal issues addressed in this report. A few observations will have to do for now.

First, the document, in keeping with the extraordinary academic standards of the Meese OLP monographs, stands as the most thorough account of the original meaning of the concept of discrimination and the statutory phrase "because of" that we have seen. It is limited only by the technology of the 1980s. Much of the evidence of original meaning employed by the report comes from congressional debates. Just as the subjective intentions of Framers do not determine the meaning of the Constitution, so the subjective intentions or expectations of legislators do not determine the meaning of statutes. (Justice Scalia made precisely this point in reverse in his address to the economic liberties conference in 1986.) Today, under modern conceptions of originalism, a more accurate account of original meaning would look to broader public understandings of terms such as "discrimination" or "because of," possibly using the relatively recent availability of broad digitized databases and computer search capabilities (a technique called "corpus linguistics"). In this instance, however, we do not believe that anyone doubts that a broad look at public understandings in the 1960s would confirm the report's conclusions about the meaning of discrimination. Of course it meant in 1964 what the OLP said it meant.

Second, a few years after the report came out, the Supreme Court took some tentative steps toward reining in—without overturning or directly challenging—the disparate impact framework.[64] Congress in 1991 amended Title VII in a way that effectively codifies the disparate impact cause of action. A modern study of the communicative meaning of Title VII, as amended three decades ago, would thus yield different results from those that the Department of Justice reached in 1987, though that would not necessarily be the case with other statutes whose texts were not amended to refer specifically to disparate impact cases.

Third, the disparate impact idea is at the root of much of what today goes under the vague and often unhelpful label "critical race theory," which rejects the notion of color-blindness because it ostensibly (and, to keep things real, sometimes actually) reinforces effects of past intentional discrimination. This is why the term "equity" has largely replaced the term "equality" in much leftist discourse. "Equity" and "disparate impact" are about results, while "equality" and "disparate treatment" (the technical legal term for what everyone in 1964 would have called "discrimination") are about processes. The OLP report grasped this basic point decades ago. Anyone who wants to understand modern debates about civil rights can benefit from reading the 158-page OLP monograph from 1987.

Fourth, the Supreme Court in 2023 took major steps toward restoring the color-blind approach to discrimination set forth by the Meese Justice Department nearly four decades earlier. We say more about that development in chapter 13.

Guidelines on Constitutional Litigation *et al.*

THE OLP MONOGRAPHS covered a vast range of topics beyond those that we have thus far mentioned. On August 31, 1988, a few weeks after Meese had resigned as attorney general, the Office of Legal Policy published a 169-page monograph entitled *Justice without Law: A Reconsideration of the "Broad Equitable Powers" of the Federal Courts.* This document, obviously written before Meese's resignation, discusses the entire tradition of equity both in England and in the United States, describes three critical principles of equity, discusses the injunctive power and the new American equity jurisprudence, and suggests limiting principles for the new equity as well as offering some suggested reforms. This OLP monograph is essentially a draft of an academic press book on equity as it stood in 1988. It was also in some ways ahead of the academy. There is currently vibrant academic interest in the equitable powers of federal courts,[65] especially the emerging trend in which a single federal district court judge can shut down the agenda of an entire administration—of either party—with a "nationwide injunction." Not only scholars but Supreme Court justices have taken notice of this issue.[66] This document offers further proof of the proposition that the Meese DOJ was in many respects operating like a law school faculty.

Other OLP documents study such things as constitutional conventions under Article V, and in particular whether such conventions can be limited to consideration of a defined set of topics such as balanced budgets or abortion, and the constitutional issues that would be posed by attempts to make the District of Columbia a state. These also have long been topics of academic interest, and the OLP monographs make characteristically important contributions to the scholarly debate. But perhaps the most intellectually intriguing OLP document did not present itself as a scholarly inquiry. It was a manual for litigators.

When Ed Meese announced that the DOJ was going to pursue originalism as its official interpretative approach, that was likely at best puzzling and at worst anathema to the career staffers who were responsible for the department's day-to-day litigation activities in district courts. They surely learned nothing about originalism in law school—and if they had even heard of originalism, interpretivism, or anything resembling it in school, it would doubtlessly have been with dismissive disdain from the professor. Once out of school as litigators, their primary object was presumably to win cases, and originalism in the mid-1980s was no more popular in the courts than in the academy. To the extent that they were seeking to push the law in some direction, their background and training in elite law schools surely meant that any such direction would be both non-originalist and leftist. So how could the Meese DOJ translate its originalist commitments into effective legal policy?

In chapter 10, we will explore how these questions were raised and (partially) answered in connection with litigation in the Supreme Court and the courts of appeal. But only a tiny fraction of cases end up in the appellate system, much less in the Supreme Court. Most of the cases take place in the district courts, managed by line attorneys. Those attorneys needed to be instructed to employ, and educated in how to use, the Jurisprudence of Original Meaning.

Accordingly, on February 19, 1988, the OLP produced *Guidelines on Constitutional Litigation*, which describes itself as "a manual on 'how to think clearly' about principles of interpretation."[67] This document, consisting of 124 single-spaced pages of dense text plus another thirty pages of appendices, is remarkable on several levels.

First, it summarizes the 1988 state-of-the-art understanding of originalism as a doctrine which says that "constitutional language should be construed as it was publicly understood at the time of its drafting and ratification."[68] Much of the document explains in some detail, with examples drawn from cases across the country's history, how this methodology can be applied (or misapplied) to specific constitutional provisions and recurring issues. But second, and more importantly, it then adds to this detailed description of originalism that "government attorneys should attempt to construct arguments based solely on the ordinary usage of the words at the time the provision at issue was ratified."[69] More specifically:

> Government briefs should clearly set out the text and original understanding of the relevant constitutional provisions, along with an analysis of how the case would be resolved consistent with that understanding. For those provisions couched in clear, unambiguous terms, little more than citing to and noting the original meaning of the terms employed will be necessary for this exegesis. For the less precise provisions, more detailed discussions of original meaning gleaned from the language, history, and context of those provisions will be necessary.[70]

Perhaps anticipating the response of career litigators that the courts would not accept originalist arguments in most settings, the *Guidelines* responded:

> The inclusion of an original meaning section will help to refocus constitutional analysis on the text of the Constitution. Not only will it serve to ensure that government attorneys give careful consideration to the original meaning of the constitutional provisions at issue, it will help to focus judges on the text of the Constitution and away from their personal preferences or from incorrectly reasoned court precedent as the appropriate basis for decisionmaking. Instead of looking exclusively to years of questionable precedents and their equally questionable accretions, the courts will at least be more likely to review the original constitutional text.[71]

Because the litigators to whom the manual was addressed are arguing to district courts, which are bound by Supreme Court precedent and the precedent of their circuit court of appeals, the government lawyers "will often have to continue to fashion arguments based on seemingly incorrect precedents."[72] In such cases, "many of these guidelines are expressed in terms of working to prevent the courts from compounding existing errors."[73] Thus, the DOJ School of Law needed to educate both its own attendees and the federal judiciary about the Constitution's original meaning.

There was, of course, no assurance that the courts were going to be receptive students. Might not an approach that emphasizes original meaning thereby lose some cases that otherwise could be won if the lawyers emphasized or sought to extend non-originalist arguments or precedents?

Of course it might. The *Guidelines* acknowledged and accommodated this possibility by making clear what the department regarded as winning or losing:

> This manual is in part intended to reassure government litigators that their first priority is to ensure faithful execution of the laws rather than to "win particular cases." More optimistically, it is intended to help government attorneys begin to measure what constitutes a "win" in terms of how closely the resulting court interpretations actually mirror the laws construed, rather than in terms of a more simplistic win-loss score sheet.[74]

Put as simply as possible, for the Meese Justice Department, the ultimate client was not Congress, the president, or the particular agency whose action was at issue in any particular case. The ultimate client was the Constitution.

* * *

THE ACADEMIC CONFERENCES sponsored by the Meese Department of Justice, the monographs produced by the Office of Legal Policy, and the day-to-day conversations that took place at work and at home show that the Meese DOJ was a beehive of intellectual and academic inquiry. Many of those ideas were clarified, developed, and put into effect by making judicial appointments, issuing Office of Legal Counsel opinions, and arguing cases in court. In addition, the alumni of the Meese DOJ have carried its legacy into many high places and institutions, including the mainstream legal academy. The DOJ School of Law was only open for a few short years, but its legacy survives today.

CHAPTER NINE
JUDICIAL SELECTION IN
THE MEESE JUSTICE DEPARTMENT

JUST AS ORIGINALISM was the official litigating position of the Meese DOJ, it was also the key to the Reagan administration's approach to judicial selection. Federal judges are appointed by the president with the advice and consent of the Senate,[1] so the final decision on whom to appoint to vacancies on the federal bench rested with President Reagan. But, as with most things, President Reagan relied heavily on the advice of Ed Meese, who "knew the president's mind better"[2] than anyone else.

Ed Meese, in his own words, knew that Ronald Reagan's "vision was that judges [who] were recommended to him for nomination believed in... [t]he original understanding of the Constitution." This meant that judges "should interpret the law, not make up the law. And that the Constitution should be interpreted and applied as it actually read, and the judges should not substitute their own political preferences, their policy ideas, or their personal biases for what the Constitution and the laws made under it actually say." The goal, in short, was "a constitutionally faithful judiciary."

As we suggested in the previous chapter, looking for *constitutionalist* judges is not the same thing as looking for *conservative* judges, if by the latter one means judges who are systematically going to rule in favor of or against particular parties, such as accused criminals. The OLP *Guidelines on Constitutional Litigation* made this clear, noting that principles of originalism "are neither 'conservative' nor liberal,'" but are simply "faithful to our Constitution."[3] The hard part was to find people who would be faithful originalists and not simply faithful conservatives (though finding even the latter was tricky enough), especially in a world in which originalism had not been widely theorized or taught.

The job was even harder because of the prominence of notions of "judicial restraint," which some people confused, and even today still confuse, with originalism. Some people argue that courts act best when they act least, even in the face of claims that seem grounded in actual constitutional law, such as the Second Amendment. Meese clarifies this distinction for us: "Well, I think the idea that judicial restraint means limiting a judge in enforcing the Constitution is the wrong construction to put on the idea of judicial restraint. Judicial restraint is not a limitation on activeness in terms of enforcing the Constitution. But it's a restraint on judges substituting their ideas or their political or policy preferences for what the Constitution actually says. So judicial restraint is a phrase that talks about restraining them from substitution of things that are not in the constitution for what's actually there. It's not a restraint on being energetic you might say in enforcing the Constitution in appropriate cases."

It was vital to the success of the Meese Revolution to pick judges who understood the differences among originalism, judicial restraint, and conservatism and whose true allegiance was to originalism and the Constitution. The vast majority of cases are heard by lower court judges, so getting those picks right was vital. Lower court judges bound and determined to resist the Supreme Court can succeed to a large degree simply because of the Supreme Court's small caseload.[4] To put this in context, we would note that in 2024 the federal circuit courts of appeals hear about sixty-two thousand cases a year, state supreme courts hear a very large number of cases that involve federal law, but the Supreme Court hears only about eighty cases a year. Obviously, the selection of federal circuit court of appeals judges and of state supreme court justices is essential to having an originalist judiciary. Later in this chapter, we will talk about the Reagan administration's selection process for lower court judges. But the Supreme Court has outsized importance—not just because it is formally the highest court and its rulings formally, even if not always practically, bind the lower courts, but because it is the most visible legal institution in the country. Getting originalism represented on the Supreme Court has ripple effects throughout legal practice, as lawyers who need to get the votes of originalist justices to win cases must learn to make persuasive originalist arguments. Law schools that fail to train lawyers to make those originalist arguments will produce losing lawyers. And, of course, because there are only nine Supreme

Court justices and more than eight hundred lower court judges, hits or misses at the Supreme Court have more consequences. Thus, we start with the process by which the Meese DOJ advised President Reagan on Supreme Court nominations.

THE MEESE SUPREME COURT SELECTION EFFORT

Sometime in 1985, Chief Justice Warren Burger gave secret notice to President Reagan and Attorney General Meese of his intention to retire at the end of June of 1986. Ken Cribb remembered Burger giving as much as a year's notice, while others remembered perhaps eight months. Notwithstanding the difficulty of imagining "secret" and "Washington, D.C." appearing in the same sentence, for close to a year there were no leaks about the upcoming Supreme Court vacancy. Steve Calabresi, for example, was told the news ten minutes before President Reagan held a press conference to announce that Associate Justice William Rehnquist was being nominated for chief justice and Antonin Scalia was being put forward to replace Rehnquist as associate justice.

Meese explained that the key to secrecy in this setting was that "it was a very small group who knew about this. ... [T]here was no one even in the White House who was told about this. The only people [besides me] that knew were the president's chief of staff, who was sworn to secrecy, and the president himself and Ken Cribb and Brad Reynolds." The secrecy was so tight that when the press conference was held on June 17, 1986, "[t]he press secretary did not know what the topic was. So the buzz went through the press, gee maybe the president's sick or maybe there's some health problem or we're going to war or something like that. So we walked in and in walks the president with Bill Rehnquist and Antonin Scalia."

How did this small group of people end up picking Chief Justice William Rehnquist and Associate Justice Antonin Scalia?

Picking a Chief Justice

MEESE HAS told us that he and President Reagan "had in mind ... right from the start" elevating William Rehnquist from associate justice to chief justice. Both men greatly admired Rehnquist's tenure as an associate justice from January 7, 1972 up to 1986, and they had no concerns at all that he would "grow" in the office or become more liberal. They felt he had a proven track record on the issues about which they cared the most: federalism, separation of powers, substantive due process, constitutional criminal procedure, and a restrained view that judges would and should enforce the original public meaning of the Constitution as it was understood by those who made it law. They also believed that Rehnquist had "the institutional knowledge of how to lead the court. ... [T]hat that was a valuable attribute that [Rehnquist] would have that obviously would not necessarily be shared with others who had not had that experience. ... So that's why he seemed to be a natural person to be chief justice."

William Rehnquist indeed checked off a lot of boxes. He had an established track record as an associate justice, he was sixty-one years old, and he was in good enough health to pass his seat on to another Republican president. He was also a very popular figure with the other justices, all of whom much preferred Rehnquist's humble midwestern persona to Chief Justice Warren Burger's pompous formality and rudeness. The problems with getting Rehnquist confirmed were already known about from his first confirmation and fourteen-year tenure on the Supreme Court. There would be no surprise witnesses popping up to accuse this happily married father of three children of sexual harassment. Republicans had a 53–47 majority in the Senate, and many moderate Democrats in those less partisan days could be counted on to cross the aisle and vote to confirm Rehnquist. Even Rehnquist's bitterest opponents conceded that he was exceptionally well qualified for the job. For President Reagan and Attorney General Meese, "this was a logical choice."[5]

The only plausible alternative was to nominate a person not already on the court to be chief justice, as President Bush did in 2005 when he nominated John Roberts as chief justice. As we discuss below, the two obvious candidates for a new position on the court were Antonin Scalia and Robert Bork, and neither had the administrative or organizational skills that would suit them for that position. The chief justice is also a chief administrator, and Rehnquist was clearly better suited for that role than Scalia or Bork.

One other factor that may have helped Rehnquist get the nod for chief justice, if any nod was needed, was that Meese's key aide, Brad Reynolds, who was one of the three people in the Department of Justice who knew about the Supreme Court vacancy, was a close personal friend of Rehnquist. When Brad was the most junior associate in the Nixon Solicitor General's Office, his office was so far down the hall on the 5th floor of the Robert F. Kennedy Department of Justice Building that it abutted Rehnquist's office as head of the Office of Legal Counsel. Bill Rehnquist and Brad Reynolds became good friends, and Brad even helped prepare Rehnquist for a Supreme Court oral argument. Later on they had houses in the same neighborhood in Northern Virginia. Brad Reynolds knew all three men who were plausible chief justice candidates—Bill Rehnquist, Robert Bork, and Antonin Scalia—but he was the closest of all to Rehnquist on a personal level.

In addition, both Brad and Ken Cribb also thought, correctly, that Rehnquist was less wedded to precedent, including some important non-originalist precedents, than Bork or Scalia. In particular, Rehnquist seemed more likely than Bork or Scalia to take on a challenge to the constitutional revolution of 1937 in which the court essentially abandoned enforcement of the Constitution's structural provisions for division of power within the federal government and between the federal and state governments. Bork and Scalia regarded those decisions as long-settled precedents, whereas Rehnquist did not think they were definitively settled law. Federalism was a major interest of President Reagan's, as he said in his first inaugural address, and it was a key issue for Ken Cribb as well. Brad Reynolds's key issue was affirmative action, and no one was to the right of Rehnquist on that.[6] Ed Meese's key issues were constitutional criminal procedure cases, and again no one, other than the retiring Warren Burger, was to the right of Rehnquist on that either.

While it was clear in 1986 that Justice Rehnquist was reliably conservative, it was less clear, as pointed out in chapter 5, that he was a true-blue originalist who would be an effective standard bearer for that methodology. We will say more about that shortly. For the moment, it is enough to observe that of anyone on the court in 1986, Rehnquist was the closest approximation to an originalist that one would find. As the saying runs, you go to war with the army you have, not the army you wish you had. To some degree, the real standard bearer for originalism would have to come from the nomination for associate justice.

Although he had already been twice confirmed by the Senate—once as assistant attorney general for the Office of Legal Counsel and again as an associate justice—the Rehnquist nomination triggered a ferocious confirmation fight in the Republican-controlled Senate. He was confirmed only by a vote of 65–33, which at the time was the closest vote ever held on a successful Supreme Court nominee. Perhaps as a portent of things to come, right as Justice Rehnquist and Judge Scalia were nominated to the Supreme Court, there was a bitter confirmation battle over Daniel Manion for a seat on the Seventh Circuit U.S. Court of Appeals. As a practicing lawyer, Manion had submitted briefs (in cases that he won) with spelling errors. The real ground for opposition was surely his deep and abiding conservatism, but in 1986 opposition to a judicial nominee on open ideological grounds was not yet mainstream. Manion was eventually confirmed in July 1986 by a vote of 51–50, with the tie-breaking vote cast by Vice President George H. W. Bush. The Democrats' mantra in the Manion fight had been something to the effect of "all we want is legal ability and quality; we don't care about judicial ideology." This put the Democrats in a rhetorical bind when Rehnquist and Scalia were nominated, because they were both obviously brilliant, highly qualified nominees of the sort the Democrats had just called for during the Manion fight. The Democrats then tried to switch gears to say that actually they cared about ideology as well, but they looked blatantly political and dishonest in doing so, and the Republicans who voted against Manion all voted to confirm the Supreme Court nominees. In this way, the bitter fight over Daniel Manion's nomination helped lead to Rehnquist's and Scalia's confirmations.

Picking an Associate Justice

ONCE THE DECISION was made to go with Rehnquist for chief justice, the next task was to pick the successor to Rehnquist as associate justice. Without letting anyone at the Department of Justice beyond Brad Reynolds and Ken Cribb know that a vacancy was imminent, Attorney General Meese appointed a select committee to explore possibilities for future vacancies. The committee chair was Reynolds, with Cribb at his right elbow, and the committee's members were the most ideologically solid and intellectually sophisticated members of a very right-wing and intellectual DOJ. Moderates like Charles Fried were barred from the room. The members of the committee, in addition to Brad and Ken, were John Bolton, Steve Calabresi, Mike Carvin, Chuck Cooper, John Harrison, Steve Markman, Steve Matthews, Lee Liberman Otis, Carolyn Kuhl, and Richard Willard. Files were prepared on possible nominees—those whom the Meese Justice Department feared as well as those whom it favored, since one could expect names to come from White House operatives and senators as well.

The overwhelming favorites of Brad's committee were Judges Bork and Scalia. John Harrison, a former Bork clerk, wrote a wonderful memo making the case powerfully for Bork; Lee Liberman Otis, a former Scalia clerk, did the same for Scalia. Steve Matthews wrote a prescient memo on Anthony Kennedy, predicting he would be quite good on almost everything except for LGBTQ rights. Meese, who had known how socially conservative Kennedy had been when they had worked together for Governor Reagan, could not imagine that his longtime friend would go that far off the reservation. Among the notable other judges whose opinions were read were Second Circuit judge Ralph K. Winter, Fifth Circuit judge Patrick Higginbotham, and Ninth Circuit judge J. Clifford Wallace, all names well known at the time to conservative legal thinkers. There were others whose work was read, but these were obviously the cream of a modest crop, with Bork and Scalia clearly leading the way. Judge Richard Posner was never read or considered.

Bork and Scalia were both intellectual giants. So how to choose between them? Scalia had at least five advantages in the selection process.

First, he had a very thin paper trail. As an academic, he did not write about mainstream constitutional law issues. His principal field was administrative law, a technical and dry subject (as Lawson can attest after teaching it for thirty-five years) that does not involve the hot-button topics that draw the ire of interest groups. His major scholarly works involved the history of judicial review of decisions of the public land office[7] and the promotion procedures for administrative law judges.[8] He was very difficult for Ted Kennedy to demagogue.

Second, he was Italian American, a first on the Supreme Court. We do not recall that being an issue in the DOJ, but White House counsel

Peter Wallison, at least, thought that it made Scalia more attractive to President Reagan.[9] No one doubts that Ronald Reagan chose Sandra Day O'Connor at least in part because she was a woman; it would not be shocking if he settled on Scalia at least in part because of his heritage. To be clear, we are not endorsing these considerations as selection criteria; we are just noting their existence and possible effect.

Third, Scalia came across as more personable than Bork. Bork was actually very warm with those close to him, but his external persona was a bit gruff and aloof. We doubt whether people in 1986 appreciated how important that might become in an era of televised hearings, but Scalia was clearly a better interviewee than Bork.

Fourth, some key actors in the DOJ believed, with some justification, that Scalia was more reliably originalist and conservative than Bork. Both Brad Reynolds and his former deputy Chuck Cooper, who had clerked for Rehnquist, favored Rehnquist and Scalia over Bork. Cooper made it clear to Steve Calabresi, a Bork partisan, that Cooper thought Scalia was a more reliable conservative than was Bork. It is probably true that in some ways Bork was actually more open-minded than was Scalia. During the course of Bork's lifetime, the judge was at different times a Marxist, a libertarian, a Burkean traditionalist, an atheist, and a Roman Catholic. On substance, Bork had little interest in structural constitutionalism such as separation of powers, while that was Scalia's wheelhouse, and it was a topic that commanded central attention in the Meese Justice Department.

Fifth, and decisively, Scalia was younger and in better health. That really mattered a lot. Ken Cribb, who was Meese's counsellor and closest advisor, remembered that "Meese took both names over, because he really believed, you know, in not hiding options from the president. He gave the president both options, and the president decided based on actuarial grounds. Ten years younger, and Scalia smoked cigars, and Bork smoked cigarettes, and that was the difference." Meese similarly recollects that he and President Reagan favored Scalia over Bork because Scalia had a longer life expectancy, and President Reagan was not at all sure that he would get another chance at filling a Supreme Court seat. As it happened, Robert Bork died on December 19, 2012, during President Obama's presidency, whereas Justice Scalia died on February 13 of the 2016 presidential election year, and Senate Republicans refused to let Obama fill the vacancy. Scalia was succeeded as an associate justice by Neil Gorsuch, a staunch originalist. President Reagan and Attorney General Meese were right to go with the actuarial tables.

Most people in the Department of Justice were elated with the dual choices of Rehnquist and Scalia. Ken Cribb recalls waiting with Brad Reynolds to hear the news of Reagan's decision. Ken said, "[T]he stakes were so high that Brad and I never left Meese's private office after Ed Meese left the Justice Department to go to the Oval Office to hear President Reagan's final choice of Supreme Court nominees.... So as soon as Meese got off the elevator, he didn't say, 'Brad' or 'Ken' or anything. He just said, 'It's Rehnquist for chief, and Scalia for associate.'" At that point, said Cribb, "I grabbed the sherry and poured three glasses.... We toasted the president, and the court, and Brad had this funny look." Ken said, "What's the matter, Brad? Didn't you think the AG could pull it off?" Brad replied, "It's not that. I'm a teetotaler. This is the first drink I've had in twenty-five years, and it's 10 a.m.!"

To be sure, not everyone in the DOJ fully shared the joy. The day when President Reagan announced the Rehnquist and Scalia nominations, Steve Calabresi, a former student of Professor Bork and a former law clerk to Judge Bork, cried. In retrospect, however, he agrees that Ed Meese and Ronald Reagan made the right call.

The Rehnquist and Scalia Legacies

ED MEESE believes that he made the right call, opining that "Chief Justice Rehnquist did an outstanding job, both in terms of his philosophical leadership of the court and also from his administrative and managerial leadership of the court.... [Y]ou had a collegiality then that I think was remarkable." Much of this rings true. Rehnquist was very well liked by his colleagues, including liberal Justice William Brennan, who far preferred Rehnquist to his stuffy predecessor. Rehnquist was especially close friends with Justice Sandra Day O'Connor, a law school classmate to whom he had unsuccessfully proposed marriage, and with Justice Byron White, a Kennedy appointee whose views were astonishingly close to Rehnquist's on everything but federalism. Rehnquist had a good relationship with Justice Anthony M. Kennedy, although they disagreed on some important cases. His relationship with Justice Scalia was, in Steve Calabresi's view, strained by the fact that Rehnquist was very pragmatic and Scalia was very intellectual and academic.[10] Notwithstanding this difference in temperament, Rehnquist wrote many important academic books while he served on the Supreme Court.[11] Rehnquist just did not have an intellectual or academic affect, whereas Justice Scalia did.

In the end, Rehnquist served for almost nineteen years as chief justice. Only John Marshall, Roger Taney, and Melville Fuller served longer, though John Roberts is on the verge of knocking Rehnquist into 5th place. By his length of tenure alone, Chief Justice Rehnquist had an outsized influence on the U.S. Supreme Court.

Ken Cribb told us that Rehnquist had promised to serve at least another ten years, if he were appointed chief justice, but Ed Meese does not recall that. Cribb regarded promoting Rehnquist as a way of keeping him on the Supreme Court and preventing him from retiring at an earlier age. Rehnquist's departure from office in 2005, when Republican George W. Bush was president with a Republican Senate, showed that Rehnquist was a brilliant poker player to the end.

In June of 2005, Justice Sandra Day O'Connor came to Chief Justice Rehnquist, who then had thyroid cancer, and said that she was planning on retiring from the Supreme Court, but she added that she would wait a year if Rehnquist was planning to retire in 2005 to avoid two vacancies on the Supreme Court at the same time. Rehnquist falsely reassured O'Connor that his cancer was under control, and he said truthfully that he did not plan to retire in 2005. O'Connor, believing this, retired, and George W. Bush nominated John Roberts to replace her to huge popular acclaim. George W. Bush was at the peak of his power in the summer of 2005, following his successful reelection, and he was much more able to nominate conservatives in 2005 than he would have been in 2006 when he was headed into a midterm election in which he would lose his majority in the Senate. Chief Justice William Rehnquist had been around Washington, D.C., for long enough to know this.

In late July, reporters asked Rehnquist, as he got into his car outside his house, when he would leave the Supreme Court. Rehnquist replied, "That is for me to know and for you to find out." Rehnquist kept his deteriorating health completely secret from his colleagues until he died in office on September 3, 2005. No chief justice had died in office since Fred M. Vinson in 1953. Justice Scalia told his law clerks that he was completely stunned by Rehnquist's death in office and that he had no idea Rehnquist was that sick.

President George W. Bush responded by re-nominating John Roberts, this time to be chief justice, and, thinking he had satisfied Federalist Society conservatives to whom he had promised in the 2000 presidential campaign that he would appoint Supreme Court justices like Antonin Scalia, George W. Bush instead nominated his personal friend Harriet Miers to be an associate justice. Conservatives erupted in outrage, with former judge Robert H. Bork declaring Miers totally unqualified to sit on the Supreme Court. Miers was forced to withdraw as a nominee, and Ed Meese recommended that George W. Bush nominate Third Circuit judge Samuel Alito instead. Alito was nominated and confirmed—in effect replacing O'Connor, the court's swing justice, with a staunch conservative originalist. Of course, the balance on the Supreme Court did not shift much, since Chief Justice Roberts was much more moderate than the staunch Chief Justice Rehnquist whom he replaced.

Rehnquist's influence, in retrospect, was measured in more than just length of service for almost nineteen years. For all of our criticisms of Chief Justice Rehnquist from an originalist perspective, we have to acknowledge his enormous accomplishments as well.

While no one today associates Chief Justice Rehnquist with originalism in any strong fashion, Meese suggests that Rehnquist "had a concept of originalism, as by that time it was starting to be called, that was very valuable. And, in a way, it was also not an ideological way of expressing it as much as it was fidelity to the Constitution as the theme." To be sure, many originalist law professors (including both of the present authors) view Chief Justice Rehnquist as a conservative legal realist who reached conservative outcomes more from policy reasons than from originalist analysis. Brad Reynolds vehemently disagreed with that assessment, arguing that in at least one crucial respect Rehnquist was even more originalist than Scalia or Bork: Rehnquist was more willing to overrule or distinguish non-originalist precedents than were Scalia and Bork. Consequently, Rehnquist's outcomes were actually more originalist even if the language of his opinions wasn't necessarily as originalist as purists might prefer. Meese agrees with Reynolds that Rehnquist's opinions "were definitely originalist opinions…, but it was a little different style of writing." Scalia, Bork, and Clarence Thomas "were more expressive," but not necessarily all that different in substance from Chief Justice Rehnquist's "shorter, more concise" approach.

A quick look at Chief Justice Rehnquist's service on the court gives some credence to Meese's and Reynolds's assessment. The Supreme Court from 1986 to 2005 was in many ways a different institution than it had been for the previous half century.

William Rehnquist's most important accomplishment as chief justice was the stunning revival of enumerated powers federalism, which took place during his tenure and which continues to play an important role on the Supreme Court. The Constitution grants to Congress only a limited set of powers, and in 1791 the Tenth Amendment confirmed that "[t]he powers not delegated to the United States by the Constitution, nor prohibited by it to the States, are reserved to the States respectively, or to the people." This is why James Madison could say in 1787 in the 45th paper of *The Federalist*:

> The powers delegated by the proposed constitution to the federal government, are few and defined. Those which are to remain in the State governments are numerous and indefinite. The former will be exercised principally on external objects, as war, peace, negotiation, and foreign commerce; with which last the power of taxation will for the most part be connected. The powers reserved to the several States will extend to all the objects, which, in the ordinary course of affairs, concern the lives, liberties and properties of the people; and the internal order, improvement and prosperity of the State.[12]

In particular, the federal Congress's power to "regulate Commerce… among the several States" was originally understood to reach only the interstate shipment of goods and the means of transport; it did not include power over in-state activities such as manufacturing, agriculture, mining, or contracting. In the early years of the New Deal, the Supreme Court followed this understanding to invalidate some of the most expansive federal regulatory regimes put forward by the Roosevelt administration and enacted by Congress. By the early 1940s, however, due to a switch in one justice's vote and a series of Roosevelt appointments, the court began treating Congress as having essentially unlimited legislative power, including power to regulate a farmer's production of wheat on his own farm for his own consumption.[13] From 1937 to 1994, no federal statute regulating private conduct was found by the court to exceed Congress's constitutionally enumerated powers.

The drought ended in 1995 in Chief Justice Rehnquist's majority opinion in *United States v. Lopez*,[14] in which a 5–4 majority of the Supreme Court, for the first time since 1937, struck down a federal law on the ground that it exceeded congressional power under the Commerce Clause. The law in question made it a federal crime to possess a gun within one thousand feet of a school. This holding was subsequently reaffirmed in another 5–4 opinion by Chief Justice Rehnquist in *United States v. Morrison*,[15] involving a statute creating a federal cause of action for women who were the victims of violence and who were not, in Congress's judgment, adequately protected by state criminal or tort law. These holdings were reaffirmed by the Roberts Court in *NFIB v. Sebelius*,[16] a case which upheld on Taxing Clause grounds the individual mandate in President Obama's healthcare law, although five justices also wrote that the law exceeded the scope of Congress's power under the Commerce and Necessary and Proper Clauses. This latter holding was an enormous victory for originalism.

It is difficult to find words to describe the importance of the federalism revolution launched by Chief Justice Rehnquist. From 1937 to 1995, it was unthinkable that *any* federal law might violate the Commerce Clause. Lawson in 1994, right on the eve of the *Lopez* decision, wrote in the *Harvard Law Review* that "in this day and age, discussing the doctrine of enumerated powers is like discussing the redemption of Imperial Chinese bonds."[17] After the Rehnquist Court's decisions on the scope of federal power, however, that was no longer correct.

Moreover, the enumerated powers revolution was even more pronounced in eviscerating congressional power to enforce the Reconstruction Amendments to the Constitution—a move, as it happens, that we are not all sure is correct as a matter of original meaning.[18] The Thirteenth, Fourteenth, and Fifteenth Amendments, enacted in the five years after the Civil War, all give Congress power to enforce their terms through "appropriate" legislation. In *City of Boerne v. Flores*,[19] a 5–4 majority of the Supreme Court, in an opinion written by Justice Kennedy, held for the first time in American history that congressional laws enforcing the Fourteenth Amendment had to be "*congruent and proportional*" and not merely "rational." (Lawyers understand that "rational" in this context is legal code for "the government wins"; it does not mean "sensible.") The Supreme Court has stuck with this test down to the present day in 2024, and it marks a severe curtailing of federal power to pass civil rights laws that do not obviously respond to defects in state processes. Although Justice Kennedy wrote the opinion in *City of Boerne v. Flores*, it reflected the passion and spirit for reviving federalism that William Rehnquist had brought back into Supreme Court jurisprudence. The case held unconstitutional a statute that had passed both houses of Congress by a nearly unanimous vote: the Religious Freedom Restoration Act (RFRA). As a result of *City of Boerne v. Flores*, RFRA applies today to only the federal government and not to the states.

The Rehnquist Court, in opinions variously written by Rehnquist, Justice Kennedy, Justice O'Connor, and Justice Scalia, limited Congress's power to authorize lawsuits against states;[20] imposed a "clear statement" rule on congressional laws seriously implicating federalism, which requires Congress to speak unambiguously when it wants to press the boundaries of the constitutional structure;[21] and forbade Congress from ordering state legislators or executives to act.[22] Chief Justice Rehnquist also authored a whole series of 5–4 opinions holding that Congress could not abrogate state sovereign immunity in federal court using its enumerated powers. In the most pro-Congress decision of that era, *Gonzales v. Raich*,[23] allowing Congress to ban possession of homegrown marijuana plants in a terminal cancer patient's kitchen, Chief Justice Rehnquist joined Justice O'Connor's dissenting opinion as did Justice Clarence Thomas.

It is doubtful whether any of the other jurists whom President Reagan could have appointed to replace Chief Justice Burger would have launched a Rehnquistian federalism revolution. Federal court of appeals judges Robert H. Bork and Antonin Scalia, to Steve Calabresi's personal knowledge, had in 1986 accepted the New Deal constitutional revolution of 1937 as a fait accompli. (Justice Scalia sided with the majority in *Gonzalez v. Raich*, though he later regretted that decision.) We are not at all certain that they would have signed on to an opinion like *United States v. Lopez* without Chief Justice Rehnquist's persistent prodding and leadership.

As discussed in chapter 3, federalism was a very important issue for Ronald Reagan. He got what he wanted when he appointed Bill Rehnquist to be chief justice of the United States.

A second key area in which Chief Justice Rehnquist moved the law was to cut back on "substantive due process," in which the court invalidates state laws based on unenumerated rights gleaned from moral theory, opinion polls, partisan politics, or wherever. The Warren Court had famously done this in *Griswold v. Connecticut*,[24] and the Burger Court went much further still in its 7–2 opinion in *Roe v. Wade*,[25] from which then justice Rehnquist dissented. Rehnquist, along with Justices White, Scalia, and Thomas, tried to get *Roe v. Wade* overruled in *Planned Parenthood of Southeastern Pennsylvania v. Casey*,[26] but lost by a 5–4 margin. But Chief Justice Rehnquist did succeed in assembling a five-justice majority in *Washington v. Glucksberg*,[27] a case involving a claimed constitutional right to physician-assisted suicide. The decision laid the groundwork for overruling *Roe* by confining substantive due process rights to rights that were "deeply rooted" in American history and tradition—a test that abortion rights could never satisfy. Indeed, in 2022, the court relied on the *Glucksberg* "deeply rooted in history and tradition" test to overrule *Roe v. Wade* in *Dobbs v. Jackson Women's Health Organization*. Ed Meese and William Rehnquist eventually won the war to get *Roe v. Wade* overruled.

The court under Chief Justice Rehnquist also put an end to the Burger Court's expansive use of the Equal Protection Clause to strike down government classifications based on disability,[28] non-citizen status,[29] and illegitimacy.[30] Under Rehnquist, the only non-race-based use of the Equal Protection Clause was for sex discrimination in *United States v. Virginia* (the "VMI" case).[31] With respect to race, the Rehnquist Court invalidated both City of Richmond, Virginia, and federal minority set-aside affirmative action programs.[32] These decisions helped set the stage for the 2023 Supreme Court case invalidating race-based college admissions programs.[33]

The Rehnquist Court was not a consistent model either of originalist fidelity to the Constitution or even adherence to a looser notion of "conservative" jurisprudence. But it has a list of accomplishments that dwarf anything traceable to the Burger Court that preceded it.

Of course, those accomplishments were not the product of William Rehnquist's single-handed efforts. His court included Justice Scalia from the start—and after 1991 included Clarence Thomas. Because Justice Scalia was also a Reagan-Meese appointee, a few words about his influence are appropriate.

Justice Scalia took his seat on the U.S. Supreme Court on September 26, 1986, and he held it until he died in office on February 13, 2016, during the middle of a presidential election. He was fifty years old when he was appointed, he was seventy-nine when he died, and he served twenty-nine years on the U.S. Supreme Court, which is the sixteenth-longest term of service among the 116 men and women who have been justices.

When he was appointed, Justice Scalia was a bracing breath of fresh air to a Supreme Court that had octogenarian William J. Brennan Jr., septuagenarians Thurgood Marshall, Harry Blackmun, and Lewis Powell, and a sixty-nine-year-old Byron R. White. Brennan was the last remaining Eisenhower appointee, White was the last remaining Kennedy appointee, Marshall was the last remaining Johnson appointee, and Blackmun was within two years of becoming the last remaining Nixon appointee, as Powell was nearing retirement.

Gary Lawson had the great privilege of clerking for Justice Scalia in the October 1986 term, his first year on the court, and Steve Calabresi had the same great privilege of clerking for Justice Scalia in the following October 1987 term. Scalia's youth, energy, and enthusiasm made him a striking contrast to the five older justices listed above, at least four of whom were clinging to their jobs on the Supreme Court when they were well past their primes in the hopes of denying President Ronald Reagan the ability to appoint their successors. Justice Brennan was mentally sharp (and personally delightful), but he was so weak physically that he had to have one law clerk hold each arm when he walked down the hallway. Justice Marshall was also failing physically, and he would lose control of his cognitive faculties at times—a fact that was occasionally publicly and sadly apparent at oral arguments. While Brennan and

Marshall outlasted Ronald Reagan's presidency, they both collapsed during the presidency of George Herbert Walker Bush. Brennan was replaced by Justice David Souter, and Marshall was replaced by Justice Clarence Thomas.

Justice Byron White was mentally and physically very able when both of us served as Supreme Court law clerks, but his twenty-five years on the bench and his untheoretical, and even anti-theoretical, approach to jurisprudence made him cynical and careless in the decision of cases. He seemed to have little interest in deciding the cases correctly. Once his law clerk came to him with a draft opinion from another justice's chambers, and the clerk carefully explained why the opinion in question mangled the relevant statute. Justice White responded by saying, "We have done worse things to statutes before," and he signed the draft majority opinion. Lawson also recalls pointing out to one of Justice White's clerks that certain language in a draft opinion from Justice White's chamber seemed needlessly to address an important and dizzyingly complex issue not directly presented or briefed by the parties in the case. The clerk agreed that the language was unnecessary and might have unpredictable consequences in the future and accordingly presented the matter to Justice White, who reportedly said, "Let the law reviews figure it out." The language stayed in.

Justice Harry Blackmun did eighty pushups every morning and was physically quite fit, but he spent his days source-citing the opinions that he assigned to his law clerks to write. We both found him to be, quite frankly, an unimpressive figure intellectually, and he did not take well to criticism, especially of his precious opinion in *Roe v. Wade*.

By 1987–1988, when Steve Calabresi clerked for Justice Scalia, one seat on the court was empty because Justice Lewis Powell had retired just before turning eighty, and Justice Anthony Kennedy was only sworn in to replace him on February 18, 1988. This meant that during the 1987–1988 term of the Supreme Court, only Chief Justice Rehnquist, Justice John Paul Stevens, Justice Sandra Day O'Connor, and Justice Scalia himself were fully functional. That adds up to four functional justices on a court with nine seats. Not only were liberal law clerks writing all the Brennan, Marshall, Blackmun, and White opinions, but the justices themselves did not welcome office visits by Justice Scalia, who wanted to drop by to talk about the cases. The Supreme Court in 1987–1988 was a geriatric home, not a court. Lawson observed only slightly better matters in 1986–1987. The lack of serious dialogue, and the seemingly lockstep ideological voting patterns, clearly frustrated former professor Scalia.

Justice Scalia, meanwhile, was full of energy and ideas, eager to engage, and asked lots of questions at oral arguments. Even Chief Justice Rehnquist lacked the energy to keep up with Justice Scalia. More importantly, Scalia began championing Ed Meese's Jurisprudence of Original Public Meaning of texts, both the Constitution and statutes, though not even Rehnquist or O'Connor were willing to go along with him. The crowning blow of the October 1987 term was the Supreme Court's 7–1 opinion in *Morrison v. Olson*,[34] in which Scalia wrote a lone dissent in a separation of powers case in which Chief Justice Rehnquist's majority opinion gutted a decade of good separation of powers case law produced by his predecessor, Chief Justice Warren Burger. *Morrison v. Olson* continues to distort doctrine in multiple respects today.

Scalia tried to form an alliance with the very cerebral Justice John Paul Stevens, who sat next to him at oral arguments and could keep up with Justice Scalia's prodigious intellect, but Stevens was too left-wing and idiosyncratic to go along with Justice Scalia's jurisprudence. (Indeed, Justice Stevens did not go along with *anyone's* jurisprudence; he long defied any categorizations other than "different drummer" and "wicked smart.") Scalia then tried to form an alliance with fellow Reagan appointee Sandra Day O'Connor, only to learn that she saw little difference between her duties as an Arizona state legislator and as a justice of the Supreme Court of the United States.[35] Scalia tried to ally with Justice Kennedy, but Kennedy was not really an originalist. It was not until Justices Clarence Thomas (1991), Ruth Bader Ginsburg (1993), and Elena Kagan (2010) arrived on the U.S. Supreme Court that Scalia felt he had friends with whom he could easily talk. And, obviously, only Justice Thomas of the three agreed with Justice Scalia on basic legal methodology.

Notwithstanding this unfriendly working environment, Scalia had a momentous impact on U.S. constitutional law. The mere presence of one, and then two, Supreme Court justices who took original meaning seriously forced lawyers to take account of that position when crafting arguments. Original public meaning textualism appeared in more and more majority, concurring, and dissenting Supreme Court opinions. In 2004, a majority opinion from Justice Scalia overturned a quarter century of case law treating the Sixth Amendment right of criminal defendants to confront witnesses against them as a mere policy to be balanced against law enforcement needs and the control of court dockets. The opinion in *Crawford v. Washington*[36] carefully parses the language, history, and context of the Sixth Amendment, and it stands as perhaps the exemplary use of originalist methodology in a Supreme Court opinion. Four years later, in *District of Columbia v. Heller*,[37] Justice Scalia wrote a quintessentially originalist opinion concerning the Second Amendment's guarantee of an individual's right to own a gun. Significantly, Justice Stevens's dissenting opinion in the *Heller* case was also crafted almost entirely in the language of originalism. These events, even if merely episodic on a court with only two originalists, were almost inconceivable in 1985.

Scalia led a more successful revolution on the Supreme Court regarding statutory interpretation, arguing vigorously for the use of text over legislative history. In 1986, it was unheard of for the court to issue an opinion in a case involving the meaning of a statute that did not include, and likely focus on, the legislative history. By the time of Justice Scalia's death, it was equally unheard of for legislative history to play a prominent role in a majority opinion, and that remains true today. In 2012, along with Bryan Garner, the country's leading legal lexicographer and the editor of *Black's Law Dictionary*, Justice Scalia wrote perhaps the most influential book on statutory interpretation ever published,[38] which has become a standard reference source for lawyers, scholars, and judges at all levels.

We could write an entire book on Justice Scalia's jurisprudence and influence, but others have already done that.[39] Justice Scalia made major contributions in just about every area of law. He was a force of nature in separation of powers cases, about which he cared deeply. He lost more often than he won, but his powerful dissenting and concurring opinions are increasingly working their way into the mainstream. He wrote some key opinions on "standing to sue," which limits who can bring cases in federal court, especially when the complaints seem better suited for legislatures than courts. And in an often-underappreciated aspect of his jurisprudence, he played a huge role in the development of criminal procedure law, especially with regard to Sixth Amendment confrontation rights and Fourth Amendment search and seizure law. His focus on the original meaning of the text of the Bill of Rights—many of whose provisions are obviously designed to protect criminal defendants—sometimes put him at odds with "conservative" justices more interested in locking up guilty crooks than in correctly interpreting the text of the Constitution. Perhaps just as importantly, Justice Scalia diligently pored over the Supreme Court's certiorari petitions, finding plausible reasons to hear fewer cases than had been the norm before his arrival (and thus providing fewer opportunities for the Supreme Court to do damage!). He single-handedly persuaded the justices to decide only eighty cases a year and to do a better job on them rather than hear 150 cases a year and decide them sloppily, as the court had been doing before Scalia was appointed to it. The court's docket today is less than half as large as it was in 1986. Judicial restraint begins by not hearing cases, and Ed Meese and Ronald Reagan wanted a more judicially restrained court. Thanks in part to Justice Scalia, they got one.

Justice Scalia spent hours arguing with his colleagues to remove language from their draft opinions that would generate unnecessary litigation and would confuse and divide lower courts. He often won these battles by threatening to concur separately or dissent. Justice Scalia told Steve Calabresi during his clerkship that the most important victories he won on the Supreme Court were the ones that the public would never see. He was referring here to his efforts to keep dicta out of his colleagues' opinions and to his reduction in the size of the Supreme Court's caseload.

While this book is about Ed Meese rather than a survey of four decades of jurisprudence, it is hard to discuss Justice Scalia's impact divorced from changes on the court during his tenure. The first shift came in 1987 when, after Justice Scalia's first year on the bench, Justice Lewis Powell was replaced by Justice Anthony Kennedy. We will say more about Justice Kennedy shortly. For the moment, it is enough to note that, while Scalia found Kennedy's style to be grating at times, especially in substantive due process cases, Kennedy was far more intellectual and conservative than the decidedly untheoretical Lewis Powell.

A more seismic change happened when, in consecutive years, William Brennan and Thurgood Marshall were replaced by David Souter and Clarence Thomas. Although Souter was a bitter disappointment to conservatives ("No more Souters!" remains a conservative rallying cry), he was immeasurably more conservative than Brennan, who was the intellectual engine of the Warren Court (and to some extent the Burger Court as well). Souter was not an originalist by inclination, but his opinions were often full of arguments from text, history, and precedent. There is no question that the Supreme Court became more conservative, and even slightly more originalist, when David Souter replaced Bill Brennan, even though the Souter appointment was a big missed opportunity for the first Bush administration.

Clarence Thomas, on the other hand, has for three decades been the court's most consistent and forceful originalist—more so than Scalia and more so even than Neil Gorsuch (though we will certainly entertain arguments on that score from Gorsuchians if they want to contest the point). Thomas is much more likely than was Scalia to resort to original meaning over precedent, which is a crucial distinction, given the volume of non-originalist precedents. Suddenly, in 1991, Scalia had a good friend on the bench, who was to his right in almost every case they decided together where they differed, which was seldom.

Two years later the ornery and cynical Justice Byron White, who derisively called Scalia "The Professor" (a rude nickname once applied to Justice Felix Frankfurter), was replaced with Justice Ruth Bader Ginsburg, Justice Scalia's closest friend when they had served together on the D.C. Circuit. Scalia and Ginsburg went to the opera together, they shared New Year's Eve together, and they were warm friends. While they disagreed sharply on methodology, and often on results, they had a mutual respect that could serve as a model in sharply polarized times. Jurisprudentially, the shift from Byron White to Ruth Bader Ginsburg was almost inconsequential. Scalia lost a vote to overturn *Roe*, but he gained a close friend. For all practical purposes, the Supreme Court was much more Scalia-friendly after this appointment than it had been before.

One year later, Justice Harry Blackmun, the author of *Roe v. Wade*, and by 1994 a Brennan-like leftist who thought capital punishment had always been unconstitutional, was replaced by moderate Democrat

Stephen Breyer, a Harvard Law School professor, a distinguished First Circuit Court of Appeals judge, and a former Senate staffer who talked Senator Ted Kennedy into championing airline deregulation. Senator Orrin Hatch gushed with praise over the appointment, which replaced the Supreme Court's last remaining hardcore leftist with an economically sophisticated intellectual who was far more congenial to Justice Scalia than Justice Blackmun had ever been. Justices Scalia and Breyer agreed on very little during their time on the court, but it was disagreement grounded in high-level legal theory rather than thoughtless politics. They became famous for their dog-and-pony shows where they would debate their differences to public audiences in characteristically civil fashion.

There then followed an extraordinarily long eleven-year gap during which no vacancies arose on the Supreme Court. In 2005, moderate Justice Sandra Day O'Connor was swapped with moderate Chief Justice John Roberts, while conservative Chief Justice William Rehnquist was swapped with arch-conservative Justice Sam Alito, an alumnus of the Meese Justice Department. This swap put a moderate in charge of the agenda at court conferences, but Roberts was more conservative than O'Connor by a long shot, especially on topics such as affirmative action, abortion, and separation of powers, and Sam Alito was just as conservative as Rehnquist had been. Neither Roberts nor Alito was (or is) an originalist in the Scalia/Thomas mold, but both are better versed in originalist lore than were their predecessors.

In 2009, Sonia Sotomayor replaced David Souter, moving the Supreme Court moderately to the left. And then, in 2010, Justice John Paul Stevens retired, a week after saying that he was going to make sure that President Obama (with a Democratic Senate) had a chance to appoint his successor. President Obama tapped former Harvard Law School dean Elena Kagan, a thoughtful and stylistically elegant liberal, to replace Stevens. According to David Axelrod, President Obama's chief election strategist and senior adviser, Justice Scalia in 2009 had lobbied the Obama administration at a White House Correspondents dinner to appoint Kagan to Justice Souter's seat. "'I have no illusions that your man will nominate someone who shares my orientation,' said Scalia. ... 'But I hope he sends us someone smart. ... Let me put a finer point on it. ... I hope he sends us Elena Kagan.'"[40] As Axelrod put it, "[I] f Scalia could not have a philosophical ally in the next court appointee, he had hoped, at least, for one with the heft to give him a good, honest fight." Justices Scalia and Kagan were good friends, honest fighters, and occasionally allies on important matters like statutory interpretation and criminal procedure.

By the time Justice Scalia died on February 13, 2016, the Supreme Court was in the process of being remade as a Reagan-Meese institution. Justice Scalia did not live to see the appointments of Neil Gorsuch, Brett Kavanaugh, and Amy Coney Barrett (a former Scalia law clerk), but his legacy infuses much of the court's current work product.

Ed Meese reflects:

> President Reagan had great expectations for both Chief Justice Rehnquist and for Justice Scalia. And I would say in both cases, the expectations were more than fulfilled. ... [With Scalia,] if you look at the entire history of the Supreme Court, there's never been a better justice of the court as far as I'm concerned, both in terms of his fidelity to the Constitution but also his qualities to judge as a human being. His integrity, his consistency, his ability to write, his ability to stand courageously, even when criticized by the news media or the legal professorate—whatever happened, he was just a man of unusually great accomplishments and stature. And I would say, no question as Chief Justice Bill Rehnquist was also excellent in what he did. And particularly, holding the court together when you have such strong positions on both sides. Yes, so I would say both worked out extremely well. And both were great losses when ultimately they passed away.

The Next Vacancy

THE YEAR AFTER the Rehnquist and Scalia appointments, Lewis Powell retired, giving Ronald Reagan and Ed Meese another opportunity to pick a justice. The decision was easy, as it had already been made the prior year when the choice had come down to Scalia or Bork. As Meese put it, "[W]hen the [Powell] vacancy did come about, there was no question that Judge Bork was at the top of the list. We didn't have to go out and have a search."

Ed Meese found out about Justice Powell's retirement before it got to the press, and he called Ken Cribb on a secure phone line from a government plane to tell Cribb the news over the weekend. Cribb immediately remembered that *National Review* founder William F. Buckley Jr. had told him after the Scalia nomination that President Reagan had personally assured Buckley that Robert Bork would be his next Supreme Court nominee. By then, Cribb was working in the West Wing of the White House for Howard Baker, who was the chief of staff. Cribb tried to call Bill Buckley but could not reach him because he was out in Texas filming a special session of *Firing Line*, which he did once a year. Cribb set the White House operators to work on finding Bill Buckley, and they tracked him down in Texas so Cribb could talk to him. Cribb told Bill Buckley that Justice Powell was retiring from the Supreme Court, and he asked Buckley to call President Reagan, who was at Camp David for the weekend.

Buckley called and reached President Reagan at Camp David, and he reminded the president of his promise to appoint Bork to the next Supreme Court seat that opened up. When White House chief of staff Howard Baker greeted President Reagan Monday morning in the Oval Office, the first thing President Reagan said to Baker was "I am going to nominate Judge Robert H. Bork to fill Justice Powell's seat on the Supreme Court." Moderate Republican White House chief of staff Howard Baker had no chance to try to sway Ronald Reagan's mind about filling the Powell vacancy. Ken Cribb had beaten him to the punch.

Too much has been written about the events of 1987 for us to discuss them at length. Several matters that were not anticipated back in 1986 changed the Supreme Court appointment process—perhaps permanently.

First, the Democrats gained control of the Senate, including the Judiciary Committee that runs judicial confirmation hearings. Justice Scalia faced a committee chaired by Strom Thurmond. Robert Bork faced one chaired by Joe Biden. Second, as Meese describes it, "there'd grown up…some very vitriolic organizations on the left, such as the so-called People for the American Way, the so-called Hawaiians for Justice, and these were…effective special interest groups of the Left with respect to judicial selection." For the first time in American history, the Bork nomination led to massive nationwide advertising campaigns against a Supreme Court nominee. "And then," Meese continues, "the third thing was that there was a definite movement within the Democrat Party [to threaten to primary southern and western moderate Democrats if they voted to confirm Bork]."

In addition, Judge Bork did not use very good judgment in the way he prepared for the hearings or answered questions from the Judiciary Committee. Bork refused to let his former law clerk Peter Keisler moot him for the hearings, thinking he was so much smarter than the senators on the Judiciary Committee that he would slip right through. As a result, when asked why he wanted to be on the U.S. Supreme Court, Judge Bork foolishly said, "Because it would be an intellectual feast!" The correct answer is: "I want to be on the Supreme Court to serve my country and the Constitution, Senator." Bork also answered specific questions about how he would rule as a judge, which he ought not to have answered. (Justice Scalia, a year earlier, had refused to tell Senator Arlen Specter whether he thought *Marbury v. Madison* was rightly decided, because the issue of judicial review might come up at some point.) The bottom line, however, was that there was simply no way a Democratic Senate was going to confirm a social conservative to be the swing justice on the Supreme Court in 1987. Bork made mistakes, but they were neither the efficient nor the final cause of his nomination's collapse.

Judge Bork's confirmation was derailed by an unhinged attack made by Senator Ted Kennedy within forty-five minutes of his being nominated by President Reagan to the Supreme Court. Senator Kennedy said the following:

> Robert Bork's America is a land in which women would be forced into back-alley abortions, blacks would sit at segregated lunch counters, rogue police could break down citizens' doors in midnight raids, schoolchildren could not be taught about evolution, writers and artists would be censored at the whim or [sic] government, and the doors of the Federal courts would be shut on the fingers of millions of citizens for whom the judiciary is often the only protectors of the individual rights that are at the heart of our democracy.[41]

Not a line in this tirade by the senator was true—or even rational. Bork had called for overruling *Roe v. Wade*; he had not called for outlawing abortion. Bork had repeatedly in print defended the correctness of *Brown v. Board of Education*, and he had never defended segregation. Bork had not supported violations of the Fourth Amendment by the police, he had not argued that schoolchildren could not be taught evolution, and he had not argued for censorship of anyone.

Senator Kennedy surely knew this. As is true of many politicians, truth was not something that he valued highly. The purpose of Senator Kennedy's tirade was to freeze in place southern Democrats, like Howell Heflin of Alabama, and western Democrats, like Senator Dennis DeConcini of Arizona, to prevent them from endorsing Bork as qualified. Senator Kennedy then drummed up Democratic primary challengers against Heflin and DeConcini to run against them if they supported Bork in the Senate Judiciary Committee, of which they were members. He did the same thing to other southern and western Democrats. The televised hearings were a farce, in which Judge Bork tried to defend originalism in a neutrally principled way, while the Democrats, along with the insipid Republican—later turned Democrat—Senator Arlen Specter, ranted in response (Howard Metzenbaum's hysterics were especially memorable). Judge Bork's nomination was defeated after a bloody four-month fight by a vote of 58–42.

In the end, none of us will ever forgive the senators who disgracefully voted against Robert Bork's confirmation. Judge Bork (with Steve Calabresi as his research assistant) gave a definitive account of this travesty of a smear campaign in 1990 in *The Tempting of America: The Political Seduction of the Law*.

Once Bork's nomination failed, who was next in line? That was a problem. In 1986, Brad Reynolds' Supreme Court selection committee came up with two top candidates for the next associate justice slot, Robert Bork and Antonin Scalia, but it failed to come up with someone for 3rd place. Attorney General Meese convinced President Reagan to nominate former Harvard Law School professor, former assistant attorney general, and then current D.C. Circuit judge Douglas Ginsburg. Doug Ginsburg is a truly brilliant individual who might well have become a historically outstanding justice, but his nomination quite literally went up in smoke when it was discovered that Ginsburg had used marijuana at parties with Harvard Law students. President Reagan might well have stuck with Ginsburg if some key Republican senators had not jumped ship. So now it was a race for 4th place.

The Democrats privately told the White House Counsel's Office that former Yale Law professor Ralph K. Winter, by then a brilliant judge on the Second Circuit Court of Appeals, was also unacceptable because he was viewed as being a Bork clone. Steve Calabresi had urged his former roommate, Peter Keisler, who was then working in the White House Counsel's Office, to pick Winter, for whom he had clerked and from whom he had taken two courses in law school.

With the 1988 presidential election impending, Attorney General Meese thought it was imperative that the next nominee be thoroughly bulletproof. And that led him to recommend the nomination of Ninth Circuit judge Anthony M. Kennedy of California, a former aide to Ronald Reagan when he was governor of California. Meese explained that he "had known Tony Kennedy for a number of years, both as a close personal friend as well as one of the principal supporters in California... of Ronald Reagan.... [H]e was very helpful in a number of the initiatives that the president was promoting.... And we did a careful search of his cases as a judge on...the Ninth Circuit. And, I, as a result of all of that thought.... [t]hat he would be an excellent member of the Supreme Court."

Justice Kennedy was a sunny, mild-mannered Californian, just as surely as William Rehnquist was a product of the Midwest where he had grown up and just as surely as Justice Scalia was a loud and in-your-face New Yorker. Kennedy was cheerful, upbeat, and optimistic. And importantly after the Bork and Ginsburg nomination, Judge Kennedy had had a thoroughly boring career. He had published no law review articles, given no revolutionary speeches, and certainly never smoked marijuana with law students. Moreover, A. B. Culvahouse, who was Howard Baker's White House counsel, asked Peter Keisler, a Federalist Society co-founder who was then working as an associate White House counsel, who Keisler thought was preferable between Kennedy and fellow Ninth Circuit judge J. Clifford Wallace. Keisler, like Meese, opted for Kennedy, who was certainly the more intellectual of the two. Keisler also favored Kennedy over Wallace because, as he told Steve Calabresi in a phone call, he thought Kennedy was more libertarian, which certainly turned out to be true! Calabresi thought that by "more libertarian" Keisler was referring to freedom of expression or freedom of religion cases. Calabresi never imagined that Justice Kennedy would become a swing justice like Sandra Day O'Connor on some key social issues.

At his confirmation hearings, Justice Kennedy handled questions ably, often dodging them. He came across as mild-mannered and unthreatening, and he was not a law professor with a beard. He was confirmed 97–0 after saying that the Constitution contains a zone of liberty beyond which government may not go.

Justice Kennedy thus arrived on the Supreme Court in difficult circumstances on February 18, 1988. Republicans and Democrats alike were watching him like a hawk. Steve Calabresi was clerking that year, and he remembers Justice Scalia returning from the first conference with the other eight justices, grinning from ear to ear. We law clerks asked him why he was so happy, and he said it was because Justice Kennedy had spent twenty minutes at the conference lecturing his colleagues on how they had been too hostile to religion, and he wanted to see that stop. Associate Justice Bill Brennan immediately sent up smoke signals that *Roe v. Wade* was in danger. Right after that, the Supreme Court issued an order asking whether it should overturn a long-settled civil rights precedent. (The court ultimately, by a 9–0 vote, left the old decision in place.) By May, the left-wing intelligentsia was gasping in horror.

Of course, within a few years the gasps of horror were on the Right, as Justice Kennedy joined Justices O'Connor and Souter in retaining constitutional protection for abortion rights. In subsequent years, Justice Kennedy wrote famous opinions giving constitutional protection to LGTBQ rights and requiring states to recognize same-sex marriages. There is thus a widespread view on the Right that while Ronald Reagan and Ed Meese hit the nail on the head with Rehnquist and Scalia, their hammer hit the thumb and the forefinger with Kennedy. Respectfully, we think this is a myopic view. Anthony Kennedy, while hardly an originalist, was likely more of a Reagan-Meese justice than Judge Bork, for all his brilliance, might have been. For leftists worried more about results than methodology, defeating Judge Bork might have been a big mistake.

Ronald Reagan's first inaugural address called for renewed attention to federalism, and it was a key priority for Attorney General Meese.

Anthony Kennedy signed on to or wrote virtually every important federalism opinion that Rehnquist, O'Connor, or Scalia produced. He signed on to the Commerce Clause revolution in *United States v. Lopez* and in *United States v. Morrison*. He signed on to the revival of state sovereign immunity and wrote one of the key opinions protecting states from being sued in federal court.[42] Justice Kennedy wrote the crucial *City of Boerne v. Flores* opinion holding that federal regulation under Section 5 of the Fourteenth Amendment had to be "congruent and proportional" to be constitutional. He joined the clear-statement and anti-commandeering opinions in *Gregory v. Ashcroft, New York v. United States,* and *Printz v. United States.* Kennedy, along with Scalia, went with the majority rather than Justice O'Connor, Chief Justice Rehnquist, and Justice Thomas in holding that Congress could regulate the growing of a marijuana plant in someone's kitchen as interstate commerce, but we are not sure that Attorney General Meese might not have joined Scalia and Kennedy on that case. Justice Kennedy was a fierce force for constitutional federalism.

Steve Calabresi, as a former student, law clerk, and research assistant to Judge Robert H. Bork, doubts whether a Justice Bork would have gone along with Chief Justice Rehnquist's federalism revolution. In all of Calabresi's conversations with Bork about the constitutional revolution of 1937, Bork never once expressed the view that it could be revisited in any way.

Similarly, Judge Bork never expressed much interest in enforcing the constitutional separation of powers, which the revolution of 1937 had largely discarded. Lawson, when he was in the Office of Legal Counsel, recalls being asked to write a memo on Bork's thinking on separation of powers. Lawson found nothing of consequence in Bork's scholarly writings, and Bork's only expressions as either solicitor general or a court of appeals judge emphasized judicial restraint in the face of dubious government structures. Justice Kennedy, by contrast, was an important part of the revival of separation of powers that has occurred during the Roberts Court, including joining Chief Justice Roberts's brutal critique of the administrative state in *City of Arlington, Texas v. FCC.*[43] On this vital subject, Justice Kennedy was more constitutionalist than conservative, in line with the Meese philosophy. We are not at all confident that a Justice Bork would have taken the same approach.

Justice Kennedy was a real leader in First Amendment law, having written the critically important opinion in *Citizens United v. FEC*,[44] which limited the government's ability to constrain campaign speech via campaign finance laws. He carried through on his 1988 promise to rein in the court's often overt hostility to religion, joining, inter alia, Chief Justice Rehnquist's powerful opinion in *Zelman v. Simmons-Harris*,[45] which upheld the constitutionality of federal money going through school vouchers to religious schools. This was a key 5–4 opinion, which repudiated prior precedent. And he signed Chief Justice Rehnquist's opinion in *Washington v. Glucksberg*, endorsing the idea that substantive due process rights have to be deeply rooted in American history and opinion.

Indeed, on virtually every subject except so-called sexual privacy rights and the death penalty for minors, Justice Kennedy was a solid constitutionalist, even if he did not always express himself in originalist terms. For anyone who is not a "single-issue voter," on either side, over those "hot-button" questions, Justice Kennedy's appointment must be rated a big success for President Reagan and Attorney General Meese.

THE MEESE LEGACY IN THE CIRCUIT COURTS OF APPEALS

The Meese Circuit Court of Appeals Selection Effort

SUPREME COURT APPOINTMENTS are vital, of course, but far more cases are decided at the lower levels of the court system. The 179 federal appellate judges decide about sixty-two thousand cases a year, and the Supreme Court reviews only eighty cases from the federal courts of appeals and the fifty state supreme courts. Federal circuit court of appeals judges are responsible for implementing—or obstructing—decisions that the Supreme Court makes. The Meese DOJ gave an unprecedented degree of thought and attention to selecting court of appeals judges.

The Meese circuit court of appeals selection effort began in the summer of 1985, just as Steve Calabresi arrived at the Meese Justice Department as a special assistant to the attorney general. As it happened, the judicial selection effort was initially entrusted to Grover Rees, a friend of Steve Calabresi's from Yale College. Rees left fairly promptly to accept an appointment as chief justice of the Supreme Court of American Samoa. He was replaced by Ken Cribb's incredibly sound and smart former roommate, Steve Matthews, who conducted the job as a deputy assistant attorney general to Steve Markman in the Office of Legal Policy. Matthews and Markman would identify candidates to interview for each court of appeals vacancy. These candidates had to be interviewed, generally for an hour, by three assistant attorneys general and then by members of Meese's personal staff, such as Steve Calabresi or John Harrison, or by trusted deputy assistant attorney generals like Lee Liberman Otis in the Civil Division or Mike Carvin in the Civil Rights Division.

These hour-long interviews took up a significant part of Steve Calabresi's day, and that was no doubt true as well for other members of the department. Calabresi was looking for candidates who were not only opposed to *Roe v. Wade*—and opposed to it for constitutionally correct reasons—but who were also willing to challenge the New Deal revolution of 1937, and its abandonment of basic constitutional principles of limited federal powers and of the separation of powers. Calabresi was acutely aware that Franklin Roosevelt appointees Felix Frankfurter and Stanley Reed had become bitter opponents of William O. Douglas and Hugo Black; that Eisenhower appointees Earl Warren and William Brennan had become opponents of John Marshall Harlan the younger and Potter Stewart; that Kennedy appointees Byron White and Arthur Goldberg had become opponents; and that Nixon appointees Harry Blackmun and William Rehnquist had become opponents. Those administrations, to the extent that they devoted any serious thought to the appointment process, were looking for judges who would rule a certain way in certain cases, not judges who had coherent constitutional philosophies that could be applied to numerous unknown cases in the future. Roosevelt got his New Deal approved, and Nixon got some guilty crooks locked up, but neither Roosevelt nor Nixon, for all their numerous appointments, secured a federal judiciary with a consistent approach to constitutionalism and law.

Steve Calabresi was determined that the associate justices he recommended to Brad Reynolds and the court of appeals judges he recommended to Ed Meese would all be people who were reasoning in the right originalist way. He wanted Reagan appointees who would join forces in opposing the huge number of Carter appointees on the federal appellate bench by presenting a textually grounded and united jurisprudential front. By and large, the Meese Justice Department was uniquely successful in attaining that goal.

Meese noted that President Reagan largely ended a practice of presidential deference to senators on federal circuit court of appeals judges (though the occasional horse trade was unavoidable), and he insisted that senators submit three candidates for federal district court appointments instead of only one. This brought about a near revolution in federal judicial selection. That President Reagan and Attorney General Meese were able to pull this off was nothing short of astonishing.[46]

Steve Calabresi never asked a judicial candidate about *Roe v. Wade* itself, but he did ask about a substantive due process right to physician-assisted suicide, which the Supreme Court found a decade later *not* to be a constitutional right. He also asked judicial candidates about their views on *Lochner v. New York*, *Wickard v. Filburn*, and *Baker v. Carr*—all cases that implicated fundamental questions about the extent of constitutional limitations and powers and about the appropriate judicial role. Finally, he asked them about originalism versus the living constitution. After an hour of this, it was pretty clear where all the judicial candidates stood on just about everything. The hapless nominees had no idea that federalism—which at the time was a non-issue in the courts—was a make-or-break issue for Calabresi, so they merrily shared their views. The most conservative nominee Steve Calabresi ever interviewed was David Sentelle, who got a seat on the D.C. Circuit. He was the only nominee to get every question right. The most liberal nominee Steve Calabresi ever interviewed was David Souter for appointment to the First Circuit. Professor Calabresi concluded he would be a John Paul Stevens–like judge, which also proved to be exactly right.

Ironically, shortly after Calabresi interviewed Souter, Calabresi's uncle, Yale Law School dean Guido Calabresi, called him. Steve Calabresi mentioned that he had just talked to a good friend of Guido's, David Souter, who was, along with Guido, a member of the Rhodes Scholarship selection committee for New England. Guido Calabresi exploded with anger and said, "You had better not be considering him for appointment as a judge because he is one of the most right-wing reactionaries I know!"

Steve Calabresi asked his uncle why he thought that, and Guido Calabresi responded that he had once had a two-hour argument with Souter in which he was unable to persuade Souter that Brennan and Marshall were right that the death penalty was always and everywhere unconstitutional! This persuaded Steve Calabresi that he was right that Souter was more like John Paul Stevens than he was like Brennan and Marshall. That was hardly ideal, but it was not catastrophic.

Ed Meese never interviewed a single court of appeals candidate, but with the team of people he had interviewing those candidates, he did not need to. Again, that team included Brad Reynolds, Ken Cribb, Chuck Cooper, Steve Markman, Steve Matthews, Richard Willard, Steve Calabresi, John Harrison, Lee Liberman Otis, and Mike Carvin, among others. No Harry Blackmuns were going to get by that group.

An unusually large number of the Reagan judicial appointees were former law professors of great distinction, including Robert H. Bork, Antonin Scalia, Ralph K. Winter, Richard Posner, J. Harvie Wilkinson, Frank Easterbrook, Stephen Williams, Douglas Ginsburg, Pasco Bowman, and John Noonan. Meese explained the rationale: "The president felt that the more you knew about a person who is being considered for nomination, the better his nominees would be. And that is why [so] many of the nominees for appellate court judges in particular were either law professors, or sitting judges on the trial courts, or in the state court systems.... You had a record essentially to look at [and] to see and to give you an indication of their adherence to the rule of law in their decision-making process and basically what they would do if they were put on the federal bench." To be sure, looking at academic records circa 1985 required making some inferences. Very few of those academics wrote on constitutional theory rather than, for example, antitrust, corporate law, or administrative law. One had to rely on general habits of reasoning which, if applied to constitutional theory, would push people as judges toward originalism. That is why the interview process mattered.

The result was a very different federal appellate bench by 1988 than had existed in 1980 when the two of us entered law school.

The D.C. Circuit

THE REAGAN REVOLUTION made a big hit with the judges it named to the prestigious United States Court of Appeals for the District of Columbia Circuit. The *en banc* majority of the court went from liberal to conservative during Meese's tenure as attorney general, building on good work done in the previous four years.

The D.C. Circuit is often considered to be second in power only to the U.S. Supreme Court. Many politically and constitutionally charged cases tend to arise in Washington, D.C. In addition, a disproportionate number of Supreme Court nominees have been drawn from the ranks of the D.C. Circuit. Finally, many D.C. Circuit clerks go on to clerk on the U.S. Supreme Court, where they play a consequential role. On vital questions of administrative law, which governs how the vast federal administrative state conducts its business, the D.C. Circuit is *more* important than the Supreme Court, because most such questions never reach the Supreme Court level and an outsized share of those cases end up in the D.C. Circuit.

Attorney General William French Smith urged President Reagan to appoint future Supreme Court nominees Robert H. Bork and Antonin Scalia, both staunch originalists, to the D.C. Circuit in 1982. The foundational nature of these two appointments cannot be overstated. Both men were towering intellectuals and forces of nature who contributed mightily to the development of originalism as a theory of constitutional interpretation. White House counsellor Ed Meese was strongly behind the Bork and Scalia appointments during Ronald Reagan's first term.

William French Smith then urged President Reagan to appoint his thirty-seven-year-old counsellor, liberal Republican Ken Starr, to the D.C. Circuit in 1983. Steve Calabresi clerked on the D.C. Circuit for Judge Bork in 1984–1985 and saw that Starr routinely joined the Jimmy Carter–appointed judges in big cases and small. Lawson clerked for Judge Scalia at the same time and had a modestly more optimistic view of Judge Starr, though Starr's writing style was sometimes over-the-top. Starr was not an originalist—and indeed did not have a discernible jurisprudential approach. Starr was subsequently named solicitor general under President George Herbert Walker Bush, where he tacked so far left that Attorney General Richard Thornburgh, urged on by future attorney general William Barr, threatened to resign in protest if Starr was nominated by Bush to the Supreme Court. President Bush instead nominated David Souter, passing over the outstanding Edith Jones (who concededly was so good that she might have had problems getting confirmed by a politicized Senate). Starr later gained fame—or infamy, depending on one's outlook—as the independent counsel investigating Bill Clinton. That job, fairly or not, permanently ended Ken Starr's career in politics and as a government official, which led to a long stint in university administration as dean of Pepperdine Law School and president of Baylor University. In the end, Starr as a judge was a good deal better jurisprudentially than the court's Democratic appointees (with the notable exception of Ruth Bader Ginsburg, who was an outstanding court of appeals judge), but we doubt that he would have made it through the Meese DOJ gauntlet if his candidacy had come up a few years later.

When Meese became attorney general on February 25, 1985, he thus inherited two superb D.C. Circuit judges (Bork and Scalia), one moderate Republican (Starr), and half a dozen mostly hostile Democratic appointees, plus an eclectic mix of senior judges who frequently sat on panels, often as randomizing elements. Attorney General Meese's first recommendation to President Reagan for the D.C. Circuit was the brilliant, but temperamental, Laurence Silberman. Silberman had served in the Nixon and Ford administrations, where he had been the author of Nixon's affirmative action plan—an idea that he had come to reject as being evil. Silberman had then also served as deputy attorney general under President Ford and was good friends with Bork and Scalia. He was widely considered to be a possible Supreme Court nominee himself, though his personality was probably too prickly to make that fully realistic.

Silberman took his seat on the court on October 28, 1985, and he continued to hear cases as a senior judge on the D.C. Circuit until his death on October 2, 2022. While serving on the D.C. Circuit, Judge Silberman was appointed by Chief Justice Rehnquist to be, in addition, a judge of the United States Foreign Intelligence Surveillance Court from 1996 to 2003. President George W. Bush then appointed Judge Silberman to be the chair of the Iraq Intelligence Commission in the executive branch in 2004–2005—a job that was compatible with Judge Silberman remaining on the D.C. Circuit.[47] As a jurist, Silberman was sharp, often acerbic, and absolutely committed to the rule of law. By any available metric, Attorney General Meese's urging of the appointment of Larry

Silberman to the D.C. Circuit was an act of brilliance. Silberman played a leading role on the D.C. Circuit for more than a third of a century. One of his former law clerks, Amy Coney Barrett, went on to clerk for Justice Antonin Scalia, and she was appointed to the Supreme Court herself by former president Donald Trump to replace Justice Ruth Bader Ginsburg, who died in the middle of the 2020 presidential election.

We should add that Ken Cribb gets some credit here due to his longtime friendship with Judge Silberman and his then wife, Ricky. Indeed, Ken was always eager to promote Judge Silberman for appointment to the Supreme Court, but the George H. W. Bush White House Counsel's Office prevented this from happening because of fears that Silberman and Justice Antonin Scalia would fight if both men, with very big egos, were on the Supreme Court together. Silberman angled for the nomination in 1987 when Judge Robert H. Bork's nomination to the Supreme Court was collapsing, but he was stopped dead by liberal D.C. Circuit judge Abner Mikva's statement that Silberman had once threatened to punch him in the nose when they disagreed about a case. As we said above, Judge Silberman was prickly.

Several months later, Attorney General Meese recommended that former senator James L. Buckley (R-NY) be appointed to the D.C. Circuit. Buckley was easily confirmed by his former friends in the U.S. Senate, in which he had served one term representing the state of New York. Jim Buckley was a very bright conservative, like his brother Bill Buckley, who had founded the conservative magazine *National Review*. Both President Reagan and Attorney General Meese were happy to appoint a very bright, committed conservative to this seat on the D.C. Circuit, where Buckley was always a reliable and thoughtful conservative presence. Judge Buckley remained eligible to hear cases on senior status until he died at the age of one hundred on August 18, 2023.

Ed Meese's third recommendation to President Ronald Reagan for appointment to the D.C. Circuit was a brilliant libertarian-conservative law professor, Stephen F. Williams. Before becoming a federal judge, Professor Williams had been the faculty advisor to the University of Colorado Federalist Society chapter. The Meese Justice Department initially tried to get Steve Williams appointed to the Tenth Circuit in Colorado, but the attempt was blocked by Republican senator Bill Armstrong, who complained that Williams was inactive in the Colorado Republican Party and had supported George McGovern for president in 1972.

Fortunately, Steve Williams's father was very close to Bill Buckley, who called Meese to vouch for Williams. The appointment went forward as an appointment to the D.C. Circuit (which has no home state senators to contend with and which is far more powerful than the Tenth Circuit), with Judge Williams taking his seat on June 16, 1986. Steve Calabresi was primarily responsible for this appointment, and he takes great pride in it. Indeed, Calabresi unsuccessfully lobbied the administration of the first President Bush to appoint Steve Williams to the Supreme Court instead of David Souter, but Williams was deemed to be unconfirmable and was thus not considered seriously. Judge Williams continued to hear cases on senior status in 2020 at the youthful age of eighty-three until he died of COVID-19 on August 20, 2020 (his father had lived to be ninety-eight). The intellectual Reagan Revolution on the D.C. Circuit was really crackling at this point.

Ed Meese's fourth recommendation for a Reagan appointment to the D.C. Circuit was Harvard Law School professor Douglas H. Ginsburg, who was appointed at the age of forty on October 14, 1986. Ginsburg had been Meese's assistant attorney general for the Antitrust Division, where he followed the economic approach pioneered by Robert Bork as a Yale Law School professor in the 1960s and 1970s. This was a spectacular appointment of a brilliant man who knew a lot about law, economics, and regulation and who could help push Ronald Reagan's deregulation efforts through the D.C. Circuit in the face of sometimes lawless opposition.

As was noted above, Ginsburg was nominated to the U.S. Supreme Court in 1987—a move both of us cheered at the time. Judge Ginsburg is still only seventy-seven in the year 2024; he has senior status on the D.C. Circuit, where he can hear cases if he wishes, and he teaches at the Antonin Scalia Law School at George Mason University.

Ed Meese's fifth and final recommendation for appointment to the D.C. Circuit was North Carolina district judge David B. Sentelle. Judge Sentelle wears cowboy boots, has a very strong personality, and is the most conservative judicial nominee Steve Calabresi ever had the pleasure of interviewing. The interview went on for over an hour and established that Calabresi and Sentelle both regretted Franklin D. Roosevelt's judicial revolution of 1937. Judge Sentelle was confirmed to the seat that Judge Scalia vacated when he was appointed to the Supreme Court. Both Ken Cribb and Steve Calabresi strongly supported the Sentelle appointment, which was particularly the work of Meese's judge-picker Steve Matthews.

Judge Sentelle played an unusually important role as a federal judge because Chief Justice William Rehnquist, with whom Sentelle played poker, appointed Sentelle the chief judge of the three-judge special court that appointed independent counsels under the Ethics in Government Act. Judge Sentelle convinced Ken Starr to become the special counsel who investigated Bill and Hillary Clinton. This was, as it turned out, a double-demolition job. It destroyed not only Ken Starr's governmental career and chances of being a squishy Supreme Court nominee but also greatly hurt the Clintons, and it may be one of many reasons why Hillary Clinton was not elected president in 2016. Judge Sentelle is eighty years old, and he continues to hear cases on senior status thirty-six years after he was appointed to the D.C. Circuit.

By the end of 1987, the four Clinton appointees on the D.C. Circuit—Abner Mikva, Patricia Wald, Harry Edwards, and Ruth Bader Ginsburg—were outnumbered by seven intellectually powerful Reagan-appointed judges on the D.C. Circuit: Robert H. Bork, Ken Starr, Larry Silberman, Jim Buckley, Steve Williams, Douglas Ginsburg, and David Sentelle. Judge Bork resigned, and the senior President Bush filled his seat with Judge Clarence Thomas, who would himself go on to fame and glory as only the second Black American in history to be appointed to the U.S. Supreme Court—and quite possibly the most thoroughgoing originalist ever to sit on the court. Judge Bork also had the pleasure of seeing one of his closest friends, Judge Ray Randolph, appointed to a D.C. Circuit seat by the first President Bush. The D.C. Circuit was transformed from being a very liberal court in the 1950s, 1960s, and 1970s into being a powerhouse bastion of the Reagan Revolution—a highly intellectual conservative and libertarian court. There is no other federal circuit court of appeals that so thoroughly embodied the Reagan Revolution in the federal courts as did the D.C. Circuit from the 1980s until 2013.

The D.C. Circuit remained a Reagan Revolution court from Ed Meese's last day in office in July 1988 until November 2013—a period of twenty-five years of continuous economic growth due in part to the D.C. Circuit's abandonment of its former hostility to deregulation. Finally, Senate Majority Leader Harry Reid abolished the filibuster of inferior federal court judges and executive branch nominees so he could break the Reaganite majority on the D.C. Circuit. While President Trump tipped many federal circuit courts of appeals back in a Reaganite direction, he lacked the vacancies needed to do that with the D.C. Circuit. But the price Harry Reid paid to take over the D.C. Circuit became apparent when Senate Republicans abolished the filibuster of Supreme Court nominees in 2017. This, in turn, paved the way for the appointment of originalists Neil Gorsuch to replace Antonin Scalia, Brett Kavanaugh to replace Anthony M. Kennedy, and Amy Coney Barrett to replace Ruth Bader Ginsburg on the U.S. Supreme Court.

The Other United States Circuit Courts of Appeals

RONALD REAGAN, following the recommendations of the Meese Justice Department, appointed a number of very distinguished judges to the other federal courts of appeals. We also give the Meese Justice Department a measure of credit for some of the George H. W. Bush appointees to these courts picked by Lee Liberman Otis, an alumna of the Meese DOJ. Ed Meese had a very close working relationship with Vice President Bush and Bush's counsel C. Boyden Gray, both of whom were in their own soft-spoken ways advocates of the Reagan Revolution. Meese employed at the Justice Department former Scalia law clerk John Schmitz, who was detailed to the vice president's office to assist Boyden Gray. Schmitz went on to persuade Boyden Gray to hire Meese alumna, and Federalist Society co-founder, Lee Liberman Otis to take charge of judicial selection for the first Bush administration.

President-Elect Bush's instructions to Boyden Gray were that he was going to retain Ed Meese's hand-picked successor, Richard Thornburg, as attorney general and that judicial selection should continue to be, run out of the White House Counsel's Office, in exactly the same way as Ed Meese had run it. Boyden Gray then made Lee Liberman Otis the Bush White House czar of judicial selection. The Reagan-Meese Revolution on judicial selection, thanks to Boyden and Lee, thus ran from 1985 until noon on January 20, 1993.

The First Circuit Court of Appeals is one of the smallest circuits, covering Massachusetts, Rhode Island, New Hampshire, Maine, and Puerto Rico. During his first term, President Reagan appointed Puerto Rican conservative Juan R. Torruella to the First Circuit, where he served with great distinction until his death on October 26, 2020. Attorney General Meese recommended that President Ronald Reagan appoint the very able moderate conservative Bruce Selya from Rhode Island. The senior President Bush appointed David Souter to the First Circuit before elevating him to the U.S. Supreme Court. Interestingly, despite its small size and relative anonymity among federal circuits, the First Circuit produced two Supreme Court justices in the 1990s, as President Clinton elevated Stephen Breyer in 1994. President Bush's best appointee to the First Circuit was undoubtedly the very cerebral Judge Michael Boudin.

Appointments to the Second Circuit, which encompasses New York, Connecticut, and Vermont, were hampered by the fact that Senator Al D'Amato (R-NY) insisted on controlling the New York state seats,[48] which he gave to lawyers with no commitment to the Meese Revolution. But there were a few bright lights. One such light that preceded Meese's tenure as attorney general was Yale Law professor Ralph K. Winter, who was appointed to a "Connecticut seat" during Reagan's first term. Winter was a leading scholar in business law, which is a subject that comes up often in the Second Circuit via its jurisdiction over federal cases from New York and the Wall Street financial district. Winter was a very smart and able judge for whom Steve Calabresi clerked in 1983–1984. Judge Winter continued to sit on cases on the Second Circuit at the age of eighty-five until his death on December 8, 2020. A second light was the appointment of bright and lively conservative Judge J. Daniel Mahoney, the former chairman of the New York Conservative Party. He and Ralph Winter became great friends. The third key appointment to the Second Circuit was of Reagan-appointed district judge John Walker, who was the first cousin of President George Herbert Walker Bush. The Reagan-Bush judge-pickers had acquired such a reputation for excellence in hiring that no one even tried to complain about nepotism when President Bush appointed his first cousin to the Second Circuit. The fourth and final key appointment to the Second Circuit was Lee Liberman Otis's successful effort to get a brilliant, New

York City, Hayekian lawyer, Dennis Jacobs, appointed in October 1992, right before President Bush lost his bid for reelection. The key here was that former Jimmy Carter secretary of state Cyrus Vance was a law partner and friend of Dennis Jacobs and loved him. He demanded that Senate Democrats confirm Dennis, and they very reluctantly did so. Jacobs is an intellectual whirlwind who took senior status during the Trump administration in 2019.

The Third Circuit covers Pennsylvania, New Jersey, Delaware, and the Virgin Islands. While President Reagan appointed some solid lawyers to that court, such as Walter Stapleton, the only Meese Revolutionary appointed was future Supreme Court justice and Meese DOJ alumnus Samuel Alito. Ronald Reagan had appointed Alito to be the U.S. attorney for the District of New Jersey at Meese's suggestion. Alito's promotion to the Third Circuit was entirely Lee Liberman Otis's doing. President George W. Bush promoted Alito to the Supreme Court at the suggestion of Meese and Leonard Leo. While Justice Alito is not a strict originalist in the Thomas/Gorsuch mode, he is a practitioner of what is sometimes called "inclusive originalism," a term coined by law professor Will Baude[49] to describe a method that looks to precedent, policy, and practice as tools to help ascertain original meaning.[50] His appointment alone makes the Meese/Reagan legacy on the Third Circuit a spectacular success.

There were three Reagan Revolutionaries appointed to the Fourth Circuit, which takes in Maryland, North Carolina, South Carolina, Virginia, and West Virginia. The Fourth Circuit was a very solidly conservative court from the 1980s until 2009, though today it has swung left. In his first term, President Reagan appointed J. Harvie Wilkinson, a former professor of law at the University of Virginia School of Law. Judge Wilkinson took his seat on August 13, 1984, and he is still on active status in 2024 at the age of seventy-nine. He is brilliant, a charming conversationalist, and is one of the brightest ornaments on the federal bench, though his approach may reflect a traditional conservative inclination to "judicial restraint" more than a potentially radical Meese-Revolutionary originalism. He has been a prolific scholar while on the bench—far more so, intriguingly, than during his time in the academy. A decade later, in 1991, President Bush, at the instigation of

Lee Liberman Otis, appointed former Scalia law clerk J. Michael Luttig, who took office on August 2, 1991. Mike was a brilliant originalist judge whom Leonard Leo and Ed Meese tried valiantly to persuade the feckless second Bush administration to appoint to the U.S. Supreme Court. Unfortunately, Judge Luttig was so mad to be passed over that he resigned his judgeship to become general counsel to the Boeing Company. In 1990, President Bush appointed Paul Niemeyer, whom Reagan and Meese had appointed to the District Court, to the Fourth Circuit, and Judge Niemeyer has ever since been one of the stars of the federal circuit courts of appeals. The Fourth Circuit has become perhaps the most far-left federal appeals court, and Judge Niemeyer's dissents are often vindicated by the Supreme Court when it reviews Fourth Circuit decisions. One of Judge Niemeyer's clerks, Michael Scudder, a former student of Steve Calabresi's, was appointed by President Trump to the Seventh Circuit seat vacated by Reagan appointee Richard Posner.

There were many Reagan Revolution stars on the Fifth Circuit (Louisiana, Mississippi, and Texas), but two especially stand out. The first is Judge Edith Jones who took office on April 4, 1985. Judge Jones was one of two finalists, along with Judge David Souter, who were interviewed by the senior President Bush to fill the vacancy created on the U.S. Supreme Court by the resignation of Justice William Brennan. To his credit, President Bush came out of the interviews much preferring Judge Jones to Judge Souter, but his staff told him, probably correctly, that Judge Jones was unconfirmable, so David Souter got the nomination. Judge Jones continues to serve with great distinction and is universally recognized as a conservative icon. The other noteworthy star Reagan appointment to the Fifth Circuit was Judge Jerry Smith, who was confirmed in late 1987. Smith is as much an icon as his colleague Edith Jones. His former law clerks include Senator Tom Cotton; longtime Institute for Justice stalwart Dana Berliner; more than half a dozen judges, including his now colleague James Ho; and a host of distinguished law professors such as Julian Ku, Aaron Nielson, Ilya Somin, and Todd Zywicki.

On the Sixth Circuit, covering Kentucky, Michigan, Ohio, and Tennessee, Reagan's second term saw three strong appointments: Danny Boggs, Alan Norris (senior status in 2001), and James Ryan (senior status in 2000). Judge Boggs in particular was recommended to the Meese DOJ by former solicitor general Robert H. Bork, for whom he had worked for two years as an assistant solicitor general arguing the government's cases in the U.S. Supreme Court. It was an inspired recommendation. Judge Boggs is a brilliant, widely read intellectual, who is famous for giving his law clerk candidates an eclectic quiz.[51] He was on the short list of possible Supreme Court nominees during George W. Bush's presidency. Judge Boggs remains on senior status, which he took in 2017, after distinguishing himself for thirty years as one of the finest Reagan appointees.

President Reagan made some truly excellent appointments to the United States Court of Appeals for the Seventh Circuit (Illinois, Indiana, Wisconsin), including Frank Easterbrook, Joel Flaum, Michael Kanne, Kenneth Ripple, and Daniel Manion. Two appointees to that court deserve special mention.

The first person warranting special mention, Richard Posner, pointedly did not make our "truly excellent" list above. In the early 1990s, Lawson told one of his colleagues at Northwestern University School of Law that if he could remove one person from the federal bench, it would not be any of the liberal icons. It would be Richard Posner.

Richard Posner is one of the smartest human beings ever to walk the planet. He was probably the 20th century's closest approximation of the 19th-century utilitarian political philosopher Jeremy Bentham—and, despite our strong substantive disagreements with Bentham on just about everything, we mean that as a compliment to Posner's breadth and intellect. As an academic, Posner and his prolific co-author William Landes revolutionized jurisprudence by popularizing "law and economics," which applied tools of economic analysis to virtually every legal problem imaginable. Posner went on to write more than forty books, many while serving on the Seventh Circuit, on everything from jurisprudence to sexuality to the relationship between law and literature, and he became the most cited federal appeals court judge in the nation. He remains one of the most important figures in American legal thought, and Lawson would have been honored to have him as a colleague on any law faculty in the world. He just had no business being a judge.

Posner hated originalism. More broadly, he hated *law*, which he saw as an irrational obstacle standing in the way of achieving good results. Indeed, one of his books was entitled *Overcoming Law*, and he constantly sparred with Justice Antonin Scalia and Professor Richard Epstein. That kind of sparring over fundamental questions of law, policy, and social organization was wonderful in the academy. It was not so wonderful on the bench. And his academic inclinations sometimes led him to write opinions deciding "cases" quite different from the ones actually presented by the parties, no doubt because the faux cases he imagined were more intellectually interesting than the real ones brought before him.[52] He was probably President Reagan's biggest mistake in judicial appointments.

Frank Easterbrook, by contrast, is a very good man and a model judge. He was Robert Bork's top assistant solicitor general when Bork was solicitor general. In 1978, he joined the University of Chicago Law School faculty, where he quickly became one of the country's leading corporate law and antitrust scholars—and had he instead concentrated his prodigious intellectual energies on constitutional theory, we suspect that our previous chapter on originalism in the academy before Ed Meese might have looked very different. He was appointed to the Seventh Circuit in 1985, on Bork's recommendation, at the age of thirty-seven, and he has served with great distinction, as much committed to the enterprise of law as Posner was against it. Easterbrook continues to serve on active status in 2024 at the age of seventy-five. He was and is an exemplary and brilliant Reagan Revolutionary judge.

The Eighth Circuit covers a lot of space and a lot of states: Arkansas, Iowa, Minnesota, Missouri, Nebraska, North Dakota, and South Dakota. Ronald Reagan made a transformative Reagan Revolutionary appointment of law professor Pasco Bowman to the Eighth Circuit, and Bowman was on Reagan's list of potential Supreme Court nominees, only to be vetoed by Senate Democrats. As with Frank Easterbrook, if Professor Bowman as an academic had pursued constitutional theory rather than business law, the history of originalism might have looked different. The same can be said of Morris ("Buzz") Arnold, an outstanding legal historian whom President Reagan appointed to the district court in 1985. In 1991, Lee Liberman Otis secured Arnold's appointment to the Eighth Circuit.

The vast Ninth Circuit, spanning Alaska, Arizona, California, Guam, Hawaii, Idaho, Montana, Nevada, the Northern Mariana Islands, Oregon, and Washington, was so thoroughly packed by the Carter administration that it is only now starting to recover. Ronald Reagan made a number of conservative appointments to that court, but only two were bona fide Reagan Revolutionaries: Diarmuid O'Scannlain and Alex Kozinski. Judge O'Scannlain is such a conservative star that in recent years he has been among the leading "feeder" judges whose law clerks go on to clerk for the Supreme Court, even though he has been on senior status since 2016.[53] Alex Kozinski was an intellectual and influential jurist, but history will likely give priority to his 2017 resignation in the face of multiple accusations of sexual harassment rather than to his remarkable record as a judge. Lee Liberman Otis in 1991 secured the appointment of another Reaganite Ninth Circuit judge, Andrew Kleinfeld, of Alaska, whom Reagan and Meese had appointed to the district court in that state.

President Reagan had many appointments to the Tenth Circuit, which covers Colorado, Kansas, New Mexico, Oklahoma, Utah, and Wyoming. Steve Calabresi's favorite recommendation was David Ebel, a former law clerk to Justice Byron White. Judge Ebel took senior status in 2006, when he was replaced by Neil Gorsuch. There were only two Reagan appointees to the Eleventh Circuit (Alabama, Florida, Georgia), but both of them—Larry Edmondson and Emmett Cox—were solid Reagan Revolutionaries. The one remaining court is the Federal Circuit, created in 1982 primarily to handle patent appeals but also having a broad jurisdiction that includes takings claims, government employment and contracting cases, and appeals from the U.S. Court of International Trade. Steve Calabresi was proudest of his recommendation of the appointments of Haldane Robert Mayer and Paul Michel.

Here is a list of all eighty-three Reagan appointees to the federal circuit courts of appeals:

D.C. Circuit

Robert Bork
Antonin Scalia
Kenneth W. Starr
Laurence J. Silberman
James L. Buckley
Stephen F. Williams
Douglas H. Ginsburg
David B. Sentelle

First Circuit

Juan R. Torruella
Bruce M. Selya

Second Circuit

Richard J. Cardamone
Lawrence W. Pierce
Ralph K. Winter Jr.
George C. Pratt

Roger Miner
Frank Altimari
J. Daniel Mahoney

Third Circuit

Edward R. Becker
Carol Los Mansmann
Walter King Stapleton
Morton Ira Greenberg
William D. Hutchinson
Anthony Joseph Scirica
Robert Cowen
Richard Lowell Nygaard

Fourth Circuit

Robert F. Chapman
J. Harvie Wilkinson III
Emory M. Sneeden
William Walter Wilkins

Fifth Circuit

William Lockhart Garwood
Patrick Higginbotham
E. Grady Jolly
W. Eugene Davis
Robert Madden Hill
Edith Jones
Jerry Edwin Smith
John M. Duhé Jr.

Sixth Circuit

Leroy John Contie Jr.
Robert B. Krupansky
Harry W. Wellford
Herbert Theodore Milburn

Ralph B. Guy Jr.
David Aldrich Nelson
James L. Ryan
Danny J. Boggs
Alan Eugene Norris

Seventh Circuit

Jesse E. Eschbach
Richard A. Posner
John Louis Coffey
Joel Flaum
Frank Easterbrook
Kenneth Francis Ripple
Daniel A. Manion
Michael Stephen Kanne

Eighth Circuit

John R. Gibson
George Gardner Fagg
Pasco Bowman II
Roger Leland Wollman
Frank J. Magill
C. Arlen Beam

Ninth Circuit

Robert Beezer
Cynthia Holcomb Hall
Charles E. Wiggins
Melvin T. Brunetti
Alex Kozinski
John T. Noonan Jr.
David R. Thompson
Diarmuid O'Scannlain
Edward Leavy
Stephen S. Trott

Tenth Circuit

John Carbone Porfilio
Stephen H. Anderson
Deanell Reece Tacha
Bobby Ray Baldock
Wade Brorby
David M. Ebel

Federal Circuit

Pauline Newman
Jean Galloway Bissell
Glenn Leroy Archer Jr.
Haldane Robert Mayer
Paul R. Michel

Eleventh Circuit

James Larry Edmondson
Emmett Ripley Cox

The Claims Court and the Federal Circuit

THE MEESE JUDICIAL SELECTION team was committed to appointing judges to the Claims Court and the Federal Circuit who understood the centrality of the Takings Clause as a bulwark of economic liberty. As a result, Ronald Reagan's former campaign counsel, Loren Smith, was appointed to the Claims Court where he rapidly became chief judge—a post he would hold for many years. The Meese team was committed to the idea that some government regulations were so intrusive that they constituted takings of private property.

Conclusion

WE COULD SAY much more about the Reagan record on judicial appointments, and there are many circuit court of appeals judges, of the eighty-three Reagan appointed, including some that we did not name here, who merit sections or even chapters of their own. The overall record, however, is enough to count President Reagan's effect on the judiciary as one of many reasons why President Reagan ranks with the likes of George Washington, Thomas Jefferson, Andrew Jackson, Abraham Lincoln, and Franklin Roosevelt as what noted political scientist Stephen Skowronek has termed a "transformative" president.[54] Ed Meese and his Department of Justice deserve at least some credit for that.

When President George H. W. Bush took office, White House counsel C. Boyden Gray replaced Ed Meese as the key lawyer who had the president's ear. Attorney General Richard Thornburgh was a rare carryover appointment from the Reagan administration after President Bush's establishment-oriented personnel shop fired 90 percent of President Ronald Reagan's political appointees. Bush owed his victory in November 1988 to Reagan's growing economy, peace with foreign nations, and hard campaign work by his seventy-seven-year-old predecessor who had gone to Orange County, California, the weekend before election day to campaign for Bush. Bush carried California and was the last Republican ever to do so as of 2020.

Two fortresses of the Reagan Revolution held out in an administration composed largely of Gerald Ford Republicans: Vice President Dan Quayle's office, which was nicknamed "Fort Reagan," and C. Boyden Gray's office, where John Schmitz got off Ed Meese's payroll and onto the White House staff. Schmitz persuaded Boyden to hire Lee Liberman Otis to be the head judge-picker, as well as hiring young conservative stalwarts like Brent Hatch and Nelson Lund. Lee Liberman Otis did an absolutely spectacular job in picking circuit court of appeals judges, and in getting Justice Clarence Thomas appointed to the U.S. Supreme Court. As a result of her hard work, George H. W. Bush's administration was as good as the Reagan administration with respect to judicial appointments.

Legal policy during the George H. W. Bush years continued on autopilot once Meese resigned as attorney general. Attorney General Thornburgh wisely made few changes to the course Meese had set, and Reagan administration alumnus Bill Barr held to that course when he replaced Thornburgh. Judicial appointments at the circuit court level were as good as they had been under Meese, but Supreme Court selection was compromised by the fact that Bush had inherited a Senate of 55 Democrats and 45 Republicans. This was not a great state of affairs, but there were still in those days enough southern and western moderate Democrats to confirm a good Supreme Court justice. Clarence Thomas, after a searing fight, was confirmed 52–48.

Boyden Gray and Lee Liberman Otis are often criticized by conservatives for the mistaken appointment of David Souter to the Supreme Court, but conservatives should remember that the most conservative and originalist Supreme Court justice of the last forty years is without a doubt George H. W. Bush's appointment of Justice Clarence Thomas. They should also reflect on the list below of President George H. W. Bush's stellar set of forty-two appointments to the federal courts of appeals.

D.C. Circuit

Clarence Thomas
Karen L. Henderson
A. Raymond Randolph

First Circuit

Conrad K. Cyr
David H. Souter
Michael Boudin
Norman H. Stahl

Second Circuit

John M. Walker Jr.
Joseph M. McLaughlin
Dennis Jacobs

Third Circuit

Samuel A. Alito Jr.
Jane Richards Roth
Timothy K. Lewis

Fourth Circuit

Paul V. Niemeyer
Clyde H. Hamilton
J. Michael Luttig
Karen J. Williams

Fifth Circuit

Rhesa Barksdale
Jacques L. Wiener Jr.
Emilio M. Garza
Harold R. DeMoss Jr.

Sixth Circuit

Richard F. Suhrheinrich
Eugene Edward Siler Jr.
Alice M. Batchelder

Seventh Circuit

Ilana Rovner
Eighth Circuit
James B. Loken
David R. Hansen
Morris S. Arnold

Ninth Circuit

Ferdinand Fernandez
Pamela Ann Rymer
Thomas G. Nelson
Andrew Kleinfeld

Tenth Circuit

Paul Joseph Kelly Jr.

Eleventh Circuit

Stanley F. Birch Jr.
Joel Fredrick Dubina
Susan H. Black
Edward Earl Carnes

Federal Circuit

S. Jay Plager
Alan David Lourie
Raymond C. Clevenger
Randall Ray Rader
Alvin Anthony Schall

AFTER TWELVE YEARS of Ed Meese–inspired Reagan appointees and Lee Liberman Otis–inspired George H. W. Bush appointees, the federal judiciary was totally transformed. Originalism, which was unknown and untheorized until Ed Meese became attorney general in 1985, had become a dominant force by noon on January 20, 1993. Even President Bill Clinton's two Supreme Court appointees, Justice Ruth Bader Ginsburg and Justice Stephen Breyer, were both moderate Democrats who were picked because they might be able to peel off a vote or two from the Republican Supreme Court majority. But Ed Meese was not done yet. In fact, he stayed in Washington, D.C., as the Ronald Reagan Chair in Public Policy at the Heritage Foundation. Meese helped produce *The Heritage Guide to the Constitution* (2005), and as discussed above he played a critical role, along with Leonard Leo, in persuading President George W. Bush to appoint Chief Justice John Roberts and Justice Samuel Alito to the U.S. Supreme Court.

Ed Meese so thoroughly persuaded Republicans of the importance of selecting originalist judges and Supreme Court justices that Donald Trump won the presidency over Hillary Clinton, in part, by promising to appoint Supreme Court justices off of a list of twenty-two originalists whom he named in a press release. A poll done after Trump won the November 2016 presidential election showed that among voters for whom Supreme Court and other federal judicial appointments was the number-one voting issue, Donald Trump led Hillary Clinton by a 57 percent to 43 percent margin. The death of Justice Scalia, who was beloved by Republicans in the middle of the 2016 campaign, and the knowledge that whoever won in November would appoint Scalia's successor motivated conservative and religious voters to turn out in big numbers to vote for Donald Trump in 2016. Justice Scalia's final legacy to the country was that the timing of his death led to the appointment to the Supreme Court of three originalist justices who would end up turning some of Scalia's dissents and concurrences into majority opinions.

In fact, Ed Meese and Ken Cribb had lunch at a National Lawyers Convention event at the Mayflower Hotel with Widener University Commonwealth Law School graduate Don McGahn, who became an ardent Federalist Society member in the mid-1990s. McGahn was thrilled to have lunch with two such famous and modest people, and he never forgot it. McGahn went on to become President Donald Trump's first White House counsel, where he played the key role in the appointment to the U.S. Supreme Court of three spectacular originalist justices: Neil Gorsuch, Brett Kavanaugh, and Amy Coney Barrett. McGahn filled his White House Counsel's Office with Federalist Society members who interviewed and picked President Trump's superb federal court of appeals and district court judges.

Ed Meese and Ken Cribb deserve a lot of credit for their kindness and humility in getting Don McGahn to become an ardent originalist and Federalist Society member in the mid-1990s. McGahn joked in a Barbara K. Olsen Memorial Lecture to the Federalist Society that the press was wrong in saying he had "outsourced" judicial selection to the Federalist Society as White House counsel. He said, instead, that he had hired originalist Federalist Society members to work for him as White House counsel and that he would call that "insourcing" not "outsourcing." In all seriousness, McGahn picked up where Ed Meese and Lee Liberman Otis had left off, and he picked much better lower federal court judges than George W. Bush was able to do because the Democrats had abolished the filibuster of lower federal court judges in 2013, which had stymied George W. Bush. Leonard Leo helped to persuade former president Trump to appoint Pat Cipollone to be his second White House counsel, and Cipollone continued to recommend originalist judges to President Trump. So the Ed Meese legacy in judicial selection lives on!

CHAPTER TEN

THE SOLICITOR AND THE GENERAL

THE SOLICITOR GENERAL'S Office in the Department of Justice "supervise[s] and conduct[s] government litigation in the United States Supreme Court."[1] This function includes arguing cases involving the United States before the Supreme Court, participating as an amicus curiae ("friend of the court") in cases in which the federal government is not a party but has some interest in the outcome or reasoning of the case, and asking the Supreme Court to review or not review cases decided by lower courts. The "SG's office" as it is known, also "review[s] all cases decided adversely to the government in the lower courts to determine whether they should be appealed and, if so, what position should be taken."[2] It is one of the most important units in the Department of Justice. The head of the office, the solicitor general, is accordingly one of the most important figures in the Justice Department[3]; some people refer to the solicitor general as "the tenth justice."[4] The lawyers who work in that office are among the most important lawyers employed by the government.

Throughout Ed Meese's time as attorney general, the Solicitor General's Office was viewed with deep suspicion by the Meese Revolutionaries—though not necessarily by Meese himself. There were good reasons for this suspicion.

First, most of the day-to-day work in the SG's Office is done by the nearly twenty assistants to the solicitor general, or "assistant SGs," who are supervised by four deputy solicitors general, only one of whom is a so-called "political appointee" chosen by the attorney general. Those assistant SGs and the three "non-political" deputies typically see the office as their careers, often staying for decades. (There are people presently in the SG's Office who served in the mid-1980s.) Professor Thomas Merrill, a deputy solicitor general from 1987 to 1990, told Steve Calabresi that the career lawyers called the political appointees—the solicitor general and the one non-career deputy—"the in-and-outers" because they left after a few, and at most eight, years. During Meese's time as attorney general, a good number of those long-serving career lawyers were

- 289 -

hardcore leftists. We doubt whether many, or even any, of the career people in the office voted for Ronald Reagan.

Second, even those assistant SGs who were largely apolitical had agendas quite far removed from the Meese Revolution. Lawyers are trained to want to win cases, which usually means hewing closely to the status quo, including the mass of non-originalist precedent that drives most court decisions.[5] The Meese Revolution was about changing the status quo toward a focus on the Constitution's original meaning. That kind of radicalism had little attraction for the career litigators, who constituted the DOJ's version of "the establishment." Charles Fried, the solicitor general under Meese and someone about whom we will say much more in a moment, wrote in his memoir: "The superb career lawyers had gradually come to imagine that the function of the office was so disconnected from the present administration that in fact it was they who should determine what positions were taken, how briefs were written, and who gets hired. … I was constantly being told that I should not intervene in cases where all I had to add was a philosophical statement about how the law should come out. I was supposed to represent the interest of 'government' in general—that is, the ability of government to go about its work, whatever it may be, as freely as possible."[6] As Fried aptly points out, this attitude carries a leftist bias, possibly even an unintentional one, "because since the 1930's the prerogatives of the federal government had been overwhelmingly invoked in furtherance of a liberal, regulatory agenda."[7] The Meese Revolution, not to mention the Reagan Revolution, was hardly about letting government "go about its work" uninhibited by constitutional niceties. The career staff was so convinced that it was the Way, the Truth, and the Light that it would sometimes give its putative boss "drafts of briefs so near to the deadline that I had no real opportunity to make changes or rewrite parts of them."[8] We will see a dramatic example of this staff insubordination later in this chapter.

The third basis for suspicion of the SG's Office was the SG himself: Charles Fried. Charles was obviously to the right of the median employee in the SG's Office, but that was rather like being to the right of the median member of the Politburo or a law school faculty. Charles Fried was not a Meese Revolutionary—not by a long shot.

Charles Fried was, however, one of the most academic and intellectual forces in Meese's Justice Department. Before joining the government, he was—and remained until his death in 2024—an extraordinarily distinguished professor at Harvard Law School, and after leaving the DOJ he spent several years as a justice on the Supreme Judicial Court of Massachusetts. Charles only retired from teaching at Harvard Law School on December 31, 2023. He served as Meese's acting solicitor general and then as the Senate-confirmed solicitor general from 1985 until 1989, and he held that job for most of the period during which Meese was attorney general. Throughout that time, Charles was a key part of the atmosphere that made the Meese Justice Department feel so much like a law school faculty. Charles Fried was a true intellectual who was widely read, had lots of interesting ideas, and was devoted to the life of the mind. He was also courteous and well-mannered in an almost aristocratic way. As Ken Cribb pointed out to us, Charles's good manners were a sign of the respect with which he treated other people. In addition, Charles had a wonderful sense of humor—one of the best senses of humor Steve Calabresi has ever encountered. Along with that courtesy and sense of humor came a strong sense of decency. Charles did not hold grudges. Even though he sparred with many members of the Federalist Society while he was solicitor general, he was a longtime faithful faculty advisor to the Federalist Society's Harvard Law School chapter, where he was revered. In sum, Charles Fried can be absolved of all of the seven deadly sins except for the one from which virtually all academics suffer—Pride. He was not Angry, Envious, Lustful, Greedy, Slothful, or Gluttonous. He often exhibited courage, wisdom, temperance, justice, and love. For all of these reasons, Ed Meese, Ken Cribb, Steve Calabresi, and Gary Lawson all really liked Charles, and we always will.

In 1991, he wrote a near-contemporaneous account of his time in the Justice Department. That book is vital for two reasons. First, it gives a detailed account of many of the key cases argued in the Supreme Court during the second Reagan term, and we encourage anyone interested in the full story of the Reagan Justice Department to read that account. Second, it gives vivid insight into why Charles Fried was a headache for the Meese Revolutionaries—and vice versa.

Charles Fried "liked [Ronald Reagan] from the start," sharing

"Reagan's gut-level dislike for the pretensions of government in general."[9] He did not, however, share Reagan's or Meese's constitutional vision.

Charles Fried was a common-law constitutionalist, meaning that he considered the text and original meaning of the Constitution no more important, and often less important, than the Supreme Court case law interpreting the text. It is unsurprising that he would think this way, since his academic specialty was contract law,[10] which in America is predominantly a common-law subject with no text with an original meaning to apply. Charles thus approached constitutional law by looking first at the case law and only secondarily, if at all, at the text or its original public meaning. As we earlier quoted him saying, "I used to tease the lawyers in my office that the ideal SG's brief would not have one word that is not in quotation marks and attributed to some prior Supreme Court opinions. This has been the texture of common lawyers' reasoning for centuries."[11] More fundamentally, Fried doubted whether originalism was feasible in practice or internally coherent,[12] though his understanding of "originalism" was a crude intentionalism that looked to 18th-century views on specific practices. It speaks worlds that this primitive understanding was the solicitor general's account of originalism, even in 1991 after the Jurisprudence of Original Meaning utterly displaced the Jurisprudence of Original Intention.

This common-law focus was consistent with Charles's overall approach to social theory, which tracked Edmund Burke's suspicion of sudden and inorganic change in social institutions. The Meese Revolution was—well, a revolution. Burkeans like Charles Fried would not easily sign onto something that so unsettles the status quo. Better to stick with the case law, for all its flaws, and maybe seek incremental change at the margins without fundamentally changing the practice.

Even if he had been a fan of originalism as its practitioners, including the attorney general, understood it, Charles would have been in a difficult, and perhaps impossible, position as solicitor general. On the one hand, he faced a Supreme Court that had a liberal majority and, until the fall of 1986, not a single originalist justice. The court's conservatives, Chief Justice Warren Burger and Justices Byron White, William Rehnquist, and Sandra Day O'Connor, were all essentially conservative legal realists (though we have noted that Ed Meese and Brad Reynolds contest this account with respect to Rehnquist). They did not fully believe in law but thought of themselves as sensible, conservative policymakers. Those in the liberal bloc thought of themselves as sensible, progressive policymakers. Hardcore originalist arguments were not likely to win many cases. For litigators playing a short, one-case-at-a-time game, that was surely reason enough to stick with quotations from prior Supreme Court opinions.

On the other hand, the Meese Revolutionaries were playing a long game, in which winning cases in 1986 or 1987 was less important than changing the legal culture as happened in 2022 and 2023. Recall from chapter 8 the *Manual for Litigation* prepared by the Office of Legal Policy. It encouraged line litigators to view "winning" less in terms of case outcomes than in terms of fidelity to the law. It instructed them to advance originalist arguments even if those arguments were not necessarily going to increase the chance of "victory" in specific cases, with the long-term goal of educating judges and other lawyers about the methodology of original meaning. That document was addressed only to litigators in the trial courts, not to the appellate lawyers in the SG's Office. No comparable document was issued instructing the SG's Office to elevate long-term legal change over short-term case victories. But the mindset that generated the OLP document in 1987 was the mindset of the Meese Revolutionaries from 1985 onward. This "conflict of visions," to quote the irreplaceable Thomas Sowell, was bound to generate pressure on Charles Fried. He had to contend with his career staff on the left and pretty much the entire civil side of the Department of Justice on the right, with his own sentiments leaning toward neither. It is no surprise that sparks sometimes flew.

Charles's chief nemesis in Meese's Justice Department was Brad Reynolds. Brad Reynolds undoubtedly thought that he would have been a better solicitor general than the Burkean Charles Fried, and Charles found his opposition unsettling. Fried said in 1991, "I can still picture the chilling way Reynolds made his points; the cold stare, the tense, high-pitched but quiet voice speaking between clenched teeth.... Working with Brad Reynolds was the toughest part of my job.... After a confrontation with him you needed a stiff drink and a long walk."[13]

Some of this tension reflected a simple personality conflict. Brad

Reynolds was a tight-lipped practicing lawyer who could be puritanical and zealous (Fried recalls Reynolds having "an almost religious sense of mission"[14]), and Fried was a gregarious European intellectual law professor. Some of the tension, however, was substantive. Even apart from Fried's antipathy toward originalism, he was not a true believer on the issues about which Brad cared deeply, such as federalism.

Apart from his run-ins with Reynolds—who, despite everything, Fried "always liked"[15]—Fried got along quite well with the key players in the DOJ. Fried and Meese were both former law professors, and they shared a love of ideas. It is no surprise that Fried "found Meese intelligent, receptive, and intellectually curious."[16] Ken Cribb, who is a died-in-the-wool intellectual with an infectious sense of humor, could make almost any social situation work out well, and he had much in common with Fried. Ken really liked and supported Fried, as did Meese. He still really liked and admired Fried up until his death in 2024.

But beneath the genuine level of personal respect and admiration shared by all the principals was a deep and profound disagreement about the nature of law and the role of the DOJ in promoting it. As it happened, Meese never told Fried what to do. As Fried recalls, "[W]hen I balked at making what seemed to me extreme or unsupportable or unwise or incorrect arguments, the Attorney General backed me up. He showed caution and hesitation."[17] Fried draws from this that Meese might not have been a revolutionary after all. He was, says Fried, "too good a lawyer to be easy as a revolutionary. . . . [So] [i]t is hard for me today—as it was when we would debate particular positions and actions—to be sure just how personally committed Meese was to all aspects of this revolutionary program."[18] So how to explain Attorney General Meese's extraordinary and groundbreaking speeches on originalism, departmentalism, and other topics? Fried has a theory:

> These speeches were written for Meese by his cadre of committed young assistants. Because those who were standing with or behind the Attorney General thought of themselves as revolutionaries, they did not trust the usual channels to deliver results. The bureaucracy could not be trusted to implement a revolutionary program. I and other political appointees could not be trusted completely: unlike the very young members of the inner circle, we

were not creatures of the movement. … Even the Attorney General could not be fully trusted. …

> The provocative public statements served a purpose; they pushed the Attorney General so far out on a limb that he was committed.[19]

We are in one sense flattered that Charles Fried thinks that a bunch of twenty-somethings two or three years out of law school could engineer a coup within the Department of Justice. We are in another sense offended that he could think us capable of plotting to undermine someone that we respected, and even revered, like Ed Meese. In any event, it seems never to have occurred to Fried that Meese gave his speeches because he believed in what he was saying and thought a revolution in constitutional law was needed, or that he gave Fried space to get things wrong simply because Meese believed that it was the correct way to run the DOJ.

Fried not only did battle with Meese's speechwriters Gary McDowell (no radicalized twenty-something he) and Blair Dorminey, but also with many of the assistant attorneys general like Chuck Cooper and Brad Reynolds and their deputies like Mike Carvin in the Civil Rights Division. The revolutionary cadre of twenty-somethings on the attorney general's personal staff also spent much of its time butting heads with the SG's Office, which perhaps explains why Fried's memoir invested it with so much power. Meese and Cribb hired two former Robert Bork clerks, Steve Calabresi and John Harrison, to monitor constitutional law issues within the DOJ. Calabresi and Harrison were specifically assigned by Cribb to keep an eye on what Fried was doing and to interview judicial candidates for the federal circuit courts of appeals. Calabresi and Harrison were both Yale Law School graduates who went on to become chaired professors at, respectively, Northwestern Pritzker School of Law and the University of Virginia School of Law. They are (says Lawson, with Calabresi recused from the decision) among the leading originalist scholars of the past four decades. The youthful "cadre" about which Fried complained was a knowledgeable and elite group of individuals who knew just as much about the Constitution as did Fried and, importantly, knew much more about originalism than did Fried.

One anecdote reveals how Fried viewed the "cadre." The Washington, D.C., Lawyers Division chapter held a monthly luncheon for Federalist

Society lawyers working in the Washington area. One day, Fried arrived at the luncheon. To his great surprise, he came face-to-face with one of his young career assistant lawyers, Samuel Alito. Fried memorably blurted out "Why Sam, I did not know you were a member of the Federalist Society. Why, this is just so awkward, so strange—kind of like running into a good friend at a bordello!" This was vintage Charles Fried: very funny and at the same time condescending. Suffice it to say that Sam Alito is today a Supreme Court justice.

Fried was also a bit of a flatterer, which could lead him to awkward situations. One of the major cases decided by the Supreme Court in 1989 concerned the United States Sentencing Commission, a body created in 1984 to prescribe uniform sentencing guidelines for federal criminal offenses. The motivation for the legislation was noble enough: it does not seem fair to have sentences for the same crimes vary wildly depending on who happens to be the judge. Narrower sentencing ranges, fixed in advance, seem much more consistent with the rule of law. The problem was that the sentencing ranges should be set by *Congress*, not by bureaucrats. This was a classic instance of Congress punting away its responsibilities to so-called experts—who might in fact be experts, and who might in fact do a better job than would Congress, but who are not the people the Constitution expects to make legislative decisions. To make matters worse, the only function performed by the commission was promulgating sentence guidelines. It did not itself administer any laws or investigate or prosecute anyone. In *Mistretta v. United States*,[20] Justice Scalia memorably described the commission as "a sort of junior-varsity Congress."[21] But he did so in dissent, in an 8–1 decision upholding the agency's constitutionality.

Meese had supported the creation of the Sentencing Commission on fairness grounds and because the Sentencing Commission's guidelines cracked down quite hard on repeat offenders, whom Meese quite rightly thought committed most crimes. Cribb, however, was aware from conversations with intellectuals in the Meese DOJ that the Sentencing Commission raised serious separation of powers problems. On the day that the *Mistretta* case came down, Meese, Fried, and Cribb were all at a reception together at the Supreme Court. Fried came up to Cribb and said, "Ken, this decision is a disaster for the separation of powers. I fear

*Attorney General Meese,
White House Chief of Staff
Howard Baker,
President Ronald Reagan,
and Ursula Meese.*

*Ken Cribb and
President Reagan
addressing the
Federalist Society
Lawyers Convention
on September 9, 1988.*

*In his remarks, the president said, "Today is
Ken Cribb's last day in our administration. Liberals all
around town are breaking out the champagne."*

*President Ronald Reagan
addressing the Federalist
Society with David McIn-
tosh, Steve Calabresi, and
Lee Liberman looking on.*

Meese sworn in as the 75th attorney general of the United States, with President Ronald Reagan, Ursula Meese, and Vice President George H.W. Bush.

Meese's official photograph as the 75th attorney general of the United States.

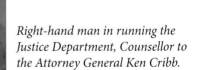

Right-hand man in running the Justice Department, Counsellor to the Attorney General Ken Cribb.

Don McGahn was counsel to President Trump's 2016 presidential campaign and then White House Counsel from 2017 to 2018. A longtime Federalist Society member and a great admirer of Ed Meese, Don persuaded the president to appoint Supreme Court justices and judges who were Meesian Originalists.

Donald Trump cemented control over the Supreme Court by original public meaning textualists. His Court of Appeals and District Court judges are on balance as good as Reagan's, but they are not conservative enough and they lack the intellectual firepower of the Meese Revolutionary judges. Trump has vowed to do better in a second term, and we both hope he gets the chance to do so.

Meese faithfully attended every Federalist Society Lawyers Convention until his health made it impossible for him to continue to do so. He continues to serve by Zoom on the Federalist Society's Board of Directors.

October 8, 2019. President Trump presented Meese with the Presidential Medal of Freedom, the highest civilian honor in the United States.

Ed and Ursula share a tender moment at the end of the Presidential Medal of Freedom ceremony.

The Burger Court in 1985 when Meese became attorney general. There were no originalists on that Court, nor was there more than one solid conservative on the Court, William H. Rehnquist.

The Roberts Court in February 2024. The Supreme Court has been transformed in the 39 years since Ed Meese took office as attorney general.

we may never, ever recover from its ill effects." About five minutes later, Ken was within earshot when Fried greeted Meese with a huge smile on his face and said, "Mr. Attorney General, today we have won a great victory for law and order!"

Managing the Deep State

IN THE END, however, Fried was not the biggest obstacle in the Solicitor General's Office to the Meese Revolution. That distinction goes to the career staff. Anyone who doubts the existence of a "deep state" has never worked in government. While we are going to criticize Fried's handling of certain cases in a moment, we want to acknowledge that he was sometimes vigilant and courageous when vigilance and courage were desperately needed. One episode speaks volumes.

The Constitution's Fifth Amendment forbids the government from taking "private property... for public use without just compensation." If the government bulldozes your home and builds a post office on the lot, it must pay for the home and the land. But what if the government doesn't take over your lot but floods it by building a dam nearby? You still "own" your land in a formal sense, but you can't do anything with it except maybe go scuba diving. Is that a taking, or does the Fifth Amendment only apply when the government actually seizes the title to your property?

As a matter of original meaning, it is actually a tricky question. The Takings Clause was added to the Fifth Amendment by James Madison without discussion or fanfare, and no one said much about it in 1791. Maybe a taking requires a transfer of title to the land, maybe it constitutes anything that deprives you of most of the land's use, and maybe it includes anything that damages the property (there are state constitutions that specifically call for compensation for property "taken or damaged"). In 1871, the Supreme Court said that flooded property was "taken" for constitutional purposes.[22] So, if flooding the property is a taking, how about regulating away the property's uses by narrowly confining by law what you can do with your property? Does that also count as property being "taken"? The Supreme Court in 1922 said "potentially sometimes yes,"[23] depending on the nature of the regulations, and for more than a century the case law has gone back and forth about when and how government regulations go so far that they effectively "take" property in the constitutional sense.[24]

In 1986, the law was not especially favorable to property owners trying to challenge regulations. A 1978 Supreme Court case, which upheld a New York City historic landmark designation that made it essentially impossible to turn a train station into a much more profitable office building,[25] gave governments broad leeway to reduce property values dramatically through regulation without triggering a just compensation requirement. That was the context for a challenge by some Native Americans to a 1983 congressional statute saying that they could only pass certain land interests at death to their tribe or to other partial owners of the same land. Thus, if the landowner's children or friends, say, were not already part owners of the land in question, the owner could not will his or her share of that land to those people. Was the statute the kind of regulation of land that amounts to a constitutional taking?

Under the case law of 1986, it was a tough argument for the Native American landowners. A 1979 case had held that the federal government could, without owing compensation, essentially ban all uses of and transactions involving eagle feathers except displaying them on a mantle.[26] Here, the Native American landowners could do more than just display their land. They simply couldn't pass it by will to their beneficiaries of choice. Nonetheless, the Eighth Circuit Court of Appeals found a taking,[27] and the Supreme Court agreed to hear the case.

There was no question that the DOJ was going to defend the statute. The precedents presented a strong case for the government, and the answer as a matter of original meaning is somewhat obscure. The question was *how* the government was going to defend the statute. And thereby hangs a tale.

The story begins, humbly enough, with Gary Lawson in the Office of Legal Counsel writing a memorandum commenting on a federal statute that tells states when they have to commence running their statutes of limitations on tort actions stemming from environmental hazards.[28] One possible issue was whether the federal statute might "take" property if it revived a cause of action for which the state's own statute of limitations had already run out. Knowing that the government was filing briefs in several takings cases coming to the court in the October

1986 term, Lawson asked to see drafts of the briefs to make sure that his memo did not contradict the government's litigating position.

In the early draft brief for *Hodel v. Irving*, the case involving the Native American lands, Lawson was surprised to see an argument—apparently authored by career SG lawyers Ed Kneedler and Larry Wallace—saying, "Moreover, every sovereign possesses the *plenary* power to regulate the manner and terms upon which property may be transmitted at death, as well as the authority to prescribe who shall and who shall not be capable of taking it" (emphasis added). Much of this statement was uncontroversial. No one doubts that governments can regulate the passage of property by will; there have long been statutes defining how to write a valid will, limiting to some extent the power fully to disinherit certain family members, and so forth. The key to the draft brief's argument was the word "plenary."

The word "plenary" in this context means "unqualified; absolute." Thus, the SG's Office was arguing that governments at all levels, including the federal government in its role as trustee for Native American lands, had total power over testation, including the ability to abolish it altogether. Thus, *any* regulation of the power to pass property by will, including its complete abolition, was just fine, and since this statute fell short of abolition, it must be fine a fortiori. There was actually language in a New Deal–era case supporting this claim of "plenary" governmental power over testation,[29] but it struck Lawson as a bit odd for the Reagan administration to be arguing that the United States could turn socialist in one generation by having governments claim all property once the current owners die. He mentioned the issue to Chuck Cooper, wrote his memo on statutes of limitations, and thought no more of it.

Only much later did he hear of the resulting firestorm throughout the Justice Department regarding the word "plenary." Richard Willard in the Civil Division, Hank Habicht in the Lands Division, Chuck Cooper at OLC, and Fried as the solicitor general all agreed that the government should not be making such an argument, even if New Deal case law supported it. Indeed, Fried announced that he could not sign his name to any brief that contained such an argument. The career SG litigators, however, saw no problem, and the language about "plenary" power over wills kept appearing in drafts. Finally, the definitive order was given to describe the government's power over wills in broad terms but specifically to avoid describing the power as "plenary."

Recall how Fried mentioned that he sometimes received briefs from his staff with little or no time to make revisions. This time, he received *printed* copies of the brief—several dozen of them—ready to be filed with the Supreme Court. The brief described the government's "plenary" power over testation, including its ability to abolish altogether people's power to pass down their property. There was then no way to make revisions to the briefs; they were in final printed form.

Charles Fried found a way. On the eve (literally the eve) of filing the briefs in the Supreme Court, he took a marker and personally, by hand, blacked out the word "plenary" in every printed copy of the brief. Today, when everything is digitized, this remarkable event is in danger of disappearing. But if one can locate a hard copy of the brief (there are nine depositories for printed SG briefs across the country), or a PDF that accurately reproduces the original document, one will see a handmade deletion in every copy. This was Charles Fried at his finest—and the career staff in the SG's Office doing what it did.

There is a coda to the story. Even after Fried's heroic effort at damage control, if one held up the marked-out portion of the printed briefs to the light, one could faintly see the word "plenary" underneath. At oral argument in *Hodel v. Irving*, when Ed Kneedler presented the government's case, Justice O'Connor asked, "Mr. Kneedler, are there any limits in your view as to what the government can do or change concerning the descent of property belonging to Indians? Do you think the government has *plenary* power to really make any kind of a regulation?" (Lawson was in the gallery during this argument and had to choke back laughter when Justice O'Connor varied her typically polite and soothing tone to give pointed emphasis to the word "plenary.") Kneedler replied, no doubt as he had been ordered to reply, "No, our submission does not go nearly that far." He then added, however, that "[t]he Court has described the power of the legislature over the descent of property in very broad terms, suggesting that the right to pass property and to receive it by descent or by will is creation of statute and not a natural right, it is a privilege that can be conditioned or even abolished, but the Court has never been confronted with a situation where it had to address that, and it isn't here." A simple "no," of course, would have sufficed, but Kneedler insisted on emphasizing at least the possibility that governments could abolish the transfer of property at death. Justice O'Connor followed up: "Well, do you take the position that it can be abolished?" Kneedler responded, "That is not part of our submission here, no," and sought to explain the limited scope of the law actually at issue in the case. Another justice (Lawson recollects Justice Stevens, but it was almost forty years ago) then chimed in, leading to an intriguing colloquy that prompted open laughter from the gallery:

QUESTION [we think by Justice Stevens]: May I follow up on the question asked by Justice O'Connor? On page 17 .... the brief states, "Every sovereign possesses the power to regulate the manner and terms upon which property may be transmitted at death as well as the authority to prescribe who shall and who shall not be capable of taking it." [Authors' note: This was the sentence containing the blacked-out word "plenary."] Doesn't that say that the government may disinherit anyone it wishes to disinherit? ... I am surprised that the Solicitor General would—

MR. KNEEDLER: I don't—we did not intend for that language to be taken to its full implications.

QUESTION: You didn't intend for it to be taken the way it reads? (General laughter.)

MR. KNEEDLER: Well, this is—Congress obviously can—I think there is an element of reasonableness in anything Congress does in a situation such as this in terms of defining who may be qualified to take property, what sort of property can pass, and within reasonable limitations. ... [W]e are not suggesting here that Congress could simply pass a statute providing for all property to escheat to the government after one generation.

Of course, Ed Kneedler and Larry Wallace were most definitely suggesting that Congress could simply pass a statute providing for all property to escheat to the government after one generation. That obviously was not the position of the Meese DOJ or Solicitor General Fried, but the career staff had its own agenda.

The Supreme Court, by the way, found the statute unconstitutional by a 9–0 vote, though there was a splintering of opinions about the reasons for that result.[30]

Privacy

THUS, THERE WERE TIMES when Fried was both an effective solicitor general and an effective messenger for the Reagan/Meese Revolution. At other times, however, there was sharp tension between the Meese message, Fried's own inclinations, and Fried's conception of victory as securing five votes in Supreme Court cases rather than laying the foundation for possible future victories. That tension was nowhere more evident than with regard to the so-called "right to privacy."

There is no right to privacy in the U.S. Constitution or in any of its twenty-seven amendments. There are provisions that expressly protect certain aspects of privacy, such as the Fourth Amendment's requirement that searches and seizures be "reasonable," and the overall scheme of enumerated federal powers gives federal actors only limited capacity to restrict privacy rights, but there is no overarching "privacy" norm that trumps express grants of constitutional power. Moreover, all of these provisions apply only to *federal* actors. The vast majority of cases complaining about privacy violations involve *state* action, for which the only relevant constitutional provision is the Fourteenth Amendment, which forbids states from abridging the "privileges or immunities" of citizens or depriving people of the equal protection of the laws or due process of law. From 1787 to 1868, when the Fourteenth Amendment was adopted, not a single state bill of rights had a right to privacy clause in it, even though all the other clauses in the U.S. Bill of Rights were replicated in state bills of rights during that time.[31] Even modern-day state bills of rights do not generally protect a constitutional right to privacy.[32] This is thin gruel for generating an overarching right to privacy against state action from the unpromising language of the Fourteenth Amendment, however appealing such a right might be as a matter of policy.

This so-called right was created out of whole cloth by the Supreme Court in *Griswold v. Connecticut*[33] to strike down a state statute forbidding married couples from using contraceptives. The statute was almost never enforced, and it could readily have been found unconstitutional without mentioning the word "privacy." The alleged purpose of the statute was to prevent adultery, and, as Justice Byron White noted in his concurrence in *Griswold*, the statute failed even a minimalist "rational basis" test because there is no plausible connection between forbidding the use of contraceptives by married couples and the prevention of adultery. Rather than follow Justice White's straightforward path, however, the Warren Court majority invoked a so-called right to privacy.

If the new right had been used only to invalidate absurd and unenforced contraception laws, *Griswold* might have been a "one-hit wonder," never to be heard from again. Less than a decade later, however, the "right to privacy" surfaced in *Roe v. Wade*[34] to strike down as unconstitutional the abortion laws of all fifty states.

As a policy matter, there were people in the Meese Justice Department—including people whom some might find surprising—who were pro-choice as a policy matter. But from a constitutionalist standpoint, the question was not whether abortion restrictions would subordinate women or save millions of innocent lives. The question was whether the United States Constitution made that call or left it up to voters, state legislatures, and state courts under their own state constitutions. For any originalist of any stripe, that was an easy question. *Roe* was an unconstitutional, and even anti-constitutional, assertion of judicial power with few equals in American history. *Roe* had to go. And from a constitutionalist standpoint, the problem was not even that *Roe* interjected the federal courts into the abortion controversy. The real problem was the judicially invented right of privacy that would continually thrust the federal courts into ever-expanding realms of policy even if the abortion issue somehow went away. The "right of privacy" had to go.

Charles Fried made it to about the halfway point. In his 1991 memoir, he acknowledged the Meese/Reagan view that "the constitutional right of privacy was seen as the deep theoretical root of the trouble," but he revealingly opined that attacking the problem at its root was "misconceived. It grew out of the same disappointed yearning for a mechanical rule of judging that gave us originalism. That is a part of the project I never signed on to."[35] Originalism was not "part of the project." It *was* the project. The Meese Revolution was not about defending abortion statutes. It was about defending originalism. Fried never got that.

Fried believed in 1961 when he clerked for Justice Harlan, in 1986

- 303 -

when he was solicitor general, in 1991 when he wrote his memoir, and surely until he died that the Due Process Clauses of the Fifth and Fourteenth Amendments have a substantive component to them that calls upon judges to use "the method of reason"[36] to strike the appropriate balance between "liberty and the demands of organized society."[37] As Fried describes the view that led to *Griswold* and *Roe*, "The words of the Constitution were the starting point" or "like the points on a graph, which the judge joins by a line to describe a coherent and rationally compelling function."[38] Fried's problem with *Roe* was simply that, in his judgment, it went too far off the graph.[39]

That is a view of due process and the judicial role that sophisticated academics have spun into elaborate theories.[40] It was not the view of Ed Meese's Justice Department, as expressed both in the attorney general's speeches and in Office of Legal Policy working papers. It was also contrary to President Reagan's speech at the investiture of Chief Justice Rehnquist and Justice Scalia, which inveighed against newly made-up constitutional rights. Reaganite originalism does not view the words of the Constitution as a "starting point" or "points on a graph." They *are* the graph. Some of the points are harder to see than others, and some of the "points" may even describe a range rather than a single discrete point, but the object of interpretation is to find the point or the range, not take them as occasions to construct a "coherent and rationally compelling [to whom?] function."

Thus, when faced with a privacy-based challenge to a state statute, an originalist would ask whether the challenged law implicates one of the "privileges or immunities of citizens of the United States" and, if so, whether the law "abridge[s]" them. That inquiry could well involve exercise of some of the reason and judgment that Fried favored, and it might even yield a decent chunk of the results that he treasured. But it would do so in a textually grounded fashion that ascertained the Constitution's meaning rather than treating that meaning as a launching pad. This was precisely Justice Thomas's position in his concurring opinion when the court finally overruled *Roe* in 2022.[41]

Charles Fried was not an originalist. Accordingly, when the Meese DOJ had its first opportunity to weigh in on abortion, as an amicus curiae in *Thornburgh v. American College of Obstetricians and Gynecologists*,[42] the brief was disappointing to many. Much of the SG's brief explained, with considerable force, how the Pennsylvania statute at issue—which did not prohibit abortion as such but regulated the procedures used in abortions, information provided to patients, and access to abortion by minors—was consistent with prior case law, including *Roe*. At the end of the brief, the government asked the court to overrule *Roe*. We cannot reproduce that entire argument here,[43] but it can fairly be described as "softcore." A large part of the argument concerned the unworkability and arbitrariness of the trimester framework established by *Roe*—a framework that the court in fact abandoned in 1992, thirty years before it formally overruled *Roe* altogether.[44] When it came time to challenge the underlying foundations of *Roe* in the invented right to privacy, the two words that best describe the argument are "academic" and "equivocal." It contains a few mentions of history and the need to ground analysis of phrases like "due process of law" in original intentions, but the real flavor of the argument is captured by a representative passage:

> History is invoked in another way to take account of developments in society and the law. Such an approach has seemed particularly plausible in determining the application of the Fourth Amendment's protections to such undreamt-of developments as wire-tapping, electronic surveillance, the searches of automobiles and airplanes. History in this sense appears as a vector, in which the original understanding is seen as the point of departure for developing values implied and the inchoate at the point of origin. But ... the Court has always taken pains to trace its point of origin back to specific constitutional provisions by a route either inferential or historical.
>
> In *Roe v. Wade*, by contrast, the connections by either route were wholly missing and the Court was forced to leap to its conclusion. Certainly the course of legal attitudes and practice, "the compelling traditions of the legal profession" (*Rochin v. California*, 342 U.S. at 171), permit no extrapolation from the past to the Court's conclusion in *Roe v. Wade*. The story traced by the Court [in *Roe*] does not show a steady and growing acceptance of a point of view until the practice in a few jurisdictions can be characterized as anomalous.

There was also, unsurprisingly, a paean to Justice Harlan's opinion in *Poe v. Ullman*, likely written by law clerk Charles Fried, described by the brief as the "classic statement" of how "a specific constitutional text is seen to harbor the germ of a theory that establishes a general and fundamental right." This is not, in either substance or style, the argument of a Meese Revolutionary.

But it might have been the argument of a Meese DOJ, nonetheless. Obviously, the brief was not constructed without input. Fried's memoir describes the consultation process, which included sign-offs by Meese and Brad Reynolds.[45] Why would Meese and Reynolds agree to this un-originalist slop?

This was perhaps the first major brief filed by the Meese DOJ. A full-throated originalist argument would have secured at most one vote on the court in 1986, and even that one (Rehnquist) probably would not have accepted the reasoning of a hardcore originalist brief. Coming out swinging would surely anchor most of the justices, including moderate swing justices like Powell and O'Connor, to be deeply suspicious of subsequent DOJ arguments. Or so one could readily imagine experienced lawyers like Meese and Reynolds thinking. And Meese surely did not want to start his tenure as attorney general by setting a precedent of telling the solicitor general how to do his job. As Fried pointed out, Meese never once told him what to do.

Having said that, a Meese Revolutionary, or even someone who took originalism at all seriously, could have found a way. One could have made all the incremental, precedent-based arguments crafted by Fried and *also* included a section, for posterity if for no other reason, instructing lawyers, judges, and even the public about original meaning. In 1987, as we have seen, the OLP instructed line litigators to do precisely that in district court cases. It could have been done for Supreme Court cases as well.

There were long-term costs to compromising on a commitment to originalism. During the first Bush administration, when Fried was no longer solicitor general, he was asked to come back to present oral argument for the government in another abortion case, *Webster v. Reproductive Health Services*.[46] He saw the argument as "a unique occasion ... to remove—from the campaign to re-establish the law in general and the effort to overrule *Roe* in particular—the albatross of originalist rigorism."[47] His oral argument emphasized that "we are not asking the Court to unravel the fabric of unenumerated and privacy rights which the Court has woven. ... Rather, we are asking the Court to pull this one thread." This half-hearted, overtly anti-originalist advocacy was bound to make the justices worry about what "pull[ing] this one thread" would do to the court's "fabric of unenumerated and privacy rights." The right way to begin an argument calling for the overruling of *Roe v. Wade* is to point to the Constitution and analogize *Roe* to past substantive due process blunders like *Dred Scott v. Sandford*. One needs, in other words, adherence to constitutional principle. It is noteworthy that in a *New York Times* op-ed that coincided with oral argument in *Dobbs v. Jackson Women's Health Organization*, Fried recanted his oral argument in *Webster* and said that if one pulled the one thread of *Roe*, the whole fabric of the right to privacy would unravel![48] Thankfully, the Supreme Court in 2022 chose the Constitution over Fried's threads, graphs, and functions.

Race

FRIED DID a much better job representing the Meese Revolution in race discrimination cases, in part because his heart was really in the fight for color-blindness in a way that was lacking in the abortion cases. It was also a lot easier to get Justice Sandra Day O'Connor's and Justice Anthony M. Kennedy's votes in a race discrimination case than in a case seeking to overrule *Roe*. Fried believed that the affirmative action push toward quotas "dangerously aggrandizes government. It is a threat to liberty and to the basic right of every person to be considered as a distinct individual and not in terms of the groups to which government says he belongs."[49] That was in keeping with the general sentiment of the Meese DOJ. But general sentiments—even sound ones—are not a basis for constitutional law. Absent from Fried's explanation for his position is its grounding in the original meaning of either the Constitution or the numerous federal statutes prohibiting discrimination on the basis of race or other characteristics.

Such grounding would require careful engagement with the categorical texts of federal statutes, such as Title VII of the Civil Rights Act of 1964, which forbids employment discrimination "because of such individual's race, color, religion, sex, or national origin,"[50] Title VI of the same act declaring that "[n]o person in the United States shall, on the ground of race, color, or national origin, be ...subjected to discrimination" in federally funded programs,[51] and the Civil Rights Act of 1866, which says that everyone in the United States must have the same rights to hold property and make contracts "as is enjoyed by white citizens."[52] It would involve serious study of the original meaning of the 1788 Constitution and the Fourteenth Amendment, which are both best understood as prohibitions on caste legislation that treats people as higher or lower based on accidents of birth or political or social connections. This kind of study of the Constitution could generate any number of conclusions: that the Constitution requires that all state and federal governmental action be color-blind; that all state and federal action be *presumptively* color-blind, with race-conscious decisions justified only in narrow and extreme circumstances, such as preventing prison riots; that all state and federal action be presumptively color-blind, but with race-conscious decisions more easily justified; or a host of other possibilities within this range. (It is hard to read the relevant federal statutes as anything other than unqualified requirements of color-blindness, though courts have managed.)

To explore these possible constitutional meanings would take us far beyond this book.[53] For present purposes, it is enough to know that during the Meese years the Supreme Court was not asking those kinds of questions. It had not asked them in the 1960s, and it was not asking them in the mid-1980s. As a result, the SG's Office was also not asking them. It was drawing on the court's muddled case law, urging incremental moves as this case or that language allowed. Frankly, Fried probably accomplished as much in terms of short-term litigation success as anyone was likely to accomplish at that time; his account of those cases is worthwhile reading.[54]

But the court never got a detailed discussion of original meaning—or even of the texts that were relevant for original meaning, which often were not the texts discussed in the case law. (Modern constitutional doctrine has fastened on the Equal Protection Clause as the chief constitutional constraint on state discrimination when virtually every originalist law professor agrees that the Privileges or Immunities Clause is the key text, and the court looks to the Due Process Clause for the doctrine of "federal equal protection" when non-discrimination is in fact built into the grants of powers to federal actors by the Constitution's fiduciary character.) This failure to focus on original meaning continues to haunt modern law; the Supreme Court's 2023 decision invalidating the affirmative action admissions policies of Harvard and the University of North Carolina[55] relies almost wholly on statements from prior opinions rather than careful textual analysis. Those statements, due in part to Fried's arguments as solicitor general but probably much more to the replacement of Warren Burger and Lewis Powell with Antonin Scalia and Anthony Kennedy respectively, push doctrine in the direction favored by Fried—and by Ed Meese and Ronald Reagan—but in the long run it is not the right way to push doctrine, whether on privacy or equality. Court opinions are neither the Constitution nor statutes.

Government Structure

THE CONSTITUTION is not primarily about rights. It is primarily about governmental structures, which are designed to secure rights without the need to list exhaustively (and surely fruitlessly) every conceivable "thou shalt not" that limits governmental power. Those constitutional structures take two forms: federalism, which divides authority between the state and federal governments, and separation of powers, which parcels out authority among federal actors within the national government. Both forms result from the enumeration of institutional federal powers; any given federal actor can only do what the Constitution authorizes it to do.

Ascertaining and implementing the Constitution's original meaning regarding federalism and the separation of powers were among the top priorities for Ronald Reagan and Ed Meese. As with many things, it was not a priority, or even a desideratum, for Fried. To be sure, Fried's policy views on at least some—not all, but some—structural issues were largely in accord with those of Reagan and Meese, but he did not seek to ground those views in original meaning or challenge faulty paradigms that distorted, and to an extent continue to distort, constitutional doctrine.

On at least one key structural issue, Fried was at odds with the administration on both jurisprudential and policy grounds. Reagan and

Meese considered federalism of paramount importance, and restoring the constitutional scheme of federalism, which had been totally abandoned by all three branches of government for the half century before the mid-1980s, was one of their chief legal aims. Fried, much more a nationalist than either Reagan or Meese, was not onboard. His 1991 memoir contains chapters on topics that he considered important, such as "Privacy" and "Race." There is no chapter on "Federalism," and very little discussion of it. He describes "run-ins with [Chuck] Cooper and [Brad] Reynolds, whom I later came to call the 'federalism police' or the 'Holy Office.'"[56] Those "police," of course, were defending the territory of Ronald Reagan, who, as we saw in chapter 4, issued a powerful executive order to his subordinates, including Fried, regarding federalism. Fried confessed that "I did not take this [federalism] project so entirely to my heart that I made it readily and instinctively my own."[57]

That is putting it mildly. Fried contributed nothing to the intellectual revival of the doctrine of enumerated federal powers, which was judicially moribund in 1985–1988. The doctrine burst back to judicial life in 1995, perhaps because of the intellectual developments and judicial appointments of Ed Meese and his federalism police. Fried also took as settled the Supreme Court's 5–4 decision in 1985 saying essentially that states have no special role in the constitutional system. That doctrine, too, was substantially eroded in the 1990s, after Fried left office, again perhaps due to the Meese/Reagan judicial appointments and spread of ideas. Today, there is vibrant law and even more vibrant scholarship concerning federalism—no thanks to Charles Fried.

The story with the internal separation of powers within the national government is more complex. Here Fried's policy preferences were more in line with Reagan's and Meese's, but again he did not connect those preferences to the Constitution's meaning. He has a chapter on the subject in his memoir that is characteristically erudite, thoughtful, and elegantly presented, as he discusses the importance of such values as accountability and transparency and the urgent need to disperse power to protect individual liberty. This is all profound, important, and at times even inspiring. What is missing from Fried's account, as it was missing from his arguments as solicitor general, is reference to the specific, calibrated scheme of separated powers created by a particular constellation of constitutional provisions. He acknowledges that

[t]he vision I offer is not literally required by the words of the Constitution. Nor did the framers' intent compel this view. No, that vision must be discerned from the structure of the document as a whole, the logic implicit in the arrangement of its parts. Most of all, it is a vision based on the best and most compelling extrapolation from what was written in that text, what was said about it, and what was dreamed of by those who inspired it.[58]

This is precisely the kind of reasoning that led Fried to a right to privacy, which in turn led to *Griswold*, which in turn led to *Roe*. Constitutional reasoning is not about visions or dreams. It is about texts, the structures in which the texts are embedded, and the background rules of interpretation that help ascertain the meanings of those texts. Or at least that is what it is about for originalists, which Fried was not.

It was clear that the Supreme Court in the 1980s was not prepared for a serious revival of separation of powers. In 1988, in *Morrison v. Olson*,[59] the court upheld, over a lone and ferocious dissent from Justice Scalia, the constitutionality of the independent counsel law, which allowed prosecutors to proceed free from presidential control in all but the most extreme instances of prosecutorial misconduct. This is impossible to square with the Constitution's language vesting "[t]he executive Power"—all of it, as Justice Scalia pointed out—in the president, but the court in that era was no more interested in the constitutional text than was Charles Fried. In 1989, the court in *Mistretta v. United States*[60] upheld the statute authorizing the Sentencing Commission to prescribe binding guidelines for federal criminal sentences, even though that seems like a squarely legislative function. The near-unanimous decision, again with Justice Scalia as the lone dissenter, declared the nondelegation doctrine essentially nonjusticiable. In 1991, Fried proclaimed the latter case "another nail in the coffin of a rigorous view of separation of the powers," and he "doubt[ed] that the ground we lost can be retrieved in this Court."[61]

He might well have been right about that court, circa 1991, with Justice Scalia as the lone originalist. Fried's precedent- and policy-based arguments in cases like *Morrison v. Olson* and *Mistretta* could have been the best that anyone could do to try to get votes in those cases.

We are not sure about that, as we will explain in a moment. But even assuming that this was so, the question is whether getting votes in those cases was the right way to craft arguments. For those playing the long game, with the hope of eventually seeing cases decided based on the Constitution rather than on snippets from past court decisions, perhaps the better strategy was to set out the Constitution's original meaning.

The SG's briefs during the Reagan administration did not do that, but alumni of the Meese DOJ did so in prodigious waves of scholarship in ensuing years. Subsequent appointments brought more and more judges and justices who take seriously the Constitution's original meaning, including—and even especially—the original meaning of structural provisions. The result has been a revival of separation of powers doctrine and theory that Fried thought unimaginable in 1991. It got no support from the Solicitor General's Office from 1985 to 1989.

Moreover, it is not at all clear that the state of doctrine regarding separation of powers in the 1980s was quite as bad as the state of doctrine regarding federalism. The latter was dead until the 1990s, but the former had shown some signs of life. In 1976, the court for the first time in four decades had found a congressional statute in violation of the Constitution's separation of powers. More importantly, it did so not by appeals to policy but by carefully studying and then quoting—more than once—the precise language of the Constitution's Appointments Clause, which specifies how important figures in the executive and judicial branches must be selected.[62] The statute provided selection procedures for all six members of the Federal Election Commission that flagrantly violated the terms of the Appointments Clause—as flagrantly as would a law trying to give Wyoming six senators or nationalizing all media. The lower court had upheld the law on the basis of forty years of prior case authority and practice, observing that the challenger's attempt to compare the law to the actual words of the Constitution was "strikingly syllogistic."[63] One would normally think of a syllogism as an especially *strong* argument ("all men are mortal, Socrates is a man, therefore Socrates is mortal"), but in separation of powers law from 1936 to 1976, syllogisms using the Constitution as a major premise were sure losers. The court's 1976 decision was "strikingly syllogistic," and it expressly rejected reliance on policy concerns

- 312 -

as a defense to the statute. This at least opened the door to arguments premised on text and original meaning.

The Reagan administration extended this modest victory in two important cases, the second of which was decided while Fried was solicitor general. In *Immigration and Naturalization Service v. Chadha*,[64] the court invalidated an enormously popular congressional device allowing single houses of Congress, and sometimes even single committees, to veto or cancel administration regulations. The court held that Congress could only make law by following the Constitution's precisely defined procedures for making law, which involves votes by both houses of Congress and presentment of the proposed laws to the president for signature or veto.[65] This was another "strikingly syllogistic" decision that eschewed policy concerns and focused on the Constitution's words and their original meanings. And Fried himself won *Bowsher v. Synar*[66] in 1986, which said that Congress could not give itself power to remove executive officials except through the constitutionally prescribed processes for impeachment. There was material from which to work to make arguments about original meaning.

To be sure, there was nothing resembling assurance that those arguments would work. For every separation of powers victory for constitutionalism in the 1970s and 1980s, there were at least as many crushing defeats. Cases like *Morrison* and *Mistretta* might have been unwinnable. But a focus on original meaning could at least have laid the groundwork for future developments.

Mistretta was a particularly tricky case. Both Attorney General William French Smith and Ed Meese had actively supported the creation of the United States Sentencing Commission by the Sentencing Reform Act of 1984 in order to promote uniformity in sentencing and assure harsher sentences for career criminals. Fried had to defend the law, even if originalists saw it as an unconstitutional delegation of legislative power to an administrative agency. But there were ways to defend the statute while still advancing the cause of originalism.

The creation of the Sentencing Commission was not an initial delegation from Congress. Congress had already effectively delegated its power to prescribe criminal sentences to courts, leaving federal district judges with virtually limitless discretion to grant or withhold sentences.

The Sentencing Commission could have been defended as a means to ensure equal treatment under law—not by creating a new delegation of power but by moving it from seven hundred district judges to a smaller group that would create uniform rules. This is not an argument that would convince all originalists (it does not convince Lawson), but it at least offers a way to uphold the statute without doing serious additional damage to the Constitution.

Loyalty

RECALL HOW SOME of Fried's subordinates in the SG's Office pursued their own agendas. Was Fried guilty of the same offense, pursuing his own agenda rather than the originalist agenda of his immediate boss Ed Meese and his ultimate boss Ronald Reagan?

It is a difficult question because of the deliberate choice by Meese, and the mediate choice by Reagan, not to tell or even pressure Fried on what to do. By express statute, Meese could have personally executed any and every function of the SG's Office if that had been his preference,[67] and we believe that the president has similar authority under Article II by constitutional command.[68] Was the decision to give Fried a free hand a tacit authorization for him to pursue his own agenda if that is what he thought best? We do not purport to answer that perhaps unanswerable question; it is a matter that goes outside of law. We do, however, have a few concluding observations about some gaps between key tenets of the Meese Revolution and the fate of those tenets in the SG's Office.

Fried discusses two episodes in which his own inclinations ran counter to the wishes of Meese and Reagan, and each is instructive.

In *Communications Workers of America v. Beck*,[69] the Supreme Court asked for the views of the solicitor general on whether unions could use compelled dues payments to support candidates and parties—invariably of a leftist sort, though the particular orientation is legally irrelevant. The federal labor laws give unions a government-assured monopoly of the labor force; once a union is certified by the National Labor Relations Board, the employer *must* bargain exclusively with that union. As a result, individual workers who do not agree with the union's political outlook find themselves compelled by federal law to pay dues that benefit candidates and parties they do not personally support. If the government directly ordered workers to donate to candidates, that would obviously violate the First Amendment. Did the same result follow when the government gave the union monopoly status by law and the union then did the dirty work? Without the monopoly status conferred by federal labor laws, the answer would be no, because the First Amendment does not apply to private entities. If the union was a wholly private institution, it could impose whatever speech restrictions or compulsions on its members that it wished without violating the First Amendment.

The Republican Party, President Reagan, and Attorney General Meese all favored the right of union members not to be compelled to fund speech with which they disagreed. Fried disagreed, because he feared that if monopoly unions were labeled as being state actors for First Amendment purposes, it would not be long before all recipients of federal funds or contracts, such as universities, business organizations, and even media firms, were deemed to be state actors too. As Fried put it, "In my constitutional catechism, the line between the public and the private must be drawn firmly."[70] Putting aside for the moment Fried's decided preference for judicial judgment, common-law reasoning, graphs, and dreams over firm lines on separation of powers, privacy, federalism, and everything else discussed in his book seemingly except the public-private distinction in *Beck*, Meese's special assistants thought that there was a sensible line to draw between government-enforced monopolies compelling speech and private corporations receiving government grants or contracts compelling speech.

The SG's Office, over the objection of Special Assistant to the Attorney General David McIntosh, sided with the unions. The Supreme Court ducked the constitutional issue entirely and ruled 5–3 against the union's compelled speech on statutory grounds. Fried had insisted that the relevant federal statutes did not forbid unions from using their compelled dues for political purposes, and as a textualist matter he was likely correct about that. Justice Scalia certainly thought so, joining the dissenting opinion in the case, so we find it hard to fault Fried for not pushing the statutory argument. Do we fault him for not taking a harder First Amendment line? Yes, though it is tricky. The public-private line for constitutional purposes is actually one place where Fried's fuzzy, judgment-based reasoning may actually be correct as a matter of original meaning. After all, the Congress of 1875 thought, with considerable justification, that it could use its Fourteenth Amendment power to prevent discrimination by state governments also to prevent discrimination by nominally private common carriers and innkeepers. Those entities were often government-sanctioned monopolies or beneficiaries of the state's eminent domain power, and there is considerable evidence that earlier generations understood them to be on the "public" side of the public-private divide for that reason. The Supreme Court rejected that argument in 1883,[71] but we are not at all sure that the court got that right as a matter of original meaning.[72] A careful originalist account of the public-private line would have been (and would still today be) extremely valuable for the court to see, but that was not in the cards.

Fried also worried a lot about how to litigate cases involving government takings of property. We already mentioned how complicated this issue can be. If the Constitution's reference to private property being "taken" refers only to instances in which the government formally takes over the title to someone's land, then the clause has very narrow application and is easy to understand and implement. But what if the government leaves the title intact but regulates so heavily that it effectively forces the landowner to do the government's bidding at the landowner's own expense? If takings include some government actions that destroy or damage property without formally transferring the title, it becomes a difficult task to sort out permissible from impermissible government actions. Since 1871, the court has held that *some* actions that don't transfer title are takings, but it has been unable to articulate a clear test for how to determine which actions require just compensation. The court has proceeded using Fried's favored method of common-law, judgment-based adjudication. The incoherent and inconsistent results do not speak well of that method, though whether that is the fault of the court or the method is a question for another day.

The October 1986 Supreme Court term is sometimes called "the Takings Term" because it presented an unusual number of cases raising key questions about the Takings Clause and its incorporation against states through the Fourteenth Amendment.[73] Though all of the cases except *Hodel v. Irving* involved state rather than federal action, the federal government had an obvious interest in how the court developed its Takings

Clause jurisprudence, so the SG's Office had to consider filing amicus briefs in those cases, and it filed briefs in two of those cases—once on the side of the government and once on the side of the property owner.

Fried was very worried that "Attorney General Meese and his young advisers—many drawn from the ranks of the then fledgling Federalist Societies and often devotees of the extreme libertarian views of Chicago law professor Richard Epstein—had a specific, aggressive, and, it seemed to me, quite radical project in mind: to use the Takings Clause of the Fifth Amendment as a severe brake upon federal and state regulation of business and property."[74] Guilty as charged. Indeed, virtually the entire civil side of the DOJ, not just the young advisers, believed that courts had under-enforced the constitutional rule against uncompensated takings of property. As Fried acknowledges, "The Attorney General…was personally committed."[75] That is not surprising, since one of Meese's good friends was San Diego Law professor Bernie Siegan, whose main scholarly project was reviving more vigorous judicial protection of traditional property rights.

Fried feared that if the Supreme Court enforced a vigorous regulatory takings doctrine, it would only be a matter of time before the court protected the expectations of "welfare beneficiaries, government job-holders, and the like."[76] As we observed in chapter 5, this was not a paranoid fear. Constitutional welfare rights had been a major project of the academic and judicial left for several decades, and one of Fried's colleagues at Harvard Law School, the mega-brilliant Frank Michelman, was among the project's leading champions. Fried was so worried that he considered resigning rather than file a brief making it easier for landowners to sue governments for damages, but he was talked out of it by his deputy, Carolyn Kuhl, because the matter was not sufficiently important ("Jeez Louise, quit over a Mickey Mouse thing like this?").[77] The landowner won the case, establishing the principle that once the government has taken your property, even for a short period of time, it has to pay you just compensation for that "temporary taking"; it can't make things right just by saying "oops" and giving it back.[78] That seems obvious, and we still puzzle over why Fried was reluctant to say so. Of course, the left was going to come back with a claim for constitutional welfare rights, but it was going to do so anyway. That claim was best met on its merits—and Charles met it and defeated it with aplomb and distinction in 1988.[79]

On the other hand, perhaps the most important property rights case of the term was *Nollan v. California Coastal Commission*, in which the California Coastal Commission would only grant landowners a permit to build on their property if they granted an easement for the general public to traverse the beach in front of their house. This practice of conditioning the grant of legally mandated permits on transfers of some portion of the property to the government—something that would be called "extortion" or a "shakedown" if done by private parties—was commonplace throughout the country. If the government had just grabbed an easement, it would obviously have to pay compensation. Could the government avoid that obligation by "asking" landowners to "donate" an easement in return for permission to build anything—including anything as small as a new mailbox—on their land?

In a 5–4 decision, in an opinion by Justice Scalia, the court held that governments could only condition permits on give-backs of land or easements when those give-backs had some kind of nexus to the regulatory scheme. In *Nollan*, building a new house would not eliminate any public access to the beach that already existed, so the imposed condition was not offsetting some problem caused by the construction. Most states already required some kind of nexus for permit conditions as a matter of their own state law. *Nollan* held that it was a federal constitutional requirement.

The SG's Office filed a brief in that case on behalf of the landowners. Fried claims, and we have no reason to doubt, that "I felt so strongly about the impropriety of the governmental action in that case that I personally strengthened the brief that had come up in the usual course of business from the Attorney General's people and the Lands Division staff."[80] Seven years later, the court expanded on *Nollan* by clarifying the tightness of the nexus requirement between permit conditions and the actual effects of the proposed land use.[81] Thus, the Meese Justice Department's takings initiative, this time with Fried's support, influenced a major property rights case six years after Meese had left office.

So was Fried the right person to be solicitor general for the Meese Revolution? Steve Calabresi originally thought not. On reflection, he thinks it is a harder call because every solicitor general is an ambassador from the president to the Supreme Court, which may not at the time share the president's constitutional vision. Fried might very well have been the best ambassador that the originalists in the Meese DOJ could have hoped for to what was at the time a very non-originalist Supreme Court.

The easier call is whether we would have had lunch or dinner with him whenever we could, or whether we would have chosen him as a co-castaway if we were stranded on a desert island. Unquestionably yes. Charles Fried was a wonderful conversationalist, hilariously funny, a true intellectual, and had the impeccable manners of a bygone era—an era in which people respected each other more than they do now. Indeed, we criticize him here out of respect as fellow academics. Charles Fried could take it—and surely dish it out in return throughout his eighty-eight-year-long lifetime. We regret that he did not live to see this book because we are certain he would have had a very interesting reaction to it!

CHAPTER ELEVEN

"AND THE REST..."

THE DEPARTMENT OF Justice employs more than one hundred thousand people across more than three dozen units, including eleven units housed in the Robert F. Kennedy Building, headed by assistant attorneys general. We can obviously only touch here on a few highlights from these disparate units within the department during Ed Meese's tenure, but several require special mention.

The Office of Legal Counsel

THE DEPARTMENT OF JUSTICE'S Office of Legal Counsel (OLC) is one of the most important government agencies that most people probably don't know about. It functions as the general counsel to the executive branch, providing legal advice on constitutional and statutory matters to the attorney general and the president. The attorney general's authority to issue legal opinions on behalf of the executive branch has long been delegated to the OLC.[1] The OLC also prepares and reviews executive orders, comments on the constitutionality of proposed legislation, and resolves disputes between government agencies about the meaning of statutes. For the great mass of legal questions about governmental operations that never reach the courts, the OLC is typically the last word, and it carefully cultivates a reputation for impartial and accurate legal advice.

Two assistant attorneys general of the OLC, William Rehnquist and Antonin Scalia, have gone on to serve with distinction on the Supreme Court, along with former OLC deputy assistant attorney general Sam Alito. William Barr was the assistant attorney general for the OLC before serving as the nation's second youngest attorney general under President George H. W. Bush and the nation's oldest attorney general under President Donald Trump. The office, despite having fewer than two dozen lawyers on staff, has long been a breeding ground for future academics. Just during the brief eight Reagan years, the OLC produced for the academy Mike Fitts, a former dean of the University of Pennsylvania

Law School and currently president of Tulane University; Harold Koh, a former dean of Yale Law School; John Manning, the current dean of Harvard Law School, on leave to serve as interim provost of Harvard University; Marc Miller, the current dean of the University of Arizona Law School; and a who's who of chaired or distinguished professors with names recognizable to anyone in the legal academy.[2] With considerable justification, former attorney general William French Smith described the OLC as "the most prestigious group of lawyers in government (except possibly for those in the Solicitor General's Office)."[3]

The assistant attorney general for the OLC under Ed Meese was Charles J. "Chuck" Cooper, a thirty-three-year-old former Rehnquist clerk and a committed Meese Revolutionary who had previously served as Brad Reynolds's deputy in the Civil Rights Division. Chuck took over the office at a difficult time, both administratively and legally.

On the administrative side, the office had been in a hiring freeze and was wildly understaffed, with barely half a dozen lawyers instead of the normal twenty or so. More importantly, the only other originalist in the OLC in mid-1985 was Gary Lawson, who joined the office just a few months before Chuck took over; the rest of the staff were career lawyers with no background in or commitment to originalism. Chuck later brought in as one of his deputies Sam Alito, who had been working in the Solicitor General's Office. (Another deputy, Allan Gerson, a former staffer to Jeane Kirkpatrick with no interest in originalism, was later hired to handle the office's considerable international law workload.) That still left the office short on lawyers and even shorter on Meese Revolutionaries.

From a legal standpoint, Chuck faced many of the problems faced by Charles Fried in the Solicitor General's Office. The OLC needed to give the president and the attorney general sound advice about the likely legal consequences of their actions, including accurate predictions of success or failure in court. There were also considerations of institutional consistency; the OLC had a large stock of prior opinions on a wide range of topics concerning separation of powers and other constitutional and statutory matters. The courts and case law circa 1985 were decidedly non-originalist, as was a large stock of the internal OLC precedents. If the president and attorney general actually followed the meaning of the Constitution and statutes rather than the policy-based judicial and executive precedents, there would be real-world consequences. But for originalism to become part of the legal fabric, it had to be woven into the OLC's work product.

Cooper navigated that problem as well as anyone could have managed. His opinions accurately represented the existing precedents, but also shined those precedents through an originalist lens so that the president, the attorney general, and anyone else could see the *right* answer as well as the *precedential* answer. Chuck Cooper was writing originalist and textualist opinions before Antonin Scalia joined the Supreme Court and emerged as a public champion of originalism and textualism.

Cooper's opinions also displayed a subtle appreciation for separation of powers and federalism, both of which he cared about as deeply as did Meese. Cooper was the chief of the "federalism police" about whom Charles Fried complained so much; he chaired the Federalism Working Group while he was single-handedly doing much of the day-to-day OLC work in his understaffed office.

A few examples show how Cooper's OLC demonstrated originalism and textualism in action before those ideas became commonplace.

One of the first OLC opinions issued under Cooper's name objected to proposed legislation giving congressional committees increased access to grand jury materials, which are typically kept under strict secrecy. The OLC opinion[4] raised concerns of separation of powers and due process. Much of the analysis was grounded in case law, but, importantly, the opinion contained a substantial discussion of original meaning, citing the Constitution's prohibition on bills of attainder, *The Federalist*, and first principles of separated powers to emphasize the federal executive's exclusive role—and therefore Congress's non-role—in prosecuting crimes. This was a clear signal that the Meese/Cooper OLC would take originalism seriously while still providing an accurate account of existing precedents. The legislation was not enacted.

The OLC, speaking through the Office of Legislative and Intergovernmental Affairs, was less successful in opposing a legislative provision that deemed certain administrative decisions "affirmed" by a court if the court did not issue a decision within ninety days.[5] Congress, in other words, would effectively decide the case. The OLC objected on strict originalist grounds that Congress was not granted the federal "judicial

Power" and thus could not exercise that power even indirectly by ordering courts to issue particular decisions in particular cases. The opinion was all about first principles of separation of powers:

> The Constitution vests all federal judicial power "in one supreme Court and in such inferior Courts as the Congress may from time to time ordain and establish." U.S. Const, art. Ill, § 1. Thus, "our Constitution unambiguously enunciates a fundamental principle that the 'judicial Power of the United States' must be reposed in an independent Judiciary." *Northern Pipeline*, 458 U.S. at 60 (plurality opinion). As Alexander Hamilton wrote in *The Federalist*, it is necessary for the Judiciary to remain "truly distinct from the Legislature and the Executive. For I agree that 'there is no liberty, if the power of judging be not separated from the legislative and executive powers.'" *The Federalist* No. 78, at 466 (C. Rossiter ed. 1961) (citation omitted). Thus, it is a violation of the separation of powers for the Legislative and Executive Branches to exercise judicial power, just as it is unconstitutional for the Judiciary to engage in lawmaking or executive functions.[6]

Congress this time ignored the Justice Department's objections and enacted the law. A decade later, a Supreme Court opinion authored by Justice Scalia vindicated the OLC analysis, saying that Congress could not by legislation retroactively undo final judgments rendered by courts.[7] The same considerations of judicial independence explain why Congress cannot force courts to issue judgments that courts do not think warranted. Congress can change the law that courts must apply, but it cannot command the results in specific cases. Before the Meese Revolution, it is quite possible that the Supreme Court would have come out the other way on this matter, perhaps instead endorsing Justice Stevens's and Justice Ginsburg's position in dissent that a strict separation of powers rule "unnecessarily hinders the Government from addressing difficult issues that inevitably arise in a complex society"[8] and that, quoting Justice Oliver Wendell Holmes, "the machinery of government would not work if it were not allowed a little play in its joints."[9] Cooper's OLC-sponsored originalism on separation of powers eventually migrated to the Supreme Court.

Just as Congress cannot tell courts how to decide cases, it cannot tell the executive how to execute the laws. Using the same originalist first principles of separated powers, Cooper's OLC explained that the Senate could not dictate the decisions made by U.S. commissioners under a treaty by conditioning approval of the treaty on those decisions.[10] Once the treaty is approved, it is up to the executive to carry it into effect, as with other laws. Neither the Senate as a body nor Congress as a whole gets to implement the treaty.

Cooper's signature OLC opinion is surely his discussion of proposed legislation creating a national lottery, the proceeds of which would go to the various Social Security trust funds. In 1986, it had been half a century since the Supreme Court had found a statute unconstitutional for exceeding Congress's enumerated powers. As a matter of case law, there were no discernible limits on Congress's power. Cooper nonetheless concluded that "Congress lacks the power to establish a national lottery."[11]

The OLC opinion did not begin by describing half a century of case law. Instead, it began "by noting that Article I, § 8 of the Constitution does not endow Congress with 'all legislative power.'"[12] Hence, "[u]nder the doctrine of enumerated powers," the bills in question "are invalid unless the creation of a national lottery falls within one of the limited grants of legislative authority conferred upon Congress."[13] The opinion conducted an analysis of the original meaning of each of the constitutional sources of funding authority, concluding that a lottery was not a "tax," "duty," "impost," or "excise" nor an exercise of authority to "borrow" on the credit of the United States. (The government can also raise money by selling public lands or other assets, but a lottery is clearly not a land sale.) This was a tour de force of originalist reasoning.

Just as the opinion did not begin by describing half a century of case law, it did not end with it either. The opinion did not describe the Supreme Court's non-originalist case law on congressional power at all. It focused entirely on ascertaining the original meaning of the constitutional provisions. This was unprecedented in modern times—as unprecedented as Attorney General Meese's speeches.

The context of this opinion was crucial. The executive branch was not deciding whether or how to defend an enacted statute in court. The law had not yet been enacted. It was advising the president whether to support or potentially veto proposed legislation. From an originalist standpoint, the relevant question for the president is *not* whether courts would likely find the bill constitutional if it passed and became a law. The relevant question is whether the *Constitution* would find the bill constitutional if it passed and became a law. A president swears an oath to "preserve, protect and defend the Constitution of the United States,"[14] which requires independent judgment—independent of both Congress and the courts—about the Constitution's meaning. This is a logical consequence of the "departmentalism" put forward by Ed Meese in his speeches, highlighting the difference between the Constitution and constitutional law. From the standpoint of original meaning, Cooper's analysis was spot on, even though that analysis had no traction in the courts or Congress. This was advice to the president on how to exercise the president's judgment, and it was advice grounded strictly in original meaning.

Nine years later, the Supreme Court revived the doctrine of enumerated powers after nearly sixty years of dormancy. The Meese Justice Department got there first. This OLC opinion stands as a model of how to conduct originalist analysis before Justices Scalia or Thomas could show the world how to do it from a more public podium.

Cooper's OLC was also ahead of the curve on statutory interpretation. One of the most important legal developments in the past three to four decades has been the rise of textualism as the principal mode of statutory interpretation, at least in the Supreme Court. Throughout the Reagan administration, and into the early 1990s, the dominant approach in the courts to interpreting statutes was a crude purposivism that tried to divine the "goals" of the statute, using a combination of legislative history and the court's own views of wise policy. A countermovement led by Justice Scalia emerged on the Supreme Court in the 1990s[15] and in a remarkably short time transformed the way that cases on statutory meaning get argued and decided. While appeals to purposes and legislative history still find support among some justices, it is today as hard to find a majority opinion relying on those considerations as it was thirty years ago to find a majority opinion that did not. When Justice Kagan in 2015 said with regard to statutory interpretation that "we're all textualists now,"[16] she was exaggerating only slightly.[17]

None of this was true in the mid-1980s, where if the statute said "dog" but some congressional committee report said "cat" or the judges thought that "cat" made better policy sense, there was a pretty good chance that a court would go with "cat." Cooper's OLC, however, took as hard a textualist/originalist line with statutes as it did with the Constitution.

The best illustration came from a tragedy: the rise of Acquired Immunodeficiency Syndrome (AIDS). AIDS first appeared in 1977, but its legal implications became pronounced in the early 1980s. AIDS was and is thankfully very difficult to transmit, but in the early years, there was enough irrational fear of being near persons who had, or were even thought to have, AIDS that it raised serious concerns about discrimination. At that time, there was no Americans with Disabilities Act, which was enacted in 1990, so the only applicable federal statute was section 504 of the Rehabilitation Act of 1973, which forbids discrimination in federally funded programs "solely by reason of"[18] disability—though the 1986 version of the statute used the term "handicap" rather than "disability." By 1986, multiple federal agencies administering programs subject to section 504 had asked the OLC to what extent discrimination based on AIDS or fear of AIDS would violate the statute.

The statute does not forbid all discrimination against people with handicaps (using the 1986 terminology). It forbids discrimination "solely by reason" of handicap. Race discrimination, for example, against someone with a handicap violates other statutes, such as Title VI of the 1964 Civil Rights Act, but not section 504, which focuses only on discrimination that is *based on* handicap. The key to the statute's scope is the definition of a "handicap."

In 1986, the statute defined an individual with handicaps as "any person who (i) has a physical or mental impairment which substantially limits one or more of such person's major life activities, (ii) has a record of such an impairment, or (iii) is regarded as having such an impairment."[19] The statute has since been amended to have a broader sweep that elides many of the issues faced by the OLC in 1986, but Cooper and his staff had to work with the quoted language.

More precisely, Cooper's key decision, which was not at all inevitable by the legal conventions of 1986, was indeed to work with the quoted language. One option was simply to decide what a good or sensible statute would say and go from there. If one were trying to predict how courts circa 1986 would decide cases, that policy-based method would probably have been a sensible approach. But as with advising the president whether to veto a lottery bill, Cooper determined that the right approach was to figure out what the statute actually means, not which misreadings of the statute might or might not survive in court. Accordingly, Chuck, Sam Alito, Gary Lawson, and some people from other departments (Lawson specifically recalls Steve Mathews contributing and believes Mike Carvin played a role as well) set out to do what literally no one had done since the statute's enactment in 1973: figure out its original meaning.

Some questions were very easy. Of course AIDS itself was a handicap under this statute, so discrimination based on that condition was obviously within the statute. The harder questions involved people who did not yet have AIDS, which is an advanced condition with many serious consequences, but who tested positive for the human immunodeficiency virus (HIV) that ultimately caused AIDS in many affected people. Someone can have a positive test for HIV but no overt symptoms at all, and certainly no symptoms that "substantially limit" any physical or mental capacities. In that respect, asymptomatic HIV infection was analogous to a genetic marker that *might* in the future lead to a disabling condition but is not itself disabling at the moment. If asymptomatic HIV infection was not a handicap under the statute, then discrimination based on that infection—or a record of such infection, or even a false belief that someone had such an infection—would not be discrimination "solely by reason" of handicap. It might be really dumb discrimination, but the statute did not prohibit all really dumb discrimination. It prohibited discrimination based on handicap.

The result was not going to sit well with the press or the Left. It meant that discrimination based on even a wildly irrational fear of transmission of HIV would not violate section 504, because it would not be discrimination "solely by reason" of handicap. Even discrimination against someone with actual AIDS would not violate section 504 if the basis for discrimination was HIV infection rather than AIDS—just as discrimination against someone with AIDS based on, for example, hair color or height would not violate section 504. These results were surely counterintuitive to those accustomed to thinking about statutes as invitations to make policy rather than legal instructions, but they were obviously what the statute prescribed, and that is what OLC said.[20] This was strict textualism in action years before such methods took hold on the Supreme Court.

Indeed, the Supreme Court had a case involving section 504 the very next year involving precisely the kinds of issues addressed by the OLC opinion, this time in the context of tuberculosis. The DOJ participated as an amicus curiae, and the solicitor general's brief adopted in full the OLC analysis of the statute. Charles Fried immediately grasped the OLC argument,[21] fully endorsed it, and produced a terrific brief. But this was a Supreme Court still wedded to reading statutes to make what the court considered good policy, and the court, with Chief Justice Rehnquist and Justice Scalia dissenting, rejected the textually obvious meaning of the statute.[22] The following year, after Cooper had left the OLC, the new assistant attorney general abandoned Cooper's reasoning, partly in response to the intervening Supreme Court case.[23]

The OLC under Chuck Cooper was a pioneer in originalist and textualist analysis. As Barbara Mandrell might say, it was doing originalism when doing originalism wasn't cool.

The Criminal Division

ED MEESE thought he had two great duties as attorney general of the United States: enforcing the law, especially the criminal law, and encouraging the legal system to emphasize original meaning textualism. If he failed at accomplishing the first duty, there would be no safe and civil society in which to accomplish the second. Meese's career was principally in criminal law, so it is no surprise that he focused much of his attention on it. As we said earlier, an entire second book could be written about the criminal law side of the Meese Justice Department, and the revolutionary nature of Meese's term as attorney general. We, unfortunately, are not qualified to write such a second book, but we can make at least a few observations from our perspective as experts in constitutional and administrative law.

Meese elevated the visibility of the criminal law enforcement effort by conducting it out of the Deputy Attorney General's Office rather than the Associate Attorney General's Office, as had been the case under former attorney general William French Smith. To Meese's good fortune, Bill Smith's associate attorney general, D. Lowell Jensen, became Meese's deputy attorney general. Jensen had worked with Meese in Alameda County, California, where he rose up the ranks from 1955 to 1981, overseeing prosecutions involving the Black Panthers and Patty Hearst. From 1981 to 1983, Jensen headed the criminal division in the Justice Department before taking more senior positions as associate and then deputy attorney general. Meese could rely on Jensen to handle the criminal side of the DOJ until Jensen was appointed as a district judge for the Northern District of California on June 25, 1986. The Criminal Division was initially in the capable hands of Stephen Trott, who took over as associate attorney general in 1986 and was eventually appointed to a Ninth Circuit judgeship in 1988. Jensen and Trott were replaced by, respectively, Arnold Burns and William Weld, who were among Ed Meese's biggest mistakes. But that is a story for another chapter.

The criminal side of the DOJ faced some big challenges in the mid-1980s. As Meese put it, "[B]etween 1960 and 1980 you had a period of time where, at least at the start of that period, almost nobody went to prison. And those that did go, were let out very quickly. And as a result, we had one of the greatest crime waves in the history of the country: violent crime is going up something like 500 percent and overall crime…something like 300 percent. And…the drug problem had…been at its height." Much of the crime came from "serious habitual offenders," whom Meese thought belonged in prison and then "kept there longer." The drug problem receded for a time and then rose again, "partially because of the crack epidemic in the major cities." The enforcement priorities were thus "continuing to keep more serious, habitual criminals in prison and secondly to deal with the drug problem."

Some of the key anti-crime initiatives, such as the Sentencing Commission, which produced guidelines for harsher penalties for career criminals, and asset forfeiture laws, came from the 1984 Comprehensive Crime Control Act, before Ed Meese's tenure as attorney general. Once he took over, Meese approached criminal law issues with the same academic and philosophical bent that characterized his whole Department of Justice. Many of his speeches focused on criminal justice. They were too numerous to summarize here, but two themes emphasized by Meese stand out.

One theme was the search for truth, which much criminal law doctrine then (and now) systematically stifled. The two most obvious doctrinal roadblocks to truth-finding are the *Miranda* rule, which excludes use at trial of confessions that do not conform to the Supreme Court's rigid norms for ensuring "voluntariness," and the exclusionary rule, which forbids trial use of evidence obtained, even indirectly, from unlawful searches and seizures. Meese thought then, and thinks now, that "it was wrong to exclude from a trial a portion of the truth for policy reasons unrelated to the particular criminal case. ... [T]here had to be better ways to discipline the police than allowing the criminal to go free."

Meese expressed this philosophy in numerous speeches, including one at Vanderbilt Law School on October 6, 1986, on "Promoting Truth in the Courtroom." "The Gospel of John, chapter 8 verse 32," Meese observed, "tells us that 'The truth shall make you free.' ...In the criminal law, however, I'm afraid that all too often the opposite is the case. Today, criminals—people who have committed violent and serious crimes and whose guilt is clear beyond any doubt—often go free because in important ways our criminal justice system obstructs the search for truth." If criminal law does not accurately seek truth, the whole enterprise is dubious. "If the truth cannot be discovered and acted on, the criminal justice system fails in its basic mission. Indeed, the state itself fails in its most fundamental responsibility."

According to Meese, the law places "hurdles ...between the facts and the judge or jury" that "are not inherent in our legal traditions or the nature of an adversary system." Instead, those obstacles to truth-finding were "born in the radical innovations of the 1960s" from people "willing to compromise the search for truth in favor of extrinsic policy objectives." Correcting those modern innovations, most notably *Miranda* and the exclusionary rule, "involves a *restoration* of enduring principles, not their abolition."

In the case of illegally acquired but otherwise admissible evidence, "the Supreme Court has made clear that the exclusionary rule is not required by the Fourth Amendment or any other provision of the Constitution. It survives today only as a judicially created *prophylactic* rule, designed to deter police misconduct." There are better ways to do that than by letting obviously guilty criminals go free. "Officers and investigators should be trained to understand and follow the rules governing searches and seizures. When those rules are violated, appropriate sanctions should be imposed. But we should discipline and deter misconduct outside the forum of the criminal prosecution itself. Make the offending constable, not the public, pay the price."

The same considerations apply to *Miranda* and its exclusion of voluntarily offered confessions when not preceded by court-ordered formalities. One could require "confessions to be tape- or video-recorded whenever practical"—which is surely something even more readily possible today, when anyone with a cell phone can record an event, than it was in 1986. "These other means would enable courts to satisfy themselves that statements were freely made...with far less cost to the truth-finding interest of the law...."

In 1965, the Supreme Court ruled for the first time that it was unconstitutional to comment on a defendant's failure to take the witness stand at trial. This, too, said Meese, is counter to the search for truth: "A defendant's failure to take the stand at trial can be just as telling as his silence before trial." Meese's bottom line was that "[i]f our citizens are to retain their trust in our system of justice, we must make sure that when we ask them [as jurors] to find the truth, we give them, consistent with our Constitution, [evidence]...to see the whole truth."

All the doctrines identified by Meese—the exclusionary rule, the *Miranda* rules, and a prohibition on commenting on a defendant's silence—are still very much alive in 2024. But the issues raised by Meese in 1986 remain the subject of vibrant debate. It was a bold stroke for him to raise them.

One of Ed Meese's most successful criminal law initiatives happened before he was attorney general. In 1982, President Reagan created the Task Force on Victims of Crime, chaired by Lois Herrington, who in 1983 was appointed assistant attorney general for the Office of Justice Programs and a decade later appointed a California state court judge. The Task Force's report was completed in 1983. According to Herrington, Ed Meese "was the one that thought up the idea of having a Victims of Crime Task Force....[H]e's the one that spearheaded that movement and that thought process."

If today it seems obvious to pay attention to crime victims, it was not obvious in the early 1980s. As Herrington explained, "Nobody was talking about victims of crime then, nobody.... When we started, there were … probably eleven states that had any kind of … legislation for victims. When we finished, every state, every state. This was Reagan and Meese's contribution. It was all driven by Meese and the president." And if today it seems routine for White House events to feature crime victims, it was Ed Meese, said Herrington, "that enabled me to bring the victims to the White House, [for the] first time ever."

Herrington describes a cabinet meeting where she discussed the plight of crime victims. David Stockman, the Office of Management and Budget director, interjected: "Mr. President, this is just an entitlement. She just wants more money for an entitlement. We cannot do this." Reagan turned to Stockman and said, "I don't think victims get themselves bashed over the head, and then go to the hospital to get medical care. I don't think that's an entitlement, David."

Another crucial figure in the victims' rights movement was Paul Cassell, who worked on this and other criminal law issues in the Deputy Attorney General's Office from 1986 to 1988. Paul had clerked (with Gary Lawson) for Judge Antonin Scalia on the D.C. Circuit and for Chief Justice Warren Burger on the Supreme Court. As a distinguished academic at the University of Utah's S. J. Quinney College of Law, Cassell for three decades has carried Meese's torch for the crime victims' rights movement.[24]

Cassell points out that in the 1780s crimes were prosecuted privately, often by the victims themselves. Moreover, the federal government initially lacked a police power, and the scope of federal criminal law was minimal,[25] so there was no need to add a Crime Victims' Bill of Rights to the U.S. Constitution. Within a century after ratification of the Constitution, most states had moved from private to public prosecutions. When that happened, the crime victim became the "forgotten man" (or woman) in the criminal law justice system. While the civil rights and women's rights movements both placed some emphasis on crime victims, the formal victims' rights movement really owes its origins to the Meese-inspired 1983 Task Force Report, which included a proposal to amend the Constitution to include victims' rights protections, such as the rights to notice of any hearings related to their case and to be present *and heard* at those hearings.

Members of the victims' rights movement eventually persuaded thirty-eight states to amend either their constitutions or laws to protect crime victims' rights. Presidents Bill Clinton and George W. Bush endorsed a federal constitutional amendment to protect crime victims' rights, but when it failed to secure adoption in the Senate, Congress passed crime victims' rights legislation in 2004.

None of this happens without Ed Meese. Meese was critical to getting the crime victims' rights movement going politically. The Task Force Report made it clear that crime victims' rights were not a "left" or "right" issue but were in fact a bipartisan project.

One more observation is appropriate before we leave criminal law. Ed Meese was prescient about something that has become a major issue in the past two decades since 9/11: the threats from both terrorism and the possible responses to it. In language that has even more resonance today than on January 21, 1987, when Meese spoke them as remarks at a "Conference on Terrorism," he said:

> [A] terrorist can claim victory if he intimidates a society or a
> group of people to the extent that he causes fear or changes in the
> living and work habits of the people or alterations in their lifestyle,
> because then the terrorist has subjugated society to his will. And
> also the terrorist can achieve significant gains if by his provocation
> he stimulates over-reaction on the part of government so that
> government takes steps that are oppressive, such as denying basic
> rights to the people or unduly interfering with their lives, or if it
> causes government itself to give up the rule of law, in which case it
> responds in kind. Such oppressive acts on the part of government
> sow the seeds within the citizenry of resentment, dissatisfaction,
> disaffection, and ultimately disloyalty, thereby serving the cause
> for which the terrorist acts.

Ed Meese understood that law enforcement is a means to an end, not an end in itself.

Other Key Units

MUCH OF WHAT HAPPENED in the Meese Justice Department carried over the fine work of the DOJ under Meese's predecessor, William French Smith. Smith was a close friend (and the personal lawyer) of Governor Ronald Reagan in California, and he performed more than ably as attorney general. Smith, unlike Meese, was not out to change the legal culture in a major way, but under his tenure a number of units within the DOJ changed course from previous administrations of both parties, and those developments continued into President Reagan's second term.

Antitrust law may cause many people's eyes to glaze over, but it is vitally important. Bad antitrust policy can cause enormous economic damage by stifling true competition and productive efficiency in the name of opposing "bigness." In William French Smith's memoirs, the first substantive topic he discussed was antitrust law.

Antitrust law changed dramatically during Smith's tenure when William Baxter, a Stanford Law professor who headed Smith's Antitrust Division, settled the government's seven-year-old campaign against AT&T, splitting it into seven regional phone companies and setting into motion a competitive revolution in telecommunications law. The Smith/Baxter Antitrust Division also dismissed as "without merit" a thirteen-year-long antitrust suit against IBM; the basis for the suit was essentially that IBM had done too good a job of offering consumers something they wanted to buy. Even more significantly, Baxter issued "Merger Guidelines" in 1982 regarding the government's prosecutorial discretion in antitrust cases, providing that henceforth the government would analyze mergers in light of consumer welfare rather than just assuming that big businesses were always benefiting from monopoly status. Mergers often promote efficiency in production and can serve as a useful check on poor corporate management, but past practice too often assumed that anything that results in fewer firms in a market must be bad. This focus on careful economic analysis and consumer welfare may seem obvious, but at the time it was a significant, and highly controversial, shift in focus. Baxter essentially codified into Department of Justice policy the consumer-oriented antitrust theories of Robert Bork, laid out in Bork's 1978 classic *The Antitrust Paradox: A Policy at War with Itself.* J. Paul McGrath continued those policies when Baxter returned to the academy in 1983, and Doug Ginsburg and Charles Rule carried through on the consumer-welfare focus under Meese.

The Civil Rights Division under Attorney General Smith was headed by Brad Reynolds, assisted by Meese Revolutionaries like Chuck Cooper and Mike Carvin. The office continued, and even expanded, enforcement of discrimination laws, including voting-rights laws, but

it questioned prior practices regarding remedies, which often amounted to quotas in employment and forced busing in education. In a 1981
speech to the American Law Institute, Smith explained that "the nation
must end its overreliance on remedial decrees aimed solely at achieving
inflexible and predetermined mathematical balance." One can imagine
that going over about as well as Ed Meese's 1985 remarks to the American Bar Association. But it reflected the consistent views of the Reagan
Justice Department across two terms and two attorneys general. As
Smith eloquently put it,

> Guiding our efforts, as we forged ahead despite the brickbats of
> the press, was a single principle: Individuals should be treated as
> individuals, without regard to race, creed, or ethnic background.
> Freedom from discrimination consists of the right to participate
> fully in our society on the basis of individual merit and desire.[26]

A law school faculty candidate saying these words today would be black-
balled at all but a handful of schools, but those were also the principles
that carried through, along with many of the same personnel, into
Meese's time as attorney general.

There was much more to the Meese legacy than we can describe here.
We have said little about the enormous workload of, for example, the
Civil Division, magnificently run by Richard Willard, or the often-underappreciated Lands Division (the federal government owns a third of
the country's land mass), headed by Meese Revolutionary Hank Habicht. One could do a book on each division, but that is not our project
here. Hopefully we have said enough to convey some sense of the intellectual ferment that permeated a Department of Justice like no other
before or after it.

CHAPTER TWELVE

UNCONSTITUTIONAL PROSECUTORS, FAKE NEWS SCANDALS, AND THE IRAN-CONTRA AFFAIR

THE LAST FIVE years of Ronald Reagan's presidency, from 1984 to 1989, were dogged by fake-news "scandals" that were pursued by a string of unconstitutionally appointed special prosecutors. Cumulatively, these baseless investigations and prosecutions took an enormous toll by distracting the Reagan Revolution's leaders from pushing forward with their program. Ed Meese, in particular, was a target of two politically motivated prosecutorial investigations, both of which concluded, after generating a mountain of bad press, that Meese had done absolutely nothing warranting this treatment. Even before "Bork" became a verb, and before unhinged attacks on distinguished legal figures like Clarence Thomas and Brett Kavanaugh became standard operating practice on the Left, Ed Meese endured scorching and false attacks on his character.

But Meese had a remarkable ability to avoid being distracted by these investigations. He knew that he had done nothing wrong and that eventually that would become apparent to everyone. In the end, he was right about the former but not necessarily about the latter: he emerged legally unscathed from these so-called scandals, but his reputation suffers even today with people who know only what they saw in press headlines almost four decades ago.

Anyone who looks behind those headlines knows two things about Ed Meese.

First, Ed Meese is one of the least avaricious people ever to serve in government—or any other line of work. Many high-level government officials and members of Congress end up on K Street in Washington, D.C., making a fortune peddling influence with congressional or executive branch insiders that they know from their time in government. Meese could, if he was so inclined, have made a fortune arguing cases for law firms before the many judges he had helped pick as attorney general. As did Jim Baker after he was done being secretary of state, Meese could have worked for the likes of the Carlyle Group, which Peter Baker and Susan Glasser (quoting Michael Lewis) describe as being "a kind of salon des refusés for the influence peddling class. ... It offers a neat solution for people who don't have a lot to sell besides their access, but who don't want to appear to be selling their access."[1] Instead, Meese left the government on August 12, 1988, to work at a conservative think tank as the underpaid steward of the Reagan Revolution for the next thirty years. Making money, or even collecting plaudits, was the last thing on his mind.

Ed Meese suffers from none of the seven deadly sins—something few of us can claim with a straight face. Instead, he exemplifies what St. Thomas Aquinas called the seven heavenly virtues: he is brave, wise, just, temperate, and full of faith, hope, and love. He is uncorruptible.

Second, Meese was and is unflappable, even in the face of the most ruthless and dishonest attacks. A cartoon that was published during his time in government (which we cannot now find on the internet) showed a desk in the midst of piles of rubble and a lamp hanging oddly from the ceiling, with Mr. Meese seated and working contentedly at the desk. The cartoon was captioned "The end of the world," and it captured Mr. Meese's complete obliviousness to the vicious political attack campaign that was carried out, appearing on the front pages of every establishment newspaper in the country to try to compel him to resign.

The weapon of choice of Meese's enemies was the independent counsel law, which expired without reauthorization in 1999 after it was used, as its champions never envisaged, against a Democrat: President Bill Clinton. A bit of background on that law is necessary before exploring the so-called scandals of the Reagan administration.

THE INDEPENDENT COUNSEL LAW

THE CONSTITUTION places the administration of federal criminal law in the hands of the president, in whom is vested the "executive Power." Congress is expressly kept out of the loop via the Bill of Attainder and Ex Post Facto Laws Clause,[2] which prevents Congress from directly or indirectly declaring anyone a criminal, and Congress is implicitly kept out of the loop by not being affirmatively granted any power to conduct criminal investigations or trials.

But what if someone close to the president—or even the president personally—is a plausible subject of criminal investigation? Can the president and the president's appointees be trusted to investigate fairly and objectively in those circumstances?

The Constitution has an answer to that puzzle (apart from the electoral process): while Congress cannot itself participate in the administration of criminal law, it can impeach and remove from office any executive official, including the president, who fails in the duty to "take Care that the Laws be faithfully executed."[3] The Constitution contains half a dozen provisions dealing with impeachment and removal of executive and judicial officials. It was something about which the founding generation thought deeply.

Impeachment and removal, however, is akin to the nuclear option. It generates an enormous cost to the polity, and the requirements of impeachment by the House and then conviction by a two-thirds supermajority vote in the Senate make it an unwieldy device for assuring evenhandedness in law enforcement. It is not surprising that some people might look for other options.

One of those options emerged in the 1970s after the theoretical possibility of criminal wrongdoing by high-level executive officials became very real in the Nixon administration. Nixon's first attorney general, John Mitchell, was convicted of multiple crimes and served nineteen months in jail. Nixon's second attorney general, Richard Kleindienst, was convicted of contempt of Congress, but, unlike John Mitchell, he escaped serving time in jail, though he was disbarred. The result was a popular law that passed overwhelmingly in both houses of Congress— and was one of the most blatantly unconstitutional and destructive laws ever enacted in this country.

In 1978, Congress enacted the Ethics in Government Act, which included provisions for appointment by three federal judges of an "independent counsel" who would pursue criminal investigations and prosecutions against high-ranking executive officials, free of supervision by the president, the attorney general, the assistant attorney general of the Criminal Division, or any other person in the president's administration. The proximate cause of this law was a series of events in the early 1970s leading up to what has come to be called "the Saturday night massacre."

President Richard Nixon employed on his White House staff a group of political dirty tricksters who were known as the White House plumbers.[4] These men broke into the Democratic National Committee's headquarters at the Watergate Hotel in Washington, D.C., on June 17, 1972, a presidential election year, looking for dirt. They were arrested by the police, who alerted the FBI that the men were all White House employees. The FBI opened a criminal investigation into the White House plumbers' activities, which included inquiries into what White House senior officials, including President Nixon, knew about the Watergate break-in.

President Nixon himself obstructed the FBI's investigation by calling the director of the CIA to ask him to tell the FBI to close the investigation of the Watergate burglary because the break-in was for top secret national security reasons, which was not true. President Nixon tape-recorded his obstruction of justice, and when the tape finally became public because of a U.S. Supreme Court decision,[5] President Nixon was forced to resign as president on August 9, 1974, to avoid certain impeachment and removal from office.

Before his resignation, between June of 1972 and May 1973, President Nixon had to fire top White House aides H. R. Haldeman and John Ehrlichman, as well as Attorneys General John Mitchell and Richard Kleindienst, some of whom were sent to jail for Watergate-related crimes. Nixon then appointed liberal Republican Elliot Richardson to be attorney general and William Ruckelshaus to be deputy attorney general. Richardson promised in his Senate confirmation hearings that he would appoint a special prosecutor within the Department of Justice to investigate President Nixon's role, if any, in the Watergate break-in. To the delight of liberal Senate Democrats, and especially Senator Ted Kennedy, Richardson appointed Harvard Law School professor Archibald Cox, Attorney General Robert Kennedy's solicitor general, to be the Watergate special prosecutor. This was a foolish move by Richardson, since Archibald Cox was not at all independent, as he was closely allied to the Democratic Party and to the Kennedy family.

In July 1973, during congressional testimony, Deputy Assistant to the President Alexander Butterfield revealed that President Nixon had tape-recorded all of his conversations in the Oval Office. Special Prosecutor Cox subpoenaed the tapes, and Nixon refused to comply. While there were strong legal grounds for maintaining that no one within the executive department could force the president to act against his will and that, in any event, the courts had no role in adjudicating internal disputes between the president and subordinates, the only argument raised by President Nixon in opposing the subpoena was a venerable doctrine called "executive privilege," which shields certain executive communications from disclosure. The D.C. Circuit Court of Appeals rejected Nixon's assertion of executive privilege on October 12, 1973.[6] A week later, on Saturday, October 20, 1973, President Nixon ordered Attorney General Richardson to fire Archibald Cox—a matter entirely within the president's authority, since there was no statute even purporting to give the special prosecutor any kind of tenure of office. Richardson then resigned because he had promised the Senate in his confirmation hearing that he would not fire a Watergate special prosecutor. President Nixon then asked Deputy Attorney General William Ruckelshaus to fire Archibald Cox, and when Ruckelshaus refused, President Nixon fired Ruckelshaus. Nixon then asked Solicitor General Robert H. Bork, who was by then acting attorney general, to fire Archibald Cox, and Bork did so. Two fired attorneys general and one fired special prosecutor in one day led to the "massacre" label.

On Monday morning, October 22, 1973, Acting Attorney General Bork met with Archibald Cox's lawyers and asked them all to remain in their jobs while promising to appoint a new Watergate special prosecutor with sterling credentials. Bork appointed Leon Jaworski, a former president of the American Bar Association who had prosecuted Nazi war crimes, to be the new Watergate special prosecutor. At the time of his appointment by Bork, Jaworski was a private citizen, and the Department of Justice organic statutes did not give Acting Attorney General Bork the power to appoint an inferior officer special counsel.[7] What Bork should have done was to name as special counsel one of the very best Senate-confirmed U.S. attorneys to carry on Archibald Cox's investigation. Jaworski himself did a terrific job of bringing Nixon to justice. The problem with Bork's appointment of Jaworski is that Bork did not have the statutory power to appoint a private citizen to be special counsel.

In any event, Jaworski pursued the subpoena for the Watergate tapes to the U.S. Supreme Court, which unanimously ordered President Nixon to hand over the tapes to prosecutors and to Congress.[8] Nixon complied with the Supreme Court's order, the tape of Nixon obstructing justice became public, and Nixon was forced to resign to avoid certain impeachment and removal from office.[9]

The lesson that ought to have been learned from all of this is that a Justice Department practice of appointing sitting U.S. attorneys as ad hoc special prosecutors for crimes committed outside the district in which they were appointed in politically sensitive cases would work just fine. Sure, President Nixon had fired Archibald Cox, but the only result of that was the appointment of Leon Jaworski, who drove Nixon from office.[10] But congressional Democrats were not content with this outcome. They wanted to make sure that a Saturday night massacre would never happen again.

Their first response, once Democrat Jimmy Carter became president, was to propose turning the whole Department of Justice into an independent agency—meaning that the DOJ officers would be removable only for statutorily specified causes rather than at will. President Carter's attorney general, former U.S. court of appeals judge Griffin Bell, was adamantly of the view that this was unconstitutional under a 1926 Supreme Court case holding that the president must be able to remove at will all officials performing purely executive functions.[11] Prosecution of criminal offenses has, for the entirety of American history, been an executive power, and turning the DOJ into an independent agency would fly in the face of this history and would limit popular control through presidential elections of government law enforcement policy. Attorney General Bell argued that precedent allowed independent agencies only in rare cases where executive branch agencies were engaged in activities that look more like what legislatures or courts normally do.[12] There was nothing "quasi-legislative" or "quasi-judicial" about the core executive powers of prosecution and taking care that the laws be faithfully executed.

Congressional Democrats backed down from that ambitious plan to transform the entire DOJ, but they were still determined to set up a new special prosecutorial process for alleged wrongdoing by high-level executive branch officials, including the president. What emerged was the Ethics in Government Act of 1978 (EIGA), which President Jimmy Carter signed into law. Under the EIGA, when allegations were made against specified high-level executive officials,[13] the attorney general was obliged to seek appointment of an independent counsel so long as there were "reasonable grounds to believe that further investigation or prosecution is warranted."[14] That made the standard for investigation whether there was a *plausible* accusation of wrongdoing, not whether there was probable cause to believe that a crime had been committed. Moreover, the appointment of the independent counsel, as well as the definition of the independent counsel's jurisdiction, was made by a three-judge special court appointed by the chief justice of the United States. Once appointed by the three-judge court, the independent counsel was removable only "for good cause, physical disability, mental incapacity, or any other condition that substantially impairs the performance of such independent counsel's duties."[15]

The EIGA was unconstitutional, and even obviously unconstitutional, on multiple grounds. First, and most basically, it deprived the president of his constitutional "executive Power" to decide whether or not, and to what degree, to prosecute legal wrongdoing where there is probable cause to believe that wrongdoing has occurred. For better or worse, our Constitution has always been understood to make the president not only commander-in-chief but also prosecutor-in-chief. Presidents George Washington, John Adams, and Thomas Jefferson all ordered particular prosecutions to be started or stopped. The constitutional remedy for misuse of this power is impeachment and removal by Congress.

Second, the Constitution requires that federal "Officers" be appointed by the president with the advice and consent of the Senate,[16] not by a three-judge court. There is an exception for "inferior Officers," who can be appointed by courts, as well as by presidents or department heads, but there is no way that an official with uncontrollable power over prosecutions can be considered an "inferior" officer.

Third, even when courts are allowed to appoint "inferior Officers," such as their own clerks, it is far from obvious that they can also be given power to appoint inferior *executive* officers—just as one would not expect the attorney general or the secretary of agriculture to be able to appoint Supreme Court law clerks.

These constitutional prohibitions on anything like the independent counsel law reflect the Framers' wisdom, as independent counsels present a host of real-world problems. Under a constitutional scheme, investigations and prosecutions of government officials would run through the Department of Justice's Public Integrity Section of the Criminal Division. That unit has a fixed annual budget, which it must spend carefully to investigate and punish the worst and most egregious wrongdoers. Independent counsels under the EIGA had no comparable budget constraints, and they would keep on investigating their targets until they could pin some wrongdoing on them. Moreover, each independent counsel's office was staffed by assistant prosecutors who were intellectually and ideologically interested in finding wrongdoing by those they were investigating. For example, many of Steve Calabresi's and Gary Lawson's Yale Law School left-wing friends signed up to work on Lawrence Walsh's Iran-Contra investigation of the Reagan administration. Then, in the 1990s, many of Calabresi and Lawson's Federalist Society friends signed up to work on Ken Starr's many investigations of Bill and Hillary Clinton. This is unjust, it is unprofessional, and it smacks of being a lynch mob. The fact that the independent counsel statute was hair-triggered by plausible allegations of wrongdoing and not by probable cause of wrongdoing made matters even worse. One can make a plausible-sounding allegation of wrongdoing against any high-level executive official.

The independent counsel law was the Article II equivalent to an Article I bill of attainder. A bill of attainder is a legislative act that declares a named individual to be a criminal and specifies how he should be punished. Perhaps the most famous bill of attainder in English and American history was the Act of Parliament in 1645 declaring the Archbishop of Canterbury, William Laud, guilty of high crimes and misdemeanors for Catholicizing the Church of England. This bill of attainder specified that the Archbishop of Canterbury should be put to death, which was then done. The appointment by a three-judge court of an independent counsel to investigate some high-level government official over merely plausible allegations of impropriety that do not rise to the level of probable cause is an executive branch equivalent of a bill of attainder. It presumes the defendant to be guilty of crimes based on mere suspicions of impropriety. Unlike a true bill of attainder, the independent counsel law did not declare guilt, but oftentimes "the process is the punishment," as the simple act of having to defend against a limitless investigation can destroy a person's life.

In a famous speech on April 1, 1940, to U.S. attorneys from all over the United States, Attorney General Robert Jackson commented on the enormous power of federal prosecutors, noting that "[b]ecause of this immense power to strike at citizens, not with mere individual strength, but with all the force of government itself, the post of Federal [U.S.] Attorney from the very beginning has been safeguarded by presidential appointment, requiring confirmation of the Senate of the United States. You are thus required to win an expression of confidence in your character by both the legislative and the executive branches of the government before assuming the responsibilities of a federal prosecutor." Independent counsels appointed under the EIGA were not "required to win an expression of confidence ... [from] both the legislative and the executive branches of the government." No president ever nominated or appointed Lawrence Walsh or Ken Starr to be a federal prosecutor. No Senate ever confirmed Lawrence Walsh or Ken Starr to be a federal prosecutor. And, notwithstanding these egregious omissions, no president or attorney general could even fire Lawrence Walsh or Ken Starr at will for prosecutorial overreach. The EIGA system of hiring and firing independent prosecutors was the worst of all possible worlds.

William French Smith summed up the consequences of the independent counsel statute aptly in 1991:

> Its application to individuals can be, and has been, devastating,
> falsely destroying reputations and forcing one to incur great
> personal debt. Moreover, it has applied artificial standards often
> unrelated to culpability, and to that extent has prevented the use
> of normal standards of prosecutorial discretion. All in all, the act
> has been used more for political purposes and the satisfaction of
> media appetite than to achieve justice, has been a nightmare to

administer, and has caused a substantial (and needless) waste of the taxpayers' money.[17]

The U.S. Supreme Court nonetheless upheld the constitutionality of the EIGA in *Morrison v. Olson*,[18] in what might be the weakest opinion of Chief Justice Rehnquist's career, with Justice Scalia the lone dissenter. Justice Scalia's dissenting opinion in that case has become a modern classic.[19] It was loudly praised by Clinton attorney general Janet Reno when she testified against renewing the EIGA in 1999, when that statute mercifully sunsetted out of existence.

Eventually, everyone came to understand the problems with the independent counsel law. Republicans were incensed by Independent Counsel Lawrence Walsh's prosecution in the late 1980s and early 1990s of the Iran-Contra Affair. From December 19, 1986, until he submitted his final report on August 4, 1993, Walsh tormented the Reagan and Bush administrations with criminal investigations, even though his convictions of former national security advisor John Poindexter and former National Security Council aide Oliver North were both overturned on appeal.[20] Walsh's most egregious act was his indictment of former Reagan and Bush administration officials on October 30, 1992, the eve of the presidential election, in violation of DOJ guidelines that forbid bringing politically charged indictments close to election time. Walsh's election-eve indictments could well have caused Bill Clinton to beat George Herbert Walker Bush in the 1992 presidential election. On December 24, 1992, outgoing president George H. W. Bush put an end to the Iran-Contra prosecution by pardoning six Iran-Contra defendants.

Democrats, for their part, soured on the law once it was turned against them through Kenneth Starr's investigations of the alleged Whitewater scandal, the death of deputy White House counsel Vince Foster, the firing of White House travel office personnel, potential political abuse of confidential FBI files, malfeasance at the Rose Law Firm, and President Bill Clinton's perjury and obstruction of justice in Paula Jones's civil lawsuit alleging sexual harassment against Clinton when he was governor of Arkansas. Starr referred this last matter to the House of Representatives, which impeached Bill Clinton, though the Senate acquitted him—with all votes on largely partisan lines.

The independent counsel law expired in 1999 and was not renewed by

Congress. As of this moment, there has not been an independent counsel statute for a quarter century. Immediately after the law expired in 1999, however, Attorney General Janet Reno promulgated regulations for the appointment of special counsels. Those regulations have infirmities of their own, at least when the special counsel comes from outside the Department of Justice, such as Robert Mueller, who investigated President Trump, and Jack Smith, who is currently bringing federal criminal charges against former president Trump, but that is a story for another time.[21] As we explained above, only one of the ninety-four Senate-confirmed U.S. attorneys who are currently in office can be appointed by the attorney general to serve as a special counsel. Surely, at least one out of ninety-four sitting U.S. attorneys ought to be professional enough and zealous enough to be an effective special counsel.

With this background in mind on the damage that can be done by independent counsels who are not constrained by the usual limitations on criminal investigations and prosecutions, we can examine the so-called scandals that hung over Meese during his time in office.

THE JACOB STEIN INVESTIGATION

ED MEESE'S FIRST ENCOUNTER with an independent counsel came in 1984 when President Reagan nominated him to replace William French Smith as attorney general. "The entire hive of liberal activist groups, 165 in all, erupted to oppose Meese's confirmation…."[22] While the obvious ground for the opposition was ideological, "[t]he Left peddled every vicious rumor and charge imaginable, hoping something would stick."[23] The Senate Democrats eventually focused on some small financial matters, and Meese had to ask William French Smith to appoint a special counsel in order to move his confirmation forward. Smith invoked the independent counsel law, and the three-judge court appointed Jacob Stein, a distinguished lawyer, to pursue the case.[24]

The independent counsel law required the attorney general to seek appointment of an independent counsel unless the attorney general determined that "there are no reasonable grounds to believe that further investigation is warranted."[25] The allegations that rose to that minimal level, which is far below finding probable cause to investigate, mostly concerned Meese's failure to report, on a complicated financial disclosure form, a $15,000 loan to his wife from a man named Edwin Thomas. It turned out that Thomas and some other of Ed and Ursula's friends who helped them out with loans when they were having problems with their mortgage (Ed Meese is among the most penurious people to serve at a high level in government) got various low-level federal jobs. Other subjects investigated included Meese's and his family's stock trading; whether Meese had obtained special treatment from government agencies for business entities in which he had a financial interest; Meese's change of status from the retired Army Reserve to the Active Reserve and his later military promotion; Meese's statements to House and Senate committees investigating how the Reagan campaign acquired possession of Democratic candidate Jimmy Carter's presidential debate briefing book; Meese's retention of cuff links given to him by the South Korean government; Meese's receipt of payments by the Presidential Transition Trust and the Presidential Transition Foundation; Meese's reporting on his financial disclosure statements of reimbursements for travel expenses; Ursula Meese's receipt of funds from the William Moss Institute; and, finally, Meese's connection, if any, with federal grants to Pepperdine University and American University. None of these allegations rose to the level of probable cause of wrongdoing. No sensible prosecutor under ordinary circumstances would have pursued any of them; the notion that Meese knowingly and deliberately traded low-level jobs for loans was absurd on its face, and the rest of the investigatory agenda was just silly. It was a perfect example of why Stalin's secret police chief Lavrentiy Beria would have loved independent counsels: "Show me the man and I'll show you the crime."

But even Beria would not have been able to prosecute Ed Meese. On September 21, 1984, after a five-month investigation, Stein issued a report finding "no basis with respect to any of the 11 allegations for the bringing of a prosecution against Mr. Meese for the violation of a Federal criminal statute." What did it take to reach that obvious conclusion? "We conducted investigative interviews with over 200 witnesses. Forty-five of the witnesses testified before a Federal grand jury impaneled on May 8, 1984, by the United States District Court in the District of Columbia. Mr. and Mrs. Meese were among those who testified. No witness refused to testify or sought immunity in consideration of testifying." The cost to taxpayers for the Jacob Stein investigation was $312,000. The Meeses were reimbursed for their legal expenses in the amount of $750,000 by court order. All in all, the totally unnecessary and wasteful Jacob Stein investigation of Ed Meese deprived the nation of one year of service by its most successful attorney general in U.S. history while costing the taxpayers $1,062,000.

THE JAMES C. McKAY INVESTIGATION

THE ATTACKS did not let up once Meese was confirmed as attorney general. Another independent counsel was appointed in 1987, and this episode again demonstrates everything that was wrong with the independent counsel law. This investigation was even more baseless than the first, if that is possible. To be sure, there were crimes involved; it's just that none of those crimes involved Ed Meese.

The facts of the case are long and complex; anyone interested can find an account from the government's perspective in *United States v. Wallach*.[26] The case began with a criminal investigation of one of Meese's law school classmates named e. bob wallach (the lower casing of the name was wallach's idea). Wallach was a left-leaning, and very successful, lawyer who left practice after Reagan's election in 1980 to move to Washington, D.C. He took an interest in the Wedtech Corporation, a small New York business that made metal parts. Wedtech's original owner was Puerto Rican, which qualified the company for government bidding preferences for minority-owned businesses. Wedtech thus got a number of military contracts without competitive bidding, even though it should have lost its minority-business designation when its ownership changed.

When it failed to get a small-engine contract with the Army, Wedtech concluded that it needed help lobbying the government for favors. Wallach offered his services—for a hefty fee—as someone who could connect Wedtech with government officials. Lynn Nofziger, Reagan's chief political affairs advisor, also was engaged by Wedtech after he left government service in 1982 and formed a lobbying firm. In 1986, an independent counsel was appointed to investigate Nofziger for possibly violating laws that prohibited lobbying so soon after leaving government service. The independent counsel, James McKay, secured several convictions against Nofziger, but they were reversed on appeal.[27]

Wedtech and wallach, meanwhile, came under the scrutiny of Rudy Giuliani. Giuliani is a familiar figure with a colorful career, including time as the chief of staff to the deputy attorney general, the associate attorney general to Attorney General William French Smith, the mayor of New York City, including during the 9/11 terrorist attack, and most recently the subject of a state RICO indictment by a Georgia district attorney. For present purposes, his relevant role was U.S. attorney for the Southern District of New York from 1983 to 1989, where he became infamous for arranging public and televised "perp walks" for financiers whom he arrested on Wall Street, but whom he later declined to prosecute because of a lack of evidence.

Wedtech was a fertile source for investigation. There were numerous charges of bribery, racketeering, and financial shenanigans, many of which resulted in prosecutions, including prosecutions of both state and federal government officials. Wallach, who received a lot of money for his influence peddling from Wedtech, was among those charged and convicted, though his conviction was also overturned on appeal when it was revealed that government witnesses in his case had perjured themselves.[28]

One might ask: what does any of this have to do with Ed Meese?

Some of the claims in the Wedtech investigations were that wallach, Meese's former law school classmate, and Nofziger, a fellow Reagan Revolutionary, both tried to contact Meese to get his help securing contracts for Wedtech. Meese testified at wallach's trial that wallach had never asked him to do anything improper. As it happened, wallach conceivably could have *asked* for something improper without Meese ever being aware of it. Ann Rondeau relates how, during the Iran-Contra investigation to be discussed shortly, the FBI wanted to search Meese's desk. He told them to search anything they wished. What did they find? Says Rondeau, "Well in the back of his center desk drawer were all these unopened letters from this guy [e. bob wallach]. ... Nobody trusted the man. ... Well, it was the funniest thing, because the FBI came in and all of the letters that e. bob wallach had written [to Ed Meese] were unopened in the back of his center desk drawer." Ed Meese did not even open the letters that were sent to him by e. bob wallach.

Meanwhile, Nofziger, one should remember, was being investigated and prosecuted by an independent counsel. As soon as Meese's name came up as a possible object of lobbying, the independent counsel's authority was expanded .to include investigation of Meese's possible improper role in aiding Wedtech.

Of course, there wasn't any such improper role to find, which is exactly what independent counsel James McKay concluded after an exhaustive investigation. McKay found "no substantial evidence that Ed Meese's involvement with matters concerning Welbilt/Wedtech violated any criminal law" nor "any evidence that Mr. Meese, at any time, knowingly received any money or thing of value from anyone in return for or on account of any official act he performed which benefited the company." McKay recommended no criminal charges against Meese. In a sane world, that would have been the end of the matter. But in the world of independent counsels, that was just the beginning.

Along with his conclusion that Meese had done nothing warranting criminal charges, McKay added an 800-plus-page report criticizing some of Meese's conduct, including opining that there might be crimes somewhere having nothing at all to do with Wedtech. This was totally contrary to standard Department of Justice practice, which is not to throw dirt on someone the DOJ has decided not to prosecute. Moreover, the investigation wound up going far beyond anything involving Wedtech, roaming into foreign policy matters involving a possible Middle Eastern pipeline jointly run by Israel, Iraq, and Jordan (the pipeline project did not pan out) and just about every aspect of Meese's life.

After a $3 million investigation spanning more than a year, McKay found nothing warranting prosecution, but he did *suggest*—something a responsible prosecutor would never do—that Meese *might* have committed some financial nondisclosure crimes. Here is what that was really about, as described in the devastating rebuttal to McKay provided by Meese's lawyer, Nathan Lewin:

> When Mr. and Mrs. Meese transferred away all their stock after
> he became Attorney General in 1985, they were unable to find the
> stock certificates for 17 shares of each of the seven "Baby Bell"
> companies. Faced with a deadline, they executed a "Transfer of
> Property" document which assigned to Mr. Chinn the ownership
> of the lost certificates. Mr. McKay now opines—three years later—
> that the "Transfer of Property" document was legally invalid.

Based upon this after-the-fact legal opinion, Mr. McKay declares, in a wholly gratuitous portion of his report, that Mr. Meese "probably violated" a provision of the Federal conflict-of-interest laws (18 U.S.C. 208(a)) because he was present at Justice Department meetings in 1985 and 1986 when certain telecommunications issues were discussed. ...

The essence of Mr. McKay's position is that Mr. Meese attempted to divest his ownership in the "Baby Bell" stocks but that attempt was, in Mr. McKay's opinion, unsuccessful. As a result, Mr. Meese is labeled a felon by Mr. McKay for failing to recognize the inadequacy of the divestiture. ... This is an unjust misapplication of established principles of criminal law.

McKay's other scurrilous allegation was equally absurd:

A squadron of five I.R.S. agents spent months scrutinizing all of Mr. Meese's personal finances for the past seven years. ...

The result of this painstaking and meticulous review was a totally clean bill of health. ...

The exhaustive review did, however, turn up one personal financial matter on which Mr. McKay and his staff disagree with a judgment made by Mr. Meese and his accountant. At issue is the capital gain on the 1985 sale of the Meeses' stock. This sale had been promised, in part, during Mr. Meese's confirmation hearings and it was accomplished in May 1985 with substantial notice to the entire Justice Department. Because the information regarding the cost of the transferred stock was not available to Mr. Meese when the deadline came for him to file his 1985 tax return, his accountant—a respected California C.P.A.—advised him to defer recognizing any gain or loss and file an amended return when he obtained the necessary information. With Mr. Meese's concurrence, the accountant filled out the tax return and filed it precisely as he had advised.

In order to avoid completing his 14-month fishing expedition with an empty net, Mr. McKay now declares that this omission—plainly done in good faith—violated two criminal tax laws. Mr. McKay's conclusion is so far beyond the scope of reasonable argument that it would be laughable if it did not have potentially serious consequences for Mr. Meese's reputation and professional standing.

Concerns about damage to reputation were not hypothetical or overblown. The *Washington Post* ran a story on McKay's final report that noted McKay's allegations of likely criminal wrongdoing, saying, "[i]t is no badge of honor for the attorney general of the United States to be told he has probably committed two criminal offenses but they don't rise to a level that merits prosecution."[29]

The politicization of law enforcement has perhaps become so commonplace that it is now taken for granted. But there are enormous costs to those kinds of practices. Some of those costs are systemic, and some are human costs to people who are subjected to onerous legal processes for no good reason. The independent counsel system exacerbated all of these problems by triggering investigations with absurdly low standards of proof and insulating even rogue prosecutors from the normal controls built into the Department of Justice. The McKay investigation of Ed Meese was a travesty.

Two-hundred and thirty-one years ago the French Revolution descended into a Reign of Terror in which fifty thousand people were guillotined, including King Louis XVI and his wife Marie Antoinette. This is what happens in a democracy when political disagreements get turned into crimes. The criminalization of political disagreements is a far more serious threat to American democracy today than are the minor activities that are the basis for the criminalization.

THE IRAN-CONTRA AFFAIR

A THIRD INDEPENDENT COUNSEL investigation during the second Reagan term did not have Ed Meese as its target. Indeed, Meese emerged from those events exemplifying the honor, dignity, and fidelity to the rule of law that one would expect. The story of those events is told at some length in Meese's 1992 book *With Reagan: The Inside Story*, which devotes four chapters to the story. We present here only the thinnest highlights.

When the shah of Iran fell in 1979, he was succeeded by a virulently anti-American Islamic fundamentalist government. The hope, however, was that more moderate elements within that government might at some point gain the upper hand, especially when the elderly (nearing eighty in 1979) Ayatollah Khomeini was gone. Accordingly, early in the Reagan second term, the administration considered a number of options to make ties to those more moderate elements, including possibly supplying defensive weapons to Iran in its ongoing and bloody war with Iraq.

Shortly thereafter, the terrorist organization Hizballah, which operated in Lebanon, held some American citizens hostage. It was hoped that moderates in Iran could exercise their influence with Hizballah to secure the release of the hostages while also bolstering their own position within the disorganized revolutionary Iranian government. The incentive for the Iranians, as noted above, was U.S.-made weapons, especially anti-tank weapons. While this is sometimes mischaracterized as "trading arms for hostages," it was much more complex. The arms shipments to Iran were under discussion before there was a hostage situation, and they had geopolitical aims broader than a hostage release. The hostages, in any event, were held by Hizballah, not by Iran, though the hope was that Iran might have some influence on Hizballah. President Reagan approved these transactions, and once they secured presidential approval there was nothing even arguably illegal about them.

Separately from events in the Middle East, the Reagan administration had developed the smart foreign policy device of bleeding the increasingly bankrupt Soviet Union to death by funding anti-communist insurgents in multiple communist countries. The insurgents would get U.S. funding while no U.S. troops would fight or die on a battlefield. The administration accordingly supported the anti-communist Contras in Nicaragua, the Mujahideen in Afghanistan who were resisting the Soviet Union's 1979 invasion, and UNITA, an anti-communist group fighting a civil war in Angola. This contributed to Ronald Reagan's victory in the Cold War without an American shot being fired or an American soldier killed.

Some Democrats in the House of Representatives, who seemed oddly supportive of the communist Sandinistas who controlled Nicaragua and who, along with Cuba and the Soviet Union, were promoting a communist insurgency in neighboring El Salvador, opposed funding the Contras. Everyone agreed that no U.S. troops should be sent into Central America (the Reagan administration never considered it), and legislation prohibited trying to overthrow the Nicaraguan government, but there was less agreement about funding the Contras to help stop Nicaragua from overthrowing the government in El Salvador. A series of appropriations laws cabined to some extent how the U.S. could support the Contras, but no law purported to ban *all* support, which in any event would have raised deep constitutional questions about control of foreign policy.

The most restrictive law, known as the "Boland II Amendment" after Representative Edward Boland of Massachusetts, read,

> During the fiscal year 1985, no funds available to the Central Intelligence Agency, the Department of Defense, or any other agency or *entity of the United States involved in intelligence activities* may be obligated or expended for the purpose or which would have the effect of supporting, directly or indirectly, military or paramilitary operations in Nicaragua by any nation, group, organization, movement, or individual.[30]

This was a very incomplete (and possibly unconstitutional) ban on all aid to the Contras. First, the Boland II Amendment "did not, and could not, bar private or third-country aid to the Contras, or the solicitation of such aid by the White House. The Boland prohibition affected only *appropriated U.S. tax funds* expended by the CIA or other intelligence agencies—not private or third-country funds."[31] Second, it did not bar humanitarian aid, whether to the Contras or otherwise. Third, the National Security Council (NSC) was not included in the list of agencies subject to the ban.

A small group of actors within the NSC, especially Lt. Col. Oliver North, took advantage of these openings to pursue ways of aiding the Contras. North tried to coordinate third-party (meaning non-U.S. governmental) aid to the Contras, which was obviously permissible. More controversially, North, along with NSC officials Bud McFarlane and John Poindexter, realized that the arms sales to Iran, which ran through Israel, could generate some modest profits for Israel, so he arranged to divert those profits to the Contras. For the reasons described above, this was not even arguably illegal if the money belonged to Israel rather than the United States, since it would not then involve U.S. funds, but it displayed terrible judgment, both because it would look bad to Congress and the public and because it amounted to usurpation by staffers of important foreign policy decisions. As Meese puts it, "McFarlane, Poindexter, and North were all career military men—highly distinguished in their field and intensely patriotic, but untrained in spotting legal and political pitfalls."[32] Ann Rondeau is a bit less diplomatic, describing the Iran-Contra initiative as a "minor league game that really messed up the major league players. ... [S]elfish people were not thinking about the larger strategic context. ..."

Meese got involved in late 1986 when it became apparent that dealings with the Iranian government were coming from so many quarters with so little coordination that even the president was not fully aware of all of them—Reagan did not initially know, for example, that Israel was a go-between for weapons shipments to Iran. Thus, in a November 1986 meeting with President Reagan in the Oval Office, along with White House chief of staff Donald Regan and National Security Advisor John Poindexter, Meese said that it was imperative that someone "do an overview—a survey of all the facts and documents—to enable the people testifying before Congress to be absolutely accurate, and to enable us to give a straightforward account to the American people."[33] President Reagan agreed and asked his most trusted friend, Ed Meese, to undertake such an inquiry and to complete it as fast as possible to get the whole story out before the American people.[34]

Meese conducted a five-day investigation in which he received critical help from Chuck Cooper, Brad Reynolds, and John Richardson. This "was not a criminal investigation, but an administrative inquiry seeking to pull together all the relevant details, so that a coherent and accurate presentation could be made to the public and to Congress... ."[35] During that investigation, Brad Reynolds found a document in North's files describing a plan to divert profits from the Iranian arms sales to the Contras. That changed the tenor of the investigation. Further inquiry revealed that North's plan had actually been implemented without the knowledge or approval of anyone other than North, McFarlane, and Poindexter. While the action skirted around legal prohibitions, it was a profound breach of chain of authority and tone-deaf politically. President Reagan, when Meese told him about the operation, had an "astonished reaction" of "absolute shock and surprise,"[36] as did Vice President George Bush and Chief of Staff Don Regan when they were informed.[37]

The press and congressional reaction to these events was predictable, though this time with some measure of justification, because *somebody* should have been keeping better track of the various foreign policy initiatives. That was Ed Meese's position in 1986. Had he been involved in the process sooner, President Reagan and the country might have been spared a great deal of trouble.

Meese, however, had another problem as well. While it seems doubtful whether anything that North, McFarlane, or Poindexter did was strictly illegal, under the independent counsel law the attorney general was *required* to request judicial appointment of an independent counsel if there were even *plausible* allegations to believe that further investigation was warranted. Was it obvious that Israel's profits from Iranian arms sales were really Israel's property? Once it became clear that North and others were running a secret operation from within the NSC, could it be said that it was *implausible* that something more would turn up? Accordingly, Attorney General Meese was compelled by the EIGA to seek appointment of a special counsel to investigate North, McFarlane, and Poindexter. The three-judge court appointed Lawrence Walsh as the independent counsel, which turned out to be one of the worst appointments in American political history.[38]

Walsh's tenure as independent counsel lasted for seven years—longer than the tenure of most attorneys general. It probably would not take seven years to figure out whether the U.S. or Israel owned the profits from Iranian arms sales—though that legal question turned out not to be the subject of Walsh's prosecutions. Instead, Walsh's investigation resulted in convictions of Poindexter for lying to Congress and destroying documents and of North for similar offenses and also for using government funds to build himself a private security fence. All of the convictions were overturned on appeal for various prosecutorial abuses, such as use of compelled testimony against the defendants.[39] Without defending North or Poindexter, it does seem a bit much to spend seven years and untold resources on such matters, much less to treat those matters as the stuff of an administration-defining scandal. But that would be the subject of a very different book.

CHAPTER THIRTEEN:

COME THE REVOLUTION?

M UCH HAS HAPPENED in the thirty-six years since Ed Meese was attorney general. The constitutional world of 2024 is very different from the constitutional world of 1988.

Roe v. Wade was seismically overruled in 2022.[1] Achieving this outcome had been the major preoccupation of originalists in the Meese Justice Department. Another major preoccupation had been getting the Supreme Court to reverse course on affirmative action. In 2023, the Supreme Court took a major step toward a color-blind interpretation of the Constitution and federal antidiscrimination statutes, invalidating race-conscious college admissions programs and thereby calling into question race-conscious employment practices as well.[2] In 2019, five justices indicated a willingness to reconsider the court's generous attitude toward Congress's subdelegation of its legislative authority to administrative agencies,[3] and in the October 2021 and 2022 terms, court majorities in multiple cases applied a "clear statement" rule that requires Congress at a minimum to speak clearly and unambiguously when granting agencies lawmaking power over important, or "major," questions,[4] tracking a similar rule regarding federalism that has been in place for three decades.[5] Justice Amy Barrett did not sign on to a clear statement rule per se, but her common sense textualism led her to the same outcome in a case in which President Biden had excused all student debt based on very dubious statutory grounds. In a series of cases from 2010 to the present, the court has emphasized that the Constitution vests "executive Power" in the president, not in the president's subordinates, and that Congress must therefore tread carefully when trying to insulate bureaucrats from presidential control.[6] The Second Amendment right to keep and bear arms, which was essentially a dead letter in 1988, is now treated on a par with the other constitutional rights that surround it in the Bill of Rights.[7] Religious liberty, which for many decades has been treated almost as badly as Second Amendment rights, now receives robust protection, ranging from allowing high school coaches to pray,[8] to allowing merchants to exercise their free speech rights rather than have government tell them how they must speak,[9] to treating religious education as education.[10] Much of the left is so unhappy with the current state of constitutional jurisprudence that it openly speaks of packing the court to get back its once-secure agenda.

But even if the Supreme Court were to be packed by the Democrats in 2025, the thirty-six-year Meese legacy of adherence to originalism would not just disappear. Instead, Republicans would simply re-pack the Supreme Court at their first opportunity. The originalism genie, which Ed Meese let out of the bottle, can never be put back in the bottle. It is now a permanent part of American legal history.

The forms of argument that take place in constitutional law are very different than they were four decades ago. Originalist arguments, sure losers in 1988, now show up routinely in opinions, and any lawyer who does not know how to make a persuasive originalist argument, along with arguments from precedent and other modalities of legal argumentation, has no business arguing a constitutional case in 2024.

Ed Meese did not bring about this change in legal practice single-handedly. But, for the reasons we have given in this book, it is unlikely that the world would look anything like it does without Ed Meese. If there has indeed been a constitutional revolution, it amply deserves to be called the Meese Revolution, which Don McGahn completed.

Many of these developments came to fruition in the October 2021 term, reinforced somewhat by the events of the October 2022 term. The court's October 2021 term thus bears some striking similarities to the 1937 Supreme Court term that, in conjunction with several succeeding terms and were dramatically transformed constitutional law.

Legal scholars often talk about the "constitutional revolution of 1937," which led to something called "the New Deal settlement," which was essentially a bipartisan agreement to ignore constitutional limits on the federal government.

The New Deal, which began in 1933, saw unprecedented innovations in government pushed through by President Roosevelt and the New Deal Congress. Those innovations vastly expanded the scope of federal regulatory authority to include such matters as agriculture, labor contracts, and, in the case of the National Industrial Recovery Act, literally every aspect of business operation. This legislative program was revolutionary in several ways.

First, under the Constitution, federal legislative authority is confined to the topics identified in the Constitution. One of those topics is "Commerce…among the several States," but for a century and a half before 1932 it had been understood that "commerce" was something distinct from manufacturing, mining, and agriculture (all of which produce the objects of commerce but are not themselves commerce), and that in-state contracting—involving labor, insurance, or anything else—was not commerce "among the several States." Roosevelt and the New Deal Congress discarded those traditional categorizations by claiming federal power to address anything that seemed to be a problem of national significance.[11]

Second, and perhaps more importantly, the *forms* in which federal governmental power were exercised changed. Administrative agencies had long helped implement the president's "executive Power" by carrying laws into effect, and that "executive Power" had long been understood to include some measure of power to interpret the laws. There had been occasional disputes about whether Congress had left executive officials with too much discretion, so that their "executive Power" looked like it was shading into exercises of "legislative Powers," but the Supreme Court in the 18th and 19th centuries never found that line crossed. The New Dealers took that as a license to give federal agencies sweeping power to promote vague goals such as pursuing "the public interest," acting in a "fair and equitable" fashion, and the like.

Third, agencies were given power not only to act like mini-legislatures by fashioning, under vacuous mandates, rules that functioned like statutes; they were also given broad authority to adjudicate disputes in the fashion of courts. But agencies are not courts. Agency officials, unlike federal judges, do not have tenure during good behavior and protections against having their salaries reduced because of decisions that do not please Congress, and there are no juries in agency adjudications. In the founding era, the jury was considered one of the chief bulwarks against government oppression and moving dispute resolution from courts to agencies dispenses with juries.

Fourth, while the Constitution takes great care to separate lawmaking, law execution, and judging across three different branches, the New

Deal model of governance placed *all* of those functions within administrative agencies. The agencies make rules under vague and essentially meaningless statutes, thus essentially making the law; the agencies then decide whether and how to prosecute under the laws that they just made; and the agencies adjudicate the disputes generated by their own decisions to prosecute under their own laws. This combination of functions within a single entity is what James Madison labeled the very definition of tyranny.

The New Deal model of governance thus largely undid the Constitution's schemes both for dividing powers vertically between the national and state governments (federalism) and for dividing powers horizontally within the national government (separation of powers).

During Franklin Roosevelt's first term, the Supreme Court invalidated at least some of these innovations. Among other things, it struck down Congress's cartelization of agriculture and coal production,[12] refused to permit Congress to regulate the fiscal affairs of states through bankruptcy laws,[13] and, most importantly, invalidated on multiple grounds, including unconstitutional subdelegation of legislative authority, the National Industrial Recovery Act, which was the centerpiece of the New Deal plan for industrial cartelization.[14]

In 1936, Franklin Roosevelt was reelected president with more than 60 percent of the vote. The Democrats controlled 76 out of 98 Senate seats and 334 out of 435 seats in the House of Representatives. In the winter of 1937, Roosevelt proposed legislation to pack the Supreme Court by adding six new justices—one for every justice over the age of seventy. Congress never enacted the plan, surely at least in part because of what happened at the Supreme Court in 1937.

The 1937 term produced two watershed decisions. One did not involve the New Deal but rather the court's approach to *state* legislation. The Constitution does not treat the state and federal governments the same way. The federal government can only do what it is authorized to do, while state governments can do anything that the Constitution (or their own state constitution) does not specifically forbid them from doing. And the Constitution contains relatively modest limitations on what states can do. Nonetheless, since shortly after the Civil War, the court had episodically found various state laws unconstitutional because they failed a means-ends test. For example, in 1905, a law limiting the hours that a person could work in a bakery was found unconstitutional because the state could not demonstrate an adequate relationship between the law and employee health to justify the limitation on contractual freedom.[15] While relatively few state laws were actually found unconstitutional under this theory, it happened often enough to be noteworthy.

In 1937, the court upheld a sex-specific minimum wage law in a state law case,[16] overruling a prior decision involving a sex-specific federal law for the District of Columbia.[17] The sweeping reasoning in the 1937 opinion rejected the entire line of cases over the previous half century that had employed so-called "substantive due process" to assess the means-ends relationships in state laws. The New Deal Supreme Court overruled *Adkins v. Children's Hospital*, a 1923 Supreme Court opinion that rendered sex discrimination laws as deserving of heightened judicial scrutiny, and it replaced that with the rational basis test for sex discrimination laws. This use of the rational basis test for sex discrimination laws was reaffirmed by the New Deal Supreme Court in its 6–3 decision in *Goesaert v. Cleary*.[18] Henceforth, said the Supreme Court in its landmark 1937 opinion rejecting substantive due process, state laws that did not violate specific constitutional guarantees needed only to have "a reasonable relation to a proper legislative purpose"[19]—a minimalist standard that virtually no law could fail. The next year, the court confirmed that a law that does not run afoul of specific prohibitions must be upheld if "any state of facts either known or which could reasonably be assumed affords support for it."[20] This dramatically reduced the court's role in policing state and federal social legislation based on judicial assessments of policy wisdom rather than express constitutional prohibitions.

At the same time, and with considerably less textual justification,[21] the court also stopped policing the federalism and separation of powers boundaries governing federal power. The decisive case was *NLRB v. Jones & Laughlin Steel Corp.*[22] The National Labor Relations Act of 1935 (NLRA) was a New Deal centerpiece. It created federal unionization rights, enforced through an administrative agency with broad powers to adjudicate claims under the statute, subject (as is typically the case with agencies) to only very deferential review by courts. Since the subject of the law was contracts generally made within a state rather than across state lines, the constitutional premise of the act was that labor unrest caused by a lack of unions was obstructing the flow of interstate commerce. Some prior cases had ruled that Congress can sometimes regulate commerce within a state in order to make effective a scheme of interstate regulation, but the reasoning behind the NRLA went far beyond those prior cases.

The Supreme Court upheld the law, setting the stage for a revolution in the understanding of the scope of national power. Just as importantly, the court rejected challenges to the *form* in which the governmental power was exercised, specifically rejecting a challenge to the diminution in civil jury trial rights that results from putting primary adjudicative responsibility in an administrative law judge in an administrative agency.

The combined effects of these decisions have given rise to many characterizations of the 1937 term, such as "the revolution of 1937," "the switch in time that saved nine" (referring to Justice Owen Roberts's decision to help make the 5–4 majority in *Jones & Laughlin Steel* and thus stave off Roosevelt's court-packing plan), or a "constitutional moment" so substantial that it amended the Constitution as effectively as would an actual textual amendment under Article V, as was argued by Yale Sterling Professor of Law Bruce Ackerman in his famous We the People book series, which coined the term "constitutional moment."

These labels might have surprised people in 1937. At that time, it was not foreordained that those 1937 decisions would have a lasting impact. It took Roosevelt's reelection in 1940 and his subsequent ability to "pack" the court by appointing eight of the court's nine justices without need for new legislation to lock in the results. The broad reasoning of *Jones & Laughlin Steel* about federal power was not cemented until a few years later.[23] The validation of the administrative state also took a few years, though once it took hold, it took hold deeply: from 1937 to 1975, *no* congressional statute was found unconstitutional by the court on separation of powers grounds. But the seeds were planted in 1937, and it seems reasonable in retrospect to mark the revolution from that date.

Years from now, will people speak of "the revolution of 2022"?

It is far too early to make that judgment. Much depends on the presidential and congressional elections of 2024, 2026, 2028, and the years to follow. Will Democrats hold the presidency and obtain a congressional majority of sufficient size to let them pack the court? Will the current jurisprudential tide outlast Justices Clarence Thomas and Sam Alito, who are in their seventies? We don't know, and neither does anyone else.

There are, however, some strong similarities between the events of 1937 (and the succeeding years) and 2022 (with support from 2023). Indeed, there are some respects in which it is *more plausible* to speak of a "revolution of 2022" today than it would have been, without the benefit of hindsight, to speak of a "revolution of 1937" back in 1938.

Nineteen thirty-seven was a revolution in results, but not necessarily a revolution in methodology. The court became far more deferential to social and economic legislation, both state and federal, than it had been in prior years. But that was driven by results rather than by any deep theory of constitutional interpretation, and the cases that cemented those results also had no clear method driving them.

Franklin Roosevelt eventually appointed nine members of the court: Hugo Black, Stanley Reed, Felix Frankfurter, William O. Douglas, Frank Murphy, James Byrnes, Harlan F. Stone, Robert Jackson, and Wiley Rutledge, replacing every pre–New Deal member of the court except for Justice Owen Roberts. They all agreed, in varying degrees, on upholding the key elements of the New Deal, but they agreed on very little beyond that. There was no overarching philosophy of interpretation that yielded that grand conclusion; it was a shared conclusion without a theoretical foundation. Black, Douglas, and Stone were activists of various stripes; Reed, Frankfurter, and Byrnes were champions of judicial restraint; and Murphy, Jackson, and Rutledge had muddled outlooks somewhere in the middle.

Beyond upholding the New Deal, the Roosevelt justices splintered on almost everything else. They disagreed sharply on the incorporation of the Bill of Rights against the states,[24] free speech,[25] the role of courts in legislative districting,[26] the constitutionality of sex discrimination,[27] and even the constitutionality of race discrimination in the Japanese internment case.[28]

The "conservative" bloc on the Roberts Court of 2023 is also not a monolith. Justices Thomas and Gorsuch do not act in lockstep with each other, much less in lockstep with Justice Alito, much less in lockstep with Justices Kavanaugh and Barrett, much less in lockstep with Chief Justice Roberts. Nor do the justices share a common jurisprudential framework. Chief Justice Roberts and Justice Kavanaugh appear to be *institutionalists* who care about the court's public reputation. Justices Thomas and Gorsuch, on the other hand, are principally *constitutionalists* who focus more sharply on deciding cases in accordance with the Constitution's original meaning. Justice Alito has feet in multiple camps, and it is too soon to try to label Justice Barrett.

Having said that, the Roberts Court justices agree *at a fundamental methodological level* more than did the Roosevelt justices. It would be a mistake to describe the current court as "originalist" in a strong sense. Precedent plays much more of a role in its decision-making than does resort to original meaning. But perhaps because of four decades of theorizing originalism after Ed Meese put it on the map in 1985, there is at least an originalist undercurrent to a good portion of the court's work product—with Justices Thomas and Gorsuch working hard to turn the undercurrent into a tidal wave.

The events of the 2021 and 2022 terms provide a good illustration of the potential, and the potential limits, of the current jurisprudential shift. Consider *Dobbs*, which overruled *Roe v. Wade* (and its many successor cases) after half a century, leaving abortion regulation to each of the fifty states. As a matter of original meaning, under any reasonable variant of original meaning, there is no plausible argument for a constitutional rule prohibiting states from regulating abortions at any stage of pregnancy. The Constitution does not specify when human life begins, so if a legislature concludes that it begins at conception, there is nothing in the Constitution to forbid that judgment. And once one concludes that one is dealing with human life, there is no plausible constitutional rule that would forbid a state from protecting it. As a matter of original meaning, that is an easy case, no matter what clauses of the Constitution one considers relevant.

So was *Dobbs* a triumph for Ed Meese's Jurisprudence of Original Meaning? In one important sense, yes. The result, as noted, flows unambiguously from originalism. Moreover, Justice Alito's opinion contains lengthy discourses on how abortion was viewed at common law, in 1868 when the Fourteenth Amendment was ratified, through the 19th century, and even in the 20th century until *Roe* in 1973. It also explains at length why constitutional meaning is not determined by prior case law, which must give way when it contradicts the Constitution.

In another sense, however, *Dobbs* was not a purely originalist decision. To be sure, it did not need to be a purely originalist decision. Even within the framework of post-1937 case law, *Roe* and its successor cases were an anomaly. Even the other "right to privacy" cases involved actions, such as the use of contraception or consensual adult sex, with few third-party effects beyond moral disapproval. Abortion, on the other hand, has had roughly sixty million devastating third-party effects in the half century since *Roe*—or at least a legislature could reasonably so believe given the Constitution's silence on who counts as a living third party. Accordingly, the majority opinion in *Dobbs* does not wholly discard the post-1937 framework, nor does it wholly discard the "right to privacy" that spawned *Roe*. It treats abortion as falling within the post-1937 "substantive due process" framework, but it limits application of that framework to rights deeply rooted in history and tradition. That is an originalist approach only if the framework is itself originalist, which it is not. A truly originalist opinion, as Justice Thomas pointed out in his concurrence, would focus on the Fourteenth Amendment's Privileges or Immunities Clause. There is no plausible construction of that clause that yields a constitutional rule against abortion regulations, but the majority opinion did not make that case.

Nonetheless, without forty years of originalist theorizing, is there any chance that the court would have taken the step that it took in *Dobbs*? Recall that the Republican-picked justices appointed before originalism had a chance to spread through the legal culture—O'Connor, Kennedy, and Souter—declined to overrule *Roe*. It took justices at least steeped in the culture of originalism, even if they do not fully embrace that culture, to get it right. This was Ed Meese's long game, and while one cannot be sure of that game's final outcome, the early returns are promising.

The same can be said of the court's recent moves toward reining in the administrative state. The court has not invalidated a federal statute on subdelegation grounds since 1935, when it found the National Industrial Recovery Act unconstitutional. In 2019, however, three justices, led by Justice Gorsuch, would have found unconstitutional a law letting the attorney general decide, with no statutory guidance, whether to apply retroactively a sex offender registration law.[29] Justice Alito agreed that the court should reconsider its subdelegation cases but did not find this the right vehicle. Justice Kavanaugh, who did not participate in that decision, later indicated that he would be willing to reconsider the prior cases as well.[30] The court has not yet taken up that challenge, which would involve careful study of the Constitution's original meaning,[31] but it has accomplished some of the same goals through statutory interpretation.

For decades, agencies had been able to take vague language, often directed to very specific problems or circumstances, and read it to provide them with extravagant authority over novel topics. Courts would often defer to those strained agency interpretations, and the post-1937 case law ensured that there were no constitutional problems with such agency assertions of authority.

In the October 2021 term, the court made several important moves. First, it continued a yearslong trend away from deferring to agency interpretations of vague statutes. A 1984 Supreme Court case, which surely intended no such thing, had long been understood to require courts to accept agency interpretations of statutes as long as they were *reasonable*, even if the court thought them incorrect.[32] In 2022, the Supreme Court on six occasions declined even to cite that decision in cases involving agency interpretations of statutes, even though many of those cases had turned in the lower courts on precisely that deference doctrine.[33] The October 2023 term presents a case in which the court is explicitly considering whether to overrule its 1984 *Chevron* decision (or at least to overrule the misperception of that decision that has driven administrative law jurisprudence for nearly forty years).[34] Even more, in three of those cases the court essentially adopted an *anti-deference* doctrine, saying that novel agency assertions of authority over important, or "major," questions require *clear* authorization by statute. Thus, for Congress to allow agencies to make law on major questions, it must openly and specifically authorize the agencies to take such action. That is the mirror opposite of the deferential-to-agencies position that governed during much of the New Deal settlement.

Those three cases from the October 2021 term are a good illustration of the operation of the administrative state under the New Deal settlement post-1937 and the possible implications of a lasting change in court doctrine.

In *Alabama Ass'n of Realtors v. U.S. Dep't of Health & Hum. Services*,[35] the Centers for Disease Control used a 1944 statute dealing with decontamination and pest control[36] to justify a nationwide moratorium on rental evictions in light of COVID,[37] arguing that persons evicted from rental housing might travel to other states or end up in denser living environments, so that a ban on evictions was "necessary to prevent the… spread of communicable diseases."[38] The agency read the statute, which spoke of fumigation and destruction of animals, to authorize it to do anything and everything it thought best to address communicable diseases—and in a world in which agencies can act unless *expressly forbidden* by statute, the agency's argument carries weight. The Roberts Court, however, found the agency's interpretation to be an obviously strained effort to find power that the agency was never granted. The Supreme Court then added that "[e]ven if the text were ambiguous, the sheer scope of the CDC's claimed authority under [§ 264] would counsel against the Government's interpretation. We expect Congress to speak clearly when authorizing an agency to exercise powers of 'vast "economic and political significance." ' "[39] Instead of declaring the statute unconstitutional (which it would be if it meant what the agency said it meant), the court reached a similar result with a rule of statutory construction.

The court used the same approach in *National Federation of Independent Business v. OSHA*,[40] in which the Occupational Safety and Health Administration construed its authority to promulgate "occupational safety and health standard[s]"[41] to allow a COVID vaccine mandate on workplaces with one hundred or more employees. This swept in more than eighty million workers in every job from meat packer to landscaper.[42] If the statute authorizes the agency to do anything and everything it thinks wise with regard to health for anyone who is working, and if one regards that kind of subdelegation of authority as constitutional, the agency wins. Three justices (Breyer, Sotomayor, and Kagan) took that view, which neatly reflects the New Deal settlement. But as with the CDC, this was an agency straining to find power that it was not given and that would be unconstitutional if it existed. OSHA is authorized to regulate *workplace* hazards. COVID, like the flu and the common cold, might well be a hazard that one could encounter in a workplace, and there might even be some specific workplaces where the conditions of employment elevate that hazard beyond its baseline level, but it is not a hazard that distinctively *results from* a workplace, such as the risk of a mine collapse, poor ventilation in an office building, or exposure to toxic chemicals at a construction site.[43] The agency's interpretation, said the Roberts Court, "would significantly expand OSHA's regulatory authority without clear congressional authorization."[44]

In a separate opinion, Justice Gorsuch, joined by Justices Thomas and Alito, expressly linked this "major questions" interpretative principle to the constitutional subdelegation doctrine: "[I]f the statutory subsection the agency cites really *did* endow OSHA with the power it asserts, that law would likely constitute an unconstitutional delegation of legislative authority."[45] Thus, as framed by Justice Gorsuch, the major questions doctrine requires not just boilerplate grants of authority to agencies to pursue health, safety, the public interest, or some other catch-all verbiage, but something that specifically and directly indicates that Congress authorized the kind of action involved. It is not strictly originalism, but it is a doctrine driven by originalist concerns for the separation of powers.

The third case from the October 2021 term, *West Virginia v. EPA*,[46] saw the Environmental Protection Agency use a provision authorizing "performance standards" for coal-fired plants to try to force power companies away from the use of coal and other fossil fuels altogether. That was obviously an absurd construction of the statute (it is not a "performance standard" for a coal plant to tell it to become a wind farm), and the Trump administration EPA repealed it.[47] A liberal D.C. Circuit panel repealed the repeal,[48] and the Biden EPA defended the lower court's position. The Supreme Court sided with the Trump EPA. Chief Justice Roberts's majority opinion noted that in prior cases involving major questions (and the composition of the nation's power grid was as major a question as will ever come), the expansive interpretations of agency authority "had a colorable textual basis,"[49] but that more was needed to validate agency action: "[S]omething more than a merely plausible textual basis for the agency action is necessary. The agency instead must point to 'clear congressional authorization' for the power it claims."[50]

Justices Gorsuch and Alito joined the majority opinion in full but added that the major questions doctrine was needed to let courts "act as faithful agents of the Constitution."[51] Thus, the major questions doctrine is not designed to protect Congress from courts or agencies. It protects, however imperfectly and indirectly, "the Constitution's separation of powers"[52] *from* a Congress that is often unconcerned with constitutional limits and an executive branch eager to run with what it is given.

The court re-emphasized the major questions doctrine in 2023 in *Biden v. Nebraska.*[53] The Biden administration tried to use a post-9/11 statute authorizing loan forgiveness for people affected by terrorist attacks to justify a nationwide student loan cancellation on the ostensible grounds of COVID. Everyone, including the Biden administration, understood that this was a straightforward election-year gambit to buy the votes of young people with student loan debt that had no basis in the statute. As with the three cases from the previous term, however, it was at least linguistically possible to take Congress's open-ended grants of authority to the agency as authorization to do whatever the agency thought best. Rather than find the statute unconstitutional, the court again said that agencies need to ground major decisions in clear authorizations rather than linguistically possible but contextually absurd interpretations of vague statutes. Justice Barrett wrote separately to deny that the major questions doctrine is a clear statement rule, but even she thought the Biden administration had erred as a matter of common sense in its reading of the relevant statute.

Dobbs as a counterpart to *West Coast Hotel* on substantive due process and the major questions cases as counterparts to *Jones & Laughlin Steel* on governmental structure are enough to prompt comparisons between October 2021 and spring 1937. But there was much more that happened in 2021–2022 that reflects the Meese legacy and potentially portends a lasting change in jurisprudence.

One of the greatest triumphs of originalism was the Supreme Court's 2008 decision in *District of Columbia v. Heller,*[54] which recognized that the Second Amendment right to keep and bear arms actually protects a right to keep and bear arms. The majority and dissent both argued along strictly originalist lines—which in the long run is more important even than the outcome. Two years later, the court said that the same principles apply to state and local legislation restricting gun owners' rights.[55] In the ensuing twelve years, lower courts and legislatures paid little attention to the rulings.

For example, New York, along with half a dozen other states, required gun permit applicants to show a "special need" to carry a gun in self-defense. (Living in a crime-ridden city run by criminal-coddling politicians did not count as a "special need." The New York state courts said so.[56]) In *New York State Rifle & Pistol Association, Inc. v. Bruen*,[57] the Supreme Court, in an opinion by Justice Thomas, struck down this "special need" requirement, focusing, as did *Heller* before it, on "constitutional text and history."[58] In 1985 such a case, if it reached the court at all, would surely have been decided by "balancing" the interests of gun owners against claimed policy reasons advanced by legislators, with a thumb on the scale for the latter. The *Bruen* decision openly rejects that kind of judicial assessment of the importance of the constitutional right. Rather, "[w]hen the Second Amendment's plain text covers an individual's conduct, the Constitution presumptively protects that conduct. The government must then justify its regulation by demonstrating that it is consistent with the Nation's historical tradition of firearm regulation."[59]

Again, the method—an attempt to ascertain the original meaning of a constitutional provision—is more important than the result. *Bruen* reflects the impact of the Jurisprudence of Original Meaning in a fashion hardly conceivable back in 1985 but now firmly a part of the constitutional dialogue.

One can tell a similar story about religious liberty, which has been precarious in this country for some time—at least when religious liberties conflict with the policy preferences of those in power. The 2022 Supreme Court broadened religious liberty protections in two key cases: *Carson v. Makin*[60] and *Kennedy v. Bremerton School District*.[61] The latter got more headlines, but the former may be more important.

In 1875, Rep. James Blaine introduced a constitutional amendment that would have forbidden the states from ever providing public funds to religious institutions, including Catholic parochial schools. Blaine's proposed amendment did not make it through the Senate, so it never came up for a ratification vote in the states. Had it done so, it might have passed: thirty-eight of the fifty states have so-called Blaine Amendments in their state constitutions. The rather obvious motive behind these amendments was anti-immigrant, and especially anti-Catholic-immigrant, animus.

In *Locke v. Davey* in 2004, the Rehnquist Court, with Justices Scalia and Thomas dissenting, found it constitutional for a state to exclude ministerial education from a state-funded scholarship program.[62] While the decision was potentially narrow, it contained some broad language suggesting that states had considerable freedom to treat religious people differently from non-religious ones. In 2020, the Roberts Court rejected a broad interpretation of *Davey*, saying in a 5–4 decision that a state-based scholarship program that provides public funds for students to attend private schools cannot discriminate against religious schools.[63] The issue returned to the Supreme Court in 2022 in *Carson v. Makin*.

Maine enacted a program of tuition assistance for parents who live in school districts so small that they do not operate a secondary school of their own. But, under Maine's program, state funding is only available for non-religious schools. The court, in a 6–3 opinion authored by Chief Justice Roberts, said that "Maine's 'nonsectarian' requirement for its otherwise generally available tuition assistance payments violates the Free Exercise Clause of the First Amendment. Regardless of how the benefit and restriction are described, the program operates to identify and exclude otherwise eligible schools on the basis of their religious exercise."[64] One could perhaps reach the same results on grounds of equal protection,[65] but either way the decision sweeps away some of the country's most long-standing interferences with the free exercise of religion. The thirty-eight state constitutional Blaine Amendments have now been trumped by the incorporated Free Exercise Clause of the First Amendment.

The counterpart to the Free Exercise of Religion Clause is the First Amendment's prohibition on laws "respecting an establishment of religion." The original meaning of that clause was obviously to make clear that Congress could not interfere with state efforts to establish religion within their borders, but by 1868 when the Fourteenth Amendment was ratified, two-thirds of state constitutions forbade establishments of religion in their state bills of rights.[66] Most of the court's Establishment Clause cases have involved state laws. For example, in 1991, Justice Kennedy wrote the opinion of the court in *Lee v. Weisman*,[67] which held that prayers at public high school graduations violated the Establishment Clause because they subtly coerced and offended some graduating students and their parents.

The Roberts Court again cut back on some of the broader implications of past cases in *Kennedy v. Bremerton School District*. Kennedy, a high school football coach, had a practice of privately praying at the fifty-yard line after football games, and many players from both teams voluntarily joined him. Kennedy was eventually fired by his school district for putting them at risk of Establishment Clause lawsuits. The Supreme Court held that Kennedy's prayer practice was constitutionally protected under the Free Exercise Clause and could not implicate the school district in an Establishment Clause challenge. Justice Gorsuch explained:

> Respect for religious expressions is indispensable to life in a free
> and diverse Republic—whether those expressions take place in
> a sanctuary or on a field, and whether they manifest through the
> spoken word or a bowed head. Here, a government entity sought
> to punish an individual for engaging in a brief, quiet, personal re-
> ligious observance doubly protected by the Free Exercise and Free
> Speech Clauses of the First Amendment. And the only meaningful
> justification the government offered for its reprisal rested on a
> mistaken view that it had a duty to ferret out and suppress reli-
> gious observances even as it allows comparable secular speech.[68]

Even more importantly, Justice Gorsuch explained the methodology behind this conclusion, noting that "[a]n analysis focused on original meaning and history, this Court has stressed, has long represented the rule" and that the lower courts "erred by failing to heed this guidance."[69] Ed Meese would grade the Supreme Court of 2022 very differently on religious liberty than he graded the Supreme Court of 1985 in his speech to the ABA.

Twenty twenty-two may or may not turn out to be a year that legal historians treat like 1937. But if the last two years turn out to be even close in significance to 1937, it will be a lasting tribute to the influence of Ed Meese—the most important person ever to serve as United States attorney general.

CHAPTER FOURTEEN

THE MOST INFLUENTIAL
ATTORNEY GENERAL

T HIS BOOK CLAIMED at the outset that Ed Meese was the most influential and powerful attorney general in American history. Giv-
en that there have been eighty-six attorneys general between 1789 and
2024, this is an ambitious claim.

Because there is no obvious metric for either influence or power for
such a position, it is probably impossible definitively to verify or falsify
this claim. This book presents the affirmative case for Ed Meese, from
his seminal role in the development of originalism to his crucial participation in judicial selection decisions to his function as Ronald Reagan's
close adviser and right-hand man, including his role in helping President Reagan win the Cold War. A direct comparison with more than
eighty other attorneys general, with their myriad and incommensurable
accomplishments, would be a book in itself.

Nonetheless, it is fair to say that the only attorneys general besides
Meese who are plausible candidates for the "most influential and powerful" title are Homer S. Cummings and Robert F. Kennedy. Meese, Cummings, and Kennedy all worked for multi-term presidents (counting
Kennedy/Johnson as a two-term presidency) during important times,
were involved in judicial selection, and played important roles beyond
the running of the Department of Justice. Several other persons also
fare well under these criteria and deserve special mention in any discussion of the office of attorney general—people like Edmund Randolph,
William Wirt, Roger Taney, Edward Bates, Amos Akerman, Robert
Jackson, Francis Biddle, Herbert Brownell, Nicholas Katzenbach, and
William French Smith—but, in our judgment, none rise to the level of
Meese, Cummings, and Kennedy in power and influence.

In the end, Meese stands out on many key criteria for greatness.[1] No
other attorney general had such a long-term influence on interpretative theory. No other attorney general placed such a long-term imprint

on the judiciary. And, perhaps with the exception of Robert F. Kennedy, during the one-thousand-day administration of his brother John F. Kennedy, no other attorney general played so many and such important roles outside the administration of the Justice Department for almost eight years. Even if Meese's tenure as attorney general was not the single most significant in American legal history (we think it was), it certainly ranks near the top.

BACKGROUND ON
THE OFFICE OF ATTORNEY GENERAL

MEESE, CUMMINGS, KENNEDY, and others from the past 150 years had the advantage of serving as attorney general when the office had a role beyond its original narrow limits. The Office of Attorney General was created by the Judiciary Act of 1789, which provided for the appointment of "a meet person, learned in the law, to act as attorney-general for the United States... to prosecute and conduct all such suits in the Supreme Court in which the United States shall be concerned, and to give advice and opinion upon questions of law when required by the President of the United States, or when requested by the heads of any of the departments, touching any matters that may concern their departments... ."[2] Under this statute, the attorney general was authorized only to represent the government in the Supreme Court and not in the lower courts. Each district had "a meet person learned in the law to act as attorney for the United States... to prosecute... all delinquents for crimes and offences, cognizable under the authority of the United States, and all civil matters in which the United States shall be concerned... ."[3] The district attorneys reported to the secretary of state, not to the attorney general, until the 1860s; the attorney general had no general supervisory authority over legal matters. There was no federal Department of Justice until 1870, when it was created in the administration of President Ulysses S. Grant.[4] Early attorneys general were expected to supplement their meager government salaries with private law practice, which would occupy most of their time and attention.

The part-time attorney general created by the Judiciary Act of 1789 did not have even a single clerk to help perform the job. Even after the Department of Justice was created in 1870, it was housed in various buildings all around Washington, D.C. It was not until 1934 that the Department of Justice moved into its current grand headquarters between Constitution and Pennsylvania Avenues and 9th and 10th Streets N.W. Any treatment of early attorneys general must bear all of this in mind.

THE EARLY ATTORNEYS GENERAL: 1789–1870

THERE WERE FOUR early attorneys general who deserve mention: Edmund Randolph, the 1st attorney general; William Wirt, the longest-serving attorney general in U.S. history; Roger B. Taney, who went on to become chief justice of the United States; and Edward Bates, who served Abraham Lincoln with extraordinary ability during the Civil War.

The 1st attorney general of the United States, Edmund Randolph, served from 1789 to 1794 under fellow Virginian George Washington. Given the nature of the office at that time, there was little he could do. He could not even order district attorneys to bring prosecutions—though President Washington could and did so in the 1793 Neutrality Proclamation. He offered his opinion to President Washington on the constitutionality of a proposed Bank of the United States, as did Secretary of State Thomas Jefferson and Secretary of the Treasury Alexander Hamilton. Randolph and Jefferson thought the Bank unconstitutional, but Washington went with Treasury Secretary Hamilton's legal opinion and signed the Bank Bill. That says something about the status of the attorney general at that time. Randolph was involved in some other legal matters, such as advising the president and various cabinet secretaries on various issues, and he played a key role in drafting the Neutrality Proclamation, which remains one of the most important statements on presidential power, asserting that the president could commit the United States and its citizens to a position of neutrality in foreign wars. In the end, Randolph had more success as a private litigator than as attorney general, representing the plaintiff in *Chisholm v. Georgia*,[5] where "he helped convince the justices that the states could be sued in the federal courts—a point which the people reversed by the Eleventh Amendment."[6]

Randolph is important primarily because he was the 1st attorney general and had an otherwise distinguished role in many other government offices—he was at the Constitutional Convention, where he was part of the Committee of Detail that drafted much of the Constitution, and he succeeded Thomas Jefferson as secretary of state. But as attorney general he did not leave a lasting stamp on jurisprudence.

Randolph was succeeded as attorney general by William Bradford, Charles Lee, Levi Lincoln Sr., John Breckinridge, Caesar Augustus Rodney, William Pinkney, and Richard Rush. Legal scholars and historians will recognize some (but only some) of these names, but not for any of their accomplishments in the office of attorney general.

More noteworthy is William Wirt, who served from 1817 to 1829—the longest tenure of any attorney general in United States history. Wirt was first appointed by President James Monroe and was continued in office by President John Quincy Adams. Wirt definitely brought previously lacking heft to the office of attorney general.

Wirt created a record-keeping system for the office (yes, the office functioned for nearly thirty years with no such system) and persuaded Congress to give him a clerk and an office (yes, the office functioned for thirty years without facilities or staff). Wirt also helped define the scope of the office by refusing, unlike his eight predecessors, to give official opinions or advice to "committees of Congress, district attorneys, collectors of customs, collectors of public taxes, marshals, [and] court martials.... 'My opinion is,' said Wirt, 'that the Attorney General is not bound by the law as it now stands, to obey these calls,'"[7] as the statute creating his office only spoke of giving opinions to the president and heads of departments Somewhat surprisingly, Congress never thought to pass a statute obligating the attorney general to give Congress legal advice. As a result, Wirt cemented the idea that the attorney general is an executive branch officer who works only for the president and the department heads.

In that role, Wirt wrote a number of important legal opinions that remain of contemporary relevance, such as opinions about the ability of the president to grant conditional pardons, to make recess appointments, and to halt federal prosecutions brought by district attorneys if the president deems those prosecutions unwarranted or unwise. He also foreshadowed the infamous *Dred Scott* decision by opining that free Blacks in Virginia were not citizens of the United States.

In his most important opinion, Wirt started a debate about presidential power that consumed considerable energy of attorneys general for much of the 19th century and remains a subject of dispute today. In *The President and Accounting Officers,*[8] Wirt declared that the president did not have legal power to revise a decision of accounting officers in the Treasury Department, because Congress had by statute given the accounting officers the last word on such matters.[9] It is certainly true that the president will not normally *wish* to get involved in the minutiae of account auditing, but that is different from saying that the president *cannot* do so, given that the Treasury auditors are clearly exercising "executive Power." Other attorneys general went back and forth on that question for decades afterward, and even today the law is not clear on the president's power to make, revise, or cancel decisions by subordinates when Congress seems to give those subordinates the final decision-making power. Wirt's opinion continues to be cited in those debates two centuries later.

In the end, Wirt may have been more noteworthy for his consequential private practice of law than for his work as attorney general. Wirt was one of several lawyers who argued for the prevailing parties in the Supreme Court in such famous cases as *Dartmouth College v. Woodward,*[10] *McCulloch v. Maryland,*[11] and *Gibbons v. Ogden.*[12] As attorney general, he did not have—and at the time surely did not have the opportunity to have—anything like the influence on law, policy, Supreme Court appointments, or presidential campaigns that later successors like Cummings, Kennedy, and Meese enjoyed. Nor did Wirt espouse or evangelize for a particular theory of legal interpretation. He was an important attorney general, but his impact was more limited than some of his modern counterparts.

John MacPherson Berrien followed Wirt, and his name will draw blanks with most legal scholars. Not so Roger Taney, who served as attorney general from 1831 to 1833 under Andrew Jackson. As attorney general, Taney was involved in many important actions, such as helping draft President Jackson's veto message of the bill that would have reauthorized the Bank of the United States. That veto message is one of the seminal documents championing the idea that all three branches of the federal government have co-equal and independent power to interpret the Constitution. It also questions the importance of Supreme Court precedents in constitutional law cases, noting that "mere Precedent is a dangerous source of authority," and it contains a powerful and prescient critique of monopolies. It effectively killed the Bank of the United States, which had existed from 1791 to 1811 and from 1816 to 1836. No Bank of the United States was ever created again until Congress and President Woodrow Wilson created the Federal Reserve Board on December 23, 1913. Taney deserves mention for this one opinion alone.

Taney also wrote a key opinion outlining the president's power as chief law enforcement officer, confirming the president's power to decline or dismiss federal prosecutions.[13] He authorized the Treasury secretary to remove the U.S. government's deposits in the Bank of the United States and to deposit them in state banks instead. And in his most infamous opinion, he defended an unconstitutional South Carolina law forbidding free African Americans from entering the state, arguing (in line with Wirt's prior opinion) that free descendants of African Americans could not become citizens of the United States. In his later role as a Supreme Court justice, Taney applied that view in *Dred Scott v. Sandford*,[14] helping to precipitate the Civil War.

Taney is certainly among the most important attorneys general. He was a vital player in President Jackson's administration. Some of his most consequential actions, however, happened when he served in other roles, and while attorney general he did not have the involvement in foreign and domestic policy or Supreme Court appointments that one can see in Meese, Kennedy, or Cummings. Nor did he advance a distinctive theory of legal interpretation.

Taney was followed by a string of attorneys general who do not stand out as uniquely influential or important: Benjamin Franklin Butler, Felix Grundy, Henry D. Gilpin, John J. Crittenden, Hugh S. Legaré, John Nelson, John Y. Mason, Nathan Clifford, Isaac Toucey, Reverdy Johnson, John J. Crittenden again, Caleb Cushing, Jeremiah S. Black, and Edwin Stanton. While some of these men were historically important in other roles, none stands out as having been a great or influential attorney general.

Edward Bates, who served under Abraham Lincoln from 1861 to 1864, deserves a closer look. Bates was attorney general during one of the most legally complex periods in American history, which tested the scope of presidential power during a civil rather than foreign war. Bates defended President Lincoln's suspension of the writ of habeas corpus without congressional action, prevented state courts from releasing drafted Union soldiers on state writs of habeas corpus (a position eventually vindicated by the Supreme Court[15]), persuaded Congress to pass a statute criminalizing the aiding of the insurrection without automatically requiring (as did the Treason Act) the death penalty, and winning *The Prize Cases*,[16] which upheld the legality of Lincoln's naval blockade of all Southern ports. Finally, Bates supported and assisted Lincoln in drafting the Emancipation Proclamation. That is more than enough to put Bates near the top of any list of important attorneys general.

He does not reach the very top tier because his role was limited. Bates did not play a key role in the selection and appointment of nominees to the U.S. Supreme Court or the district courts. The federal courts of appeals did not even exist yet nor did the inferior courts have jurisdiction to hear federal questions until 1875. He did not propound a "Batesian" mode of judging or interpretation the way that Ed Meese put forth originalism. He was not Abraham Lincoln's key adviser on domestic and foreign policy in the way that Ronald Reagan relied on Meese.

After Bates, the next four attorneys general were James Speed, Henry Stanbery, William M. Evarts, and Ebenezer R. Hoar, some of whom performed with distinction in other jobs but not as attorneys general. Hoar was the first person appointed attorney general who served as head of the Department of Justice, which was created in 1870. But it was President Ulysses S. Grant's second attorney general, Amos T. Akerman, who achieved greatness in the job despite serving only for a single year from 1870 to 1871.

THE RISE OF THE
DEPARTMENT OF JUSTICE: 1871–1933

WHEN THE DEPARTMENT of Justice was created, supervision of the district attorneys, today called U.S. attorneys, was transferred from all other government agencies to the new DOJ. The fledgling agency was given enormous new responsibilities because of a slew of post–Civil War federal statutes protecting civil rights. By 1871, under Amos Akerman, the Justice Department had indicted three thousand Ku Klux Klansmen and had secured six hundred sentences, with ringleaders confined in a federal prison in New York. Had he served longer, Akerman would surely be better known, and his impact might have been greater. As it happened, Akerman served only one year in office before President Grant foolishly asked for his resignation because Akerman refused to permit federal financial assistance to some western railroads. Akerman's firing and replacement for three and a half years with the dim-witted George Henry Williams may have single-handedly ruined President Grant's second term—and possibly ruined Reconstruction itself. Akerman had the Ku Klux Klan on the run after only a year in office, and he would have been a far more effective representative for Reconstruction than was George Williams. Akerman's short time in office, however, ensured that his impact would not compare to some other attorneys general. As with Bates, he also did not have a theory of judging or interpretation, and he did not play a central role in policy-making outside of law enforcement.

A list of the twenty-three men who served as attorneys general from 1871 to 1933 makes a revealing contrast with Ed Meese: George Williams, Edwards Pierrepont, Alphonso Taft (father of William Howard Taft), Charles Devens, Wayne MacVeagh, Benjamin Brewster, Augustus Garland, William Miller, Richard Olney, Judson Harmon, Joseph McKenna, John W. Griggs, Philander Knox, William Henry Moody, Charles Bonaparte, George Wickersham, James C. McReynolds, Thomas Gregory, A. Mitchell Palmer, Harry M. Daugherty, Harlan Fiske Stone, John Sargent, and William Mitchell. Some of these names will be familiar to students of American law, including future chief justice Harlan Fiske Stone and future associate justices Moody, McKenna, and McReynolds. But they are remembered as justices, not as attorneys general. And even as justices, and certainly as attorneys general, none of these figures publicly articulated a consistent theory of interpretation or judging, nor did any play a role as attorney general as broad or significant as the role played by Ed Meese.

THE NEW DEAL AND POST–NEW DEAL ATTORNEYS GENERAL

THE CLOSEST COMPETITION to Meese, in our view, is Homer S. Cummings, the 55th attorney general, who served under President Franklin

D. Roosevelt from March 4, 1933, to January 2, 1939, making him the fourth-longest-serving attorney general in history after William Wirt, Janet Reno, and Eric Holder. He was a key politico who helped FDR get the Democratic nomination for president in 1932; in that respect, Cummings is similar to Meese, who helped Ronald Reagan get the 1980 Republican nomination. He was also an important intellectual figure while attorney general, publishing two books and a collection of his papers during his time in service.[17]

One of those books is a well-done history of all the attorneys general from 1789 to 1933. Another is the published version of a three-day academic lecture series given by Cummings at the University of Virginia School of Law. It discusses the changing meaning of the word "liberty" over time but makes no real contribution to legal theory and has had no lasting impact.

Like Meese, Cummings delivered a major address to the American Bar Association six months into his tenure as attorney general. Cummings's speech was entitled "Modern Tendencies and the Law," and his topic was federalism. Commenting on the case law of the time that regarded "commerce" as an enterprise distinct from production, Cummings said,

> Today almost every economic and social problem is both local and national. Manufacturing, merchandising, transportation, agriculture, mining, oil production, problems of employment and unemployment, of strikes and the settlement thereof, are upon a national scale, or, if local in scope, are national in effect. ...
>
> To my mind, the law is not a mere body of precedents. I visualize it as a living, vital, growing thing, fashioned for service and constantly being refashioned for further service. Its function is to serve. It changes and grows.[18]

Cummings reiterated these sentiments in a speech to the Bar Association of the District of Columbia on December 5, 1936, entitled "The Right Arm of Statesmanship." Cummings also gave an important speech to the Association of the Bar of the City of New York entitled "The American Constitutional Method" on December 18, 1935. The speech complained at length about the Supreme Court's unanimous decision in *Schechter Poultry v. United States*[19] striking down the National

Industrial Recovery Act, which would have cartelized most of the nation's economy.

While Cummings's speeches did not have the theoretical or doctrinal sweep or depth of Ed Meese's, Cummings came closer than any other attorney general to matching Meese's public influence. He criticized Supreme Court decisions, argued for a "living constitution" approach to interpretation, and advanced a view of constitutional federalism. It is fair to say that Cummings's speeches were more political and less scholarly than Meese's, and Cummings did not have an Office of Legal Policy generating scholarly works elaborating a comprehensive theory of textual interpretation or a Department of Justice functioning like a law school, complete with academic conferences.

Cummings also played a central role in the development of President Franklin D. Roosevelt's unsuccessful plan to pack the Supreme Court. Building on early legislation proposed by Cummings,[20] President Franklin D. Roosevelt proposed in early 1937 adding up to six new justices to the Supreme Court—one for every justice already on the court who was seventy years of age or older and who refused to retire. That term, the court began upholding New Deal laws that previously would have been in serious jeopardy, and retirements then paved the way for Roosevelt to shift the court with his appointees without need for new legislation.

Attorney General Cummings also took important steps in legal and judicial reform. He got Congress to create an Administrative Office to aid the federal courts. He shepherded the creation of senior status for federal judges, in which judges who are sixty-five and have served at least fifteen years can take senior status at full pay. Cummings helped revolutionize federal civil and criminal procedure by persuading Congress to allow the Supreme Court to propose formal rules of procedure, in law as well as equity, that take effect unless Congress alters them. Cummings encouraged construction of the famous federal prison at Alcatraz in San Francisco Bay, expansion of the number of federal crimes, enhanced police training, and the creation of new lower federal court judgeships. He also helped President Roosevelt choose Hugo Black, William O. Douglas, Stanley Reed, and possibly Felix Frankfurter as Supreme Court justices.

Note that Hugo Black and William O. Douglas were committed judicial activists whereas Stanley Reed and Felix Frankfurter were committed advocates of judicial restraint. They agreed on getting rid of the pre-1937 Supreme Court case law, but they disagreed on everything else! FDR did not have the impact on the Supreme Court that Meese did because his attorneys general did not articulate a theory of judging in the way Meese did or in the way the six Republican-appointed Supreme Court justices in 2024 have done.

Cummings's record makes for an impressive résumé. It stacks up to Meese's resume of accomplishments better than that of any other attorney general. Cummings comes up just short, however, in two vital respects. First, while Cummings sharply criticized the justices standing in the way of the New Deal, he did not have—or at least did not articulate—a thought-out theory of legal interpretation that extended beyond the results of the moment. Consequently, Cummings had little long-term impact on interpretative theory, while Meese was the central figure in the development and rise of theorized originalism. Second, Cummings did not have a role outside the traditional confines of an attorney general comparable to Meese's broad role in the Reagan administration, including helping win the Cold War, serving for nearly eight years as the most important member of the National Security Council (which did not exist yet), or chairing the Domestic Policy Council during President Reagan's second term. Cummings had no role in the development of domestic policy outside law.

Cummings was an enormously important and effective attorney general. But it goes to Meese by slightly more than a nose.

After Cummings, President Roosevelt had some other important attorneys general, but they were better known for activities conducted in other offices. Frank Murphy (1939–1940) went on to serve with distinction on the U.S. Supreme Court, but his main accomplishment during his one year as attorney general was to establish a Civil Liberties Unit in the Criminal Division of the Justice Department.

Robert H. Jackson (1940–1941) had a long career in the Department of Justice before becoming attorney general, serving as (in reverse order) solicitor general, the assistant attorney general for the Antitrust Division, the assistant attorney general for the Tax Division, and assistant general counsel for the Bureau of Internal Revenue. As attorney general, Jackson had two big accomplishments during his one year in office. First, he tried unsuccessfully to get Congress to legalize wiretapping by the Federal Bureau of Investigation. Second, he helped President Roosevelt organize the Lend-Lease agreement, which allowed the United States to supply materials to help the United Kingdom stave off an attack by the Nazis by supplying military equipment to the U.K. in exchange for permission to operate some U.S. bases on U.K. territory. He simply was not attorney general long enough to leave a stamp on the office. His most famous accomplishments, including his most important theoretical writings, came as a Supreme Court justice and the prosecutor at the Nuremberg trials rather than as attorney general. His book *The Struggle for Judicial Supremacy* (1941) describes FDR's battle with the conservative Supreme Court in the 1930s, but it fails to put forward an affirmative theory of the judicial role or of legal interpretation.

Attorney General Francis Biddle (1941–1945) aligned the Justice Department with the emerging civil rights movement for Black Americans—a policy legacy that has endured for decades. He also resisted—sometimes successfully, sometimes less so—the internment of Japanese-, German-, and Italian-Americans during World War II. That is more than enough to put him on the map, but Biddle did not have the foreign, defense, and domestic policy portfolios held by Meese as attorney general. Nor did Biddle have much influence over judicial selection. One Supreme Court vacancy opened up on Biddle's watch, and against Biddle's advice FDR named Wiley Rutledge to that seat. Finally, while Biddle was a strong, effective, and intellectual attorney general, he did not put forth a consistent and coherent theory of interpretation for posterity.

President Harry S. Truman's attorneys general—Tom Clark, J. Howard McGrath, and James P. McGranery—were not intellectual leaders in any respect. They were caretakers for the New Deal. The same can be said of President Dwight D. Eisenhower's attorneys general: Herbert Brownell (1953–1957) and William Rogers (1957–1961). Brownell was significant because it fell to him to implement the U.S. Supreme Court's landmark opinion in *Brown v. Board of Education*.[21] Brownell did a superb job of recommending lower court judges who would implement *Brown*, especially in the then Fifth Circuit, which encompassed the entire South. He also presided over the creation in 1957 of the Civil Rights Division of the Justice Department. Neither he nor his successor as attorney general, William P. Rogers, however, had a meaningful theory of constitutional interpretation, as demonstrated by their guidance to President Eisenhower, a retired general, in the legal task of making appointments to the Supreme Court. Attorney General Brownell recommended that President Eisenhower appoint two extreme legal-realist leftists, Chief Justice Earl Warren and Associate Justice William J. Brennan Jr. He also recommended the appointment of three moderate associate justices: John Marshall Harlan, Potter Stewart, and Charles Whittaker. As with FDR's Supreme Court appointees, the Eisenhower/Brownell appointees had no coherent philosophy. Eisenhower's attorneys general were important figures in important times, but they did not leave a lasting impact on the office or on the law.

THE WARREN AND BURGER COURTS

PRESIDENT JOHN F. KENNEDY (JFK) appointed his thirty-five-year-old younger brother, Robert F. Kennedy (RFK), to be attorney general solely because President Kennedy's father insisted on it. (President Kennedy himself thought this was a bad idea.) Bobby Kennedy had little to no legal experience in his background, and he had worked as assistant counsel to the infamous Senator Joe McCarthy of red-baiting fame. He even published a book attacking labor unions and communists.[22] The New York Times and the New Republic both opined that RFK was not qualified to be attorney general. A voice vote to approve Kennedy's confirmation was held because, on a roll-call vote, "[h]e would have been lucky to get 40 votes."[23]

Neither JFK nor RFK articulated any theory of judging, and their twin Supreme Court appointments of conservative Democrat Byron White and ultra-liberal Democrat Arthur Goldberg essentially canceled each other out while adding nothing to any theoretical debate about methods of interpretation or philosophies of judging.

There was, however, one important similarity between RFK and Ed Meese: they were both the best friends and closest allies of the presidents they served. The power and influence of the Department of Justice was thus probably as high as it has ever been in American history under both Bobby Kennedy's and Ed Meese's tenures as attorney general. A key difference between JFK/RFK and Reagan/Meese, though, is that the

Kennedy brothers exercised power together for only one thousand days, whereas Ronald Reagan survived his attempted assassination and served together with Meese in some capacity for almost eight years. They were also succeeded by fellow Republican George H. W. Bush, who kept the Reagan-Meese judicial appointments coming for a total of twelve years thanks to Boyden Gray and Lee Liberman Otis. They were thus able to accomplish much more simply by virtue of having more time. It also helped Reagan and Meese that they had a coherent philosophy of both law and government that kept most of their actions focused on securing long-term goals.

In addition, both RFK and Meese played critical foreign-policy roles for their respective presidents. Bobby Kennedy is widely credited with having peacefully ended the Cuban Missile Crisis.[24] Meese, from 1981 until 1988, played a key role in helping President Ronald Reagan win the Cold War. RFK, however, did not play the big role in non–Justice Department domestic affairs that Meese played for Ronald Reagan.

RFK made two contributions as attorney general that stand out as especially significant. First, he made desegregation and protecting civil rights a top priority of his brother's presidency. Under RFK's stewardship, the Justice Department played a lead role in drafting the Civil Rights Act of 1964. Kennedy put his very able hand-picked deputy attorney general, and successor for two years as attorney general, Nicholas Katzenbach in charge of getting the Civil Rights Act passed. Katzenbach went on in President Lyndon Johnson's administration to draft and secure passage of the Voting Rights Act of 1965. Robert F. Kennedy was thus a key legal architect of the legislation that ended formal *de jure* race discrimination in the United States

Second, RFK arm-wrestled his solicitor general, Harvard Law School professor Archibald Cox, into supporting the so-called "one-person, one-vote"[25] cause in the Supreme Court, which was vindicated in revolutionary Supreme Court decisions like *Baker v. Carr*,[26] *Wesberry v. Sanders*,[27] and *Reynolds v. Sims*.[28] Solicitor General Cox started out as an adamant opponent of involving the judiciary in reapportionment because he was a New Deal advocate of judicial restraint; Kennedy worked mightily to change his mind.[29] The rule against large disparities in district size forever transformed American politics both in elections for the U.S. House of Representatives and in elections for state legislatures. Prior to these decisions, some districts had ten times as many people in them as did others. In general, rural areas were over-represented at the expense of cities and the newly emerged suburbs. There was no norm of redistricting every ten years after the census, and some states had gone for as long as sixty years without passing a redistricting bill. The over-representation of rural areas in both the House of Representatives and the state legislatures made those bodies more conservative politically than was the nation as a whole.

RFK was thus a key participant in some of the most important legal developments in modern times. But he did not have anything like Meese's, or even Homer Cummings's, influence on theories of constitutional and statutory interpretation, which translates into influence decades down the road. The events in the early 1960s were momentous, but they did not match the judicial revolution of 1937, which Cummings helped to engineer, or the judicial revolution of 2022–2023, which Meese helped to engineer, not to mention Meese's role in winning the Cold War. Perhaps with more time RFK could have been a contender, but history deprived him of that opportunity.

Robert F. Kennedy recommended that Nicholas de B. Katzenbach (1964–1966) succeed him as attorney general when Kennedy resigned on September 3, 1964, to run successfully for the U.S. Senate from New York. After President Lyndon B. Johnson first offered the position to someone else, who declined, there were months of speculation that President Johnson did not want to pick someone so close to RFK. President Johnson eventually nominated Katzenbach to be attorney general in January of 1965, and he was confirmed and appointed on February 11, 1965.

As attorney general, Katzenbach further argued for civil rights, successfully defending the Civil Rights Act of 1964 in the Supreme Court and seeking a court order preventing Alabama from interfering with Martin Luther King Jr.'s march from Selma to Montgomery.[30] Katzenbach went on to help Congress draft and pass the Voting Rights Act of 1965, which revolutionized voting rates by Black Americans. Notwithstanding these considerable accomplishments, Katzenbach did not have the broad and lasting influence or impact of a Meese, Cummings, or Kennedy.

The next eight attorneys general, from 1966 to 1981, were Ramsey Clark, John N. Mitchell, Richard Kleindienst, Elliot Richardson, William Saxbe, Edward Levi, Griffin Bell, and Benjamin Civiletti. Some of these names are familiar (and even infamous), but none leaps out as an all-time great attorney general. Certainly, none articulated a theory of judicial interpretation or of the judicial role, and none played the foreign, defense, and domestic policy roles that Meese did. Some of them were more than able public officials, two (Mitchell and Kleindienst) were convicted, some (such as Levi) were top-notch intellectuals, but none was a historically significant attorney general.

THE MEESE REVOLUTION AND BEYOND

WILLIAM FRENCH SMITH (1981–1985), Ed Meese's predecessor, was an excellent attorney general, but on metrics of influence and importance he does not quite reach the top. Nonetheless, Meese inherited a first-rate Department of Justice, which obviously helped him accomplish as much as he did. Even though Smith was more an establishment figure than a Meese Revolutionary, he deserves at least part of the credit for the success of the Meese Revolution.[31]

As attorney general, Smith helped secure passage of the Comprehensive Crime Control Act of 1984, which vastly increased the uniformity and fairness of federal criminal sentencing, provided for civil forfeiture of assets used in illegal activities, and abolished parole for federal prisoners. Antitrust law changed dramatically under Smith and Assistant Attorney General William Baxter, focusing on consumer welfare rather than a mindless opposition to "bigness" and mergers. Smith's Civil Rights Division, under Brad Reynolds, laid the groundwork for decades of law and policy opposing racial preferences, no matter the victim, leading to the Supreme Court's 2023 decision limiting the use of racial preferences in college admissions.

In the end, Smith was an important but not pathbreaking attorney general. He played no real role in judicial selection, except in the picking of Justice Sandra Day O'Connor, who was a huge disappointment to conservatives. He also played no role in changing or discussing theories of interpretation. Smith played no major role in foreign, defense, or domestic policy. Smith's memoirs of his years as attorney general do not mention originalism even once. He certainly helped pave the way for Ed Meese, but he was no Ed Meese.

Meese's immediate successor as attorney general was Richard L. "Dick" Thornburg (1988–1991). Thornburgh continued many of Meese's policies, especially on judicial selection, but he did not use the office actively to promote an originalist philosophy. He was a solid caretaker in an establishment Republican administration, which is not at all a small accomplishment, but he had little lasting influence on the office or the long-term path of the law.

The men and women who have served as attorney general since Thornburgh are William "Bill" Barr, Janet Reno, John Ashcroft, Alberto Gonzales, Michael Mukasey, Eric Holder, Loretta Lynch, Jeff Sessions, Bill Barr again, and Merrick Garland. As with other lists, some of these people were very able attorneys general, but none put forward a coherent theory of legal interpretation the way that Ed Meese did, nor were they as involved as Meese with judicial selection, foreign and defense policy, and domestic policy more generally.

Thus, if one is trying to select the most influential attorney general in American history, one comes down to Homer Cummings, Robert Kennedy, and Ed Meese. For the reasons given in this book, we go with Meese, but everyone can make up their own minds about that.

CONCLUSION

STEWARD OF THE MEESE AND REAGAN REVOLUTIONS

E D MEESE RESIGNED as attorney general on August 12, 1988, so that
his good friend George Herbert Walker Bush would not have to
say in his fall 1988 presidential campaign whether he would keep Meese
on as attorney general if he won the election. Meese had been thoroughly demonized by the left despite, and probably because of, his numerous
accomplishments. But his influence on American law and life did not
end in 1988. To this day, Meese continues to be a force for originalism,
the rule of law, conservatism, and common decency. In 2023 and 2024,
Meese signed a large number of amicus briefs in the Supreme Court,
an amicus brief in the D.C. Circuit, and one in a Florida District Court.
These briefs argued 1) that a federal wealth tax would be a direct tax that
has to be apportioned among the states; 2) that litigants prosecuted for
securities fraud have a Seventh Amendment right to a civil jury trial; 3)
that the special counsel, Jack Smith, who is prosecuting former president Trump was unlawfully appointed; and 4) that former president
Trump was not disqualified from running for president in 2024. The
Supreme Court adopted Meese's position in ruling that Trump is not
disqualified from running for president by Section 3 of the Fourteenth
Amendment. Meese also wrote an op-ed in 2022 calling for the overruling of *Roe v. Wade,* just before *Dobbs v. Jackson Women's Health
Organization* was up for oral argument. He is still in the thick of the
fight for originalism at the age of ninety-two.

His first move after leaving government was to arrange for Richard
Thornburgh, a conservative lawyer and a personal friend of the elder
President Bush, to be appointed by President Reagan to replace him
as attorney general. Meese thought that Thornburgh was the most
conservative person President Bush might choose to keep in that post.
The gambit worked, and Thornburgh served as attorney general from
1988 to 1991, essentially continuing all of Meese's policies, though not

Meese's role as an intellectual engine of and public spokesman for constitutionalism and originalism. In particular, the Bush administration continued Meese's approach to judicial selection. President Bush told his superb White House counsel C. Boyden Gray "to keep judicial selection going just as it had been going under Ronald Reagan and Ed Meese." Gray did that by appointing Federalist Society co-founder Lee Liberman Otis to be a senior associate counsel in Gray's office in charge of judicial selection. As is detailed in chapter 9, Meese did not have to worry about judicial selection between 1989 and 1993. The senior Bush's administration had a stellar record on judicial appointments, David Souter aside—which is all the more remarkable considering the strong Democrat majority in the Senate during that time.

Meese, upon finishing his tenure as attorney general, was offered full-time positions by both the Heritage Foundation in Washington, D.C., and the Hoover Institution at Stanford University in California. Meese accepted the Heritage job as the organization's first Ronald Reagan Distinguished Fellow (a title he still hold as emeritus), but he agreed to work with Hoover one week every month. At the Hoover Institution he worked on domestic policy issues, attended and participated in conferences, and helped to lobby donors. At the Heritage Foundation, Meese chaired the Center for Legal and Judicial Studies from its creation in 2001 until 2013, and he was the head of the advisory board that supervised production of the invaluable *Heritage Guide to the Constitution*. He also held a monthly conference of conservative and libertarian public interest law groups, so that they could coordinate their litigation strategies. Finally, Ed Meese played and continues to play down to the present day a critical role as a member of the Federalist Society's board of directors. He has spoken at many Federalist Society National Lawyers Conventions and at other events as well.

Meese also played a critical role in the judicial appointments made in the early 2000s by President George W. Bush. The trigger was Sandra Day O'Connor's announced retirement on July 1, 2005, giving President Bush a Supreme Court vacancy.

Andy Card, Bush's White House chief of staff from 2001 to 2006, held an initial meeting with Bush's chief political advisor Karl Rove, White House counsel Harriet Miers, Leonard Leo, and Ed Meese. Everyone in the room knew that Bush very much wanted to appoint his former White House counsel and then current attorney general Alberto Gonzalez. Everyone in the room knew that Gonzalez was neither conservative enough nor capable enough to be a Supreme Court justice. As one source puts it, they "needed Meese's help to block the appointment of ... Gonzalez, who would be a disaster."

Leo recalls that Meese "played a very, very important role in those meetings..., reminding the White House that this was a defining issue.... [a]nd that there needed to be a very strong, clear signal in the nomination of someone who had a demonstrable record. Meese's presence was vital because it was important for someone with seasoning and experience" to explain, with credibility, why someone like Alberto Gonzalez was the wrong choice. As alternatives to Gonzalez, Meese and Leo jointly suggested the appointments of either D.C. Circuit judge John Roberts, Third Circuit judge Sam Alito, Fourth Circuit judge Mike Luttig, or then Tenth Circuit judge Michael McConnell.

Bush nominated John Roberts, the least conservative person on the list and a solid establishment figure, to replace O'Connor.

Within a few months, however, a second vacancy unexpectedly opened. Before resigning, O'Connor had asked Chief Justice William H. Rehnquist if he was going to retire due to his throat cancer. Rehnquist assured O'Connor that his health was fine. Two months later, on September 3, 2005, Rehnquist died of throat cancer, startling even his closest friends on the Supreme Court, from whom he had kept secret the seriousness of his health problems.

President Bush, pleased about all the liberal support John Roberts was getting as an O'Connor replacement, doubled down on Roberts, a former Rehnquist clerk, and switched Roberts's nomination to chief justice. Now Bush needed another nominee to replace O'Connor.

Perhaps believing that Roberts was enough to placate conservatives,[1] Bush, following the recommendation of Democrat Senate majority leader Harry Reid, nominated his longtime personal friend and White House counsel Harriet Miers to the second Supreme Court vacancy. Miers was, rightly or wrongly, perceived as a Bush crony with no other administration or judicial experience, and conservatives raised a firestorm of criticism, decrying her lack of a clear record or coherent interpretative philosophy. Former judge Robert H. Bork crystalized the opposition to Miers by declaring her unacceptable both intellectually and as to judicial philosophy. Bush's nomination speech talked at length about Miers's "character" and "heart," her service to the bar, her trailblazing as a woman, and her compassion for the poor, but contained only two short throw-away sentences about judicial philosophy or interpretative theory: "Harriet Miers will strictly interpret our Constitution and laws. She will not legislate from the bench."[2] For conservatives schooled in the Meese/Reagan approach to judicial selection, this was appalling. Robert Bork called the nomination "a slap in the face to the conservatives who've been building up a conservative legal movement for the last twenty years."[3] The nomination was quickly withdrawn.

Leonard Leo recounts that he and Meese did not even have to suggest Sam Alito as the replacement nominee, because Harriet Miers herself, guided by her conservative deputy White House counsel Bill Kelly, a former Scalia law clerk and distinguished Notre Dame law professor, had already decided that she wanted Sam Alito as the next nominee. Mike Luttig, says Leo, was also a candidate "that all of us knew... but I always felt that Ed [Meese] was very high on Alito."[4]

Ed Meese thus played a critical role in President George W. Bush's decisions to appoint John Roberts and Sam Alito, rather than Alberto Gonzalez and Harriet Miers, to the Supreme Court. Whatever doubts today's conservatives have about John Roberts, they should keep in mind what else might have happened.

Meese played a key role in two other important decisions during the George W. Bush administration. First, in 2006 President Bush appointed Meese to a bipartisan Iraq Study Group to evaluate why our efforts to reform Iraq and eliminate Islamic terrorism in that country were failing. Meese, former defense secretary William Perry, Senator Charles "Chuck" Robb, and the group's co-chair former secretary of state Jim Baker all concluded that we did not have enough troops on the ground because then defense secretary Donald Rumsfeld had recommended a small, technologically skilled invading force. Meese and the others persuaded both the study group and President Bush that a surge in U.S. troops on the ground was needed as was being requested by the general in command of U.S. forces in Iraq. President Bush followed the Iraq

Study Group's advice, and the surge worked brilliantly. Iraq today is politically stable and is not a haven for Islamic terrorists. This is yet another good deed that Ed Meese has done for the country for which he sought and received no credit.

Second, the Bush administration also consulted Meese about the appointment of federal district judge Michael Mukasey as attorney general. This was a matter of extreme delicacy, because Bush's second attorney general, Alberto Gonzales, had been caught up in a scandal where it appeared that White House political advisor Karl Rove might have been causing the firing or hiring of U.S. attorneys for partisan political failure to prosecute Democrats. The situation was potentially as explosive as Iran-Contra, and Bush desperately needed an attorney general whose integrity was beyond reproach and who had superb political skills. Congress demanded that Gonzales resign or face near-certain impeachment and removal from office.

The Senate, which would have to confirm Gonzales's replacement, had a Democratic majority at this time. Democratic senator Charles "Chuck" Schumer suggested his friend, New York District Court judge Michael Mukasey, who had an impeccable record for propriety and was also a solid conservative. (Conservative Second Circuit judge Ralph K. Winter, a Reagan appointee for whom Steve Calabresi had clerked, told Calabresi privately that he thought Judge Mukasey would be a spectacularly good attorney general.)

Ed Meese was asked secretly by the Bush administration to interview Judge Mukasey and report back on whether he would be a suitable attorney general. Meese strongly supported Mukasey's appointment, and he believes (as do we) that Mukasey did an outstanding job as Bush's third and final attorney general. Mukasey served with Meese (and the two of us) on the board of directors of the Federalist Society until May 2023.

Meese's involvement in the nation's affairs continued with the next Republican president. Meese and former Heritage Foundation president Ed Feulner played a role in advising President-Elect Donald Trump's transition team after the 2016 presidential election. Vice President Elect Mike Pence persuaded Trump that Chris Christie, the former governor of New Jersey, needed to be replaced as head of Trump's transition team. Trump agreed, and Meese and Feulner provided some guidance to the Trump transition team. This role was especially urgent because Trump had never held elective office before becoming president, knew no one well in Washington, D.C., and had given little thought to a transition because he, like everyone else, probably expected Hillary Clinton to win right up until election night. Meese had been in charge of President-Elect Ronald Reagan's transition in 1980 and 1981, so he knew what a successful transition needed. Meese and Feulner both ended up playing roles in the Trump transition, which is just another reflection of the importance of Meese's thirty-three-year role at the Heritage Foundation as the steward of the Reagan Revolution.

The Trump administration's judicial appointments continued the legacy begun by Ed Meese and Ronald Reagan and both of the two Bush presidents. President Trump made three Supreme Court appointments: Neil Gorsuch, Brett Kavanaugh, and Amy Coney Barrett. Meese describes all three as "outstanding...judges who have been faithful to the Constitution." President Trump also appointed fifty-four circuit judges and 174 district court judges, most of whom have been steeped in and absorbed the post-Meese originalist and constitutionalist framework. According to an *Atlantic* article published on July 10, 2019—which is well before the last Trump judge was confirmed—President Trump had appointed ten former Clarence Thomas law clerks, seven former Anthony Kennedy law clerks, and five former Antonin Scalia law clerks to the federal bench. At the time this *Atlantic* article was printed, "roughly one-fifth of Justice Thomas's former clerks [were] either ... in the Trump administration or [had] been nominated to the federal bench" by former president Donald Trump.[5] Justice Thomas had been on the bench for twenty-eight years at that point, so "one-fifth of Justice Thomas's former clerks" was a formidable number indeed. The revolution in the law launched by the Meese Justice Department in 1985 thus lived on from 1988 to 2024. We are not aware of any other attorney general whose tenure so influenced the actions of his successors more than thirty years after he had left office.

* * *

THIS THEN CONCLUDES our intellectual biography of Ed Meese. Everyone who knows Ed Meese personally—and we have by now talked to a whole lot of people—is always struck by Ed Meese's extraordinary modesty, kindness, lack of desire for either wealth or power, and by his essential goodness as a human being. And Ed Meese has been faced with all the temptations to human vice that are imaginable living at the seat of government power near Washington, D.C., for eight years during the Reagan administration, as the president's best friend, and for thirty-five years after that as the steward of the Reagan Revolution. Ed Meese lives in a modest condominium with a modest vacation house, and he never cashed in on the fame and glory he had earned through his eight years in the Reagan administration. Ed Meese is: brave, wise, just, temperate, and full of faith, hope, and love. He has lived a perfect life of service to other people and to his country, and to the world.

Ed Meese is, like Ronald Reagan himself, a quintessential product of the American heartland. He is a sunny, upbeat, optimistic Californian just like President Reagan. Ed Meese's hand was at work in every success President Reagan achieved, and, to top things off, Ed Meese is also the most intellectually consequential attorney general in American history, whether one agrees with originalism or opposes it. The bottom line is that Ed Meese is an unusually virtuous and accomplished man who nonetheless led a revolution in legal interpretation, while also serving as President Ronald Reagan's right-hand man and counsellor in implementing the Reagan Revolution.

As this book is being written in early 2024, Ed Meese is ninety-two years old, sharp as a tack, and continues to serve as a vital member of the Federalist Society's board of directors. He is always the most mature person in the room when the Federalist Society board of directors holds a meeting.

Perhaps Ed Meese's most important roles, however, are husband to Ursula and father to Michael, Dana, and his late son Scott. Michael and Dana have offered observations that seem a fitting conclusion to this book.

When Mike learned about this book, he said,

> I think what you're writing is the equivalent of Fred Greenstein's book written about Eisenhower, which was called *The Hidden-Hand Presidency*.[6] In the same way that people did not ever give Eisenhower credit [for] all of the things that he did.... And Eisenhower didn't ever care about the credit. ... My father's

emulating those World War II generals who, setting aside MacArthur, didn't really care about the credit. ... [H]aving observed his father and the others from the greatest generation growing up ... , he thought that's what a public servant did.

This elegantly captures Ed Meese's rare combination of effectiveness, bravery, and modesty. People underestimated President Eisenhower, and people for more than four decades have underestimated Ronald Reagan and Ed Meese. Ed Meese was a *hidden-hand* transformational attorney general!

Dana captured more key features of her father's character:

[M]y dad is exactly how he is. There's no facade. There's no pretense. A lot of humility, very humble, very focused on what his purpose is. He's always very kind, very thoughtful, does not get stressed. He does not. Very rarely did I ever see him lose his temper or get really upset about anything. He handles everything in stride and is just focused on his purpose. And with that, his first and foremost priorities in his life are his faith and his family...

He's always a good listener ... and very reasoned in his decisions. He's very, and I have to say I didn't realize this until I saw it in myself, but he is very justice-oriented, ensuring that the right thing is done [is] more important [to him] than the political ramifications, or whatever the circumstances are. He is always doing the right thing.

As a husband, Dana recalls that "one of the few and only times I ever saw him get upset by the cruelty of the press and the media was when they took after my Mom. When they started being cruel to her." He was not worried about press criticism of himself. Dana remembers "[o]ne time that the press was just brutal on him. And I had enough, and I packed my bags, and I went down to the foyer in our house. And I said, 'Okay, that's it, we're going. Let's leave. I'm done.'... And my Dad just started laughing, and he said, 'Who cares what they say? We know it's not true. We know the truth. It doesn't matter what they say. We know what we're here for. We know what our purpose is, and quite honestly, the more brutal they are, obviously, that shows how effective we're being.'" But attacks on his wife were another matter. "Their relationship," says Dana, "is truly second to none. He adores her."

In 2019, President Trump awarded Ed Meese the Presidential Medal of Freedom. This is the United States' highest civilian honor and award for service to our country. For reasons of substance, character, and legacy, no one deserves that honor more than Ed Meese.

ACKNOWLEDGMENTS

THIS BOOK COULD never have been written without the tireless help of Justin Braga who spent hours on the telephone with all the interviews of the many people Steve Calabresi interviewed for this book. Justin saw to it that transcripts of each of those interviews were compiled and were sent to Steve Calabresi, who then used them to compile much of the original manuscript. Gary Lawson then generated the rest of the first draft of the manuscript by writing many chapters about Reagan's and Meese's speeches, about the genesis of originalism, and about the Meese Justice Department as a kind of intellectual "hotbed"—resembling a national law school more than a typical government cabinet department. While Calabresi and Lawson in the end co-wrote this book, we could never have done so without Justin Braga's countless hours of work from the spring of 2016 to the spring of 2024—a period of eight years.

Steve Calabresi is grateful to the following people, each of whom he interviewed for one hour. The number of interviews with each person appears in parentheses after their names: Ed Meese (8); Ken Cribb (5); Brad Reynolds (2); John Richardson (2); Steve Matthews (2); Lee Liberman Otis (2); Dana Meese (2); Mike Meese (1); George Meese (1); Charles Fried (1); Chuck Cooper (1); Gary McDowell (1); Blair Dorminey (1); Steve Markman (1); Mark Levin (1); Lois Herrington (1); Ann Rondeau (1); Becky Dunlop (1); David McIntosh (1); John Harrison (1); Leonard Leo (1); Terry Eastland (1); Paul Cassell (1).

Two people, Ed Meese and Ken Cribb, read the near-final book manuscript and corrected many errors and helped us enormously in improving the book. Ed Meese answered countless phone calls from Steve Calabresi with questions about details in the book. Steve Calabresi is also especially grateful to Mark Levin for writing the foreword to this book and to John Richardson, who helped in countless phone calls over the last eight years with many superb suggestions. John Richardson was a really big source of help in writing this book. Rhys Gilkenson and Steve Calabresi's daughter, Elizabeth, helped with the cover art for which we are very grateful.

All of the photographs of Ed Meese together with Ronald Reagan are used with the permission of the Heritage Foundation, which owns them. Ed Meese's assistant at the Heritage Foundation, Katie Samalis, was a huge help in locating these photographs and securing our permission to use them. The photographs of Ed Meese receiving the 2019 Presidential Medal of Freedom and of President Trump are credited to the White House Flickr and to the White House, and they are in the public domain. The photographs of the Supreme Court justices in 1985 and in the fall of 2023 are credited to the Supreme Court, which has posted them as official photographs on the Supreme Court website. The Meese family photographs are used with the permission of Ed Meese and his family. Special thanks to Mike Meese for finding and sending us these photographs. He did yeoman's work on this. The photographs of Judge Robert H. Bork, Justice Antonin Scalia, Ken Cribb, William Bradford Reynolds, Charles Fried, Chuck Cooper, Richard Willard, John Richardson, Mark Levin, Stephen J. Markman, David McIntosh, Justice Antonin Scalia, Judge Robert H. Bork, Justice Samuel Alito, Vice President and later President George H. W. Bush, Boyden Gray, and Don McGahn are used with the permission of the Federalist Society. Special thanks to Federalist Society president Eugene Meyer for granting permission to use these photographs.

Steve Calabresi is also deeply grateful to Gary Lawson, his best friend, for his help in finishing a book project which had become too big for him to handle well alone. Gary is in every sense of the word a true and equal co-author of this book. Steve Calabresi is also grateful to Yale Sterling Professor of Law Akhil Reed Amar, his second-best friend, for encouraging him strongly to write this book and for helping him in getting an agent to publish it. Finally, Steve Calabresi is also grateful to his former teacher, Yale Sterling Professor of Law Bruce Ackerman, for inventing the concept of "a constitutional moment" in his legendary We the People book series. While we know that Ackerman will not agree with us that Ed Meese successfully made a constitutional moment in the way that President Franklin D. Roosevelt did in 1937, we both think Ackerman's concept of the making of a constitutional moment is very helpful in understanding Ed Meese's life's work. We also draw on a more recent book by Ackerman in arguing that President Reagan and Attorney General Meese made a conscious and successful effort to constitutionalize their charisma in the Federalist Society, whose mission is, in part, to encourage the picking of judges who say what the law is and not instead what it should be, as Lee Liberman Otis wrote forty-two years ago in our mission statement.

Although former attorney general Edwin Meese III was interviewed countless times for this book and called with hundreds of small questions, the book is not an authorized biography, and it reflects Calabresi and Lawson's own scholarly assessment of Ed Meese's legacy and not the former attorney general's assessment. Calabresi and Lawson worked in the Meese Justice Department and formed their own opinions about it, which are reflected in this book, and not all of which Ed Meese shares. Calabresi and Lawson have been law professors for more than three decades now, and we have seen the ripples in the judicial appointments process, in the writing of originalist judicial opinions, and in the teaching of constitutional and administrative law caused by Ed Meese's momentous service to the United States as its 75th and, in our opinion, most consequential and best attorney general. We are determined to tell the story of "The Meese Revolution" in constitutional law: "The Making of a Constitutional Moment."

Steve Calabresi is grateful to the Northwestern Pritzker School of Law and to the school's superb dean, Hari Osofsky, for her generous support of his research and writing. He is especially grateful to the Barber family for donating the Clayton J. & Henry R. Barber Chair, which he holds at Northwestern. Calabresi is also grateful to Yale Law School, and to its dean, Heather Gerken, and before her to Dean Robert Post, for their support and sustenance of his scholarship. Together, they have allowed Calabresi to co-teach with his second-best friend in the world, Sterling Professor of Law Akhil Reed Amar, for twelve years now beginning in the fall of 2013 and continuing through the fall of 2024. This has greatly shaped Calabresi's thinking about both originalism and constitutional law.

Most of all, Steve Calabresi is grateful to his wife, Mimi Tyler Calabresi, and to his four wonderful children, Robert, James, Elizabeth, and Tyler, who make it possible for him to do everything he does. Words cannot express Steve Calabresi's love and gratitude to his wonderful wife and children.

Gary Lawson is grateful to Steve Calabresi for including him in this project. This book is authored by "Calabresi and Lawson" in the same way that *A Day in the Life* was authored by "Lennon and McCartney." Yes, Paul wrote a bit for the middle, but it was really John's song. Yes, Lawson wrote some bits in the middle for this book, but this project has been Steve Calabresi's brainchild for many years. Lawson came to the book after most of the hard work was done, and he is more an uncle than a parent to it.

While Professor Lawson is currently at the University of Florida's Levin College of Law, all of his work on this book was done while he was a William Fairfield Warren Distinguished Professor at Boston University School of Law. He is grateful to Boston University for twenty-four amazing years, and he especially thanks Dean Angela Onwuachi-Willig for unfailing support of scholarship. And he thanks Patty Lawson for her patience, her love, our children, and our cats.

ENDNOTES

INTRODUCTION

1 U.S. (4 Wheat.) 316 (1819).

2 60 U.S. (19 How.) 393 (1857).

3 198 U.S. 45 (1905).

4 *See*, e.g., A.L.A. Schechter Poultry Corp. v. United States, 295 U.S. 495 (1935); United States v. Butler, 297 U.S. 1 (1936).

5 469 U.S. 528 (1985).

6 *See* National League of Cities v. Usery, 426 U.S. 833 (1976).

7 367 U.S. 643 (1961).

8 384 U.S. 436 (1966).

9 He was affiliated with Harvard Law School as a "senior fellow" from 1971 to 1976, but after 1965 Mr. Berger did not hold a tenure-track appointment as a law professor—despite being one of the most cited legal theorists of all time.

10 142 S. Ct. 2228 (2022).

11 410 U.S. 113 (1973).

12 142 S. Ct. 2111 (2022).

13 *See* District of Columbia v. Heller, 554 U.S. 570 (2008).

14 142 S. Ct. 2587 (2022).

15 142 S. Ct. 2407 (2022).

16 2023 WL 4239254 (2023).

17 *See* Gary Lawson, "Conservative or Constitutionalist?," Georgetown Journal of Law and Public Policy 1 (2002): 81–84.

18 *See* Homer S. Cummings, The President's Proposals for Judicial Reorganization (Washington, D.C.: U.S. Government Print Office, 1937); Robert H. Jackson, The Struggle for Judicial Supremacy: A Study of a Crisis in American Power Politics (New York: Knopf, 1941); and Francis Biddle, In Brief Authority (Garden City, NY: Doubleday, 1962).

19 *See* Pub. L. No. 97-377, § 793, 96 Stat. 1830, 1865 (1982) ("None of the funds provided in this Act may be used by the Central Intelligence Agency or the Department of Defense to furnish military equipment,

military training or advice, or other support for military activities, to any group or individual, not part of a country's armed forces, for the purpose of overthrowing the Government of Nicaragua or provoking a military exchange between Nicaragua and Honduras.").

20   No position or argument in this book reflects the views of the Federalist Society, which is a 501(c)(3) non-profit corporation, which sponsors debate and discussion and holds symposia, but which never adopts any points of view.

21   *See* William Inboden, The Peacemaker: Ronald Reagan, the Cold War, and the World on the Brink (New York: Dutton, 2022), 358–59.

CHAPTER ONE

1   Kate Coleman, "The Roots of Ed Meese: Reagan's Polemical Attorney General Has Prompted a Major Constitutional Debate, Surprising Those Who Knew Him in His Pragmatic Early Days, in the Quiet Hills of Oakland and during the Turbulent '60s," Los Angeles Times, May 4, 1986.

2   Coleman, "Roots of Ed Meese."

3   Coleman, "Roots of Ed Meese," at 6.

4   Coleman, "Roots of Ed Meese," at 7–8.

5   Coleman, "Roots of Ed Meese," at 16.

6   Lee Edwards, To Preserve and Protect: The Life of Edwin Meese III (Washington, D.C.: Heritage Foundation, 2005), 15.

7   Edwards, To Preserve and Protect, at 17–18.

8   *See* Bernard H. Siegan, Economic Liberties and the Constitution (Chicago: University of Chicago Press, 1980).

CHAPTER TWO

1   Some good places to start are Martin Anderson, Revolution (San Diego: Harcourt, 1988) and Steven F. Hayward, The Age of Reagan: The Conservative Counterrevolution, 1980–1989 (New York: Crown Forum, 2009).

2   Lynn Rosellini, "'Honey, I Forgot to Duck,' Injured Reagan Tells Wife," New York Times, March 31, 1981, https://www.nytimes.com/1981/03/31/us/honey-i-forgot-to-duck-injured-reagan-tells-wife.html.

3   For a contemporary takedown of the Carter economic policy, see Bruce
     Bartlett, Reaganomics: Supply Side Economics in Action (Westport,
     CT: Arlington House, 1981), 167–81.

4   If anyone thinks we are unfairly characterizing the speech, the text can
     be found in numerous internet sources, including 1979 WL 505624.

5   *See* Kevin Mattson, "'Crisis of Confidence,'" Slate, October 22, 2021,
     https://slate.com/news-and-politics/2021/10/jimmy-carter-energy-
     crisis-malaise-speech-biden-supply-chain.html.

6   *See* https://www.google.com/search?client=firefox-b-1-d&scasv=a
     62499659915de61&q=reagan+carter+there+you+go+again&tbm=
     vid&source=lnms&saopQJegQIDBAB&biw=1920&bih=871#fpsta
     te=ive&vld=cid:a97e95b7,vid:qN7gDRjTNf4,st:0.

7   To those who might be tempted to object that it was "We the People"
     and not the states who created the federal government: "We the
     People" most definitely created the Constitution, see U.S. Constitution
     preamble, but the Constitution did not create the federal government.
     The Constitution fundamentally altered the character and power of the
     federal government, to the point of remaking it into a different kind of
     institution, but that government as an entity existed before 1788, which
     is why it could hold property and make treaties in the years before the
     Constitution. That pre-1788 entity was in fact created by the states, as
     President Reagan indicated.

8   For a discussion of the background and importance of this imagery,
     see Steven G. Calabresi, "'A Shining City on a Hill': American
     Exceptionalism and the Supreme Court's Practice of Relying on
     Foreign Law," Boston University Law Review 86 (2006): 1335, 1347–50.

CHAPTER THREE

1   Martin Anderson, Revolution (San Diego: Harcourt, 1988), 123.

2   Edwin Meese III, With Reagan: The Inside Story (Washington, D.C.:
     Regnery Gateway, 1992), 80.

3   Chris Whipple, The Gatekeepers: How the White House Chiefs of Staff
     Define Every Presidency (New York: Crown, 2017), 105.

4   Whipple, Gatekeepers, at 109.

5   Whipple, Gatekeepers, at 109.

6   *See* Anderson, Revolution, at 223–33. Anderson was a key player in the
     details and implementation of the cabinet council system. See Meese,
     With Reagan, at 76.

7 Anderson, Revolution, at 224.

8 Anderson, Revolution, at 224.

9 Anderson, Revolution, at 225.

10 Meese, With Reagan, at 76.

11 Anderson, Revolution, at 226.

12 Anderson, Revolution, at 228.

13 Anderson, Revolution, at 230.

14 Fred I. Greenstein, The Hidden-Hand Presidency: Eisenhower as Leader (Baltimore: Johns Hopkins University Press, 1994).

15 *See* Anderson, Revolution, at 109–88.

16 *See* William Inboden, The Peacemaker: Ronald Reagan, the Cold War, and the World on the Brink (New York: Dutton, 2022), 102.

17 Martin Anderson once again provides invaluable background on President Reagan's long-standing commitment to missile defense. See Anderson, Revolution, at 63–108.

18 Lee Edwards, To Preserve and Protect: The Life of Edwin Meese III (Washington, D.C.: The Heritage Foundation, 2005), 61.

19 *See* Anderson, Revolution, at 260.

20 Whipple, Gatekeepers, at 111.

21 Anderson, Revolution, at 313.

22 Inboden, Peacemaker, at 118.

23 Anderson, Revolution, at 313.

24 Anderson, Revolution, at 307. This assessment of Al Haig seems to be widely shared. See Inboden, Peacemakers, at 162; Whipple, Gatekeepers, at 112.

25 For an account considerably more favorable to Shultz, see Inboden, Peacemaker, at 17.

26 For the details of this utterly bogus "scandal," see Meese, With Reagan, at 110–11.

27 Perhaps even deeper, given the length of Clark's association with Reagan? At least one interviewee, Becky Norton Dunlop, told us that "I think Clark had a closer personal relationship with the president."

28 Meese, With Reagan, at 114.

29 Peter Baker and Susan Glasser, The Man Who Ran Washington: The Life and Times of James A. Baker III (New York: Doubleday, 2020), 195.

30   Sean Wilentz, The Age of Reagan: A History, 1974–2008 (New York: Harper, 2008), 227. We note, with some interest, that this book's award-winning author managed to write a nearly 600-page tome with no mention of Ed Meese's policymaking role in the Reagan administration.

31   Whipple, Gatekeepers, at 106.

32   Anderson, Revolution, at 238.

33   Baker and Glasser, Man Who Ran Washington, at 220.

CHAPTER FOUR

1   50 U.S.C. § 3021(b) (2018).

2   50 U.S.C. § 3021(c)(1).

3   50 U.S.C. § 3021(c)(1).

4   See George P. Shultz, Turmoil and Triumph: My Years as Secretary of State (New York: Charles Scribner's Sons, 1993).

5   Margaret Thatcher, The Downing Street Years (New York: HarperCollins, 1993), 463.

6   For a balanced look at Gorbachev, see Steven F. Hayward, The Age of Reagan: The Conservative Counterrevolution 1980–1989 (New York: Crown Forum, 2009), 420–28.

7   Walter J. Boyne, "El Dorado Canyon," Air Force 82, no. 3, March 1999.

8   Martin Anderson, Revolution (San Diego: Harcourt, 1988), 170.

9   Edwin Meese III, With Reagan: The Inside Story (Washington, D.C.: Regnery Gateway, 1992), 65.

10   Anderson, Revolution, at 169.

11   Shultz, Turmoil and Triumph, at 748.

12   Shultz, Turmoil and Triumph, at 826–27.

13   Shultz, Turmoil and Triumph, at 834.

14   E.O. 11541, § 2(a), Federal Register 35, no. 128 (1970): 10735. The council's current structure, which stems from breaking up the original DPC into the Domestic Policy Council and the National Economic Council, dates from a 1993 executive order from Bill Clinton. See E.O. 12859, Federal Register 58, no. 159 (1993): 44101–2.

15   Domestic Policy Council Low Income Opportunity Working Group, Up from Dependency: A New National Public Assistance Strategy; Report to the President by the Domestic Policy Council Low Income

Opportunity Working Group (Washington, D.C.: U.S. Government Printing Office, December 1986), 1.

16   *See* DPC, Up from Dependency, at 2–4.

17   DPC, Up from Dependency, at 51.

18   *See* DPC, Up from Dependency, at 31, 52–53.

19   *See* DPC, Up from Dependency, at 52.

20   DPC, Up from Dependency, at 53–55.

21   Domestic Policy Council Working Group on Federalism, The Status of Federalism in America: A Report of the Working Group on Federalism of the Domestic Policy Council (Washington, D.C.: U.S. Government Printing Office, November 1986), 1.

22   U.S. Const. art. I, § 8, cl. 3; see DPC, Status of Federalism, at 13–14, 20–28.

23   DPC, Status of Federalism, at 30–37.

24   DPC, Status of Federalism, at 43 (emphasis in original).

25   DPC, Status of Federalism, at 44.

26   E.O. 12612, Federal Register 52, no. 210 (1987): 41685–88.

27   E.O. 12612 § 2.

28   E.O. 12612 § 3(a) & (c).

29   E.O. 12612 § 4(c).

30   E.O. 12612 § 6(b)–(c).

31   Franklin D. Roosevelt, "State of the Union Message to Congress," Franklin D Roosevelt Presidential Library and Museum, January 11, 1944, https://www.fdrlibrary.org/address-text.

32   *See* Paul Matzko, "The Sordid History of the Fairness Doctrine," Cato Institute, January 30, 2021, https://www.cato.org/article/sordid-history-fairness-doctrine.

33   *See* 47 C.F.R. § 73.123 (1969).

34   *See* General Fairness Doctrine Obligations of Broadcast Licensees, Federal Register 50, no. 169 (1985): 35418–55.

35   *See* Red Lion Broadcasting Co. v. FCC, 395 U.S. 367 (1969).

36   Peter Keisler went on to become assistant attorney general of the Justice Department's Civil Division—and for a brief time in 2007 acting attorney general. For several decades, he has been among the nation's preeminent communications lawyers. He is also an extraordinary

human being, and he would be an outstanding federal judge today if not for the shameless obstructionism of partisan Democratic senators in 2006.

37   In re Syracuse Peace Council, 2 FCC Rcd. 5043 (1987).

38   Ronald Reagan, "Statement on the President's Commission on Privatization," Ronald Reagan Presidential Library & Museum, September 3, 1987, https://www.reaganlibrary.gov/archives/speech/statement-presidents-commission-privatization.

39   The classic work on federal lands is Paul W. Gates, History of Public Land Law Development (Washington, D.C.: U.S. Government Printing Office, 1968).

40   *See* Yellowstone National Park Protection Act, ch. 72, § 4, 28 Stat. 73 (1872).

41   Hayward, Age of Reagan, at 404.

CHAPTER FIVE

1   There are many key positions in the Department of Justice that do not, as a legal matter, have to be filled by lawyers. The solicitor general must be "learned in the law," 28 U.S.C. § 505 (2018), but there is presently no such requirement for any other position, including attorney general and U.S. attorney. "Learned in the law" requirements for those positions did exist at earlier times but were repealed in 1948 because "[s]uch requirement is not made of United States judges and no reason appears to make a distinction respecting United States attorneys." 28 U.S.C. § 541 note (2018).

2   In the 118th Congress, spanning January 2023 to January 2025, "30% of House Members, and 51% of Senators, have law degrees and have practiced law." Jennifer E. Manning, Membership of the 118th Congress: A Profile (Washington, D.C.: Congressional Research Service, March 11, 2024), 2.

3   343 U.S. 579, 634–35 (1952) (Jackson, J., concurring).

4   James B. Thayer, "The Origin and Scope of the American Doctrine of Constitutional Law," Harvard Law Review 7, no. 3 (1893): 129, 138, https://www.jstor.org/stable/1322284.

5   Stuart v. Laird, 5 U.S. 299, 309 (1803).

6   Robert H. Bork, "Styles in Constitutional Theory," South Texas Law Journal 26, no. 3 (1985): 383, 383.

7   This was much truer forty years ago than it is today when a substantial percentage of those entering the legal academy have advanced degrees and advanced training in disciplines such as political science, economics, statistics, sociology, psychology, philosophy, and history. There were important interdisciplinary scholars in the legal academy of the 1980s, but that kind of cross-discipline training for law professors has become far more prevalent in recent years.

8   Domestic Policy Council Working Group on Federalism, The Status of Federalism in America: A Report of the Working Group on Federalism of the Domestic Policy Council (Washington, D.C.: U.S. Government Printing Office, November 1986), 43n176.

9   A short summary of contemporary approaches can be found in Steven Gow Calabresi and Gary Lawson, The U.S. Constitution: Creation, Reconstruction, the Progressives, and the Modern Era (St. Paul, MN: Foundation Press, 2020), 55–61.

10 For a more technical taxonomy of constitutional methods prominent during the era when Ed Meese was about to enter the scene, which defends a version of the second approach described above (a form of "living constitutionalism") but fair-mindedly describes the other approaches as well, see Stephen R. Munzer and James W. Nickel, "Does the Constitution Mean What It Always Meant?," Columbia Law Review 77, no. 7 (1977): 1029–62.

11 Charles Evans Hughes, "Speech before the Elmira Chamber of Commerce," May 3, 1907, in Addresses of Charles Evans Hughes: 1906–16, 2nd ed. (New York: G. P. Putnam's Sons, 1916), 179, 185. Hughes later walked back the extreme implications of that comment. See H. Jefferson Powell, "Constitutional Virtues," Green Bag 9, 2d (2006): 379, 381.

12 Bork, "Styles in Constitutional Theory," at 384.

13 See, e.g., John Hart Ely, Democracy and Distrust: A Theory of Judicial Review (Cambridge, MA: Harvard University Press, 1980), 28. If this was a book on constitutional theory, we would engage with Professor Ely's claim, as the clauses that he (and other scholars) considers "open-ended," such as the Ninth Amendment and the Fourteenth Amendment's Privileges or Immunities Clause, actually have reasonably determinate original meanings. But that would have to be the subject of another book.

14 Ely, Democracy and Distrust, at 87.

15 John Hart Ely, "Constitutional Interpretivism: Its Allure and Impossibility," Indiana Law Journal 53, no. 3 (1978): 399.

16   Ely, "Constitutional Interpretivism," at 400.

17   Erwin Chemerinsky, "Empty History," Michigan Law Review 81, no. 4 (1983): 828, 834. See also Chemerinsky, "Empty History," at 834n42 ("[a]lthough there are still a few scholars who attempt to defend interpretivism, the clear weight of scholarly opinion…is that the Court is in no way obliged to follow the intent of the framers"). Professor Chemerinsky has been the dean of two major law schools, has authored one of the leading treatises on constitutional law, and as of 2024 is president of the Association of American Law Schools.

18   Thomas C. Grey, "Do We Have an Unwritten Constitution?," Stanford Law Review 27, no. 3 (1975): 703, 705. Professor Grey's article (which may involve the first academic usage of the term "interpretivist") was describing this attitude, not expressing it. While he sharply disagreed with originalism and interpretivism, he was actually urging that it be treated more seriously than his academic colleagues seemed willing to treat it.

19   See Gerald Gunther, Constitutional Law: Cases and Materials (1975), appendices A-1 [Justices] and B-1 [Constitution].

20   To be sure, the database does not include every law review from that era. For example, the 1978 article we cite by John Hart Ely is not included in that database.

21   See Joseph D. Grano, "Judicial Review and a Written Constitution in a Democratic Society," Wayne Law Review 28, no. 1 (1981): 1–76.

22   See Lillian R. BeVier, "The First Amendment and Political Speech: An Inquiry into the Substance and Limits of Principle," Stanford Law Review 30, no. 2 (1978): 299, 304. BeVier states that "the only legitimate sources of constitutional principle are the words of the Constitution itself, and the inferences that reasonably can be drawn from its text, from its history and from the structure of government it prescribes."

23   See Robert F. Nagel, "Book Review: American Constitutional Law," University of Pennsylvania Law Review 127, no. 4 (1979): 1174–94.

24   See, e.g., Grover Rees III, "Throwing Away the Key: The Unconstitutionality of the Equal Rights Amendment Extension," Texas Law Review 58, no. 5 (1980): 875. Professor Rees was also the first speaker at a Federalist Society event; he debated Yale Law School professor Burke Marshall as the first invitee of the Yale Federalist Society. Professor Rees did not get tenure at the University of Texas. Instead, he went on to an even more distinguished career that included important work in the Reagan Justice Department and as the United States' first ambassador to East Timor.

25   *See* Bernard H. Siegan, Economic Liberties and the Constitution
     (Chicago: University of Chicago Press, 1980), 8, 10.

26   John Hart Ely, "The Wages of Crying Wolf: A Comment on Roe v.
     Wade," Yale Law Journal 82 (1973): 920, 949.

27   Henry P. Monaghan, "The Constitution Goes to Harvard," Harvard
     Civil Rights-Civil Liberties Law Review 13 (1978): 117, 124 (emphasis in
     original).

28   One scholar, for example, described Professor Ely's approach as "neo-
     interpretivism." See Larry Alexander, "Modern Equal Protection
     Theories: A Metatheoretical Taxonomy and Critique," Ohio State Law
     Journal 43, no. 1 (1981) 3, 9.

29   *See* David P. Currie, The Constitution in the Supreme Court: The First
     Hundred Years, 1789–1888 (Chicago: University of Chicago Press, 1985).

30   *See* Philip B. Kurland, Politics, the Constitution, and the Warren Court
     (Chicago: University of Chicago Press, 1970).

31   For a brief sketch of what an interpretative theory requires, see Gary
     Lawson, "Reflections of an Empirical Reader (Or: Could Fleming Be
     Right This Time?)," Boston University Law Review 96 (2016): 1457–79.

32   Siegan, Economic Liberties, at 8.

33   Siegan, Economic Liberties, at 10.

34   Many of Professor Alexander's theoretical contributions were
     foreshadowed in 1981. See Alexander, "Modern Equal Protection
     Theories," 28.

35   Professor Baker would subsequently become a voice for originalism,
     famously co-teaching an annual seminar on separation of powers with
     Justice Antonin Scalia, but his scholarly focus in the 1970s and 1980s
     was criminal law rather than constitutional law or theory.

36   381 U.S. 479 (1965).

37   410 U.S. 113 (1973).

38   Griswold v. Connecticut, at 521–22 (Black, J., dissenting).

39   U.S. Const. amend. IV.

40   Katz v. United States, 389 U.S. 347, 364 (1967) (Black, J., dissenting).

41   In re Winship, 397 U.S. 358, 377 (1970) (Black, J., dissenting).

42   Akhil Reed Amar, "Some Thoughts on the Gorsuch Appointment,"
     in "Trump 100 Days," special issue, University of Illinois Law Review
     Online (2017).

43 David A. Strauss, "The Death of Judicial Conservatism," Duke Journal of Constitutional Law and Public Policy 4, no. 1 (2009): 1, 4.

44 Indeed, we are not convinced that he was correct about original meaning in either of the last two cases mentioned above. The statute in Griswold might well have been unconstitutional (it is a harder question than almost anyone in the modern legal world, on any side, will acknowledge), but not for the reasons given by any of the justices in the case.

45 William H. Rehnquist, "The Notion of a Living Constitution," Texas Law Review 54, no. 4 (1976): 693, 695.

46 Rehnquist, "Notion of a Living Constitution," at 695.

47 Rehnquist, "Notion of a Living Constitution," at 696–97.

48 Fay v. New York, 332 U.S. 261, 282 (1947) (Jackson, J., dissenting).

49 See Rehnquist, "Notion of a Living Constitution," at 699–700.

50 Hans Linde, a professor at the University of Oregon Law School and later a long-serving justice on the Oregon Supreme Court, was sometimes cited as an interpretivist because of his arguments in favor of grounding decisions in constitutional terms rather than overt policymaking terms. See Hans A. Linde, "Judges, Critics, and the Realist Tradition," Yale Law Journal 82, no. 2 (1972): 227, 253–55. Judge Linde is a figure who defies easy description, see Patricia M. Wald, "Hans Linde and the Elusive Art of Judging: Intellect and Craft Are Never Enough," Texas Law Review 75, no. 1 (1996): 215–36, and his sometimes inclusion—not by his own description—as an "interpretivist" powerfully illustrates how hard it was forty years ago to find people to fit that label.

51 Raoul Berger, Government by Judiciary: The Transformation of the Fourteenth Amendment (Cambridge, MA: Harvard University Press, 1977).

52 Raoul Berger, Government by Judiciary: The Transformation of the Fourteenth Amendment, 2nd ed. (Carmel, IN: Liberty Fund, 1997).

53 In a rebuke to all of us who feel old in our sixties, Berger published more than forty scholarly articles after the age of eighty and two dozen after turning ninety. For a summary of Berger's contribution to legal thought, see Johnathan G. O'Neill, "Raoul Berger and the Restoration of Originalism," Northwestern University Law Review 96, no. 1 (2001): 253–81.

54 See Raoul Berger, Executive Privilege: A Constitutional Myth (Cambridge, MA: Harvard University Press, 1974).

55 *See* Raoul Berger, Federalism: The Founders' Design (Norman, OK: University of Oklahoma Press, 1987).

56 347 U.S. 483 (1954).

57 *See* Calabresi and Lawson, U.S. Constitution, at 1318.

58 Gerald E. Lynch, "Book Review: Democracy and Distrust: A Theory of Judicial Review," Columbia Law Review 80, no. 4 (1980): 857, 857n1.

59 Richard B. Saphire, "Judicial Review in the Name of the Constitution," University of Dayton Law Review 8, no. 3 (1983): 745, 753.

60 Raoul Berger, "Mark Tushnet's Critique of Interpretivism," George Washington Law Review 51, no. 4 (1983): 532, 533–34.

61 Alexander, "Modern Equal Protection Theories," at 4.

62 Robert H. Bork, "Neutral Principles and Some First Amendment Problems," Indiana Law Journal 47, no. 1 (1971): 1–35.

63 *See* Robert H. Bork, "The Impossibility of Finding Welfare Rights in the Constitution," Washington University Law Quarterly 1979, no. 3 (1979): 695–701.

64 Bork, "Neutral Principles," at 1.

65 Bork, "Neutral Principles," at 19.

66 Bork, "Neutral Principles," at 8.

67 *See* Bork, "Neutral Principles," at 13.

68 Professor Calabresi was privileged to work with Judge Bork on that book as his research assistant.

69 *See* Richard H. Fallon Jr., "Legitimacy and the Constitution," Harvard Law Review 118, no. 6 (2005): 1787, 1833n208; John O. McGinnis, "Comparing the Court and the fed: Democratic Dilemmas of Elite Institutions," Wake Forest Law Review 57 (2022): 173, 213.

70 Richard Nixon, RN: The Memoirs of Richard Nixon (New York: Grosset and Dunlap, 1978), 419.

71 Nixon, RN, at 424.

72 Harvard Law Review 7, no. 3 (1893): 129–56.

73 Thayer, "Origin and Scope," at 144.

74 Thayer, "Origin and Scope," at 144.

75 *See* Steven G. Calabresi, "Originalism and James Bradley Thayer," Northwestern University Law Review 113, no. 6 (2019): 1419–54; Gary Lawson, "Thayer versus Marshall," Northwestern University Law Review 88, no. 1 (1993): 221–25.

76   The precise phrase "presumption of constitutionality" has shown up in more than one hundred Supreme Court cases since the publication of Thayer's article. Many of those cases invoke the presumption of constitutionality in favor of state as well as federal laws—something about which Thayer was noncommittal. See Thayer, "Origin and Scope," at 154–55.

77   Bork, "Neutral Principles," at 3–4.

78   *See,* e.g., William Baude, "Is Originalism Our Law?," Columbia Law Review 115, no. 8 (2015): 2349–2408.

79   60 U.S. (19 How.) 393 (1857). For our originalist assessment of Dred Scott, see Calabresi and Lawson, U.S. Constitution, at 953–54.

80   As Judge Bork phrased the old proverb during his confirmation hearings, "Even the Devil can quote scripture."

81   *See,* e.g., United States v. Brown, 381 U.S. 437 (1965); Powell v. McCormack, 395 U.S. 486 (1969).

82   290 U.S. 398 (1934).

83   U.S. Const. art. I, § 10, cl. 1.

84   Blaisdell, 290 U.S. at 448–49.

85   410 U.S. 113 (1973).

86   *See* Planned Parenthood of Southeastern Pa. v. Casey, 505 U.S. 833 (1992).

87   Roe, 410 U.S. at 153.

88   Ely, "Wages of Crying Wolf," at 947.

89   *See* Dobbs v. Jackson Women's Health Org., 597 U.S. – (2022).

90   Philip B. Kurland, "The Irrelevance of the Constitution: The Religion Clauses of the First Amendment and the Supreme Court," Villanova Law Review 24, no. 1 (1978): 3–27.

91   *See* Philip B. Kurland, "The Irrelevance of the Constitution: The First Amendment's Freedom of Speech and Freedom of Press Clauses," Drake Law Review 29, no. 1 (1979–80): 1–13.

92   Kurland, "Irrelevance of the Constitution: The Religion Clauses," at 3–4.

93   U.S. Const. amend. I.

94   Act of April 30, 1790, ch. IX, 1 Stat. 112, §§ 1, 3–4, 8–9, 14.

95   Act of April 30, 1790, ch. IX, 1 Stat. at 114, § 14.

96   Act of April 30, 1790, ch. IX, 1 Stat. at 119, § 33.

97   U.S. Const. amend. V.

98   U.S. Const. amend. V.

99   *See* U.S. Const. amend. XIV, § 1.

100   U.S. Const. amend. VIII.

101   Trop v. Dulles, 356 U.S. 86, 100–101 (1958).

102   408 U.S. 238 (1972).

103   428 U.S. 153 (1976).

104   Those limitations, still in force today and in fact growing over time, include forbidding the death penalty for rape, see Coker v. Georgia, 433 U.S. 584 (1977), for minors, see Roper v. Simmons, 543 U.S. 551 (2005), and ultimately for any crime other than murder. See Kennedy v. Louisiana, 554 U.S. 407 (2008). An entire body of jurisprudence regulates the procedures that must be used during the trial and sentencing phases of capital crimes.

105   Just to be clear: more particularized challenges to specific applications of the death penalty—grounded in claims of discrimination or disproportionality—are certainly within the bounds of possibility for originalists. Our point is only that categorical abolition of the death penalty in the name of the Constitution is not a plausible originalist position. And litigation in the 1970s was seeking abolition—a goal that has not been abandoned today and that some modern justices continue to advance.

106   *See* Gregg, 428 U.S. at 176–77.

107   *See* Gregg, 428 U.S. at 168–76, 179–83.

108   *See* Gregg, 428 U.S. at 183–206.

109   *See* Gregg, 428 U.S. at 207 (White, J., concurring).

110   *See* Roberts v. Louisiana, 428 U.S. 325 (1976).

111   *See* Roberts v. Louisiana, 428 U.S. at 337 (White, J., dissenting).

112   *See* Gary Lawson, "Limited Government, Unlimited Administration: Is It Possible to Restore Constitutionalism?," The Heritage Foundation, January 27, 2009, https://www.heritage.org/political-process/report/limited-government-unlimited-administration-it-possible-restore.

113   For a short and readable account of these developments, see Adam Mossoff, "What Is Property? Putting the Pieces Back Together," Arizona Law Review 45, no. 2 (2003): 371, 371–74.

114   Thomas C. Grey, "The Disintegration of Property," in Property, ed. J. Roland Pennock and John W. Chapman, NOMOS XXII (New York:

New York University Press, 1980), 69, 72.

115 Charles A. Reich, "The New Property," Yale Law Journal 73, no. 5 (1964): 733, 771.

116 Reich, "New Property," at 779.

117 Reich, "New Property," at 778.

118 Reich, "New Property," at 785–86.

119 *See* Fred R. Shapiro and Michelle Pearse, "The Most-Cited Law Review Articles of All Time," Michigan Law Review 110, no. 8 (2012): 1483, 1489.

120 *See* David A. Super, "A New New Property," Columbia Law Review 113, no. 11 (2013): 1773, 1871–74 (2013).

121 U.S. Const. amend. V.

122 Frank I. Michelman, "Foreword: On Protecting the Poor through the Fourteenth Amendment," Harvard Law Review 83, no. 1 (1969): 7–282.

123 *See* Frank I. Michelman, "In Pursuit of Constitutional Welfare Rights: One View of Rawls' Theory of Justice," University of Pennsylvania Law Review 121, no. 5 (1973): 962–1019; Frank I. Michelman, "Welfare Rights in a Constitutional Democracy," Washington University Law Review 1979, no. 3 (1979): 659–93.

124 Michelman, "Welfare Rights," at 659.

125 *See* Bailey v. Richardson, 182 F.2d 46 (D.C. Cir. 1950), aff'd by an equally divided Court, 341 U.S. 918 (1951).

126 Joint Anti-Fascist Refugee Committee v. McGrath, 341 U.S. 123, 168 (1951) (frankfurter, J., concurring).

127 *See* Cafeteria & Restaurant Workers Union, Local 473, Afl-cio v. McElroy, 367 U.S. 886 (1961).

128 394 U.S. 618 (1969).

129 397 U.S. 254 (1970).

130 *See* Goldberg v. Kelly, 397 U.S. at 262 ("Appellant does not contend that procedural due process is not applicable to the termination of welfare benefits.").

131 Goldberg v. Kelly, 397 U.S., at 262n8.

132 Goldberg v. Kelly, 397 U.S., at 264–65 (footnote omitted).

133 *See* Dandridge v. Williams, 397 U.S. 471 (1970).

134 *See* Williams v. Dandridge, 297 F.Supp. 450 (D. Md. 1969).

135 *See* Dandridge v. Williams, 397 U.S. at 508 (Marshall, J., dissenting).

136 Some later cases have limited the scope of Goldberg v. Kelly, both with regard to what kinds of interests are protected by due process of law, see Board of Regents of State Colleges v. Roth, 408 U.S. 564 (1972), and when elaborate procedures have to be provided before termination of benefits. See Mathews v. Eldridge, 424 U.S. 319 (1976).

137 *See* David A. Strauss, The Living Constitution (Oxford: Oxford University Press, 2010).

138 448 U.S. 56 (1980).

139 *See* Crawford v. Washington, 541 U.S. 36 (2004). For a discussion of the importance of Crawford to modern originalism, see Gary Lawson, "Confronting Crawford: Justice Scalia, the Judicial Method, and the Adjudicative Limits of Originalism," in "In Memoriam: Justice Antonin Scalia (1936–2016)," special issue, University of Chicago Law Review 84 (2017): 2265–89.

140 *See* U.S. Const. amend. VI ("In all criminal prosecutions, the accused shall enjoy the right to a speedy and public trial, by an impartial jury of the State and district wherein the crime shall have been committed; which district shall have been previously ascertained by law, and to be informed of the nature and cause of the accusation; to be confronted with the witnesses against him; to have compulsory process for obtaining witnesses in his favor, and to have the Assistance of Counsel for his defence.").

141 The Supreme Court did not apply the Sixth Amendment's Confrontation Clause to state in addition to federal criminal cases until 1965. See Pointer v. Texas, 380 U.S. 400 (1965).

142 Ohio v. Roberts, 448 U.S. at 64.

143 Ohio v. Roberts, 448 U.S. at 64.

144 Berger v. California, 393 U.S. 314, 315 (1969).

145 Ohio v. Roberts, 448 U.S. at 63.

146 Ohio v. Roberts, 448 U.S. at 64.

147 *See* Ohio v. Roberts, 448 U.S. at 65.

148 *See* Crawford v. Washington, 541 U.S. at 53–54.

149 Ohio v. Roberts, 448 U.S. at 66.

150 Crawford v. Washington, 541 U.S. at 61.

151 Lawson, "Confronting Crawford," at 2275.

CHAPTER SIX

1   28 C.F.R. § 0.25 (2022).

2   304 U.S. 144 (1938).

3   If you say the simple words "footnote four" to lawyers or law students, they will know exactly to what you are referring.

4   Even Steven Hayward's epic 600-plus page account of the Reagan years has no entry in its index for Ken Cribb.

5   "About," Intercollegiate Studies Institute, https://isi.org/about-us.

6   "Office of Legal Policy," U.S. Department of Justice, https://www.justice.gov/olp.

7   "Douglas Ginsburg: Fallen Supreme Court Nominee," UPI, November 7, 1987, https://www.upi.com/Archives/1987/11/07/Douglas-Ginsburg-Fallen-Supreme-Court-nominee/7130563259600.

8   Linda Greenhouse, "High Court Nominee Admits Using Marijuana and Calls It a Mistake," New York Times, November 6, 1987, https://www.nytimes.com/1987/11/06/us/high-court-nominee-admits-using-marijuana-and-calls-it-a-mistake.html.

9   "About the Office," U.S. Department Office of Legislative Affairs, https://www.justice.gov/ola. While the OLA has formal responsibility for submitting administration comments on legislation to Congress, much of the work is done within the OLC. (Lawson, as a staff attorney in the OLC, drafted multiple memoranda for Bolton's signature commenting on the constitutional aspects of proposed legislation.)

10   Mark Landler, Maggie Haberman, and Eric Schmitt, "Trump Tells Pentagon Chief He Does Not Want War with Iran," New York Times, May 16, 2019, https://www.nytimes.com/2019/05/16/world/middleeast/iran-war-donald-trump.html?module=inline.

11   See Joseph F. Zimmerman, "Federal Preemption under Reagan's New Federalism," Publius: The Journal of Federalism 21, no. 1 (1991): 7–28.

12   See Charles Fried, Order and Law: Arguing the Reagan Revolution—A Firsthand Account (New York: Simon and Schuster, 1991), 45, 49, 54, 126.

13   Fried, Order and Law, at 65.

14   Fried, Order and Law, at 66.

15   Fried, Order and Law, at 66.

16   367 U.S. 497 (1961).

17   367 U.S. at 542 (Harlan, J., dissenting).

18   381 U.S. 479 (1965).

19   410 U.S. 113 (1973).

20   Analysis of these cases—and of Dobbs v. Jackson Women's Health Org., 142 S. Ct. 2228 (2022), which finally overruled Roe after half a century— would go far beyond the scope of this book. But we note that Griswold's result was not obviously wrong as a matter of original meaning. To the possible chagrin of some conservatives, the original meaning of the Fourteenth Amendment might well support something close to the framework laid out in Justice Harlan's Poe v. Ullman dissent. And in any event, the state of Connecticut's offered defense of the birth-control law in 1965 was so transparently weak that the Griswold Court could, and maybe should, have decided the case without saying much about the Constitution. See Steven Calabresi and Gary Lawson, The U.S. Constitution: Creation, Reconstruction, the Progressives, and the Modern Era (St. Paul, MN: Foundation Press, 2020), 1471–73. The deeply flawed reasoning employed in the Griswold case, however, which largely tracked the reasoning of Justice Harlan's dissent in Poe, generated the constitutionally absurd result in Roe. As we said in chapter 5, how one decides cases is more important than the outcomes.

21   See Steven G. Calabresi, Note, "A Madisonian Interpretation of the Equal Protections Doctrine," Yale Law Journal 91, no. 7 (1982): 1403–29.

22   Interestingly, Fried's biggest ally at that 1982 conference was Antonin Scalia, who urged conservatives in the audience to consider advocating a federal statute forbidding all local rent control.

23   Fried, Order and Law, at 187.

24   See Steven G. Calabresi and Daniel Lev, The Legal Significance of Presidential Signing Statements (Berkely, CA: Berkeley Electronic Press, 2006).

25   See generally Steven G. Calabresi and Christopher S. Yoo, The Unitary Executive: Presidential Power from Washington to Bush (New Haven, CT: Yale University Press, 2008).

CHAPTER SEVEN

1   See Frederick Schauer, "Legal Realism Untamed," Texas Law Review 91, no. 4 (2013): 749, 754–56 ("most versions of Realism maintain that legal doctrine ordinarily does not determine legal outcomes without the substantial influence of nonlegal supplements.... [L]egal outcomes will often then be the product. ... the ideological or policy preferences of judges ... [,] the judge's view of the complete array of facts presented by individual cases [or] .... the conscious or subconscious personal

predilections, biases, and idiosyncrasies of particular adjudicators.").

2   Lawson recalls attending a speech—he believes it was to the 1984–1985
    D.C. Circuit law clerks—at which Justice Rehnquist was fed a softball
    question about the constitutionalization of criminal procedure. Instead
    of talking about the meaning of the Constitution, he talked about how
    he enjoyed deciding criminal procedure cases because they raised such
    interesting questions of policy.

3   "Speeches of Attorney General Edwin Meese, III," U.S. Department of
    Justice, April 22, 2021, https://www.justice.gov/ag/speeches-attorney-
    general-edwin-meese-iii.

4   That label "the Bill of Rights" is very modern. It did not become
    commonplace until the 20th century. See Gerard N. Magliocca, "The
    Bill of Rights as a Term of Art," Notre Dame Law Review 92, no. 1
    (2016): 231–69.

5   See Barron v. Baltimore, 32 U.S. (7 Pet.) 243 (1833).

6   See, e.g., Akhil Reed Amar, The Bill of Rights: Creation and
    Reconstruction (New Haven, CT: Yale University Press, 1998).

7   It's complicated. Attorney General Meese was technically correct that
    Bill of Rights provisions do not literally bind the states, but many of
    the rights described in the Bill of Rights might well be "privileges or
    immunities" that are directly protected against states by the Fourteenth
    Amendment. The First Amendment's Establishment Clause, which
    prompted Attorney General Meese to raise the incorporation issue,
    raises possibly unique issues of incorporation because of its explicit
    focus on protecting state prerogatives. For some quick thoughts of
    ours on the subject, see Steven Calabresi and Gary Lawson, The U.S.
    Constitution: Creation, Reconstruction, the Progressives, and the
    Modern Era (St. Paul, MN: Foundation Press, 2020), 1552–55; Steven
    G. Calabresi and Sarah E. Agudo, "Individual Rights under State
    Constitutions When the Fourteenth Amendment Was Ratified in 1868:
    What Rights Are Deeply Rooted in American History and Tradition?,"
    Texas Law Review 87, no. 1 (2008): 7, 31–32.

8   The Federalist Society, created in 1982, was originally an organization
    of and for law students. Once the organization was formed, it was
    clear that there was enormous pent-up demand throughout the legal
    community for a forum promoted to discussion and debate of ideas,
    including ideas such as originalism that were largely shut out of law
    schools and mainstream legal culture. In 1985, the Federalist Society
    was just starting to expand into a Lawyers Division—which today has
    120 local chapters and seventy thousand members.

9   Robert H. Bork, The Tempting of America; The Political Seduction of
     the Law (New York: Touchstone, 1990), 168.

10   Attorney General Meese underestimated the creativity of the academy.
     See Anthony D'Amato, "Aspects of Deconstruction: The 'Easy Case' of
     the Under-Aged President," Northwestern University Law Review 84,
     no. 1 (1990): 250–56.

11   142 S. Ct. 2228 (2022).

12   Saikrishna B. Prakash, "Unoriginalism's Law without Meaning,"
     Constitutional Commentary 15 (1998): 529, 529–30, 541–42.

13   Ryan D. Doerfler and Samuel Moyn, "The Constitution Is Broken and
     Should Not Be Reclaimed," New York Times, August 19, 2022, https://
     www.nytimes.com/2022/08/19/opinion/liberals-constitution.html.

14   Philip Hamburger, Is Administrative Law Unlawful? (Chicago:
     University of Chicago Press, 2014), 371 (quoting Columbia University
     Professor John Burgess).

15   The Federalist, no. 51 (James Madison).

16   Steven Gow Calabresi et. al., The U.S. Constitution and Comparative
     Constitutional Law: Texts, Cases, and Materials (St. Paul, MN:
     Foundation Press 2016).

17   Even Justice Brennan, in his October 1985 speech, invoked the image
     of the "shining city on a hill." He thought that status depended on "our
     ceaseless pursuit of the constitutional idea of human dignity." We think
     it depends on our ceaseless pursuit of the idea of constitutionalism and
     the accurate vision of human nature on which it rests.

18   5 U.S. (1 Cranch) 137 (1803).

19   See Keith E. Whittington, Political Foundations of Judicial Supremacy:
     The Presidency, the Supreme Court, and Constitutional Leadership in
     U.S. History (Princeton, NJ: Princeton University Press, 2007). But see
     Steven Gow Calabresi, The History and Growth of Judicial Review, vol.
     1, The G-20 Common Law Countries and Israel (New York: Oxford
     University Press, 2021): 169–79 (disagreeing with Whittington to some
     extent).

20   For a long discussion of this point, see Gary Lawson and Christopher D.
     Moore, "The Executive Power of Constitutional Interpretation," Iowa
     Law Review 81, no. 5 (1996): 1267–330.

21   See Michael Stokes Paulsen, "The Irrepressible Myth of Marbury,"
     Michigan Law Review 101, no. 8 (2003): 2706–43.

22   See U.S. Const. art. I, § 7, cl. 2 (defining the procedures for enacting "a

Law").

23   60 U.S. (19 How.) 393 (1857).

24   The clause gives Congress power "to make all needful Rules and Regulations respecting the Territory or other Property belonging to the United States." U.S. Const. art. IV, § 3, cl. 2.

25   Sanford Levinson, "Could Meese Be Right This Time?," Tulane Law Review 61, no. 5 (1987): 1071, 1074–75.

26   Levinson, "Could Meese," at 1078.

27   514 U.S. 549 (1995).

28   New York v. United States, 505 U.S. 144 (1992).

29   Indeed, one of us found it unthinkable even in 1994, when he wrote, "[I]n this day and age, discussing the doctrine of enumerated powers is like discussing the redemption of Imperial Chinese bonds. There is now virtually no significant aspect of life that is not in some way regulated by the federal government. This situation is not about to change." Gary Lawson, "The Rise and Rise of the Administrative State," Harvard Law Review 107, no. 6 (1994): 1231, 1236. The next year, the Supreme Court decided Lopez, resuscitating the idea of enumerated powers. Lawson does not have a career as a weather forecaster or fortune teller.

30   See Steven Gow Calabresi and Lucy D. Bickford, "Federalism and Subsidiarity: Perspectives from U.S. Constitutional Law," in Federalism and Subsidiarity, ed. James E. Fleming and Jacob T. Levy, NOMOS LV (New York: New York University Press, 2014), 123.

31   See Steven Gow Calabresi and James Lindgren, "The President: Lightning Rod or King?," Yale Law Journal 115, no. 9 (2006): 2611–22.

32   Buckley v. Valeo, 424 U.S. 1 (1976).

33   INS v. Chadha, 462 U.S. 919 (1983).

34   295 U.S. 602 (1935).

CHAPTER EIGHT

1   Paul Baumgardner, "Originalism and the Academy in Exile," Law and History Review 37, no. 3 (2019): 787, 788.

2   Baumgardner, "Originalism," at 804.

3   United States v. Carolene Products Co., 304 U.S. 144, 152n4 (1938).

4   Usery v. Turner Elkhorn Mining Co., 428 U.S. 1, 15 (1976). No justice in 1976 objected to this formulation.

5   *See* Bernard H. Siegan, Property Rights: From Magna Carta to the Fourteenth Amendment (New Brunswick: Transaction Publishers, 2001); Bernard H. Siegan, Economic Liberties and the Constitution, 2nd ed. (London: Routledge, 2005); Bernard H. Siegan, Property and Freedom: The Constitution, the Courts, and Land-Use Regulation (New Brunswick: Transaction Publishers, 1997); Bernard H. Siegan, The Supreme Court's Constitution: An Inquiry into Judicial Review and Its Impact on Society (New Brunswick: Transaction, Inc., 1987); Bernard H. Siegan, The Rise and Fall of Economic Due Process: When the Supreme Court Championed and Then Curtailed Economic Freedom (Los Angeles: International Institute for Economic Research, 1983).

6   *See* Bernard H. Siegan, Economic Liberties and the Constitution (Chicago: University of Chicago Press, 1980), 7–21.

7   *See* Richard Epstein, Takings: Private Property and the Power of Eminent Domain (Cambridge, MA: Harvard University Press, 1985).

8   *See* Richard Epstein, "The Proper Scope of the Commerce Power," Virginia Law Review 73, no. 8 (1987): 1387–455.

9   U.S. Department of Justice Office of Legal Policy, Report to the Attorney General on Economic Liberties Protected by the Constitution (Washington, D.C.: U.S. Department of Justice, March 16, 1988), executive summary.

10 *See,* e.g., Tyler v. Hennepin County, Minn., 143 S. Ct. 1369 (2023) (saying that when states sell property at tax sales to pay delinquent property taxes, the states must give back any surplus proceeds to the property owner and cannot simply "take" the owner's equity stake in the property).

11 *See* Antonin Scalia and Richard A. Epstein, Scalia v. Epstein: Two Views on Judicial Activism (Washington, D.C.: Cato Institute, 1985).

12 As an aside, Scalia's views on statutory interpretation have largely prevailed on the Supreme Court, which no longer relies on legislative history to any significant extent when interpreting statutes, though lower courts continue to consult those materials with some frequency.

13 One of the earliest mainstream scholarly works to take originalism seriously reached the same conclusion. See H. Jefferson Powell, "The Original Understanding of Original Intent," Harvard Law Review 98, no. 5 (1984): 885–948.

14 Terry Eastland, "The Power of Giving the Right Speech at the Right Time," Washington Examiner, December 7, 2018.

15 Eastland, "Power."

16   Eastland, "Power."

17   Domestic Policy Council Working Group on Federalism, The Status of
     Federalism in America: A Report of the Working Group on Federalism
     of the Domestic Policy Council (Washington, D.C.: U.S. Government
     Printing Office, November 1986), 43n176. Lawson confesses to
     authoring those words in 1986.

18   347 U.S. 483 (1954) (finding segregated public schools unconstitutional).

19   388 U.S. 1 (1967) (finding laws against racially mixed marriages
     unconstitutional).

20   See, e.g., Steven G. Calabresi and Michael Perl, "Originalism and Brown
     v. Board of Education," Michigan State Law Review 2014, no. 3 (2014):
     429–573; Steven G. Calabresi and Andrea Matthews, "Originalism and
     Loving v. Virginia," Brigham Young University Law Review 2012, no. 5
     (2012): 1393–476.

21   The appendices include, inter alia, speeches we have discussed in this
     book by Ed Meese, Antonin Scalia, and William Brennan. Anyone
     who wants to read the texts of those speeches can find them, along
     with a wealth of other material, at https://www.ojp.gov/pdffiles1/
     Digitization/115083NCJRS.pdf.

22   Office of Legal Policy, Original Meaning Jurisprudence: A Sourcebook
     (Washington, D.C.: U.S. Department of Justice, March 12, 1987).

23   OLP, Original Meaning, at 34.

24   OLP, Original Meaning, at 14.

25   OLP, Original Meaning, at 20.

26   OLP, Original Meaning, at 21.

27   OLP, Original Meaning, at 24.

28   James E. Fleming, "Fidelity, Change, and the Good Constitution,"
     American Journal of Comparative Law 62, no. 3 (2014): 515, 518.

29   Margaret Jane Radin, "Reconsidering the Rule of Law," Boston
     University Law Review 69, no. 4 (1989): 781, 816.

30   Robin West, Progressive Constitutionalism: Reconstructing the
     Fourteenth Amendment (Durham, NC: Duke University Press, 194),
     309.

31   West Virginia State Board of Education v. Barnette, 319 U.S. 624, 639
     (1943).

32   Fay v. People of State of New York, 332 U.S. 261, 282 (1947).

33   Civil Rights Act of 1866, 14 Stat. 27–30. The law was enacted on April

9, 1866, and reenacted in 1870 following ratification of the Fourteenth Amendment. The provisions remain good law today. See 42 U.S.C. §§ 1981–1988 (2018).

34   *See* John Hart Ely, Democracy and Distrust: A Theory of Judicial Review (Cambridge, MA: Harvard University Press, 1980), 14.

35   83 U.S. 36 (1873).

36   For a few of our thoughts on the subject, see Steven Gow Calabresi and Gary Lawson, The U.S. Constitution: Creation, Reconstruction, the Progressives, and the Modern Era (St. Paul, MN: Foundation Press, 2020), 1242–44.

37   Yale Law Journal 101, no. 7 (1992): 1385–474.

38   *See* McDonald v. City of Chicago, 561 U.S. 742, 805 (2010) (Thomas, J. concurring in part and concurring in the judgment).

39   384 U.S. 436 (1966).

40   Miranda, 384 U.S. at 444.

41   Stephen J. Markman, "Miranda v. Arizona: A Historical Perspective," American Criminal Law Review 24, no. 2 (1986): 193–242.

42   *See* Dickerson v. United States, 530 U.S. 428 (2000).

43   Office of Legal Policy, Report to the Attorney General on the Law of Pre-Trial Interrogation (Washington, D.C.: U.S. Department of Justice, February 12, 1986), 93–96.

44   For a comprehensive study of the evolution of the exclusionary rule, from a scholar who supports the rule, see Tracey Maclin, The Supreme Court and the Fourth Amendment's Exclusionary Rule (New York: Oxford University Press, 2013).

45   People v. Defore, 150 N.E. 585, 587 (1926).

46   232 U.S. 383 (1914).

47   116 U.S. 616 (1886).

48   Wolf v. Colorado, 338 U.S. 25 (1949).

49   367 U.S. 643 (1961).

50   Akhil Reed Amar, The Constitution and Criminal Procedure: First Principles (New Haven, CT: Yale University Press, 1997).

51   Amar, Constitution and Criminal Procedure. To be fair to defenders of the exclusionary rule, the founding-era remedy for unlawful searches and seizures—a civil lawsuit against the offending government agents—has been rendered near-nugatory by the mid-20th-century

rise of doctrines of "official immunity," which shield government officials from liability for even illegal actions unless those actions were egregiously wrong. Letting guilty criminals go free seems like an odd second-best result, but the sentiment is understandable.

52 McNabb v. United States, 318 U.S. 332, 341 (1943).

53 Office of Legal Policy, Report to the Attorney General on Federal Habeas Corpus Review of State Judgments (Washington, D.C.: U.S. Department of Justice, May 27, 1988), i.

54 It is certainly not our place here to offer a general critique of mainstream law reviews—almost all of which are edited by second- and third-year law students rather than faculty. (Yes, second- and third-year law students decide what gets published in the Harvard Law Review, Yale Law Journal, and virtually every other law journal.) Lawson only notes that about fifteen years ago, he was told—very politely and without the slightest tint of rancor—by the editor-in-chief of one of the country's top law reviews that the editor considered it his moral obligation not to publish anything that might present originalism in a positive light.

55 See Steven G. Calabresi and Sarah E. Agudo, "Individual Rights under State Constitutions When the Fourteenth Amendment Was Ratified in 1868: What Rights Are Deeply Rooted in American History and Tradition?," Texas Law Review 87, no. 1 (2008): 7, 31–36.

56 In the present sample of two, for instance, Lawson has never professed religious beliefs as far back as his memory goes.

57 Lawson's faculty as of early 2024, for instance, has more Jewish atheists (including himself) than Evangelicals. Oddly enough, this imbalance seems of little concern to law school offices allegedly committed to a diversity that reflects the country's population.

58 Office of Legal Policy, Report to the Attorney General: Religious Liberty under the Free Exercise Clause (Washington, D.C.: U.S. Department of Justice, August 13, 1986), 15n23 ("As far as we can determine, no structural or language-intensive analysis of the Free Exercise Clause has been made.).

59 OLP, Religious Liberty, at 12.

60 42 U.S.C. § 2000e-2(a) (2018).

61 Griggs v. Duke Power Co., 401 U.S. 424 (1971).

62 Office of Legal Policy, Report to the Attorney General, Redefining Discrimination: "Disparate Impact" and the Institutionalization of Affirmative Action (Washington, D.C.: U.S. Department of Justice,

November 4, 1987), i, 1.

63   OLP, Redefining Discrimination, at 2. The one exception is a 1982
     amendment to one provision of the Voting Rights Act of 1965 that sets
     out an "effects" test.

64   Wards Cove Packing Co. v. Atonio, 490 U.S. 642 (1989).

65   *See,* e.g., Owen W. Gallogly, "Equity's Constitutional Source," Yale Law
     Journal 132, no. 5 (2023): 1213–319.

66   *See* Dep't of Homeland Security v. New York, 140 S. Ct. 599 (2020)
     (Gorsuch & Thomas, JJ., concurring in the grant of stay).

67   Office of Legal Policy, Guidelines on Constitutional Litigation
     (Washington, D.C.: U.S. Department of Justice, February 19, 1988), 1.

68   OLP, Guidelines, at 3. See OLP, Guidelines, at 3–6 (explaining the
     methodology in more detail).

69   OLP, Guidelines, at 3.

70   OLP, Guidelines, at 10.

71   OLP, Guidelines, at 10.

72   OLP, Guidelines, at 3.

73   OLP, Guidelines, at 3.

74   OLP, Guidelines, at 2.

CHAPTER NINE

1   U.S. Const. art. II, § 2, cl. 2.

2   Terry Eastland, "The Power of Giving the Right Speech at the Right
    Time," Washington Examiner, December 7, 2018.

3   Office of Legal Policy, Guidelines on Constitutional Litigation
    (Washington, D.C.: U.S. Department of Justice, February 19, 1988), 1.

4   A possibly apocryphal story—though it rings true—circulated on the
    D.C. Circuit in the 1980s about J. Skelly Wright. He was supposedly
    asked about an opinion he wrote that flagrantly flew in the face of
    governing Supreme Court precedent. According to the story, his
    response was, "Well, they can't reverse 'em all."

5   Brad Reynolds recollected that President Reagan's first thought was
    to replace Warren Burger with Robert Bork and that Ed Meese had to
    talk Reagan into doing Rehnquist instead. Meese, who was probably
    in a better position to get this story right, says that from the beginning
    both he and President Reagan wanted to replace Warren Burger with

William Rehnquist.

6   In 1979, the Supreme Court held that affirmative action does not violate Title VII's explicit prohibition on basing employment decisions on race or sex. See United Steelworkers v. Weber, AFL-CIO v. Weber, 443 U.S. 193 (1979). Justice Rehnquist (with Chuck Cooper as his law clerk) wrote a blistering dissent in that case.

7   *See* Antonin Scalia, "Sovereign Immunity and Nonstatutory Review of Federal Administrative Action: Some Conclusions from the Public-Lands Cases," Michigan Law Review 68, no. 5 (1970): 867–924.

8   *See* Antonin Scalia, "The ALJ Fiasco—a Reprise," University of Chicago Law Review 47, no. 1 (1979): 57–80.

9   "Glimpses of the Supreme Court Nominating Process, from White House Insiders," Washington Post, April 25, 2010.

10   Lawson concurs in this judgment. He remembers Justice Scalia being particularly incensed at a memorandum from Chief Justice Rehnquist near the end of the October 1986 term that said something to the effect of "It's time to stop thinking and start voting." Chief Justice Rehnquist wanted the term to end in a timely fashion. Justice Scalia, in his first term on the court, wanted to get things right.

11   *See* William H. Rehnquist, The Centennial Crisis: The Disputed Election of 1876 (New York: Knopf, 2004); William H. Rehnquist, All the Laws but One: Civil Liberties in Wartime (New York: Knopf, 1998); William H. Rehnquist, Grand Inquests: The Historic Impeachments of Justice Samuel Chase and President Andrew Johnson (New York: Morrow, 1992); William H. Rehnquist, The Supreme Court: How It Was, How It Is (New York: Morrow, 1987).

12   In one of his less prescient moments, Madison also noted that federal tax collectors "will be principally on the sea-coast, and not very numerous."

13   *See* Wickard v. Filburn, 317 U.S. 111 (1942).

14   514 U.S. 549 (1995).

15   529 U.S. 598 (2000).

16   567 U.S. 519 (2012).

17   Gary Lawson, "The Rise and Rise of the Administrative State," Harvard Law Review 107, no. 6 (1994): 1231, 1236.

18   For our thoughts, see Steven Gow Calabresi and Gary Lawson, The U.S. Constitution: Creation, Reconstruction, the Progressives, and the Modern Era (St. Paul, MN: Foundation Press, 2020), 876.

19   521 U.S. 507 (1997).

20   *See* Seminole Tribe of Florida v. Florida, 517 U.S. 44 (1996); Alden v. Maine, 527 U.S. 706 (1999).

21   *See* Gregory v. Ashcroft, 501 U.S. 452 (1991).

22   *See* New York v. United States, 505 U.S. 144 (1992); Printz v. United States, 521 U.S. 898 (1997).

23   545 U.S. 1 (2005).

24   381 U.S. 479 (1965).

25   410 U.S. 113 (1973).

26   505 U.S. 833 (1992).

27   521 U.S. 702 (1997).

28   Cleburne v. Cleburne Living Center, 473 U.S. 432 (1985).

29   Plyer v. Doe, 457 U.S. 202 (1982).

30   Trimble v. Gordon, 430 U.S. 762 (1977).

31   518 U.S. 515 (1996).

32   City of Richmond, VA v. J.A. Croson Co., 488 U.S. 469 (1989); Adarand Constructors v. Peña, 515 U.S. 200 (1995).

33   Students for Fair Admissions, Inc. v. President and Fellows of Harvard College, 143 S. Ct. 2141 (2023).

34   487 U.S. 654 (1988).

35   Having said that, Lawson does not recall ever meeting another human being as genuinely gracious as Sandra Day O'Connor. And while she took heat for being an "affirmative action" appointee brought up prematurely from the Arizona state appellate court system, she contributed significantly to the Rehnquist Court's federalism revolution. But she was not by any stretch an originalist or deep theoretician.

36   541 U.S. 36 (2004).

37   554 U.S. 570 (2008).

38   *See* Antonin Scalia and Bryan A. Garner, Reading Law: The Interpretation of Legal Texts (St. Paul, MN: Thomson/West, 2012).

39   For a good introduction to Justice Scalia's jurisprudence, see Jeffrey S. Sutton and Edward Whelan, eds., The Essential Scalia: On the Constitution, the Courts, and the Rule of Law (New York: Crown Forum, 2020). For a modest addendum to the book, see Gary Lawson, "Deep Tracks: Album Cuts That Help Define The Essential Scalia," New York University Journal of Law and Liberty 15, no. 1 (2021): 169–232.

40   David Axelrod, "David Axelrod: A Surprising Request from Justice Scalia," CNN, March 9, 2016, https://www.cnn.com/2016/02/14/opinions/david-axelrod-surprise-request-from-justice-scalia/index.html.

41   Robert H. Bork, The Tempting of America: The Political Seduction of the Law (New York: Touchstone, 1990), 268.

42   Alden v. Maine, 527 U.S. 706 (1999).

43   569 U.S. 290, 312–28 (2013) (Roberts, C.J., dissenting).

44   558 U.S. 310 (2010).

45   536 U.S. 639 (2002).

46   Of course, it didn't always work out as planned. Lawson, a Seattle-area native, recalls a vacancy on the Washington district court for which the state's two liberal Republican senators, Dan Evans and Slade Gorton, submitted three names: "Bill Dwyer, Bill Dwyer, Bill Dwyer." William Dwyer was an eminently distinguished lawyer, but he was a staunch Democrat with no interest in the Reagan judicial philosophy. He got the appointment.

47   The Constitution forbids members of Congress from simultaneously serving in other branches, but it does not prevent people from simultaneously serving in both judicial and executive capacities. See Steven G. Calabresi and Joan L. Larsen, "One Person, Office: Separation of Powers or Separation of Personnel," Cornell Law Review 79, no. 5 (1994): 1045–157. That is how, for example, Chief Justice Earl Warren could lead the Warren Commission investigating the death of President Kennedy.

48   There is no formal legal requirement that circuit judges come from any particular state. But as a matter of custom and practice, the Senate normally will only confirm people for regional courts of appeals who have close associations with the states within those circuits. Thus, there are informally "New York seats," "Connecticut seats," and "Vermont seats" within the Second Circuit.

49   See William Baude, "Is Originalism Our Law?," Columbia Law Review 115, no. 8 (2015): 2349, 2355.

50   For a detailed look at Justice Alito's jurisprudence, see Steven G. Calabresi and Todd W. Shaw, "The Jurisprudence of Justice Samuel Alito," 87, no. 3 (2019): 507–78.

51   You can take the 2005 version of the quiz at Andrew Wolfson, "Can You Pass Judge Boggs' Quiz?," Courier Journal, January 11, 2017.

52   His Seventh Circuit colleagues, of course, bear some responsibility for going along with his inventions instead of calling him out. Inventions? Really? Yes, really. When Lawson started teaching at Northwestern in 1988, he heard frequent complaints from the clinical faculty members who litigated cases before the Seventh Circuit that Judge Posner wildly distorted the facts and arguments in cases. Lawson, who knew of Posner almost entirely through his brilliant and engaging scholarship, chalked it up to grousing by hard-left professors about a Reagan appointee—until Lawson was called by a local Chicago lawyer to consult on drafting a certiorari petition to the Supreme Court on a Posner opinion. After reading the case record, Lawson was stunned to see that, just as his colleagues had maintained, there was such a gross disconnect between the case presented by the parties and the case described in Posner's opinion that it was impossible to frame a discrete question for the Supreme Court to review. After advising the lawyer that the chances of getting certiorari granted in the case did not warrant the filing fee, Lawson wrote (for a song) a petition asking the court for summary reversal, meaning reversal of the case without even hearing oral argument, to send a message to lower courts that they cannot simply make up cases to decide when they don't like the ones that are brought to them. Of course the petition was denied. But that was the moment when Lawson decided that Richard Posner was the worst judge in the country.

53   Josh Blackman, "The Volokh Conspiracy," Reason, August 12, 2021.

54   Stephen Skowronek, The Politics Presidents Make: Leadership from John Adams to Bill Clinton (Cambridge, MA: Belknap Press, 1997).

CHAPTER TEN

1   "About the Office," U.S. Department of Justice Office of the Solicitor General, June 16, 2023.

2   "About the Office."

3   The statute creating the Office of Solicitor General requires that the appointee be "learned in the law." 5 U.S.C. § 505 (2018). Interestingly there is no such statutory requirement for any of the other DOJ positions, including attorney general, deputy attorney general, associate attorney general, or the assistant attorneys general. See 5 U.S.C. at §§ 502–4, 506.

4   See Lincoln Caplan, The Tenth Justice: The Solicitor General and the Rule of Law (New York: Knopf, 1987).

5   This Solicitor General's Office mindset of caring first about case law and only secondarily about text and original public meaning perhaps helps explain why Chief Justice John Roberts and, to a lesser degree, Justice Samuel Alito—both veterans of the Solicitor General's Office—care more about case law as Supreme Court justices than do Justices Clarence Thomas and Neil Gorsuch (and perhaps Brett Kavanaugh and Amy Coney Barrett, though it is too soon to make those judgments). Chief Justice John Roberts was the principal deputy solicitor general of the United States from October 1989 to January 1993. John Roberts then spent the next decade in private practice in Washington, D.C., trying to get five votes and a win for his clients. This made him much more of a case law guy than an originalist.

6   Charles Fried, Order and Law: Arguing the Reagan Revolution—A Firsthand Account (New York: Simon and Schuster, 1991), 36–37.

7   Fried, Order and Law, at 37.

8   Fried, Order and Law, at 40.

9   Fried, Order and Law, at 13–14.

10   *See* Charles Fried, Contract as Promise: A Theory of Contractual Obligation (Cambridge, MA: Harvard University Press, 1981).

11   Fried, Order and Law, at 66.

12   *See* Fried, Order and Law, at 62–65.

13   Fried, Order and Law, at 27, 41.

14   Fried, Order and Law, at 41.

15   Fried, Order and Law, at 41.

16   Fried, Order and Law, a 47.

17   Fried, Order and Law, at 49.

18   Fried, Order and Law, at 49.

19   Fried, Order and Law, at 51.

20   488 U.S. 361 (1989).

21   Mistretta, 488 U.S. at 427 (Scalia, J., dissenting).

22   *See* Pumpelly v. Green Bay Co., 80 U.S. (13 Wall.) 166, 177–81 (1871). Technically, the case involved a provision in the Wisconsin constitution rather than the Fifth Amendment, but the wording of the provisions was identical.

23   *See* Pennsylvania Coal Co. v. Mahon, 260 U.S. 393 (1922).

24   For anyone who wants to pursue the matter, good introductions to the

complex problems raised by governmental takings are Ilya Somin, The Grasping Hand: Kelo v. City of New London and the Limits of Eminent Domain (Chicago: University of Chicago Press, 2016); Richard A. Epstein, Takings: Private Property and the Power of Eminent Domain (Cambridge, MA: Harvard University Press, 1985); and David Dana and Thomas W. Merrill, Property: Takings (New York: Foundation Press, 2002).

25　*See* Penn Central Transportation Co. v. City of New York, 438 U.S. 104 (1978).

26　*See* Andrus v. Allard, 444 U.S. 51 (1979).

27　*See* Irving v. Clark, 758 F.2d 1260 (8th Cir. 1985).

28　If that sounds fascinating rather than tooth-grinding, you can read the memo at 10 Op. O.L.C. 32 (1987).

29　*See* Irving Trust Co. v. Day, 314 U.S. 556, 562 (1942).

30　Hodel v. Irving, 481 U.S. 704 (1987).

31　Steven G. Calabresi and Sarah E. Agudo, "Individual Rights under State Constitutions When the Fourteenth Amendment Was Ratified in 1868: What Rights Are Deeply Rooted in American History and Tradition?," Texas Law Review 87, no. 1 (2008): 7–120; Steven G. Calabresi, Sarah E. Agudo, and Kathryn L. Dore, "State Bills of Rights in 1787 and 1791: What Individual Rights Are Really Deeply Rooted in American History and Tradition?," Southern California Law Review 86, no. 6 (2012): 1451–550.

32　Steven G. Calabresi, James Lindgren, Hannah M. Begley, Kathryn L. Dore, and Sarah E. Agudo, "Individual Rights under State Constitutions in 2018: What Rights Are Deeply Rooted in a Modern-Day Consensus of the States?," Notre Dame Law Review 94, no. 1 (2018): 49–154.

33　381 U.S. 479 (1965).

34　410 U.S. 113 (1973).

35　Fried, Order and Law, at 72.

36　Fried, Order and Law, at 74.

37　Poe v. Ullman, 367 U.S. 497, 542 (1961) (Harlan, J., dissenting). As noted earlier, we suspect that Charles Fried wrote those words as Justice Harlan's law clerk. He uses them to begin his chapter on "Privacy" in his memoir. See Fried, Order and Law, at 71.

38　Fried, Order and Law, at 74.

39   Fried, Order and Law, at 76–81.

40   *See,* e.g., James E. Fleming, Constructing Basic Liberties: A Defense of Substantive Due Process (Chicago: University of Chicago Press, 2022).

41   Dobbs v. Jackson Women's Health Org., 142 S. Ct. 2228, 2301–2 (Thomas, J., concurring).

42   476 U.S. 747 (1986).

43   It can be found at https://www.justice.gov/sites/default/files/osg/briefs/1985/01/01/sg850181.txt.

44   *See* Planned Parenthood of Southeastern Pa. v. Casey, 505 U.S. 833 (1992).

45   *See* Fried, Order and Law, at 33–35.

46   492 U.S. 490 (1989).

47   Fried, Order and Law, at 85.

48   Charles Fried, "I Once Urged the Supreme Court to Overturn Roe. I've Changed My Mind," New York Times, November 30, 2021, https://www.nytimes.com/2021/11/30/opinion/supreme-court-roe-v-wade-dobbs.html.

49   Fried, Order and Law, at 90.

50   42 U.S.C. § 2000e-2(a) (2018).

51   42 U.S.C. § 2000d.

52   42 U.S.C. §§ 1981–1982.

53   For some of our joint thoughts, see Steven Gow Calabresi and Gary Lawson, The U.S. Constitution: Creation, Reconstruction, the Progressives, and the Modern Era (St. Paul, MN: Foundation Press, 2020), 1181–87, 1243–44. For some of Calabresi's extensive writings on the subject, see Steven G. Calabresi and Michael W. Perl, "Originalism and Brown v. Board of Education," Michigan State Law Review 2014, no. 3 (2014): 429–573; Steven G. Calabresi and Andrea Matthews, "Originalism v. Loving v. Virginia," Brigham University Law Review 2012, no. 5 (2012): 1393–471. For Lawson's tentative thoughts, see Gary Lawson and Guy Seidman, "A Great Power of Attorney": Understanding the Fiduciary Constitution (Lawrence, KS: University Press of Kansas, 2017), 151–71.

54   *See* Fried, Order and Law, at 89–131.

55   Students for Fair Admissions v. President and Fellows of Harvard College, 143 S. Ct. 2141 (2023).

56   Fried, Order and Law, at 35.

57   Fried, Order and Law, at 188.

58   Fried, Order and Law, at 170–71.

59   487 U.S. 654 (1988).

60   488 U.S. 361 (1989).

61   Fried, Order and Law, at 170.

62   Buckley v. Valeo, 424 U.S. 1 (1976).

63   Buckley v. Valeo, 519 F.2d 821, 889 (D.C. Cir. 1975).

64   462 U.S. 919 (1983).

65   U.S. Const. art. I, § 7, cls. 2–3.

66   478 U.S. 714 (1986).

67   28 U.S.C. § 509 (2018).

68   Whether the president could personally carry out executive functions, such as writing and filing briefs, in the face of statutes designating particular federal officers to perform those functions is a tricky constitutional question. Fried says no—see Fried, Order and Law, at 192 (statutory executive duties "cannot be discharged personally by the President even if he wants to do so")—while we think the answer is yes. See Gary Lawson, "Command and Control: Operationalizing the Unitary Executive," Fordham Law Review 92, no. 2 (2023): 441–61. The president does not need statutory authority to file briefs in the Supreme Court, just as George Washington in the 1793 Neutrality Proclamation did not need a statute in order to direct the district attorneys to prosecute all offenses against the law of nations. At a minimum, the president could have issued instructions about what to do or not to do that would invalidate any action by subordinates contrary to those instructions. President Reagan never issued such instructions with respect to the Solicitor General's Office. Even the president's executive order on federalism pointedly exempted briefs and arguments in court from the requirement to comply with the president's focus on federalism.

69   487 U.S. 735 (1988).

70   Fried, Order and Law, at 178–79.

71   The Civil Rights Cases, 109 U.S. 3 (1883).

72   See Calabresi and Lawson, U.S. Constitution, at 860–61.

73   In addition to Hodel v. Irving, discussed earlier, see Nollan v. California Coastal Comm'n, 483 U.S. 825 (1987); First English Evangelical Lutheran Church v. Los Angeles County, 482 U.S. 304 (1987); Keystone

Bituminous Coal Ass'n v. DeBenedictis, 480 U.S. 470 (1987).

74 Fried, Order and Law, at 183.

75 Fried, Order and Law, at 184.

76 Fried, Order and Law, at 185.

77 Fried, Order and Law, at 185.

78 *See* First English Evangelical Lutheran Church v. Los Angeles County, 482 U.S. at 317–19.

79 *See* Schweiker v. Chilicky, 487 U.S. 412 (1988).

80 Fried, Order and Law, at 185n26.

81 *See* Dolan v. City of Tigard, 512 U.S. 374 (1994).

CHAPTER ELEVEN

1 *See* 28 C.F.R. § 0.25(a) (2023).

2 Without meaning to leave anyone out, alumni from 1981 to 1988 in the OLC include Rebecca Brown, Harold Bruff, Gary Lawson, Nelson Lund, John McGinnis, Geoffrey Miller, Mike Rappaport, the late Thomas Sargentich, Peter Shane, David Strauss, and Cass Sunstein. Put them at a school with the four deans mentioned above and you might have the best law faculty in the country.

3 William French Smith, Law and Justice in the Reagan Administration: Memoirs of an Attorney General (Stanford, CA: Hoover Institution Press, 1991), 23.

4 *See* Charles J. Cooper, "Legislation Providing for Court-Ordered Disclosure of Grand Jury Materials to Congressional Committees," 9 O.L.C. 86 (1985).

5 *See* Phillip D. Brady, "Constitutionality of a Judicial Review Provision Providing for Automatic Affirmance of Agency Decisions," 9 O.L.C. 118 (1985).

6 Brady, "Constitutionality," at 121.

7 *See* Plaut v. Spendthrift Farm, 514 U.S. 211 (1995).

8 Plaut v. Spendthrift Farm, 514 U.S. at 262 (Stevens, J., dissenting).

9 Bain Peanut Co. of Texas v. Pinson, 282 U.S. 499, 501 (1931) (quoted in Plaut, 514 U.S. at 266 (Stevens, J., dissenting)). The Solicitor General's Office, under Attorney General Janet Reno and Solicitor General Drew Days, filed a brief defending the statute, essentially on the ground that it did not fall squarely within any past precedent invalidating

congressional laws. Justice Scalia's opinion for the court, as with Chuck Cooper's OLC opinion a decade earlier, was all about first principles of separation of powers.

10   *See* Charles J. Cooper, "Constitutionality of Proposed Conditions to Senate Consent to the Interim Convention on Conservation of North Pacific Fur Seals," 10 O.L.C. 12 (1986).

11   Charles J. Cooper, "Congressional Authority to Adopt Legislation Establishing a National Lottery," 10 O.L.C. 40 (1986).

12   Cooper, "Congressional Authority," at 41.

13   Cooper, "Congressional Authority," at 41.

14   U.S. Const. art. II, § 1, cl. 8.

15   For example, Justice Scalia, later joined by Justice Thomas, refused to join any portion of a majority opinion that relied on legislative history.

16   *See* (and/or hear) Harvard Law School, "The Scalia Lecture: A Dialogue with Justice Elena Kagan on the Reading of Statutes," YouTube, November 25, 2015, https://www.youtube.com/watch?v=dpEtszFToTg.

17   The movement toward textualism is a bit less dramatic in the lower courts than on the Supreme Court, though that is a story for another day. See Abbe R. Gluck and Richard A. Posner, "Statutory Interpretation on the Bench: A Survey of Forty-Two Judges on the Federal Courts of Appeals," Harvard Law Review 131, no. 5 (2018): 1298, 1324 (noting that forty-one out of forty-two surveyed court of appeals judges reported using legislative history to help interpret statutes).

18   29 U.S.C. 794 (2018).

19   29 U.S.C. § 706(8)(B) (1982).

20   The OLC opinion of June 20, 1986, is not published. The substance of the opinion can be gleaned from a law review article Lawson authored in 1989 explaining and expanding the analysis. See Gary Lawson, "AIDS, Astrology and Arline: Towards a Causal Interpretation of Section 504," Hofstra Law Review 17, no. 2 (1989): 237–316.

21   Not everyone immediately, or ever, grasped the argument. Many critics either did not grasp it or chose, for strategic reasons, to misrepresent it. Lawson in 1986 wrote the only op-eds of his life correcting some of those misinterpretations or misrepresentations, followed three years later by the lengthy article cited in the previous note. Within the Justice Department, Brad Reynolds did not immediately grasp the argument. Lawson is not sure that Reynolds ever actually grasped it; Reynolds was entirely unable to explain the opinion at a meeting of agency general

counsels, where Chuck Cooper had to take over the meeting from him. It was never clear to Lawson why Reynolds was initially chosen to present the OLC opinion at that meeting, as Reynolds had no role at all in producing it.

22 *See* School Board of Nassau County v. Arline, 480 U.S. 273 (1987).

23 Douglas W. Kmiec, "Application of Section 504 of the Rehabilitation Act to HIV-Infected Individuals," 12 O.L.C. 209 (1988). For Lawson's detailed critique of this 1988 OLC opinion, see Lawson, "AIDS, Astrology and Arline."

24 *See* Paul G. Cassell and Margaret Garvin, "Protecting Crime Victims in State Constitutions: The Example of New Marsy's Law for Florida," Journal of Criminal Law and Criminology 110, no. 2 (2020): 99–139; Paul G. Cassell, "The Victim's Rights Amendment: A Sympathetic, Clause-by-Clause Analysis," Phoenix Law Review 5, no. 2 (2012): 301–39; Paul G. Cassell, "Protecting Crime Victims in Federal Appellate Courts: The Need to Broadly Construe the Crime Victims' Rights Act's Mandamus Provision," Denver Law Review 87, no. 3 (2010): 599–631; Paul G. Cassell and Steven Joffee, "The Crime Victim's Expanding Role in a System of Public Prosecution: A Response to the Critics of the Crime Victims' Rights Act," Northwestern University Law Review Colloquy 105 (2010): 164–83; Paul G. Cassell, "Treating Crime Victims Fairly: Integrating Victims into the Federal Rules of Criminal Procedures," Utah Law Review 2007, no. 4 (2007): 861–970; Paul G. Cassell, "Recognizing Victims in the Federal Rules of Criminal Procedure: Proposed Amendments in Light of the Crime Victims' Rights Act," Brigham Young University Law Review 2005, no. 4 (2005): 835–926.

25 The entire federal criminal code in 1790 included fewer than two dozen crimes and took only a few pages to list. See Crimes Act of 1790, ch. IX, 1 Stat. 112 (1790).

26 Smith, Law and Justice, at 91.

CHAPTER TWELVE

1 Peter Baker and Susan Glasser, The Man Who Ran Washington: The Life and Times of James A. Baker III (New York: Doubleday, 2020), 519.

2 U.S. Const. art. I, § 9, cl. 3.

3 U.S. Const. art. II, § 3.

4 To be clear, dirty tricks were not an invention of the Nixon

administration; they have been part of American politics since the beginning. See Victor Lasky, It Didn't Start with Watergate (New York: Dial Press, 1977).

5   *See* U.S. v. Nixon, 418 U.S. 683 (1974).

6   *See* Nixon v. Sirica, 487 F.2d 700 (D.C. Cir. 1973) (en banc).

7   We explain this in Steven G. Calabresi and Gary Lawson, "Why Robert Mueller's Appointment as Special Counsel Was Unlawful," Notre Dame Law Review 95, no. 1 (2019): 87–153.

8   *See* U.S. v. Nixon.

9   For an inside account of these events, see Robert H. Bork, Saving Justice: Watergate, the Saturday Night Massacre, and Other Adventures of a Solicitor General (New York: Encounter Books, 2013).

10   *See* Terry Eastland, Ethics, Politics, and the Independent Counsel: Executive Power, Executive Vice, 1789–1989 (Washington, D.C.: National Legal Center for the Public Interest, 1989).

11   Myers v. United States, 272 U.S. 52 (1926).

12   Humphrey's Executor v. United States, 295 U.S. 602 (1935).

13   28 U.S.C. § 591(b) (1982).

14   28 U.S.C. § 592(b).

15   28 U.S.C. § 596(a)(1).

16   *See* U.S. Const. art. II, § 2, cl. 2.

17   William French Smith, Law and Justice in the Reagan Administration: The Memoirs of an Attorney General (Stanford, CA: Hoover Institution Press, 1991), 178.

18   487 U.S. 654 (1988).

19   *See* (and hear), Gary Lawson, Richard H. Pildes, and Theodore B. Olson, "The Great Dissent: Justice Scalia's Opinion in Morrison v. Olson," The Federalist Society, October 7, 2018, https://fedsoc.org/commentary/videos/the-great-dissent-justice-scalia-s-opinion-in-morrison-v-olson.

20   North's convictions were tossed out in United States v. North, 910 F.2d 843 (D.C. Cir. 1990), and Poindexter's were tossed in United States v. Poindexter, 951 F.2d 369 (D.C. Cir. 1992).

21   For a long telling of the problems with the current DOJ regulations, see Calabresi and Lawson, "Why Robert Mueller's Appointment."

22   Steven F. Hayward, The Age of Reagan: The Conservative Counterrevolution, 1980–1989 (New York: Crown Forum, 2009), 408.

23 Hayward, Age of Reagan, at 408.

24 Judi Hasson, "Former Watergate Defense Lawyer Jacob A. Stein Was Named … ," UPI, April 2, 1984, https://www.upi.com/Archives/1984/04/02/Former-Watergate-defense-lawyer-Jacob-A-Stein-was-named/5885449730000.

25 28 U.S.C. § 592(b)(1) (1976).

26 935 F.2d 445 (2d Cir. 1991).

27 *See* United States v. Nofziger, 878 F.2d 442 (D.C. Cir. 1989).

28 *See* United States v. Wallach, 935 F.2d at 450.

29 "The McKay Report," Washington Post, July 19, 1988, https://www.washingtonpost.com/archive/opinions/1988/07/19/the-mckay-report/139fb4da-8943-4976-a8da-cde8259301db.

30 Continuing Appropriations Act for Fiscal Year 1985, Pub. L. No. 98-473, § 8066(a), 98 Stat. 1837, 1935 (1984) (emphasis added).

31 Edwin Meese III, With Reagan: The Inside Story (Washington, D.C.: Regnery Gateway, 1992), 276–77.

32 Meese, With Reagan, at 287.

33 Meese, With Reagan, at 297.

34 Meese, With Reagan, at 243.

35 Meese, With Reagan, at 243.

36 Meese, With Reagan, at 289. Ann Rondeau recalls President Reagan describing "bile in his throat" when he learned of North's actions.

37 Meese, With Reagan, at 300.

38 Because the EIGA was obviously unconstitutional, Meese could have simply ignored the statute and waited for Congress to impeach and remove him. Rather than prompt that kind of constitutional crisis, Meese instead gave parallel appointments to Walsh and his staff under the internal Justice Department rules for special counsels that had been used before 1978.

39 *See* United States v. Poindexter; United States v. North, 920 F.2d 940 (D.C. Cir. 1990).

CHAPTER THIRTEEN

1 Dobbs v. Jackson Women's Health Org., 597 U.S. 215 (2022).

2 Students for Fair Admissions v. Harvard, 600 U.S. 181 (2023).

3   Gundy v. United States, 139 S. Ct. 2116 (2019).

4   *See* Alabama Ass'n of Realtors v. U.S. Dep't of Health & Hum. Services, 141 S. Ct. 2485 (2021); National Federation of Independent Business v. OSHA, 142 S. Ct. 661 (2021); West Virginia v. EPA, 142 S. Ct. 2587 (2022).

5   *See* Gregory v. Ashcroft, 501 U.S. 452 (1991).

6   *See* Free Enterprise Fund v. PCAOB, 561 U.S. 477 (2010); Lucia v. SEC, 138 S. Ct. 2044 (2018); Seila Law LLC v. CFPB, 140 S. Ct. 2183 (2020); Collins v. Yellen, 141 S. Ct. 1761 (2021); United States v. Arthrex, 141 S. Ct. 1970 (2021).

7   New York State Rifle & Pistol Association, Inc. v. Bruen, 142 S. Ct. 2111 (2022).

8   Kennedy v. Bremerton School Dist., 142 S. Ct. 2407 (2022).

9   303 Creative LLC v. Elenis, 143 S. Ct. 2298 (2023).

10   Carson v. Makin, 142 S. Ct. 1987 (2022).

11   To be sure, this was a position that some people also took in the founding era. See Steven Gow Calabresi and Gary Lawson, The U.S. Constitution: Creation, Reconstruction, the Progressives, and the Modern Era (St. Paul, MN: Foundation Press, 2020), 591–97. If the Constitution had been written differently, they might have been right. But that is not how the Constitution was ultimately written.

12   United States v. Butler, 297 U.S. 1 (1936) (Agriculture Adjustment Act); Carter v. Carter Coal Co., 298 U.S. 238 (1936) (Bituminous Coal Conservation Act).

13   Ashton v. Cameron County Water Improvement Dist., 298 U.S. 513 (1936).

14   Schechter Poultry v. United States, 295 U.S. 495 (1935); Panama Refining Co. v. Ryan, 293 U.S. 388 (1935).

15   Lochner v. New York, 198 U.S. 45 (1905).

16   West Coast Hotel Co. v. Parrish, 300 U.S. 379 (1937).

17   Adkins v. Children's Hospital, 261 U.S. 525 (1923).

18   335 U.S. 464 (1948).

19   300 U.S. at 398 (quoting Nebbia v. New York, 291 U.S. 502, 537 (1934)).

20   United States v. Carolene Products Co., 304 U.S. 144, 154 (1938).

21   The question whether and to what extent there is textual justification for examining the substance of state and federal legislation is a topic

that would require a separate book. Suffice it to say that it is more complex than many, especially those who espouse "judicial restraint," are inclined to think. The fiduciary character of the Constitution provides some basis for a moderate level of means-ends scrutiny of federal legislation, while the Fourteenth Amendment's Privileges or Immunities Clause could well require similar scrutiny of state laws that affect certain interests. The Supreme Court's review process, from the Civil War onwards, has never been grounded in either fiduciary standards or the Privileges or Immunities Clause and thus has dubious constitutional justification.

22 301 U.S. 1 (1937).

23 *See* Darby v. United States, 312 U.S. 100 (1941); Wickard v. Filburn, 317 U.S. 111 (1942).

24 Adamson v. California, 332 U.S. 46 (1947).

25 West Virginia State Board of Education v. Barnette, 319 U.S. 624 (1943).

26 Colegrove v. Green, 328 U.S. 549 (1946).

27 Goesart v. Cleary.

28 Korematsu v. United States, 323 U.S. 214 (1944).

29 Gundy v. United States, 139 S. Ct. 2116 (2019). For a detailed account of the case, see Gary Lawson, "'I'm Leavin' It (All) Up to You'; Gundy and the (Sort-of) Resurrection of the Subdelegation Doctrine," Cato Supreme Court Review 2019 (2019): 31–68.

30 *See* Paul v. United States, 140 S. Ct. 342 (2019) (statement of Justice Kavanaugh respecting the denial of certiorari).

31 For some of the complexities involved in that task, see Gary Lawson, "A Private-Law Framework for Subdelegation," in The Administrative State before the Supreme Court: Perspectives on the Nondelegation Doctrine, ed. Peter J. Wallison and John Yoo (Washington, D.C.: American Enterprise Institute, 2022).

32 Chevron U.S.A., Inc. v. NRDC, 467 U.S. 837 (1984). For the bizarre story of how that case generated a doctrine nowhere within the contemplation of its authors, see Gary Lawson and Stephen Kam, "Making Law out of Nothing at All: The Origins of the Chevron Doctrine," Administrative Law Review 65, no. 1 (2013): 1–75.

33 For a detailed account of all six cases, see Gary Lawson, "The Ghosts of Chevron Present and Future," Boston University Law Review 103, no. 6 (2023): 1647–715.

34 *See* Loper Bright Enterprises v. Raimondo, 45 F.4th 359 (D.C. Cir. 2022),

cert. granted, 2023 WL 3158352 (2023).

35   141 S. Ct. 2485 (2021).

36   Public Health Service Act, Pub. L. No. 78-410, § 361, 58 Stat. 682, 703–4 (1944) (codified at 42 U.S.C. § 264(a)).

37   Congress had previously authorized such a moratorium on a limited basis, see Pub. L. No. 116-136, 134 Stat. 281 (2020), but that authorization had expired when the agency acted.

38   42 U.S.C. § 264(a); see Federal Register 85, no.173 (2020): 55292, 55294–95 ("Evicted renters must move, which leads to multiple outcomes that increase the risk of COVID-19 spread. Specifically, many evicted renters move into close quarters in shared housing or other congregate settings. ... [M]ass evictions would likely increase the interstate spread of COVID-19.").

39   Alabama Ass'n of Realtors v. U.S. Dep't of Health & Hum. Services, 141 S. Ct. at 2489 (quoting Util. Air Regul. Grp. V. EPA, 573 U.S. 302, 324 (2014) (quoting FDA v. Brown & Williamson Tobacco Corp., 529 U.S. 120, 160 (2000))).

40   142 S. Ct. 661 (2021).

41   29 U.S.C. § 652(8) (2018).

42   *See* COVID-19 Vaccination and Testing; Emergency Temporary Standard, Federal Register 86, no. 212 (2021): 61402–61555 (to be codified at 29 C.F.R. Pts. 1910, 1915, 1917, 1918, 1926, 1928).

43   National Federation of Independent Business v. OSHA, 142 S. Ct. at 665.

44   National Federation of Independent Business v. OSHA, 142 S. Ct. at 665.

45   National Federation of Independent Business v. OSHA, 142 S. Ct. at 669 (Gorsuch, J., concurring).

46   142 S. Ct. 2587 (2022).

47   *See* Repeal of Carbon Pollution Emission Guidelines for Existing Stationary Sources: Electric Utility Generating Units, Federal Register 82, no. 198 (2017): 48035, 48037–39; Final Rule Repealing the Clean Power Plan and Approving Related Updated Guidelines, Federal Register 84, no. 130 (2019): 32520–32584.

48   *See* Am. Lung Ass'n v. EPA, 985 F.3d 914, 945–57 (D.C. Cir. 2021).

49   West Virginia v. EPA, 142 S. Ct. at 2609.

50   West Virginia v. EPA, 142 S. Ct. at 2609 (quoting Util. Air Reg. Grp. v. EPA, 573 U.S. at 324).

51   West Virginia v. EPA, 142 S. Ct. at 2616 (Gorsuch, J., concurring in the

judgment).

52 West Virginia v. EPA, 142 S. Ct. at 2617.

53 143 S. Ct. 2355 (2023).

54 554 U.S. 570 (2008).

55 McDonald v. City of Chicago, 561 U.S. 742 (2010).

56 *See* In re Bernstein, 85 App.Div.2d 574, 445 N.Y.S.2d 716 (1981).

57 142 S. Ct. 2111 (2022).

58 Bruen, 142 S. Ct. at 2128–29.

59 Bruen, 142 S. Ct. at 2129–30.

60 142 S. Ct. 1987 (2022).

61 142 S. Ct. 2407 (2022).

62 540 U.S. 712 (2004).

63 Espinoza v. Montana Dep't of Revenue, 140 S. Ct. 2246 (2020).

64 Carson v. Makin, 142 S. Ct. at 2002.

65 Steven G. Calabresi and Abe Salander, "Religion and the Equal Protection Clause: Why the Constitution Requires School Vouchers," Florida Law Review 65, no. 4 (2013): 909–1087.

66 Steven G. Calabresi and Sarah E. Agudo, "Individual Rights under State Constitutions When the Fourteenth Amendment Was Ratified in 1868: What Rights Are Deeply Rooted in American History and Tradition?," Texas Law Review 87, no. 1 (2008): 7–120.

67 505 U.S. 577 (1992).

68 Kennedy v. Bremerton School District, 142 S. Ct. at 2432–33.

69 Kennedy v. Bremerton School District, 142 S. Ct. at 2428.

CHAPTER FOURTEEN

1   Note that our criteria for greatness in this chapter do not include whether power or influence was exercised beneficently. If that criterion were added, Ed Meese, in our judgment, would win in a landslide. Others, with different views of beneficence, might see matters otherwise. We are trying hard to avoid being influenced by our preferences in this regard.

2   Act of September 24, 1789, ch. XX, § 35, 1 Stat. 73, 93.

3   Act of September 24, 1789, ch. XX, § 35, 1 Stat. 73, 92.

4   *See* Homer Cummings and Carl McFarland, Federal Justice: Chapters
     in the History of Justice and the Federal Executive (New York:
     Macmillan, 1937), 16–17; Jed Handelsman Shugerman, "The Creation of
     the Department of Justice: Professionalization without Civil Rights or
     Civil Service," Stanford Law Review 66, no. 1 (2014): 121, 122.

5   2 U.S. (2 Dall.) 419 (1793).

6   Cummings and McFarland, Federal Justice, at 31.

7   Cummings and McFarland, Federal Justice, at 82.

8   1 Opp. Att'y Gen. 624 (1823).

9   For details on the opinion and the ensuing debate regarding it, see
     Gary Lawson, "Command and Control: Operationalizing the Unitary
     Executive," Fordham Law Review 92, no. 2 (2023): 441–61.

10   17 U.S. (4 Wheat.) 518 (1819).

11   17 U.S. (4 Wheat.) 316 (1819).

12   22 U.S. (9 Wheat.) 1 (1824).

13   The Jewels of the Princess of Orange, 2 Op. Att'y Gen. 482 (1831).

14   60 U.S. (19 How.) 393 (1857).

15   *See* Tarble's Case, 80 U.S. 397 (1872).

16   67 U.S. (2 Black) 635 (1863).

17   *See* Homer Cummings, Liberty under Law and Administration (New
     York: Charles Scribner's Sons, 1934); Homer Cummings and Carl
     McFarland, Federal Justice: Chapters in the History of Justice and the
     Federal Executive (New York: Macmillan, 1937); Homer Cummings
     and Carl Brent Swisher, Selected Papers of Homer Cummings:
     Attorney General of the United States, 1933–1939 (New York: Charles
     Scribner's Sons, 1939).

18   Homer Cummings, "Modern Tendencies and the Law," American Bar
     Association 19, no. 10 (1933): 576, 577–78.

19   296 U.S. 495 (1935).

20   *See* Cummings and Swisher, Selected Papers, at 146–54.

21   347 U.S. 483 (1954).

22   *See* Robert F. Kennedy, The Enemy Within (New York: Harper, 1960;
     New York: Ishi Press, 2017, republished).

23   Kourtney Geers, "In the Cloakroom and on the Floor: Interview #1,"
     Document Cloud, June 1, 2009, (quoting Senate Majority Leader
     Lyndon Johnson's secretary Bobby Baker).

24   *See* Victor Navasky, Kennedy Justice (New York: Atheneum, 1971).

25   "One-person, one-vote" is a marketing slogan, but it is not a legal rule.
      It is not the rule adopted by the Supreme Court in the 1960s, and it
      is not the rule that RFK's Justice Department endorsed. A true one-
      person, one-vote rule would require all elections to be held at-large
      rather than by district, because population shifts render impossible
      exact equality at voting time across districts. The actual legal rule
      forbids large disparities in voting populations across districts, not all
      disparities.

26   369 U.S. 186 (1962).

27   376 U.S. 1 (1964).

28   377 U.S. 533 (1964).

29   *See* Navasky, Kennedy Justice, at 314–66.

30   *See* Nicholas deB. Katzenbach, Some of It Was Fun: Working with RFK
      and LBJ (New York: W. W. Norton, 2008).

31   William French Smith, Law and Justice in the Reagan Administration:
      The Memoirs of an Attorney General (Stanford, CA: Hoover Institution
      Press, 1991).

CONCLUSION

1   George W. Bush was many things, but "conservative" was not among
      them. Conservatives were livid in the lead-up to the 2000 election
      because the establishment had settled on him before the primaries even
      began (much as it had settled on Jeb Bush as the candidate in 2015).
      Anyone reading Human Events—one of Ronald Reagan's favorite
      publications—in 1999 would have seen a steady stream of concern
      about a George W. Bush candidacy. Conservatives, however, never
      coalesced around an alternative candidate, and Bush sailed to victory.
      Conservatives eventually rallied around Bush because of a combination
      of 9/11 and the hysterical leftist reaction to him (giving rise to the "Bush
      derangement syndrome" label). But events like the Miers nomination,
      not to mention Bush's support for amnesty for illegal immigrants,
      reflected a deep tension between Bush and the conservative movement
      that never went away.

2   Office of the Press Secretary, "President Nominates Harriet Miers as
      Supreme Court Justice," news release, The White House, October 3,
      2005 .

3   Tucker Carlson, "Bork Calls Miers Nomination a 'Disaster,'" NBC

News, October 7, 2005, https://www.nbcnews.com/id/wbna9623345.

4   At an earlier point, Attorney General Gonzalez had privately asked Leo what President Bush should do if Chief Justice Rehnquist retired. Leo recommended Antonin Scalia for chief justice and Luttig, a former Scalia clerk, to replace Scalia as associate justice. Gonzalez called that the most conservative possible answer that Leo could have given—which it was.

5   Emma Green, "The Clarence Thomas Effect," The Atlantic, July 10, 2019, https://www.theatlantic.com/politics/archive/2019/07/clarence-thomas-trump/593596.

6   Fred I. Greenstein, The Hidden-Hand Presidency: Eisenhower as Leader (Baltimore: John Hopkins University Press, 1994).

INDEX

ABA. *See* American Bar Association

Ackerman, Bruce, 142

Adams, John, 343

Adams, John Quincy, 378

Adkins v. Children's Hospital, 363

Age of Reagan: The Conservative Counter-revolution 1980–1989, The, 56–57

Akerman, Amos T., 375, 381–82

Alabama Ass'n of Realtors v. U.S. Dep't of Health & Hum. Services, 369

Alexander, Larry, 117, 122

Alito, Samuel, 4, 5, 10, 19, 23, 155, 164, 187, 207, 247, 258, 277, 285, 286, 296, 321, 322, 328, 365, 366, 368, 370, 371, 395, 396

Allen, Richard, 59

Altimari, Frank, 282

Amar, Akhil Reed, 166, 217, 226

American Bar Association (ABA), 1, 2, 4, 6, 12, 127, 141, 175, 176, 195, 197, 213, 216, 336, 341, 374, 383

Americans with Disabilities Act, 327

Anderson, Martin, 15, 18, 56, 65

Anderson, Stephen H., 283

Anti-Ballistic Missile Defense Treaty (ABM Treaty), 68

Antitrust Paradox: A Policy at War with Itself, The, 123, 335

Aquinas. *See* Thomas Aquinas, Saint

Archer, Glenn Leroy, Jr., 283

Armstrong, Bill, 272

Arnold, Morris S., 285

Ashcroft, John, 391

Axelrod, David, 258

Baker, Howard, 13, 16, 93, 95, 263

Baker, James A., III (Jim), 14, 18, 59, 60, 338; advisory commission chaired by, 20; "canary in the mine shaft" func-

tion of, 64; duties of, 60; qualities of, 61, 71; tension between Haig and, 73

Baker, John, 117

Baker, Peter, 338

Baker v. Carr, 268, 388

Baldock, Bobby Ray, 283

Baldrige, Malcolm, 56

Balkin, Jack, 217

Barbara K. Olsen Memorial Lecture, 287

Barksdale, Rhesa, 285

Barnett, Randy, 217

Barr, William "Bill," 155, 163, 321, 391

Barrett, Amy Coney, 4, 10, 19, 24, 259, 272, 275, 287, 359, 366, 371, 398

Batchelder, Alice M., 285

Bates, Edward, 375, 377, 380, 381, 382

Bator, Paul M., 160

Baude, Will, 277

Baxter, William, 335, 390

Beam, C. Arlen, 282

Becker, Edward R., 67, 282

Beezer, Robert, 282

Bell, Griffin, 342, 390

Berger, Raoul, 5, 8, 121, 122, 123, 124, 167, 217

Berliner, Dana, 278

Berrien, John MacPherson, 379

BeVier, Lillian, 116

Biddle, Francis, 10, 375, 386

Biden, Joe, 39, 44, 62, 260, 359, 370, 371

Biden v. Nebraska, 371

Bill of Rights, 136, 179, 220, 256, 359

Birch, Stanley F., Jr., 285

Bissell, Jean Galloway, 283

Black, Hugo, 10, 118, 119, 120, 121, 124, 134, 267, 365, 384

Black, Jeremiah S., 380

Black, Susan H., 285

Blackmun, Harry, 138, 252, 253, 257, 258, 267, 269

Black Panthers, 32, 330

Black's Law Dictionary, 255

Blaine, James, 372

Blaine Amendments, 373

Boggs, Danny, 278–79, 282

Boland, Edward, 355

Boland Amendment, 12, 99

Boland II Amendment, 355

Bolton, John, 152, 172, 243

Bonaparte, Charles, 382

Bork, Robert H., 4, 5, 8, 123, 124, 131, 141, 149, 151, 156, 160, 161, 165, 168, 169, 217, 241, 250, 261, 262, 263, 265, 269, 270, 272, 273, 274, 278, 341, 396

Boudin, Michael, 276, 285

Bowman, Pasco, II, 269, 282

Bowsher v. Synar, 313

Boyd v. United States, 226

Boyne, Walter J., 83

Bradford, William, 378

Breckinridge, John, 378

Brennan, William J., Jr., 1, 5, 180, 181, 182, 183, 184, 220, 245, 252–53, 257, 264, 267, 269, 278, 387

Brest, Paul, 114, 196

Brewster, Benjamin, 382

Breyer, Stephen, 257–58, 276, 286, 369

Brezhnev, Leonid, 64

Brorby, Wade, 283

Brown v. Board of Education, 122, 217, 262, 386

Brownell, Herbert, 375, 386

Brunetti, Melvin T., 282

Buckley, James L., 274, 281

Buckley, William F., 260

Burger, Warren, 9, 127, 139, 175, 199, 214, 239–41, 250–52, 254, 292, 309, 333, 387–90

Burke, Edmund, 292

Burns, Arnold, 330

Bush, George H. W., 16, 17, 53, 80, 151, 163, 242, 253, 270, 272, 284, 286, 346, 388, 393

Bush, George W., 17, 19, 20, 277, 246, 286, 287, 334, 394, 396

Butler, Benjamin Franklin, 380

Butterfield, Alexander, 341

Byrnes, James F., 10, 365

Calabresi, Steven G., 13, 15, 19, 52, 96, 146, 153, 155, 160, 161, 164, 165, 167, 168, 169, 170, 171, 196, 217, 226, 239, 243, 244, 246, 250, 253, 262, 264, 265, 267, 268, 269, 273, 274, 281, 291, 295, 344

Cannon, Lou, 34, 56

Card, Andy, 394

Cardamone, Richard J., 281

Cardozo, Benjamin, 226

Carlyle Group, 338

Carnes, Edward Earl, 285

Carson v. Makin, 372, 373

Carter, Jimmy, 6, 16, 105, 270, 277, 342, 343, 348

Carvin, Mike, 172, 207, 243, 267, 269, 295, 335

Casey, William J., 14, 15, 16, 17, 53–54, 59, 72, 75

Cassell, Paul, 333

Central Intelligence Agency (CIA), 72, 355

Chapman, Robert F., 282

Chisholm v. Georgia, 377

Christie, Chris, 397

CIA. *See* Central Intelligence Agency

Cipollone, Pat, 287

Citizens United v. FEC, 266

City of Arlington, Texas v. FCC, 265

310, 312, 315, 323, 359, 362, 363, 383, 384

Federalist, The, 23, *161, 201, 205, 248, 323, 324*

Federalist Society, 6, 15, 19, 21, 142, 161, 162, 168, 170, 171, 183, 187, 209, 247, 263, 272, 275, 286, 287, 296, 344, 394, 397, 399

Fernandez, Ferdinand, 285

Feulner, Ed, 397

Fifteenth Amendment, 110, 249

Fifth Amendment, 130, 132, 219, 223, 224, 227, 297, 304, 317

First Amendment, 3, 95–96, 116, 129, 179, 228, 266, 315, 373, 374

Fitts, Mike, 321

Flaum, Joel, 67, 282

Ford, Gerald R., 16, 17, 34, 35

Foster, Vince, 344

Founders' Constitution, The, 117

Fourteenth Amendment, 110, 116, 121–22, 129, 130, 131, 133, 136, 137, 166, 179, 180–81, 187, 217, 219, 220, 221, 228, 249, 250, 265, 302, 304, 308, 316, 366, 367, 373, 393

Fourth Amendment, 120, 186, 225–26, 256, 262, 302, 305, 331

Fowler, Mark, 94

Fox News, 96

Frankfurter, Felix, 10, 124, 127, 257, 267, 365, 384

Free Speech Movement, 32

Fried, Charles, 95, 157–63, 146, 161, 165, 207, 243, 290, 291, 292, 293, 299, 302, 303, 306, 309, 317–18

Fuller, Melville, 246

Furman v. Georgia, 130, 131

Gaddafi, Muammar, 83

Garcia v. San Antonio Metropolitan Transit Authority, 2

Garland, Augustus, 382

Garland, Merrick, 391

Garwood, William, 67, 282

Garza, Emilio M., 285

Gibbons v. Ogden, 379

Gibson, John R., 282

Gilpin, Henry D., 380

Ginsburg, Douglas H., 151, 152, 172, 262, 263, 269, 273, 274, 281, 335

Ginsburg, Ruth Bader, 254, 257, 271, 272, 274, 275, 286

Giuliani, Rudy, 350

Glasser, Ira, 195

Glasser, Susan, 338

Goesaert v. Cleary, 363

Goldberg, Arthur, 267, 387

Goldberg v. Kelly, 134

Gonzales, Alberto, 19, 20, 391, 397

Gonzales v. Raich, 250, 251

Gorbachev, Mikhail, 18, 48, 69–70, 79, 81–82, 93–94, 101

Gorsuch, Neil, 4, 6, 10, 19, 23–24, 187, 245, 257, 259, 275, 281, 287, 365, 366, 367, 370, 371, 374, 398

Government by Judiciary: The Transformation of the Fourteenth Amendment, 5, 121

Graglia, Lino, 162

Grano, Joseph, 116

Grant, Ulysses S., 97, 376, 381, 382

Gray, C. Boyden, 275, 283, 284, 388, 394

Great Depression, 128

Great Society, 35, 41

Greenberg, Morton Ira, 282

Greenstein, Fred, 399

Gregg v. Georgia, 131

Gregory, Thomas, 382

Gregory v. Ashcroft, 265

Grey, Thomas, 132

Griggs, John W., 382

Griswold v. Connecticut, 118, 159, 251,

Jurisprudence of Original Intention, 3–4, 9, 177, 178, 180, 183, 216, 292

Jurisprudence of Original Meaning, 216, 217, 234, 292, 366, 372

Jurisprudence of Original Public Meaning, 187, 216, 254

Jurisprudence of Original Subjective Intentions, 187

Kagan, Elena, 5, 157, 254, 258, 259, 326, 369

Kanne, Michael Stephen, 282

Katzenbach, Nicholas de B., 375, 388, 389

Kavanaugh, Brett, 4, 10, 19, 24, 259, 275, 287, 337, 366, 368, 398

Kay, Richard, 117

Keisler, Peter, 95, 261, 263

Kelly, Bill, 396

Kelly, Paul Joseph, Jr., 285

Kennedy, Anthony M., 15, 19, 152, 156, 163, 165, 199, 243, 245, 250, 253, 254, 256, 263–66, 275, 307, 309, 367, 373–74

Kennedy, John F., 14, 22, 245, 252, 267, 376, 387–88

Kennedy, Robert F., 9, 14, 340, 375, 376, 387–88, 389, 391

Kennedy, Ted, 41, 243, 258, 261–62, 340

Kennedy v. Bremerton School District, 7, 372, 374

King, Martin Luther, Jr., 389

Kirk, Russell, 30

Kirkpatrick, Jeane, 55, 75

Kissinger, Henry, 17, 59, 73

Kleindienst, Richard, 339, 340, 390

Kleinfeld, Andrew, 281, 285

Kneedler, Ed, 299, 300, 301

Knox, Philander, 382

Koh, Harold, 322

Kozinski, Alex, 281, 282

Krupansky, Robert B., 282

Ku, Julian, 278

Kuhl, Carolyn, 165, 166, 172, 207, 243, 317

Ku Klux Klan, 220, 381–82

Kurland, Philip, 117, 129

Laffer, Arthur, 65

Law and Justice in the Reagan Administration: The Memoirs of an Attorney General, 8

Law, Legislation, and Liberty, 30

Lawson, Gary, 52, 87, 154, 155, 164, 167, 217, 249, 252, 265, 291, 298, 314, 322, 328, 333, 344

Laxalt, Paul, 12, 17, 101

Leavy, Edward, 282

Lee, Charles, 378

Lee, Rex, 159, 160

Lee v. Weisman, 374

Legaré, Hugh S., 380

legislation: Americans with Disabilities Act, 327; Civil Rights Act (1866), 220, 308; Civil Rights Act (1964), 230, 231, 307, 327, 388, 389; Comprehensive Crime Control Act (1984), 330, 390; Economic Recovery Tax Act (1981), 18, 65; Ethics in Government Act, 274, 339, 343; Fairness in Broadcasting Act (1987), 95; Homesteading Act, 97; Judiciary Act (1789), 376; National Industrial Recovery Act, 360, 362, 367, 383–84; National Labor Relations Act, 363; Rehabilitation Act (1973), 327; Religious Freedom Restoration Act, 250; Sentencing Reform Act (1984), 313; Treason Act, 381; Voting Rights Act (1965), 388, 389

Leo, Leonard, 7, 19, 277, 278, 286, 287, 394, 396

Lerner, Ralph, 117

Levi, Edward, 390

Levin, Mark, 19, 96, 171

Levinson, Sanford, 114, 195

ground of, 1–24; as constitutional revolution, 360; important component of, 87; judges of, 238, 239, 275, 277; legal minds of, 147, 149, 170; long game of, 293; manifesto of, 175; obstacles to, 291, 297; originalism and, 110; race discrimination cases of, 307; steward of, 393–401

Merrill, Thomas, 289

Metzenbaum, Howard, 262

Miami Herald Publishing Co. v. Tornillo, 96

Michel, Paul, 281, 283

Michelman, Frank, 133, 317

Miers, Harriet, 19, 394, 396

Mikva, Abner, 274

Milburn, Herbert Theodore, 282

Miller, Marc, 322

Miller, William, 382

Miner, Roger, 282

Miranda v. Arizona, 3, 223–25

Missouri Synod, 27

Mistretta v. United States, 296, 311

Mitchell, John N., 9, 339, 340, 390

Mitchell, William, 382

Monaghan, Henry, 116

Mondale, Walter, 16, 39

Monroe, John, 378

Moody, William Henry, 382

Morrison v. Olson, 254, 311, 346

Mueller, Robert, 347

Mukasey, Michael, 20, 391, 397

Murphy, Frank, 10, 365, 385

Nagel, Robert, 116

National Federation of Independent Business v. OSHA, 369

National Industrial Recovery Act, 360, 362, 367, 383–84

National Labor Relations Act (NLRA), 363

National Review, 30, 260, 272

National Security Council (NSC), 12, 14, 59, 60, 63, 72, 75, 79, 80–81, 99–101, 346, 355, 385

Nelson, David Aldrich, 282

Nelson, John, 380

Nelson, Thomas G., 285

New Deal, 2, 10, 34, 35, 41, 107, 118, 124, 128, 129, 145, 153, 199, 202, 210, 248, 250, 267, 299, 360, 361–62, 363, 365, 368, 369, 382–87, 388

Newman, Pauline, 283

New York State Rifle & Pistol Association, Inc. v. Bruen, 7, 372

New York v. United States, 265

NFIB v. Sebelius, 249

Nielson, Aaron, 278

Niemeyer, Paul V., 285

Ninth Amendment, 129, 219–22

Nixon, Richard M., 34, 41, 50, 54, 59, 64, 156, 159, 160, 200, 252, 341, 342; affirmative action plan of, 271; appointees of, 252, 267; campaign of, 125; creation of Domestic Policy Council by, 85; criminal wrongdoing in administration of, 339; Kissinger and, 73; White House plumbers employed by, 340

NLRA. *See* National Labor Relations Act

NLRB v. Jones & Laughlin Steel Corp., 363

Nofziger, Lyn, 55, 349, 350

Nollan v. California Coastal Commission, 318

noninterpretivism, 111–12, 113, 116, 118, 124

Noonan, John, 269, 282

Norris, Alan, 278, 282

North, Oliver, 99, 346, 355, 356

NSC. *See* National Security Council

Nygaard, Richard Lowell, 282

Obama, Barack, 2, 244–45, 249, 258

O'Connor, Sandra Day, 163, 199, 244, 245, 246, 250, 253, 254, 258, 264, 265, 292, 300, 301, 306, 307, 367, 390, 394, 395

Office of Legal Counsel (OLC), 4, 11, 87, 144, 150, 163, 321–29

Office of Legal Policy (OLP), 22, 151, 207–36, 293, 306; mission of, 208; monograph (*Guidelines on Constitutional Litigation*), 234, 237; monograph (*Original Meaning Jurisprudence: A Sourcebook*), 217–18; monograph (*Redefining Discrimination: "Disparate Impact" and the Institutionalization of Affirmative Action*), 230; monograph (*Religious Liberty under the Free Exercise Clause*), 229; monograph (*The Search and Seizure Exclusionary Rule*), 226; monograph (*The Sixth Amendment Right to Counsel under the Massiah Line of Cases*, 226–27; monograph (*Wrong Turns on the Road to Judicial Activism: The Ninth Amendment and the Privileges or Immunities Clause*), 219–21; responsibility of, 151

Office of Legislative Affairs (OLA), 152

Ohio v. Roberts, 135

OLA. *See* Office of Legislative Affairs

OLC. *See* Office of Legal Counsel

Olney, Richard, 382

OLP. *See* Office of Legal Policy

Olson, Ted, 164

originalism, 4–6, 8–11, 15, 21, 22, 50–51, 110–11, 114–16, 117–18, 121–28, 130, 141, 142–44, 154, 157–58, 167, 175–76, 178, 183–85, 187–92, 193, 195, 197, 202, 203, 207, 209, 212–18, 222, 226, 232, 234–35, 237–38, 241, 247, 249, 255, 262, 268, 269, 270, 277, 279, 280, 286, 292, 294, 295, 303, 304, 306, 313, 322–24, 329, 360, 366, 367, 370, 371, 375, 381, 385, 391, 393–94, 399

Original Meaning Jurisprudence: A Sourcebook, 217

O'Scannlain, Diarmuid, 281, 282

Osterweis, Rollin G., 30

Otis, Lee Liberman, 7, 153, 165, 166, 170, 182, 243, 267, 269, 275, 277, 281, 286, 388, 394

Palmer, A. Mitchell, 382

Patrick, Dennis, 96

Paulsen, Michael Stokes, 155

Peacemaker: Ronald Reagan, the Cold War, and the World on the Brink, The, 57

Pence, Mike, 397

Perry, William, 396

Pierce, Lawrence W., 281

Pierrepont, Edwards, 382

Pinkney, William, 378

Plager, S. Jay, 285

Planned Parenthood of Southeastern Pennsylvania v. Casey, 251

Poe v. Ullman, 158, 306

Poindexter, John, 346, 355, 356, 357

Porfilio, John Carbone, 283

Posner, Richard, 67, 243, 269, 278, 282

Powell, Lewis, 138, 163, 252, 253, 256, 259, 260, 306, 309

Prakash, Saikrishna, 188

Pratt, George C., 281

President Reagan: The Role of a Lifetime, 56

Presser, Stephen, 117

Printz v. United States, 265

privatization, 97, 98, 170

prophylactic rule, 331

Quayle, Dan, 284

Rader, Randall Ray, 285

Randolph, A. Raymond, 274, 285

Randolph, Edmund, 375, 377

Rappaport, Michael, 155, 207, 217

Reagan, Nancy, 36, 39, 60, 74

Reagan, Ronald, 6, 7, 22, 52, 58, 148, 151, 161, 167, 183, 214, 252, 309, 314; Brandenburg Gate speech of, 47–48; Bush as vice president under, 17; commands to Meese from, 142; defense of Constitution by, 95–96; Domestic Policy Council of, 154; Economic Bill of Rights of, 170; Farewell Address of, 45, 57, 191; first solicitor general under, 159; as governor, 16, 30, 32–34; importance of federalism to, 197–201, 251; Iran-Contra Affair and, 79, 80, 99–100, 337; judges to courts of appeals appointed by, 275–83; judicial appointees of, 19, 281–83; judicial nominees of, 4, 9; justices picked by, 244–45, 259, 264, 272; Meese as right-hand man to, 11, 14, 99; Meese's loyalty to, 1, 86; official policy of Justice Department of, 141; policy formulation, 59–77; presidential campaign of, 35; as product of the American heartland, 399; Republican nomination of, 383; rolling back of communism under, 46; scandals of presidency of, 337–57; second term of, 79–101; "Shining City on a Hill" Farewell Speech of, 85; Strategic Defense Initiative as priority for, 68; tax cuts of, 18; as transformational president, 15, 283; transition of, 398; unabashed defense of freedom by, 47; vision of, 237

Reagan Revolution, 8, 37–58, 59, 92, 161, 171, 284, 290; advocates of, 275; card-carrying members of, 172; in the courts, 67; Eighth Circuit appointee of, 280; Eleventh Circuit appointee of, 281; fake-news "scandals" and, 337; Fifth Circuit stars of, 278; fortresses of, 284; Fourth Circuit appointees of, 277; functions vital to success of, 64; judges named to D.C. Circuit by, 269–70, 273; key elements of, 37; Meese as promoter of, 8, 398; Meese's role in, 16, 105; Reagan, 38–40;

Reaganism, 40–52, 57–58; Reaganites, 52–57; steward of, 393–401

Reconstruction, 382

Reconstruction Amendments, 249

Red Lion Broadcasting Co. v. FCC, 94, 96

Reed, Stanley, 10, 267, 365, 384

Rees, Grover, 116

Regan, Donald, 12, 71, 75, 77, 91, 101, 214, 356

Rehabilitation Act (1973), 327

Rehnquist, William H., 9, 15, 19, 50, 51, 120–21, 124, 127, 138, 150, 156, 163, 164, 175, 199, 239, 240–41, 245–52, 253, 254, 258, 259, 263, 265, 267, 271, 274, 292, 304, 321, 329, 346, 373, 395

Reich, Charles, 132–33, 135

Reid, Harry, 275, 276

Religious Freedom Restoration Act (RFRA), 250

Reno, Janet, 346, 347, 383, 391

Report to the Attorney General on the Law of Pre-Trial Interrogation, 223

Revolution: The Reagan Legacy, 56

Revolutionary Constitutions: Charismatic Leadership and the Rule of Law, 142

Reykjavik Summit, 81

Reynolds, William Bradford (Brad), 149, 151, 155–57, 165, 172, 214, 239, 242, 262, 269, 293, 295, 335, 356, 390

Reynolds v. Sims, 388

RFRA. *See* Religious Freedom Restoration Act

Richardson, Elliot, 340, 390

Richardson, John, 19, 171–72, 356

Ripple, Kenneth Francis, 282

Road to Serfdom, The, 30

Robb, Charles "Chuck," 20, 396

Roberts, John G., 4, 10, 19, 24, 155, 240, 246, 247, 258, 265, 286, 366, 369, 373, 395, 396

Roberts, Owen, 364, 365

Specter, Arlen, 261, 262

Speed, James, 381

Stahl, Norman H., 285

Stanbery, Henry, 381

Stanton, Edwin, 380

Stapleton, Walter, 277, 282

Starr, Kenneth W., 67, 270, 271, 274, 281, 346

Status of Federalism in America, The, 87

Stevens, John Paul, 5, 253, 254, 255, 258, 268, 269, 301, 324

Stewart, Potter, 119, 223, 267, 387

Stockman, David, 333

Stone, Harlan F., 10, 365, 382

Strategic Defense Initiative (SDI), 68

strict construction. *See* judicial restraint

Struggle for Judicial Supremacy, The, 386

Students for Fair Admission, Inc. v. President and Fellows of Harvard College, 7

Suhrheinrich, Richard F., 285

Supreme Court, cases of: *Adkins v. Children's Hospital,* 363; *Alabama Ass'n of Realtors v. U.S. Dep't of Health & Hum. Services,* 369; *Baker v. Carr,* 268, 388; *Biden v. Nebraska,* 371; *Bowsher v. Synar,* 313; *Boyd v. United States,* 226; *Brown v. Board of Education,* 122, 217, 262, 386; *Carson v. Makin,* 372, 373; *Chisholm v. Georgia,* 377; *Citizens United v. FEC,* 266; *City of Arlington, Texas v. FCC,* 265; *City of Boerne v. Flores,* 250, 265; *Communications Workers of America v. Beck,* 314; *Crawford v. Washington,* 255; *Dartmouth College v. Woodward,* 379; *District of Columbia v. Heller,* 255, 371, 372; *Dobbs v. Jackson Women's Health Organization,* 7, 187, 251, 307, 366, 393; *Dred Scott v. Sandford,* 2, 128, 194, 219, 307, 380; *Furman v. Georgia,* 130, 131; *Garcia v. San Antonio Metropolitan Transit Authority,* 2; *Gibbons v. Ogden,* 379; *Goesaert v. Cleary,* 363; *Goldberg v. Kelly,* 134;

Gonzales v. Raich, 250, 251; *Gregg v. Georgia,* 131; *Gregory v. Ashcroft,* 265; *Griswold v. Connecticut,* 118, 159, 251, 302–3, 311; *Hodel v. Irving,* 299, 300, 316; *Home Building & Loan Ass'n v. Blaisdell,* 128; *Immigration and Naturalization Service v. Chadha,* 313; *Kennedy v. Bremerton School District,* 7, 372, 374; *Lee v. Weisman,* 374; *Lochner v. New York,* 2, 35, 268; *Locke v. Davey,* 373; *Loving v. Virginia,* 217; *Mapp v. Ohio,* 3, 226; *Marbury v. Madison,* 192, 261; *McCulloch v. Maryland,* 2, 379; *Miami Herald Publishing Co. v. Tornillo,* 96; *Miranda v. Arizona,* 3, 223–25; *Mistretta v. United States,* 296, 311; *Morrison v. Olson,* 254, 311, 346; *National Federation of Independent Business v. OSHA,* 369; *New York v. United States,* 265; *New York State Rifle & Pistol Association, Inc. v. Bruen,* 7, 372; *NFIB v. Sebelius,* 249; *NLRB v. Jones & Laughlin Steel Corp.,* 363; *Nollan v. California Coastal Commission,* 318; *Ohio v. Roberts,* 135; *Planned Parenthood of Southeastern Pennsylvania v. Casey,* 251; *Poe v. Ullman,* 158, 306; *Printz v. United States,* 265; *Red Lion Broadcasting Co. v. FCC,* 94, 96; *Reynolds v. Sims,* 388; *Rochin v. California,* 305; *Roe v. Wade,* 7, 19, 113, 118, 129, 159, 188, 196, 197, 198, 219, 222, 251, 253, 257, 261, 264, 267, 268, 303, 305, 307, 311, 359, 366, 393; *Schechter Poultry v. United States,* 383; *Shapiro v. Thompson,* 133; *Students for Fair Admission, Inc. v. President and Fellows of Harvard College,* 7; *Thornburgh v. American College of Obstetricians and Gynecologists,* 304; *United States v. Carolene Products,* 145; *United States v. Lopez,* 199, 249, 251, 265; *United States v. Morrison,* 249, 265; *United States v. Virginia,* 251; *United States v. Wallach,* 349; *Washington v. Glucksberg,* 251, 266; *Webster v. Reproductive Health Services,* 306; *Weeks v. United States,* 226; *Wesberry v. Sanders,* 388; *West*